A KICK AGAINST THE PRICKS

A KICK AGAINST THE PRICKS

THE AUTOBIOGRAPHY

David Norris

TRANSWORLD IRELAND

TRANSWORLD IRELAND
An imprint of The Random House Group Limited
20 Vauxhall Bridge Road, London SW1V 2SA
www.transworldbooks.co.uk

A KICK AGAINST THE PRICKS
A TRANSWORLD IRELAND BOOK: 9781848271371

First published in 2012 by Transworld Ireland,
a division of Transworld Publishers
Transworld Ireland paperback edition published 2013

This book is a work of non-fiction.

Extract from 'Love From A Short Distance' by Bono reproduced by kind permission.
Extract for *All for Hecuba* by Michael Mac Liammóir reproduced with the kind
permission of the Lilliput Press.

A CIP catalogue record for this book
is available from the British Library.

Addresses for Random House Group Ltd companies outside the UK
can be found at: www.randomhouse.co.uk
The Random House Group Ltd Reg. No. 954009

The Random House Group Limited supports The Forest Stewardship Council® (FSC®), the
leading international forest-certification organisation. Our books carrying the FSC label
are printed on FSC®-certified paper. FSC is the only forest-certification scheme supported
by the leading environmental organisations, including Greenpeace. Our paper
procurement policy can be found at www.randomhouse.co.uk/environment

Typeset in Sabon by Falcon Oast Graphic Art Ltd.
Printed and bound by CPI Group (UK) Ltd, Croydon, CR0 4YY.

2 4 6 8 10 9 7 5 3 1

This book is dedicated to the unconquerable spirit of those like Noël Browne, Victor Griffin and Tom Hyland who I have been lucky enough to call friends and whose passionate integrity has been a continuing inspiration. It is also dedicated to Miriam Gordon Smith and Muireann Noonan, who remained 100 per cent steadfast not only throughout the ups and downs of my political career but also in the preparation of this book.

'And when we were all fallen to the earth, I heard a voice speaking unto me and saying in the Hebrew tongue, Saul, Saul, why persecutest thou me? It is hard for thee to kick against the pricks.'

Acts, 26:14

'Being enraged I would kick against the pricks.'

Euripides, *The Bacchae*

'If you strike against the pricks with your fists you hurt your hands more than the pricks.'

Plautus

Prick – a kind of sharpened goad used to prod oxen in what those in control considered the correct direction – was from ancient times a source of metaphor. I also use it in full consciousness of its *double entendre* as a metaphor for my lifelong struggle against the establishment.

CONTENTS

Warning to Readers

This material should be consumed whole and in its original wrapping. Unauthorised toxic bundles of selected quotations may appear in the media. The public are advised to be cautious about such products as their ingestion may lead to mental confusion and moral constipation, with possibly fatal intellectual or spiritual consequences. Be especially cautious of sensational headlines. They often equate to the old Quaker dictum 'First thee tells the lie, then thee asks the question.' As Pascal wisely remarked in his *Pensées*: 'Words arranged differently have different meanings and meanings arranged differently have different effects.'

References to real people are as accurate as possible especially in cases where those concerned possess a reasonable degree of reality. I have tried to be fair and truthful throughout my life and have attempted to obey the biblical injunction to turn the other cheek, although frequently not before delivering a resounding slap in return to my attackers. I freely acknowledge that I have yet to attain that perfect state of Christian forbearance to which one is supposed to aspire, and as my years advance seem less and less likely to do so before I am welcomed into Abraham's capacious and forgiving bosom.

Finally I would remind readers of that old superstitious rhyme about magpies:

> *One for sorrow, two for joy,*
> *three for a girl, four for a boy,*
> *five for silver, six for gold*
> *and seven for a story that will never be told.*

No human life, certainly not one as complicated as mine, can be compressed within the pages of a single book, but there are in any case some stories that will go to my grave with me. They concern nothing that would bring me into disrepute but they might inadvertently cause hurt to people I care about; and my purpose throughout life has been to do good rather than harm. The old medico-legal dictum, *'Primum non nocere'* – 'do as little harm as possible', is I think one that should be observed.

PROLOGUE

CHRISTMAS 2010 WAS A CHILDHOOD DREAM IN DUBLIN – A REAL white Christmas. The snow around lay thick and deep and cast an unusual mantle of pristine purity even over the north inner city. A young newly engaged couple living temporarily in a flat across the street from my house took the opportunity to build a wonderful, traditional, larger-than-life-size snowman. He had a battered felt hat, little black eyes of coal, a carrot nose and orange-peel mouth. I even seem to remember a small tattered scarf. Beside him was built from solid snow, like the blocks of an igloo, a throne on which the young couple photographed each other. Other people drifting up the street also took the opportunity; there was a sense of happiness and celebration. I went back inside for my camera and took a few snaps myself.

Then up the street came the sound of what might be taken as merriment, the nasal voices of three teenage girls united in-harmoniously in the chorus of a pop song. Then they spotted the snowman. First of all like everyone else they took a few photographs on their telephones, but quickly the playfulness turned nasty. One of them knocked the hat off, then the nose was tweaked away. The most adventurous of the three started shoving at the head until with the help of her two accomplices she pushed it over to the ground. Then a frenzy of destruction took place until the only remnants of the snowman were a scatter of smeared lumps. It was apparently only the human form that attracted their instinct for vandalism; the throne lay isolated, unoccupied. As they passed the bewildered creators of the image one of them sneered, 'We killed your fuckin' snowman for you, mister.'

It was a sad moment but an illustrative one. One frequently hears it said that there are two kinds of people: good and bad, the ugly and the beautiful, the vivacious and the dull, and so on. But it seemed to me on that early Christmastide evening that there are also two kinds of personalities: one to whom the arrival of something that bespeaks creativity and the positive find themselves drawn towards it to join in the fun, while the other force is a sinister instinct, equally attracted, drawn to everything that is positive however, not to celebrate but instead to enjoy the thrill of destruction.

I have always tried as far as I could to tell the truth, even when it was painful to myself. But I have on occasion pulled back from full revelation to spare others. There are times when, having told a story so often, I wonder if I am embroidering things somewhat, as storytellers frequently do. But this book's kernel is the truth as I believe it to be.

I do not in any sense consider myself a hero, nor have I constantly aimed at the heroic. I am an ordinary man placed from time to time in extraordinary circumstances which I have attempted to face with what courage I could muster, sometimes alone and sometimes with valiant companions. I have had many good friends and comrades but there is no doubt that my attitudes, my beliefs, my constant attempts at honesty, perhaps to some also the grating sound of my voice, have alienated others, and I have been aware for some time of enemies in the thickets. This book may no doubt add to their number, but if one is going to make enemies by the honest expression of opinion, why stop at one or two? To walk on one corn could be considered an error of judgement but to plough on through thickets of misshapen calloused and carbuncled digits at least suggests a sense of deliberation.

Now I am for the first time attempting to do for myself what I have throughout my life attempted to do for others – provide a personal justification. This book constitutes in Newman's phrase an 'apologia pro vita mea'. An apologia not in the popular sense of an apology, for I apologise to no one for my actions or my words, but in the classical sense of an explanation, and one which I hope will be, if not accepted, at least considered by the civilised reader.

As I write, this is a new year. Another Christmas is over, but for me, apart from the religious and spiritual elements that have always been the most significant, there was no Christmas this year. No Christmas tree scented the hallway of my Georgian house in central Dublin, no holly decorated my grandmother's marble clock, my grandfather's Regency bookcase. A few cards were sent out as a matter of duty and thanks to those who remained loyal in a difficult time. No presents except recycled fripperies at the last moment from my treasure chest of curiosities collected during my global travels. No celebration except – a slightly incongruous luxury considering my precarious financial state – on Christmas Eve a meal in Frère Jacques which has become a tradition. Every year I take my family and perhaps a close friend or two to lunch at that splendid French restaurant and then on to the carol service at St Patrick's Cathedral which I have been attending now for over sixty of my nearly seventy years.

And why this austerity, this grimness? Not certainly because I did not succeed in becoming the ninth President of Ireland. That has surely been compensated for by the election of President Michael D. Higgins, a man of profound intellect and a poet, but most important of all a man who has always spoken out with passionate eloquence and with encyclopaedic knowledge of human-rights legislation both national and international, on behalf of the marginalised; rather it was because of the impact of the unrestrained, indecent and inaccurate attacks upon my character motivated by a casual nastiness, revenge for some of my political actions and an almost universal desire among the print media to increase circulation by the promotion of scandal rather than accurate reporting. There has never been an election like the 2011 presidential election in Ireland. Nor in my lifetime have I known any citizen who was not a criminal singled out and collectively targeted by the media for such abuse as I was.

Even in my beloved eighteenth century, of course, there were scandals, lampoons, lies, character assassinations and an unpleasant odour from Grub Street, but that rank stink has intensified, especially since the general implementation in the gutter press in Ireland as well as in the UK of the moral and ethical standards of organisations presided over by Rupert Murdoch.

I remember many years ago, when researching James Joyce and his circle, coming across an essay by one of Joyce's fellow students, Arthur Clery, in which he coined a remarkable phrase: 'The nation that takes for its Sunday lunch an English Sunday newspaper may one day find a change in its Friday diet.' In those days of course for the overwhelmingly Roman Catholic population of Ireland Friday was a day of spiritual observance, perhaps even penance, when meat was forbidden and fish the ordained meal of the day. What Clery meant was that there would be a corruption of the standards of Irish journalism and morality by a debased British press. The flooding of the Irish market with low-class, vulgar English journalism has proved his point and I remember with embarrassment now how patronisingly I felt towards him when I read the sentence first, and categorised him merely as an insular, xenophobic Catholic quasi-intellectual. All that he may indeed have been, but he was also certainly prophetic, as recent years have confirmed.

Through one of the vagaries of human life I myself had a

part-time career as a journalist with a tabloid newspaper. I was proud and excited to be accepted as a member of the National Union of Journalists even though qualification for entry requires no particular skill of literacy or intellect, professional training or apprenticeship, merely the capacity to demonstrate that one can earn a certain proportion of one's income by the pen. I have since learnt a healthy scepticism of the trustworthiness of journalists.

Finally may I say that the inscription on the tin remains an accurate description of the contents. For all my religious and spiritual beliefs, my humanitarian record and all the rest of it, in this case what you see is what you get, for it *is*, at least in part, a kick against the pricks. After a lifetime of experience I can say without fear of contradiction that there are plenty of them in public life, whether they be politicians, journalists, churchmen, professional hypocrites or fundamentalists of various kinds.

One of my colleagues warned me against re-entering the presidential race in September 2011, saying it would be a crucifixion. However what of course she overlooked was the fact that in the Christian religion crucifixion is followed by resurrection. And so it has been proven. Within a few months I was back: early January in Cyprus. The log fire was roaring, snow on Mount Olympus and my friend Nora there to dispute with on topics of politics, religion and sex. It was an evening of laughter and fun.

And that is what one aspect of resurrection and recovery means. In the words of Hilaire Belloc, which I have used as the title for the last chapter of this book:

> From quiet homes and first beginning,
> Out to the undiscovered ends,
> There's nothing worth the wear of winning,
> But laughter and the love of friends.

CHAPTER I

My Family and Other Animals

THE CLINIQUE REINE ELISABETH WAS A LONG, LOW, WHITE ART Deco building deep in the heart of Africa. Built in Leopoldville in the 1930s, it served the medical needs of the colonial administrators and their families who lived in the Belgian Congo. And it was there, on 31 July 1944, that I, David Patrick Bernard FitzPatrick Norris, was born.

I was conceived from the conjugal union of one man and one woman, legally registered and conducted according to the rites of the Anglican Communion, viz. to wit and to woo, John Bernard Norris, born in Richmond, London, in 1895, and Aida Margaret FitzPatrick, born in Mountrath, County Laois, in 1901. That town, located in what was then still officially designated the Queen's County, was a little unkindly described by the late Lord Killanin and Frank O'Connor as 'a decayed market town'.

Both my parents, as far as I know, were as deeply committed to heterosexual monogamy as they were to their strong but rather Middle Church form of Christianity. I state these facts at the beginning to correct the kind of confusion about my nature that contaminates certain right-wing conservative groups who affect an adherence to the Christian religion. They appear to believe that I either emerged surreptitiously from the hot tap in

1

the bathroom or, a more likely proposition, that whereas men may indeed come from Mars and women from Venus, I in fact materialised from even more remote regions of the universe, charged with an extraterrestrial mission of outstanding significance, i.e. the destruction by insidious means of the human family unit, especially that version presided over by the ageing celibates of the Vatican.

Were such an exotic origin capable of confirmation I would embrace it with alacrity. But, alas, my beginnings are as banal as almost everyone else's.

Since I am now of a certain age there could not have been even the suggestion of a test tube or other kind of well-intentioned modern assistance to my conception. My parents did it all on their own, *au naturel* so to speak. Their first ten childless years of marriage were triumphantly ended by the birth of my older brother, John, and it took just less than half that time for what, one hopes, were their modestly pleasurable efforts to produce me.

I say I hope it was a modestly pleasurable exercise because, in my mother's family at least, sex was regarded as a subject too squalid and unhygienic to be referred to in public – and certainly not in front of the young: a kind of regrettable, almost veterinary necessity for the continuation of the species. This may seem odd to the younger generation, but it was a fairly widespread fact of life in the first half of the twentieth century. Sexuality was just not visible, even among animals in the farming community, a fact confirmed to my infant imagination by the arrival of a postcard from a rather prim cousin, with a photo on the front of market day in Roscrea. No one except myself appeared to have noticed – and certainly no one commented upon – the fact that bang in the centre of the rustic scene a complacent cow could be clearly seen enjoying the energetic attentions of a bull.

I arrived on the Equator in the middle of summer and at precisely 1 p.m., lunchtime. A few months after my birth I received my first review, in the beautiful handwriting of my mother in one of her many letters home: *You asked me what David is like – well he is exactly what John Richard was like at that age, only fatter and more placid. He is always smiling.*

My parents had been living in Africa for more than a decade. Their extraordinary journey had begun at a tennis party in south County Dublin in 1930. One of my father's sisters, Daisy, had married an Irishman called Agnew Montgomery Martin, who owned lands near the family home at Flimby Hall in County Clare. Monty was a bit of a character, who also had properties in London and Brighton, and three houses on Lower Pembroke Street, just off Fitzwilliam Square in Dublin, which he called the Arcadia Club and leased out to the gentry as serviced apartments with butlers, silver tea services – the works.

Monty and Daisy were high-livers and loved the theatre, especially patronising the Gate. They became friendly with Micheál Mac Liammóir and Hilton Edwards, and allowed them to stay free of charge when they were short of cash. In a wonderful passage in his memoir *All for Hecuba*, Mac Liammóir described Daisy – whom he called Tessie – making cocktails and coming out with a stream of political commentary, literary criticism and salacious gossip:

'Cosgrave's party is going out soon', Tessie would say, looking like a blonde Brazilian butterfly as she rattled the cocktail shaker on high in the big basement kitchen, 'and De Valera's coming in. Glad? I'm not. Things will be just as lousy as they are now, and they'll let all those I.R.A. boys out of jail and then we'll all be murdered in our beds. In our beds,' she continued . . . 'heard about Denis Johnston and that Abbey girl, you know her name, Shelah Richards? Married next month. Don't suppose they'll ask me to the wedding. All very Protestant and smart though. They might just as well ask me. God knows I'm English enough. Can't understand Irish prods. Neither fish, fowl nor the other thing . . . And long skirts are coming back. That woman with no nose in Baggot Street went to Paris last week and met Paddy Perrott on the top of the Eiffel Tower and he told her son, and he's in with Poiret. Of course it's a tremendous secret, so don't say I said a word. Awful to be sued by Schiaparelli, wouldn't it? Maud Gonne is going to see your show tonight. Maud Gonne Mad they used to call her. Lovely woman, though, all the men mad about her. Yeats is going to live in Rathfarnham. Oh yes, he's fed up with Merrion Square. Well wouldn't you be with all those old cats playing bridge all day? . . .

Even though she died five years before my birth, Daisy sounds just like me.

The Montys invited my father over to spend some time in Dublin after the collapse of his business in the 1929 crash, and one weekend they all went off to a house near Greystones to join a tennis party. The rambling mansion was the home of Lord Chief Justice Cherry and it was there my parents first set eyes on each other and began a romance that lasted until my father's death, two decades later.

My father had been something of a hero during the First World War, nursing the Merchant Navy vessel HMS *Sceptre* back to port after it had been attacked by German submarines in 1917. For his efforts he had received a Lloyds Medal – popularly known as the marine VC – and a reward of £900, which could have bought you two substantial houses in London at the time. Instead he invested it in setting up an engineering company. He was very enterprising and a keen inventor, coming up with designs for silent hydraulic elevators for plush hotels in London. In the Congo, where he worked for Lever Brothers, he designed and invented machines to extract oil from palm nuts, which was then used to make margarine.

My mother had a wonderfully optimistic spirit and was devotedly in love with this dashing Englishman. That spirit carried her through, especially when you consider that she was whisked from the bogs of Laois to the dark heart of Africa, pausing only at St Ann's Church on Dawson Street at eight o'clock one September morning in 1930 to marry the man she loved.

The newlyweds sailed from Antwerp, down through the Bay of Biscay to the mouth of the Congo. They exchanged their liner for a paddle steamer, later for a smaller boat as the river narrowed. This continued on up the river until, in small canoes, they reached their new home.

The European intervention in the Congo was evil, with the mass-murdering King Leopold II treating it as his personal possession from 1885 until 1908. The true heroes who exposed that sorry chapter were the novelist Joseph Conrad and the Anglo-Irish diplomat Roger Casement. Conrad's *Heart of Darkness* caught exactly the atmosphere of racist bestiality fostered by the Belgian company that was in the control of the King, and Casement's persistent and dramatic reports of the depravity could not be overlooked and led to an inquiry.

My father was chief engineer with Lever Brothers in the Congo, and later responsible for maintaining the supply of raw materials needed by the Allies in Europe, so they eventually had a comfortable life in Leopoldville (now Kinshasa), although they certainly roughed it when they were living in the bush. My father had been wounded in the First World War and also managed to contract anthrax in Africa from a badger-hair shaving brush. My mother nursed him through that, but then she caught rheumatic fever and was flat on her back for a full year. That episode damaged a valve in her heart, whose failure eventually killed her thirty years later.

She was very good at languages and learnt several of the local tongues, including Kikongo and Swahili, compiling dictionaries and grammars in little notebooks, where she recorded words and phrases phonetically, with an explanation of their meaning in English or French. They had a Congolese butler called Martin who loved them as they loved him, and wanted to come home with them in the end, but it was impossible to get him in to Ireland, just as I was to find later with my partner Ezra.

In her letters home my mother described Christmas in Africa, which at times reads like a Somerville and Ross story.

We had a quiet Christmas. There was nothing to give John Richard but I had been keeping a drawing book, a Kipling story-book and the story of Pinocchio, and I found a little ebony walking stick with ivory top and bought that. With a tin of biscuits and a jar of home made fudge, that was everything Santa Claus brought – with one exception!

Seeing that his Christmas was going to be on the mean side I begged a donkey colt belonging to the company, and a friend, M Bosquet, who is a good horseman, had a saddle and bridle made and got a little native boy to ride it to break it in!

It arrived on Christmas morning just after Santa Claus had been disposed of! John was most excited but it never entered his head that it might be just bringing a message. He said 'Mummy, Mummy, there's a horse with long ears and a thing for me to sit on when I ride him!' He had to have a ride at once. I can't say that the 'breaking in' had been very successful. The impression I had was that it had never had anyone on its back before! It escaped three times on Christmas Day and had to be chased by the cook, houseboys, waterboys, gardener, chauffeur, sentries, etc each time. They are all terrified of it so when I go near it I feel as if I were a lion-tamer giving an exhibition! John loves it, talks to it, brushes it and scratches its head. Yesterday afternoon I yoked it up and got the chauffeur to come and help me give John a ride. The famous 'Cooper's Ass' wasn't in it! I had to call the cook as well to push its hind quarters down as it kept 'histing' them. John enjoyed it but I'm sure I lost several pounds of fat.

We enjoyed the carols from King's College and thought of you all when we listened to the King's broadcast.

Another family event recorded in my mother's letters was John's fourth birthday, at which he greeted a visitor with 'Please, I am politely four.' The party, in the garden, was enlivened by the arrival of some interlopers, who thought the sight of adults under the trees, the extensive and beautifully laid-out flowerbeds and children playing meant it was a public park! The next morning, she wrote, John awoke to ask her, 'Am I still four?'

My father had a strongly developed sense of justice and was frequently called upon to arbitrate in local disputes. He operated as a type of bush magistrate, taking notes, summoning witnesses and adjudicating on matters. He dealt severely with some Belgian men who were found to be having sex with the wives of the locals, and he had the malefactors deported in disgrace.

Mother was also a keen naturalist; she adored animals, and was adept at coaxing them out of the jungle and domesticating them. She was a friend of Sir Julian Huxley, the first director of UNESCO and founder of the World Wildlife Fund, and at the time head of London Zoo. She presented him with the first Bosman's potto to be held in captivity, which she brought back to London in her cabin. This lovely creature, resembling a loris or lemur with grey fur, is found in the canopy above the rainforest. A photograph of the animal appeared on the front page of the London *Evening Standard*, the original of which I have framed over the fireplace in the library. She was rewarded with life membership of the zoo.

John Junior had arrived in 1940, four and a half years before my birth, but it was my arrival that spurred their decision to return to live in Dublin. Leaving my father behind, my mother, brother and I came home on the Belge-Maritime du Congo vessel the *Copacabana* early in 1945. The Second World War was still on-going, and the U-boats prowling the Atlantic made the crossing very difficult for my mother on her own with two small children. John remembers the ship coming under attack from the air, and the sound of the shell casings as they rattled on the wooden deck as the ship's anti-aircraft guns fired on the Luftwaffe planes, and my mother's rush to hide us in the cabin.

The ship was blacked out at all times and the food and living conditions weren't great. We were met at Portsmouth by my uncle, who was well connected in the military and had managed to secure a car. He got us to the boat to neutral Ireland through the rubble of the Blitz, but my mother was at her wits' end after the exhausting journey. The arrival of people from the Canadian Red Cross with a sustaining cup of cocoa was something she still talked about fondly years later.

We then set off straight for the old homestead in Co. Laois, where we stayed with my grandparents in Mountrath. We lived in Laois for a year or so, of which my only memory is watching my mother as she looked back at the edge of town as we left it for our new life in Dublin. My father had returned from Africa to organise the purchase of a house in the city, and to help us move there. They had looked at a house on Ailesbury Road which had been built by a relative of my mother's family, but my father, being English and practical rather than sentimental, didn't think the damp coursing was up to scratch. So they bought a much more modern detached 1930s house in a cul-de-sac off Sandymount Avenue called Wilfield Park.

It was before my second birthday, but I remember crossing the bridge at Ballsbridge, with its illuminated globe lighting, and then the sound of my father's shoes clopping across the bare boards of the new house before he headed off on his bicycle in his tweed suit to buy a two-bar electric fire. Another infant memory is of lying in the pram under the trees, looking through the leaves at the sun and listening to the birds. I was irritated by the strap restraints, and loudly complained as I struggled to free myself from them.

I treasure those fragments of memory as I only saw my father on three occasions after we returned from Africa, and then just for four- or six-week breaks. I wasn't *entirely* happy with his visits as I was forced to take a siesta and I would be plonked in the bed alongside him. Of course I could hear other children of my age playing outside and thus couldn't sleep and became fidgety, which led to a stern reprimand.

I remember my father and brother playing cricket in the evening in the back garden. It was a game in which I wasn't particularly interested, but at which John was a feared fast bowler. As a batsman his prowess was more erratic but on one occasion he scored a six-and-out when he put the ball in through the French windows of the dining room, where my mother was entertaining some friends, and out again through the corner window, just missing the wireless set.

My father was a serious man, interested in world politics. He loved Ireland and wanted to learn Irish and get involved in public life when he finally made his home here, if his health permitted. He still suffered from his First World War injuries and walked with a stoop. The last summer we saw him was in 1949, when I was five years old. For me, his arrival home was always an occasion for joy as he would bring me the clear boiled-sugar fruit sweets that were given to him on the plane. They came in a packet of four, and I ached for them. That was what his return meant to me, but on his last visit he forgot to bring them, and I howled the house down.

One day he took me with him up to Donnybrook – probably to get me out from under my mother's feet – where there was a Ford motor dealer's showroom opposite the rugby grounds. He bought a second-hand Ford Prefect with a beautifully smelling leather interior.

I remember driving to Kerry in that car, and its registration number – ZF8. My father was a keen golfer so we visited Killarney and Ballybunion. We went to the beach and took in the views of the ruined castle. On our return we diverted to Blarney, where I was forced to kiss the stone which promises a life of loquaciousness to those who do so. I was always being forced to do things I didn't want to; I also hated trips to Dublin Zoo, where I would be put up on a howdah on the back of Sarah the elephant, to be led around by the keeper, who was the broadcaster Pat Kenny's father.

One day in late 1949 my father brought me into town with him to buy his airline ticket at the Aer Lingus head office, which was then in Cathal Brugha Street. We all went out to Collinstown Aerodrome, now Dublin Airport, to say goodbye before he flew to London where he caught his connection to Leopoldville. There were very few planes to be seen, and they were all Douglas DC3s emblazoned with the livery of Aer Lingus; I remember that the plane took off with its nose raised at a dramatic angle before levelling off. We stood on the roof balcony of the beautiful banana-shaped Art Deco building beside the control tower to wave him off.

After 1949 we were on our own again in our comfortable life in Ballsbridge. My mother would let us know how Father was doing through the frequent letters and occasional phone calls they exchanged. She busied herself about the garden and in the kitchen, where she was a gifted cook with a special talent for French haute cuisine.

My father should have retired before 1950, but the company and the Belgian government prevailed upon him to stay for another six months. This had already happened several times. He was overworking and the stress began to tell on him.

One afternoon my mother received a telegram saying that he had been taken ill. Over the next number of days further messages came, saying his condition was worsening, and then that there was little hope. Finally my mother got another telegram, after which she took John and myself into the dining room to tell us that our father had died. She put her arms around us and said we would all have to stick together now, as there were only the three of us left. At such a young age I wasn't really aware of what was going on and I had hardly met my father. I knew I was expected to cry like the other two and nearly gave myself a hernia squeezing out a couple of miniature teardrops. I was only five and a half at the time and I was more upset that we wouldn't have a motor car any more.

It transpired that my father had died on the day of the first telegram, but this succession of messages was somebody's way of breaking the news gently to us. As a humane gesture it didn't work, as my poor mother was in a terrible state of apprehension waiting for the postman and telegraph boy, hoping against hope for a gleam of good news, and it would have been better to receive the grim news all at once. He had suffered a massive coronary thrombosis and was dead at the age of fifty-six.

We had a comfortable house in a fashionable part of Dublin, and some very good furniture, mostly inherited from my mother's family, but we hadn't much money. The only things sent back from Africa were the medal of the Order of his Belgian knighthood and his set of left-handed golf clubs. The pension from Lever Brothers was small, but as a result of the Belgian knighthood we continued to receive another small pension from that government, which helped a bit. But there was no assistance whatsoever for widows from the Irish State at the time, a fact made doubly unjust because if it was my mother who had died, my father would have got a housekeeper's allowance, even though he was the breadwinner.

It was very difficult for my mother, who had for many years in Africa been used to a large domestic staff and a fleet of motor cars at her disposal. In Dublin she employed a maid, who lived in for a time, and a gardener when needed, but the car was the first thing to go. Over the centuries the FitzPatricks had alternated between one generation who were *flaithiúlach* and devil-may-care, and the next one which picked up the pieces. My mother was very prudent, and kept immaculate household accounts in which she rigidly adhered to her weekly budget. She and her sister regarded debt as sinful: everything was paid for and if you couldn't afford it you couldn't have it.

We also had prayers every day before breakfast. The maid, Nelly, was excused because she was Roman Catholic. The rest of us had to turn our chairs around to form a *priedieu* and listen to Mother say the collect of the day. Then we said the Our Father and the beautiful Second Collect from Matins, which still haunts me:

O Lord, our heavenly Father, Almighty and everlasting God, who hast safely brought us to the beginning of this day; Defend us in the same with thy mighty power; and grant that this day we fall into no sin, neither run into any kind of danger; but that all our doings, being ordered by thy governance, may be righteous in thy sight.

Although our postal address was Ballsbridge, we were closer to Sandymount, and it was in that pretty village that we did most of our shopping. Every day the staff from Findlater's rang to take my mother's grocery order, which was later delivered by Christy in his van. When one visited Findlater's, purchases would be made at the counter and then, through a system of pulleys and springs, the bill and money would be carried in a little wooden container across the ceiling to the cashier, who sat in an elevated box with a glass front. She would reach up, open the cylinder and carefully examine the transaction, and then with a jerk of the lever send the stamped bill and your change whizzing back via the pulleys.

There were many lovely little shops around the green, including the hardware shop with its unique curved window which is still a feature of Sandymount. This was run by Miss Milligan, a matronly woman from Cork who wore her white hair in a bun. The whole process of shopping there was a delight, from the pervading smell of paraffin to the creaky wooden floorboards and the huge embossed metal cash register which checked off the pounds, shillings and pence.

I loved the newsagent's shop, run by an affable couple called Harry and Lily Mapother. Harry always had the inside track on politics. The two old ladies next door who ran the Gem cake shop were very genteel and wore mink coats to Mass, while Mrs Murray, who only gave up driving aged 103, was the postmistress.

Across the green was Roddy's sweet shop, full of glass jars of gobstoppers, liquorice torpedoes, aniseed dates, acid drops, clove rock and bull's-eyes; and Batt's chemist shop occupied the corner where the bank now stands. The green itself was a generally well-kept amenity, giving a real village feel to Sandymount, but it became the scene of an appalling tragedy one day when a boy fell while climbing a chestnut tree in search of conkers. He plummeted on to the railings and was impaled through his chin.

My family loved horses, but paradoxically didn't approve of gambling. So it was always a great treat every Easter when my friends Michael Moran, John Doherty and I were loaded into the Doherty family's comfortable old Vauxhall saloon to head off to Fairyhouse racecourse. It was a colourful event, with the legendary Prince Monolulu, an alleged Cherokee Indian who wore the full rig-out, including magnificent feathered headdress, tassled leather clothing and moccasins, and who sold tips. We always parked at Ballyhack, where Mr Doherty produced a volcano kettle. This was a most interesting little alloy instrument into which newspapers could be stuffed and then lit to produce instant boiling water.

On one occasion I picked the first, second and third in the Irish Grand National, and can now disclose how I did it, perhaps for the enlightenment, if not the enrichment, of the reader. We were allowed to place threepence of our pocket money each way on our selection. I'd had a disastrous run, so for the Grand National I punted 3d. each way on each of the dozen or so horses in the race. After the race was over I carefully and discreetly discarded the nine losing dockets, retaining numbers 1, 2 and 3. One of my friends thought it would be great fun to see what stinkers I had chosen again, so with feigned reluctance I produced my tickets, which to everyone's astonishment showed I had scooped the pool. I think in fact I just about broke even.

My grandmother and Aunt Constance came to live with us for a while. It was not a successful arrangement, however, because my aunt could be very domineering and my mother didn't appreciate her attempts to take control. They moved out to Dun Laoghaire or, as my grandmother insisted, Kingstown. She always sealed her letters with sealing wax, and between that and the roaring fires she enjoyed, the family were convinced she would burn the place down. Our visits there often culminated in tears and a sudden departure. I always looked back to see my aunt in the porch, looking forlorn. She was difficult, but I adored her and even at that age I recognised a kindred spirit.

I have very clear memories of my grandmother as a regal presence in our lives, though without the frigid imperiousness of my other grandmother. I was desolate when she died in 1955. She was buried in Co. Laois after a funeral service in St John the Evangelist in Mounttown. The choir sang 'Abide with Me' and 'Rock of Ages' and I couldn't hear those hymns for twenty years afterwards without bursting into tears. Her death was a horrible wrench.

I met my father's mother on just one occasion, although at one time she lived in the same district of Dublin as us. I was four, and accompanied my father on the visit. My memories are of an imperious old lady in a white lace cap who chastised me for fidgeting. After my father's death I wasn't allowed any more contact with her, which is rather sad, as she actually lived on in Dublin till I was ten. She died in a house on the North Circular Road, close to the Phoenix Park, and had definitely been on the slide since the death of 'the Montys'.

My parents' families never got on, and looked down on each other simultaneously. That may be a mathematical impossibility but it was a social reality for us. My mother didn't approve of the Norrises, apart from my father, believing they were too flighty. Her family didn't approve of looking for publicity or appearing in the newspapers at all, and despised politics as 'a vulgar trade'. The FitzPatricks certainly wouldn't have thought much of me and my subsequent adventures!

But if the subject of the Norrises came up in conversation I would stick up for my father's family and point out that his grandmother was a baroness in her own right (who, I discovered thanks to Douglas Appleyard, a Stoker connection who is a gifted genealogist, rejoiced in the name of Wilhelmina Augusta van Kamperdijk), to which my aunt would reply that it wasn't a real title, because it wasn't British. 'They hand those out like peanuts in Europe, and in any case one look at your grandmother's nose would tell you what she was – a Middle European Jewess.' To the somewhat surprised discomfiture of my aunt, I was delighted by this prospect.

My father's sister, Pauline, was one of the very first women aviators, holding a flying licence from 1917, and was married to a much-decorated American flying ace called Dean Lamb. He occupies a footnote in military history as he is reputed to be the first man to have been involved in an aerial dogfight – he and his adversary fired pistols at each other out of two rickety biplanes in the skies above Mexico before World War I:

> Over Naco the enemy airmen entered into a pistol argument, which ended with no casualties. Circling to re-load, Lamb held his gun inside his shirt when ejecting the shells and loaded from his belt, the pistol between his legs and one hand on the wheel. It was the first air duel on record.

I recently managed to acquire a rare copy of his autobiography, *The Incurable Filibuster: The Adventures of Colonel Dean Ivan Lamb*. You get some idea of the nature of the man right at the beginning of the book when he tells of his experiences in New Orleans, aged nineteen. Gambling was prohibited within the city so he took a streetcar out to Jefferson County one night. He lost all his money, but not before realising the deck was stacked and the croupier fiddling the cards. He went to a local lawyer friend, who gave him sage advice: 'Accept the fact you were a bloody fool and learn a lesson from it – don't go back because they'll probably put a bullet in you.' However, next day Lamb did go back, this time with a Colt revolver. As soon as he caught the croupier cheating again he pulled the gun, revealed the swindle and forced them to hand over the pot. He backed his way out of the saloon with the gun in one hand and the money in the other, before he jumped on the St Charles streetcar, gave the startled driver a $100 bill and told him to drive like hell to the end of the line.

Pauline and Dean divorced on the grounds of his adultery in 1930, and Lamb was later accused of misappropriating $30,000 in diamonds and rubies entrusted to him by a diplomat friend in Manhattan. He claimed during a trial that made the front page of the *New York Times* that he had sent the gems to his sister in Ohio just before her home burnt to the ground. He was acquitted for lack of evidence. Whatever the truth of this, he was certainly a Gatsbyesque figure of the Jazz Age, and at this distance I'm prepared to find his exploits entertaining, although I completely understand why my mother wished to keep her distance. She would have felt his career justified her own mother's dictum, 'Don't stir mud,' but since childhood I have always found puddles – and the mud they conceal – irresistible. Especially when a good stir reveals a trove of diamonds and rubies.

After the divorce Pauline had married her sister's widower, Ernest Augustus Hamilton, another American air ace, by whom she had two children. With Douglas Appleyard's help I traced her children as far as I could but there is no record of them after 2006, while my father's third sister had a daughter who moved to Belgium, so there may be other Norris cousins around the place. I think my interest in meeting some member at least of my father's family is understandable, because without it part of my ancestry is extinguished. I have seen a live elephant, a live kangaroo and a live hippopotamus, but besides my brother, a childhood memory of my father and a fleeting glimpse of his brother Max, I have yet to see a live Norris.

I regret not getting to know more of my father's family, especially as, unbeknown to me, several of them made their homes in Ireland. One evening in 1975 I heard Humphrey Lyttelton on the BBC play a request for his old school chum Maxwell Norris, who lived in Mullinacuffe, Co. Wicklow. He was my uncle, but that was the first I had heard of any of my father's family being alive. The next weekend I was free I took my Aunt Constance to lunch in Hunter's Hotel in Wicklow and suggested a drive out towards Tinahely. I stopped various locals to ask the way, to the great consternation of my aunt, who realised what I was up to. I eventually found their cottage and knocked on the door. His wife, Gabriella, answered, and I caught a glimpse of Maxwell, in a blue boiler suit, dashing away down the garden. They were always short of money so perhaps he thought I was one of his creditors.

Gabriella said they were no longer in business selling herbs – I had also discovered that Max wrote on gardening for the *Irish Independent* and was a celebrated herbalist – so I left without revealing who I was. Just a few weeks later he was out for a walk on a summer evening when a motorcycle came around the corner and flattened him. It took him several hours to die at the side of the road, but that was still long before the ambulance arrived. Gabriella, deeply traumatised, went to Dublin with the ambulance and never returned to Mullinacuffe.

Max had an enormous collection of books which disappeared as word spread and vans started arriving from all over Ireland to raid their home. One bibliophile told me that he had gone down to rescue the books and had found Max's diaries, which he had then put through my letterbox. But he had got the number of the house wrong and the diaries disappeared, presumably thrown in the bin. I went down again and found the cottage almost in ruins, but did manage to salvage one incomplete handwritten diary of Max's, which contained reminiscences, one on how dull Sunday was as a boy in suburban London, and another, intriguingly, concerning Gabriella's sister who, according to Max's diary, knew the inside story of 'Anastasia', who had claimed to be the last survivor of

Tsar Nicholas II of Russia's family after the massacre at Ekaterinburg. Alas, on the details of the story Max remained silent.

Gabriella took a suite in the Burlington Hotel until the money ran out, and was then moved to a council cottage. I got in touch and corresponded with her and she told me of her extraordinary background. Her family were comfortably off, part of a strange Hungarian Protestant minority in Romania. They lived in Odorhei and, while their fortunes had fallen along with the collapse of the Austro-Hungarian Empire, she had still sometimes mixed in exalted circles. She was a skiing champion, and was a guest of Prince Paul of Romania at his ski lodge, while her brother was a good friend of Miklos Horthy, son of the Regent of Hungary. The family were later persecuted by the Nazis before the final straw when everything was seized by the communists. As a result Gabriella developed a neurotic fear and loathing of anything associated with communism.

She escaped to London, where she studied cosmetology and became the make-up artist for the celebrated tenor Richard Tauber, renowned for songs such as 'Good Night, Vienna' and 'Girls Were Made to Love and Kiss', and lived with him and his wife in his suite in the Dorchester Hotel. She then had the misfortune to meet Max, who took her for a walk across the Sahara Desert and proposed. They married and moved to Ireland, but money was never plentiful.

Years later I went down to Wicklow to do a charity show and, as Mullinacuffe was close by, asked the organiser Paddy O'Toole, a steadfast supporter of mine for the presidency, if there were any locals who might remember Max. He told me there would be someone there in the evening, who turned out to be the old lad who was parking the cars. He knew Max well and said that although a product of the public school system he was a great fellow with no affectations. He confirmed he used to play a lot of jazz music – he had been a friend of Louis Armstrong, who had stayed with them in London when he was over on tour –

and also revealed that he was a yoga fanatic and had appeared on an early *Late Late Show* doing a demonstration.

I only made real contact with Gabriella in 1990, when I traced her and started to write to her. She had become a recluse and she wrote back enigmatically:

> Dear Mr Norris,
> The histories of some families are so complex that they are more like a ball of wool with which two kittens have been playing and sharpening their nails on for weeks. They remain tangled and impossible to unravel – ever.
> It was nearly half-a-century ago when I entered the enigmatic circle of the Norris family, with its unfathomable and fateful mystery . . .

She was a very determined character and refused to accept any offers of help. She was living in awful conditions and eventually I asked a neighbour to persuade her that a new fridge and bed I had delivered to her had actually come from the St Vincent de Paul charity and that she would be evicted by the council if she didn't accept these new things. Sometime later I got a call to say she hadn't been seen for a few days so I went round and saw that she had collapsed and was lying on the floor. She wouldn't let us in so we called the police and an ambulance, and eventually I had to push a large garda through a half-open window. He got the door open and I went in and introduced myself; something clicked with her, so she would only agree to go to St Vincent's Hospital if I went with her in the ambulance. I had her house renovated and painted to await her return, but she never did.

I have sometimes been asked if I am a member of the 'Ascendancy', apparently because of the tonality of my voice. The answer is no. I am part of the *Descendancy*. Our family has been coming down in the world since 1169 AD and although in my lineage I can count not just Kings of Ossory and Leinster but indeed a couple of High Kings of Ireland, I am afraid that with me we have attained Ground Zero.

I suppose the fact that I was deliberately deprived of information about one side of my family, coupled with the storytelling of the other side, may have given me my interest in genealogy. However, this interest is purely human and entertaining. My view has always been that we are all descended from frogspawn at the time of the Big Bang, and that if one went back far enough we would find an equal number of princes, paupers, prostitutes and pawnbrokers in every family. I don't believe that anyone has the right to consider themselves superior because of an accident of birth. As a friend of mine, Pat Landers, once said to me, it's not the nest you come from that matters, it's how well and how far you can fly. However, it is fascinating if you are lucky enough – and with the growth of the internet many more people are – to be able to find a thread in the family tapestry and follow it back through history.

That is why, when I was contacted fifteen years ago by the Fitzpatrick Clan Society – who knew of my antecedents – I was delighted to join. Full credit must go to the indefatigable Ronan Fitzpatrick from Tallaght, who organises the clan gatherings. The Fitzpatricks are indeed an Irish clan, and an interesting one at that. The name is widespread in Ireland and many assume it to be Norman, but it is in fact a Normanised version of the much older Irish clan Mac Giolla Padraig. This comes from the Gaelic phrase 'son of the servant of Patrick', which refers to a fifth-century princeling who was given by his father to serve as a guide to St Patrick. Naturally the further one goes back the wilder and less credible the narrative becomes, although there is often a grain of truth in what appears the craziest fantasy. In any case, we're all part of the tribe, or clan, something in the manner of the Knox family in Somerville and Ross's delightful stories of the Irish R.M., encompassing all the classes and trades but bound together by a clan loyalty.

At the first meeting of the society there was a very nice American family who appeared to have oceans of money and produced an inscribed vellum scroll showing their descent as far back as Noah. They made a very good case to be the true descendants of the ancient Kings of Ossory. It was all great fun as we bowed and scraped and called them 'milord' and 'milady'. Then a most interesting woman said that she was, in the midst of all this royalty and nobility, one of the 'ordinary' Fitzpatricks. 'My folks left the Queen's County in the early 1840s. They made their way to New Orleans where they worked on the levees.' She pointed out that a huge number of Irish worked on building these structures, and a disproportionate number were among the 13,000 who died in an ensuing cholera epidemic. However, she was no 'ordinary' Fitzpatrick but a senior scientist with NASA with access to DNA-tracing facilities. I rushed forward and offered my veins to be opened and my blood shed in the interest of documentation of the family. However I was spurned because I was only a Fitzpatrick on my mother's side. I got my cousin David Fitzpatrick, an orthopaedic surgeon, to volunteer some saliva, which was then sent off to NASA in a special container.

We both got a bulky package from the US a few months later. 'Did you understand that stuff?' he asked when he rang me. 'I can't make head or tail of all this XY sort of stuff and I'm a doctor.' I told him to look at the last page, where the immortal line rang out about the FitzPatricks of Deerpark, myself, my cousins and one or two others being the last remnants of the ancient, royal and noble house of Ossory.

Some years before, a distant cousin, Denys FitzPatrick, had contacted me through Hugh O'Callaghan, son of an Olympic gold medallist and himself a celebrated athlete, to explore our shared ancestry. Denys was the grand-nephew of Barney Fitzpatrick, Lord Castletown, and became the last man to hold the ancient title of the Mac Giolla Padraig. I visited him in Florida, where he was fêted by the society ladies for his connection to

English royalty – he was an 'unofficial' grandson of Edward VII through his father, one of the Skeffington-Smiths.

I did a launch for one of Trinity's campus companies, a genealogy concern called Eneclann, and in return they offered me 500 worth of the firm's services. I told them I was descended from John Fitzpatrick, the second and last Earl of Upper Ossory (there was a bit of bastardy there too), and asked them to find the missing link to my mother's family. Most of the records had gone up in smoke in the Custom House in 1921, and the rest became difficult to access when there was a dramatic change of circumstances at the local rectory. But Eneclann narrowed the field down to four likely candidates, of which my favourite was a man called Michael Valentine FitzPatrick, who enters history briefly, and not entirely gloriously, as the proprietor of a dunghill at the rear of no. 3 Coote Terrace, Mountrath. I wrote back to say they could forget the others as I wanted warmly to embrace Michael Valentine since I thought his dunghill was the perfect antidote to snobbery. I told them I would be commissioning a new coat of arms featuring, instead of the order of the garter, a garter of ordure.

Denys was friendly with the Duke of Windsor, who, due to the antics of his uncle Edward VII, was in fact his cousin. He, or rather his dogs, had a bit-part in the Bing Crosby film *The Road to Morocco*. He told me how Dorothy Lamour was terrified of the lions that had been hired from Los Angeles Zoo, so he offered the use of his two Great Danes and the make-up studio did the rest. Denys was gay, and friendly with a Russian aristocrat called Count Felix Yusupov, who is best known as the man who assassinated Rasputin. Yusupov, an exceptionally handsome man, presented Denys with his jewelled waistcoat, which Denys told me he had lost at a raucous weekend party in New England; but my own view is that he either sold it or pawned it.

On my grandmother's side, my mother and aunt had occasionally talked about their Stoker relatives, many of whom were medical men (there were eleven doctors named Stoker in the Dublin medical directory at one stage), including Sir Thornley Stoker, who lived in the magnificent Georgian Ely House in Ely Place which is now occupied by the Knights of St Columbanus. The Stokers were also great furniture makers – I still have a lovely early-nineteenth-century cabinet made in Maryborough by my great-grandfather Joseph Creighton Stoker.

The best-known scion of the family, however, was Sir Thornley's brother Bram, the author of *Dracula*. When *Dracula* was made Book of the City a couple of years ago in Dublin, the remnants of the Stoker family called around to my home for tea. After an academic symposium on Dracula, one of his close relatives turned to me and said, 'Well, that was all frightfully intellectual, and I'm *sure* terribly clever, but Bram told my father the real story of the origins of that book. It seems he had been reading about Transylvania and the vampires when Sir Henry Irving [the celebrated London actor for whom Bram acted as manager] called by and invited him out for a gut-buster of a meal. Off they went to the Café Royal, where they devoured a mountain of dressed crab and guzzled bottle after bottle of champagne, after which Bram came home and had the most violent gut ache all night. That gave him such awful nightmares that when he awoke the next morning he had *Dracula* written in his head.'

My grandfather's family, like many old Irish families, had a strong mixture of Anglican and Catholic blood. It's a curious and little-known fact that the central stems of most of the old Irish families who managed to hold on to their Gaelic titles and acquire new English ones became members of the Church of Ireland – the O'Grady of Kilballyowen, the McGillycuddy of the Reeks, the O'Hara, the O'Morchoe and the Mac Giolla Padraig. However, the holders of the most romantic titles, the O'Connor Don, descendant of the last High King, and MacDermot, Prince of Coolavin, remained true to the old faith.

In my grandfather's family this theological mongrulity, as Myles na Gopaleen might have called it, was well known. He had inherited the rosary beads of a famous early-nineteenth-century ancestor, Daniel Delany, Bishop of Kildare and Leighlin from 1783 to 1814. The beads remained in the family and were inherited by two spinster cousins who died some years ago. I phoned the house to make sure they were safe but the Cork relative who was clearing it out said, 'Oh, those old things. I thought they were a skivvy's necklace and threw them in the bin. They went out on Thursday.' It was rather sad to lose such relics, but they were of course quite cheap and unornamented, being from the Penal period. However, although the physical object is lost, his story is still instructive. For Bishop Delany founded both the Brigidine Sisters and Patrician Brothers. When the Sisters celebrated their recent bicentenary, I was invited as guest speaker to talk about the family. I did some research and found I was descended from Delany on both sides of my mother's family. The story, which I have authenticated, was that Dr Delany's mother was one of the FitzPatricks of Ossory, but because of the Penal Laws they were in reduced circumstances.

His parents died suddenly and tragically young, whereupon the young Delany was fostered to his FitzPatrick relations in Mountrath, who were staunch Anglicans. Despite this they honoured his father's dying wish that the son be brought up as Catholic. With the help of some neighbours my antecedents decently and bravely raised the money for him to be educated in France, a risky act for a Protestant family in the Penal times. He became a priest and eventually a bishop.

Over one hundred years later, my mother's brother, Uncle Dick, had to abandon his education at King's Hospital in Dublin. It was a brutal regime where the alcoholic headmaster used to wake up the boys at night to beat them, and the neglect and deprivation led to Dick contracting diphtheria. (Fortunately, King's Hospital is now a well-run school.) My grandparents brought him back to Laois, but when the Patrician

Brothers got to hear about this they took him in and gave him a top-class classical education, which ensured he won every prize in Latin, Greek and Hebrew when he was at Trinity.

He studied divinity there and had as tutors Revd Dr Newport White and Revd Sir J. P. Mahaffy. Newport White was the man who came up with the celebrated quip – often misattributed to later figures – when a boorish man approached him in his club and said, 'I say, old boy, can you tell me where you can take a piss around here?': 'I do think I can help you,' he replied. 'If you go down the corridor and turn left, you will see a door that is marked "Gentlemen". But don't let that deter you.'

To me, Mahaffy was a treacherous character and a frightful snob who had been Oscar Wilde's tutor in Trinity but who abandoned him cruelly when the heat came on. 'We no longer speak of Mr Wilde in Trinity' was his heartless jibe at the time of the great writer's tragic fall from grace. He took the young Oscar to Greece with him on one occasion, and on his return completed a book about social life among the Ancient Greeks. In this was a chapter detailing the sexual morality of the time as described in Plato's *Symposium*. However, when this came under attack from his fellow clerical academics in Oxford and Cambridge, the cowardly Mahaffy suppressed the chapter. So much for intellectual freedom in Trinity in the nineteenth century! However, he was at least partly responsible for Wilde's renowned wit, the basis for which is quite simple – one takes a platitude and inverts it. A classic example of this would be the Victorian cliché 'Drink is the curse of the working classes', which becomes 'Work is the curse of the drinking classes'.

Uncle Dick thought he was wonderful, however, and I still have a letter Mahaffy wrote to a commanding officer, General Fry, recommending my uncle for a transfer: '. . . an excellent youth, highly educated man . . . please do what you can'.

Uncle Dick, or Lieutenant R. W. Fitz-Patrick (he insisted on the hyphen *and* capital P), did well in the British army, rising to the rank of colonel and becoming chaplain to the Brigade of

Guards. He believed in horses, the royal family and God, in that order. His love of horses got him into trouble when he returned to Co. Laois in the 1920s and set off riding around the fields wearing his British Army uniform.

He had quite an exciting time of it after the First World War, travelling in what was still an extensive British Empire. He was based a lot of the time around the Mediterranean Sea, and enjoyed particularly his time in Malta, where he attended parties thrown by Mabel Strickland, a famous hostess who owned the *Times of Malta*. There were more parties in Alexandria, hosted by King Farouk of Egypt, and he returned from Palestine with an enormous stack of photo-negatives on glass plate, which I still have in its hand-made wooden box.

He became chaplain to the royal family, and grew close to Queen Mary after her son ran off with the twice-divorced American Wallis Simpson. He missed his own mother in Ireland, while the old Queen was desolate for her son, with whom she cut off all contact, so there was a natural affinity despite the difference in status. My mother disapproved of the elopement, saying Edward 'was a bloody fool to give up being Admiral of the Fleet to be third mate to an American tramp'. She was a keen follower of royal affairs and had no difficulty in seeing herself both as Irish and British. We were required to stand for 'God Save the King', with which the BBC concluded its broadcasts each day, and she wept when George VI died.

My grandfather should have inherited a considerable landholding, but instead all he got was four encumbered farms. He never succeeded in getting out of debt, although he would turn his hand to anything that was decent and legal to make a buck. At one stage, he ran the post office in Mountrath. Queen Mary asked Uncle Dick one day, 'You often speak of your father. May I ask what is his profession?', to which, with typical sardonic humour, he replied, 'He's a postman, ma'am.' Queen Elizabeth clearly liked my Uncle Dick, as she used her prerogative to allow him to stay on well past the usual period of office, and he once enlisted most of the ladies of the royal family to embroider the kneelers for the Guards Chapel. 'Mr Fitz-Patrick, you're a natural autocrat!' Queen Mary told him, which was quite a remark from a former empress to a commoner. When she died he was one of a very few non-royal people allowed into her crypt to place some lily-of-the-valley on her coffin.

Uncle Dick's regular visits to Dublin were a highlight of my childhood. He floated into our lives, wafting aftershave and wearing jewellery, practically indictable offences in dull, grey 1950s Dublin. He had extraordinary Munchausenesque stories about his travels and the people he met, and the wonderful view he was granted of major historic events such as the funeral of King George VI and the coronation of Queen Elizabeth II. He knew Winston Churchill, and was friendly with his wife Clementine, who wrote several letters to him after his retirement, which I still have.

Uncle Dick always travelled with a selection of books, into which I dipped occasionally. He had catholic tastes, greatly enjoyed *Borstal Boy*, and wrote to tell Brendan Behan so. Behan sent him back a postcard which read:

Reverend Richard, a chara,
Thanks very much for the kind note. I had some experience of the
C of E druids in the nick, and they were all decent chaps.
Yours, Brendan

My mother, however, did not appreciate Behan's masterpiece and when she caught me reading it she flicked through it, only to find it filled with what she regarded as foul language, and promptly deposited it, with a tongs, in the flames of the kitchen range.

After the Guards Chapel Uncle Dick withdrew to Ashwell in Rutland, where an old army friend, Colonel Hanbury, had the feudal right to appoint the vicar. His Burley-on-the-Hill estate had its own chapel, and Uncle Dick also had care of St Mary's, Ashwell. He made a great success of the job, installing central heating and packing out the services with his colourful sermons, for example on the Ten Commandments. He would illustrate each by allotting it to a different parishioner, ascribing adultery to 'Lady —, who, as we speak, is committing it in the stables with the head groom.'

After his death and burial in Laois, his military friends organised a memorial service for him in Ashwell, and my cousin David FitzPatrick and I went over. One of his friends, an army chaplain, did the oration, and, as he was a bit rotund, got stuck climbing into the pulpit. With all the huffing and puffing he dropped his speech but reassembled the pages in the wrong order. Towards the end of one page there was a flourish of rhetorical questions.

'Some of you are probably asking, "What is the meaning of life? What is it all about?" Some of you may be pondering the eternal question, "Where is our brother Richard now?"'

With that he turned to the next page, but it was the wrong one and he got completely confused, looked straight down at the congregation and spluttered, 'Well, I haven't got the slightest idea, and I doubt if any of you have either. In the name of the Father, Son and Holy Ghost, amen,' and sat down.

It was a moment of wonderful, devastating, theological honesty. My cousin and I creased ourselves laughing, to the frozen disapproval of the Guards officers.

I've always loved the idea of a family, and throughout my life have always tried to assemble the elements of it, which is probably why I clung to the remains of my relationship with Ezra later through so many vicissitudes. But as a child I had a reasonably ordered life. We had a part-time gardener who came to the house in Ballsbridge once a week called Flynn who had trained at Lord Killanin's estate in Spiddal. I'm deeply ashamed to recall that I used to call him by his surname, but I was just a boy and that was the way it was then. He stayed with me long after my mother died and when I moved to Greystones in the

1970s I would collect him once a week in Harold's Cross and bring him out to tend my garden. Flynn was a gentle man and a gentleman, with a lovely open face, a fresh complexion, white hair and blue eyes. He never used a bad word, of any shade, and I never heard him say a negative thing about anybody. It was an aesthetic pleasure to watch him work and to admire the precise geometry of his borders, beds and drills. Even the birds loved him, and when he would leave his spade in the ground invariably a robin would fly to sit on the handle.

We had one maid, Nelly, in the early 1950s. She was a small, mousy woman who would do anything for you and I was heartbroken when she was 'let go'. She lived in the centre of the city, and was quite elderly. I think my mother suspected she might have tuberculosis, but I argued and begged that she be kept on. I was concerned about how she would survive as an elderly single woman in those days when there were no social supports. Another maid, Mrs Kavanagh, said we were savages from Darkest Africa, so we confirmed her fears one day when my mother was out by dancing semi-naked along the banisters with knives in our teeth and chanting threats to disembowel her.

Another dominant figure in my childhood was Mrs McDonnell, a woman from Wexford who became more a friend of the family than an employee. She was very good to my mother in difficult times, and afterwards came with me to Dundrum and then Greystones. She had a Honda 50 autoscooter which she drove from East Wall, through the city and out over Bray Head to my home, in all weathers. It gave me a feeling of continuity in my life and she too acted as a maternal presence.

Aunt Constance was a marvellous woman, and after my mother's death she moved into my life in her place and became a wise, guiding, loving presence for the next forty years. She had lived in England for a while after their home in Laois was sold in 1946. She was employed as companion to an elderly couple who were members of the Barrow-Cadbury family. They loved her and offered to leave her their magnificent house if she would stay on, but she wanted to come home to Ireland. She had kept on a few acres outside Mountrath into the late 1950s, but even they were eventually sold. I was desperately sad when I heard that. Although I was only thirteen, I was aware that it was breaking a link to the land that had been in the family since before the Norman Invasion.

My mother herself was not, perhaps, conventionally pretty, but she had a noble face full of humour and warmth. There were times when I disloyally wished she could have been as glamorous as some of my friends' mothers. I wished that she could have dyed her hair, backcombed it up into a fashionable American style, and worn earrings or high-heeled shoes. But there was little chance of that; the shoes were certainly out, since she was large-boned and crippled with the rheumatoid arthritis she had developed in Africa. She also had an aristocratic disdain for the type of cheap adornment I then thought sophisticated.

Dublin in the 1950s was a very different place to the city in which I live today. It was an age of courtesy, deference and good manners. There was almost no public drunkenness at all – and when it did occur it was a truly shocking sight. The mood of the times was such that most women – and certainly ladies – simply didn't go into pubs, which would have been regarded as out-rageous behaviour. Grafton Street was, in the words of Noel Purcell's song, 'a wonderland'. I remember my mother being dismayed when Cavendish's opened a furniture store which sold items on hire purchase, or 'never never', in Grafton Street – she saw the street as a social preserve, a boulevard that was the natural habitat for a certain type of person. But I loved Cavendish's because one of the great Dublin entertainers, Peggy Dell, would occasionally play ragtime on a piano in the window. She always had a cigarette dangling from her lips, and when ash would periodically drop on to the keys, she would brush it away with a magnificent arpeggio. Just off Grafton Street, on Wicklow Street, a lady with the face and hairstyle of a Roman matron used to play a heavily ornamented and gilded concert harp while a discreet mother-of-pearl conch shell lay at her feet to collect the financial tributes of passers-by. The shops on the street had a style that reflected their clientele. Gibson Price was a gentlemen's outfitters which also made the royal racing colours and carried a crest showing royal approval above its doorway.

There were several restaurants and cafés where we would stop for refreshments, such as the upmarket Mitchell's – now a fast-food joint – Jammet's, Fuller's and Ferguson's. They all had their own distinct delicacy, Fuller's being a white-iced walnut sponge cake and Ferguson's the most delicious cream-filled meringues. We particularly enjoyed the classically Quaker produce of good wholesome food and yellow Jersey milk in Bewley's Oriental Café.

The original Brown Thomas had a very sophisticated appearance, with a richly carpeted marble staircase and immaculately groomed staff. The window displays were done by established artists such as Norah McGuinness, commissioned by the store owner, Senator Edward McGuire. I can still recall the heady scent of expensive perfume as you walked through the door. Now only Weir the jewellers remains as an example of what a 1950s Grafton Street store was like.

In some ways my mother was haunted by Africa. She would from time to time try to reach out to her past, such as the occasion she bought an avocado in Smyths on the Green, the first time such food had been seen in Dublin, or when we would visit the Botanic Gardens in Glasnevin. On those excursions she would seek out the palm house and sit on a bench inside in the stifling heat, inhaling the tropical odour and recalling her happy days in the Congo.

She had an intensely difficult life, partly because she continued to be very much in love with my father until the day of her death. She was aged forty-nine when he died, and showed no interest in having an active social life thereafter. She was a wonderful gardener and spent many hours in our garden, which had been part of the orchard of the big house that stood near by. Our back wall was part of the original estate, and was very high, with large lumps of limestone and mortar, and birds nested in the cracks. She did much of the work herself, and every springtime we had an ocean of daffodils and narcissi under the trees in the back garden. She loved fruit too, and grew many varieties, including white, yellow and red raspberries. I inherited her love of the garden, and had my own little patch where I could grow my own favourites.

She also had a wonderful natural gift for happiness, something which I have inherited from her. It was always in her nature to be happy, and to want others to be happy. She was the epitome of George Herbert's wonderful poem:

> *A man that looks on glass,*
> *On it may stay his eye;*
> *Or if he pleaseth, through it pass,*
> *And then the heaven espy.*

She delighted in laughter, and music, and she loved me; I was glad I was able, despite the Victorian reserve in our family, to tell her I loved her too before she died.

CHAPTER 2

Borstal Boy

ONE WARM, SUNNY MORNING IN THE LATE AUTUMN OF 1948, my brother John took me by the hand and walked me down through Wilfield Park and Gilford Park towards Park Avenue. There was plenty of bustling activity as we watched the bread man making his deliveries and heard the strains of the BBC radio programme *Housewives' Choice* drifting through the open windows. I had a glorious sense of freedom – but as I looked up at the high garden walls of Mrs Newman's school I realised that was about to end.

I recently came across the ancient prospectus for the school that my mother must have received. It listed all the activities available, of which I most enjoyed art classes, with the lovely smell of the big tins of powdered paint. I relished sloshing it around and was always most displeased that I couldn't get what I wanted on to the paper and usually ended up with a purple-brown splodge.

I had a nasty shock one day when I discovered that I couldn't read. My grandmother had a book of Russian fairy tales which she would read to me, but after she had been sent into exile in Dun Laoghaire, I decided I would now read it myself. I was furious and called out to my mother, 'This book must be in Russian – because I can't read it!' I didn't realise you had to *learn* how to read – I thought you just looked at the words and immediately read. I did learn to read – and write – and when I was five years old I produced my first 'book', a moral tale called 'The Proud Potato', which dealt with class distinctions in the vegetable world.

Sunday was the day we went to church, and it was normal to attend two or three services over the course of the day. We went to St Mary's parish church, on the corner of Simmonscourt and Anglesea Roads, where Canon Powell was the rector. The children had Bible class there in the vestry, leaving the main service just before the sermon, which would have been regarded as above our infant heads. Every one of us had a little booklet and each week we were given a stamp which also recorded our attendance. The stamp had an illustration telling a story from the gospels. I loved the Bible stories, especially the New Testament parables, which struck me with their simple, eternal wisdom.

St Mary's was a traditional middle-of-the-road Church of Ireland parish, but I also went to St Bartholomew's in Clyde Road, which had a top-class choir for which you had to audition. We learnt quite a bit of musicianship there, singing Bach and Mozart. It was very High Church Anglican, with incense, vestments and candles; I loved it, but my mother did not approve of such things. She told me how, on a visit to London in the 1930s, she attended a church in Westminster where the incense was billowing and the chanting was all in Latin. She summoned the verger and asked was it a Roman Catholic church. He replied, 'Certainly not, madam,' to which my mother retorted, 'Well it ought to be,' and promptly left.

For a time I found certain aspects of Roman Catholicism quite attractive. I hated being left outside when my neighbour and best friend Michael Moran went to make his first confession. I could think of nothing more delicious than confiding my darkest thoughts to a handsome young priest and receiving forgiveness at his hands. I loved the waft of incense that came through the doorway, the light thrown by the candles, the colourful Stations of the Cross – it was all so sensual.

We were about eight or nine years old when a row blew up between Michael and myself over a Dinky toy. I had almost won the battle but loosened my grip fatally when I was met with the jibe 'Yah – you're not even a Catholic.' I went home to my mother in floods of tears. She asked me what was wrong and I told her Michael had said I wasn't a Catholic. 'Of course you are, darling,' she said. 'Every Sunday you say the Creed – "I believe in one holy, catholic and apostolic church." You are just not part of *the Roman Error* like Michael.' I hadn't a clue what this was, but unlike George Bush I could recognise a weapon of mass destruction when I saw one, and armed with the phrase, I threw it back at the heretic, with considerable success.

Michael Moran is one of my best friends to this day. More than sixty years ago we had a little gang in Wilfield Park. Our enemies were the boys and tomboys from Wilfield Road, who we suspected of ungentlemanly practices such as putting stones in their snowballs. Our response was to seek out higher technology – we got hold of a power-hose and, lying in wait, washed them off the street.

Michael's family owned Moracrete, at one time the largest cement producers in Ireland, and had an air-raid shelter built under their rockery. We commandeered this as the headquarters of the Adventurers Underground Society. In that damp, musty concrete basement we would plan our adventures by candle-light. I was the ringleader and would suggest all kinds of schoolboy devilment. Would we set fire to Mrs Connell's hedge? Would we climb the huge wall that surrounded the big house? Would we walk the roof of the henhouse? A member of our little band fell right through that roof one day and several birds died of fright, but he managed to extend his arms sideways so he didn't fall to the ground and, as he was suspended in the chicken wire, we were able to lift him out and resume our pose as suburban angels before the storm broke.

I had the advantage of being an alpha male with lots of organising skills, but that was also allied to a wild imagination. The result was involvement in some ambitious stunts. One day I convinced the others that we could fly, if we tried hard enough, concocted a potion of raspberry leaves, gooseberries and mud and recited a spell of my invention. Michael and John had seen plenty of my outlandish schemes and insisted I go first – but alas I was no Harry Potter. I climbed on to the roof of the outhouse, smeared a garden twig with the flying potion and, like Icarus, took to the skies. The result was a sprained ankle and a ride home in a wheelbarrow.

As we got a little older our territory expanded and we would make our way up to Sandymount Strand, where we would watch people from Irishtown as they set lines to catch plaice, flounder and dab. At weekends the people from the inner city would come out too, because it was the only beach within walking distance. In those days you could go into the Martello tower, where a little sweetshop also sold a kettle of boiling water for a halfpenny. The visitors would bring with them that peculiarly Dublin measure 'a screw of tea' and 'a screw of sugar' – which were cones of newspaper screwed tight – to make their refreshments.

In those days the sea came in as far as Irishtown, with high tide coming right up to the sea wall on Strand Road. The parks along that road had not yet been made from infill and there was almost no industry in the area except for the fascinating early-twentieth-century electricity-generating station on Pigeon House Road. The old red-brick station had seven chimneys and it was the first thing a visitor to the city saw as they sailed into the bay – most famously welcoming a returning Brendan Behan at the end of *Borstal Boy*.

One day, I resolved to make the most ambitious foray yet, an excursion necessarily made without parental consent. I walked across Sandymount Strand and the beach at the Shellybanks, past the Cockle Lake. Eventually I left behind the humming electricity station and the great Georgian block of the hotel opened by Mr Pigeon that gave its name to the whole Pigeon House area, passing the sewerage ponds where the excrement of hundreds of thousands of Dubliners lay settling as part of the process of extracting the solids. Its odour no doubt lent variety to the inhalations of the convalescents in the tuberculosis sanatorium next door.

I climbed on to the Great South Wall and headed out towards the Poolbeg Lighthouse at its tip, almost four miles from home. This was a place that always fascinated me, as it could be seen from many parts of the city. It also had a wonderful deep, vibrating foghorn which I often heard from my bedroom on wintry nights, eating into my imagination – an isolated wave- and mist-bound lighthouse so far away across the darkened waves of the bay.

On impulse I knocked on the door. After a few minutes the lighthouse keeper answered, and very kindly invited me in. There he told exciting stories of his former life as a sailor roaming the seven seas. But most thrilling of all was his pet monkey, which was amazing as such creatures were normally only ever seen in zoos. The monkey was tethered on a chain and sat in the observation window, jabbering away. It was the most exciting thing I had ever seen. I couldn't contain myself once home and blurted out the whole story, which earned me a walloping for travelling so far afield without permission.

Another adventure was the ferry ride across the Liffey at Ringsend, which cost threepence. That experience immediately connected many years later when I read the Joyce story 'An Encounter', where the two boys cross the river in the ferry. Lots of little episodes growing up connected with Joyce – the oul' wans with their prams struck a chord with Cissie Caffrey, and we of course had our own Martello tower in Sandymount which many tourists, and even some Joycean authorities, confused with the one out in Sandycove.

There was more upset when my father's solicitor in London, a doddery old man, tried to insist that my brother and I attend his old public school, Christ's Hospital in Sussex. We were horrified and refused to go, and my mother agreed and enrolled us in St Andrew's College which was then on Wellington Place, about a mile from our home in Sandymount. St Andrew's had been an excellent school when my parents left Ireland for Africa in the 1930s, and I'm glad to say it is so once again, but in the 1950s it was going through what could be euphemistically termed 'a rough patch'.

I enjoyed my first year there under the tutelage of form mistress Phyllis Sleator, with her lovely Northumbrian burr and her greying hair drawn back in a bun. She had beautiful handwriting and taught me well: I finished top of the class, with excellent grades in everything except arithmetic. I recently came across this school report among my papers and reread it with pleasure. 'David has worked much harder this year and gained first place in the examinations.'

But my idyllic life had started to change with my father's death, and further turmoil was to follow. My mother had found it very difficult to cope with losing her husband, and financial worries began to crowd in too. She should have been left comfortably off, but my father's hapless solicitor had invested his funds in hare-brained schemes such as Rhodesian railroads and various other allegedly blue-chip funds, and the estate, instead of multiplying in value, had dwindled back to pre-World War I levels. She took a job as a matron and French teacher in 'the Hall' – St Margaret's Hall, a school for young ladies along the Grand Canal near Mespil Road – and John and I were enrolled at St Andrew's as boarders. She only lasted six months at the Hall, but we were to have no early release from our prison. I suspect she found it difficult to cope with us and wanted some time on her own, being still devastated by my father's death, and in a misguided way wanted us to have some male role models.

I was aged about eight and suffered from agonies of home-sickness. I found the place, and the attitudes of the other boys, very crude. Many of the boarders seemed to be misfits of one sort or another – one or both parents were missing, or dead, or drinkers. Irish Protestant boarding schools of the era were 'yellow pack' versions of British public schools: possessing all of the defects and none of the virtues of that system.

There was one old fellow called the Sergeant, ex-army and now the school handyman, who had the face of a rat under a peaked cap and who encouraged a system of spying. He had a corps of what he called 'agents', spies who were encouraged to tell tales on their fellow pupils. The place was run by fear – fear of informants and fear of the staff.

The school was presided over by Dr P. J. Southgate, an eccentric who resembled a cartoon figure of an absent-minded professor. Indeed, the school was a male version of St Trinian's, and Dr Southgate the equivalent of Alastair Sim, who played Arabella Fritton in the famous films. That would all have been terribly entertaining if it hadn't had such disastrous effects.

Underneath Dr Southgate were employed people of various degrees of qualification and disqualification. The teachers were gods and could not be questioned or impugned in any way. There was a maths teacher who was presumed to have come from an obscure public school in England, which lent him airs. He wore an ironed gown and rimless glasses, but was an arrogant, violent man who sadistically beat the boys. I also recall seeing one pupil – almost certainly suffering from what we would now recognise as dyslexia – beaten into the corner like a dog by another teacher because he was having difficulty reading and writing.

The way the pupils were treated was Dickensian; it was our own Dotheboys Hall in the heart of prosperous suburbia. One boy from the west of Ireland, who had wet the bed, had his nose rubbed in the wet sheets while we watched his humiliation. Sixty years on I can still see him, with buck teeth and yellow hair, as the tears rolled down the cheeks of his tormented face. I joined an alliance with this boy, an early example of my defensive treatment of social pariahs, which was both principled and practical as I, too, had become an outsider in the dormitory. Someone had tried to steal a book of Bible stories that my grandmother had given me and I got into a huge fight which left me ostracised by the rest of the boarders.

My desperate friend continued to be bullied and abused until, one evening, he wandered out of the school gates on to the road, where he was knocked down and killed by a car. A story was put about that he had been going to the shops for sweets, but I am convinced he was running away. His funeral was at St Bartholomew's and I sang in the choir. As the coffin entered the church, followed by his sorrowing parents, my voice wavered. I too had been traumatised by the tragedy and for the rest of the service I just opened and closed my mouth soundlessly.

I had one serious run-in with the Sergeant, who coached boxing to the boarders on Saturday mornings. As a pacifist I did not believe in boxing so I resolutely refused to fight and told the Sergeant that, as I was a conscientious objector, I would refuse to hit back. There were a few half-hearted taps to my shoulder, which I ignored, so the Sergeant told my sparring partner to hit me on the nose so as to provoke a response.

I said, 'I wouldn't do that if I were you.'

But my opponent did as he was told, 'following orders' as usual, and hit me a bang on the nose. This is a highly unpleasant experience, and one I was not prepared to leave unavenged. I lashed out with my foot – and fractured his ankle, a circumstance which was certainly not contemplated by the Queensberry Rules.

For this crime I was condemned to spend Saturday mornings on my own in a room overlooking Wellington Place, where I was permitted to draw and paint. This had a positive result, as one drawing won first prize in a competition run by the London School of Drawing. It showed a rabbit, lying mournfully with its ears drooping through the bars of his hutch – the objective correlative, as T. S. Eliot would say, of my condition.

I was only caned once at St Andrew's. At the start of each year we were given a list of supplies, which was pasted inside our trunks. On the list I was given there was no mention of tracing paper, so when we were required to trace a map I knew I would be in trouble. I went to the kitchen staff and begged for some greaseproof paper, but they wouldn't give me any, so I swiped some sheets of Bronco lavatory paper. This was a hard, wrinkly paper, but it was impossible to disguise as the word 'Bronco' was stamped on every sheet. That didn't go down well with the teacher and I was sent to the headmaster's office.

I sat outside waiting in terror, but in a peculiarly detached way. I had a horrible feeling of being outside the system, because I was sitting in this timeless world while classes went on in the rest of the school. I looked at the wall and thought, *None of this is real*. The caning was very real, however, and destroyed any last vestige of respect I had for the system where a middle-aged scholar lost in the mists of Greek poetry had to address himself to the task of bambooing the backside of a terrified child.

I had been the victim of a gross injustice, and I never let it happen again. The second time a cane was produced to beat me unjustly, I took the law into my own hands. I had been accused of knocking an eccentric old lady off her bicycle but as I hadn't left the grounds it couldn't have been me. But they took her word and never did any investigation. I wasn't going to stand for that and I snatched the cane away, broke it in two and threw it back at the shocked teacher.

One of the unfortunate side-effects of having been pampered by my mother and the maids was that I wasn't able to tie my shoelaces. The penalty for that crime was to be deprived of breakfast, and after it happened a few times I was driven to desperation. With another boy, I sneaked into the kitchen to see what we could scavenge. Finding nothing to hand, we feasted on scraps from the bin.

I was traumatised by the whole experience of boarding at that awful school, and despaired that there was no authority to whom you could complain. I begged Mother to take us away but she was obdurate and insisted that we stay. I ran away frequently and was usually returned to St Andrew's by the gardaí, but on one occasion I got as far as Sandymount, where Mother rang the school and I was brought back.

My brother John, in addition to possessing a brilliant intellect, was a very fine sportsman, excelling at rugby and cricket. I was quite athletic too, and we both won prizes for swimming: he won a cup, I a set of Dinky road-traffic signs in a little yellow cardboard box. The open-air swimming pool was on the Stillorgan Road, where RTÉ is now, and had been built by the old boys during the war. It seemed almost Californian in its luxury to us, but there were gaping cracks between the bricks surrounding the pool in which you could painfully catch your toe if you weren't careful.

But basically, the sports ground was a place to escape the daily routine and sunbathe on a grassy bank less than a mile from the school. There was one curious series of incidents which made me terrified of trips there for a time. An older boy had started to chase me, and when he caught me he would try to take my trousers down. I was quite fast and able to evade him, but he was older and bigger and when he did catch me he was able to overpower me. I had no understanding of what was going on but my reaction was one of naked fear. I began to hate Tuesday afternoons, knowing that we had to go up to the cricket field and dreading he would be there, my heart thumping with terror when he was. I eventually told one of the teachers what was happening and asked him to stop the boy.

Nothing more was said until one day I happened to look out of the dormitory window only to see a big black sedan pull up outside the school and the boy being led out and put in the back seat with his trunk packed in beside him. It was very sad, and cruel, that his time at the school ended with his unfortunate father being summoned to collect him. Expulsion was no way to deal with such behaviour – the boy should have been helped, as should I, for I was traumatised too. But I was left in terrified ignorance because of the cowardice of the school authorities in neglecting to deal openly with the situation, opting instead to cover the episode in a cloak of silence. I felt ashamed, but, worse, I didn't know why. I didn't understand what it was all about and didn't associate it with anything sexual at all. I felt guilty that he was expelled on my account. But nothing was ever said. Not long afterwards I extricated myself from St Andrew's and made my way to somewhere that suited me much better.

The High School was a completely different style of institution to St Andrew's and I loved it from my very first day in Harcourt Street. It was a day school close to home, with no corporal punishment, and possessed a strong classical tradition under its headmaster, Dr R. W. Reynolds.

He was a noted Greek scholar, but to him Ancient Greece was not something long dead – it was a place and time still very much alive. He would put on plays in Classical Greek, an activity that increased when the school purchased grounds at Danum in Rathgar. The school eventually moved there, but before that we used it as a venue for outdoor dramas by Sophocles and Euripides.

These dramatic performances could be competitive – our opponents were usually St Columba's College or Portora Royal School, and we strove hard for victory which, to us, seemed to be achieved by whichever team managed to be the first to bore the opposition into submission. Portora, a public school near Enniskillen, won hands-down the year they were permitted to put on one of the very first performances of *Waiting for Godot* by Samuel Beckett, a past pupil who had been taught by Dr Seale, a celebrated classicist and cousin of my great-aunt. A critic once said that *Godot* is a play where nothing happens, twice. As schoolboys we didn't see the humour in it at all, and by act two we were well and truly bored and in a mutinous mood. On another occasion I was dismissed from the annual Greek play for being 'totally lacking in bodily grace' – perhaps so, but it didn't help that one of my classmates had stuck a nettle up my Grecian tunic – a simplified garment a bit like a male version of a mini-skirt.

It was at High School that the spark of talent I displayed under Miss Sleator was fanned into life again. Instead of teachers who actively disliked their students, or couldn't care less about their education, here were people motivated by a love of their subject and a desire to pass it on. That is the mark of the real teacher, such as I found later in Trinity with Brendan Kennelly.

One of the senior teachers, Sammy Evans, had taught my mother in Wesley College during the First World War, and was still around in the 1950s in High School. He was passionate about history and geography and could make his subjects come alive. Frank Peters was our Irish teacher, thanks to whose good teaching methods and generosity I still have a love of the language. I got a good honours result in the Leaving Certificate in Irish, which we learnt through the old-style Gaelic script.

I was also taught for a while by Dr Kenneth Milne, who started a drama society and would give up his evenings to coach us. I met him in Christ Church Cathedral recently and he reminded me that he gave me my first theatrical role – that of a newt in a one-act comedy called *Rock Bottom* – but best of all he introduced us to Dylan Thomas, via the wonderful BBC radio broadcast of *Under Milk Wood* in a performance led by Richard Burton.

I was curious, and greedy for knowledge, wanting to do every subject. But at a certain point I had to choose between science and Greek, and I went for science. Despite my failings at maths I was good at science subjects. I did my best to conquer arithmetic, but I was far too imaginative. I discovered too late, and fatally, the importance of the decimal point in logarithms. I did one of these old-fashioned questions in my exam which asked what was the price per ton of coal when, say, five hundredweight, seven stone and eleven pounds cost £5. 10s. I worked out that a ton cost over £17 million, and added a note that this showed how the Second Inter-Party Government was completely unable to cope with inflation.

My favourite teacher, a man who became a great friend afterwards, was Jack Cornish. He had the head of a Roman emperor – he looked like the famous bust of Nero – and a great sense of style. Jack was the son of a Methodist minister and was a pupil at Wesley College when my mother and aunt were there. That was very typical of the closed Dublin Protestant community at the time, where everyone knew everyone else.

He was a slightly eccentric but quite brilliant man, and I saw him as a romantic figure like Sherlock Holmes. The boys knew him as 'the Nipper', but I never found out why. He had a powerful intellect and strong personality, but never once raised his voice in class. I always thought that he hadn't quite achieved his potential; with his sense of style and beautiful way of expressing himself, he was an unfulfilled artist.

His teaching was inspirational, however, as he introduced us to eighteenth-century writers such as Joseph Addison, Richard Steele and Charles Lamb. Jack had been at Trinity with Samuel Beckett and Owen Sheehy-Skeffington, and as a classicist was very precise about the use of language – he hated when we misused words such as 'nice' or 'gorgeous', which have very precise meanings that are now largely ignored. He gave me extra tuition, especially in my final year, and it was largely thanks to him that I developed such a love of English literature.

Jack's real passion was rugby, which he believed was a type of chess. He was a tactician who did not see the game as just kicking, grunting, pushing and heaving. He always wore a very well-cut tweed sports jacket and finely pressed grey slacks – and when he had to go out to coach rugby he would just exchange his shoes for a pair of rugby boots, tucking his trousers into his socks. I wasn't a bad rugby player out on the right wing, but because I was knocked about a bit by several bouts of pneumonia I never made it past the second XV. Jack's proudest moment was when he coached High School's senior team to the Leinster Schools Senior Cup for the only time, by beating Belvedere College in 1973.

After I left school we would meet for a meal every six months or so. He judged eating-places by the quality of their Melba toast, and for our outings he would seek out the best place currently serving it around the city. We often ended up in the most unlikely places. Jack's tipple was Gordon's gin and Rose's lime, with two cubes of ice. His taste in reading was equally eccentric – although I am a great lover of detective fiction, I disagreed with him on his fondness for Ian Fleming, to whom he was devoted long before he became popular through the James Bond movies.

Among my other favourites on the staff was our science teacher, Mr Gardiner, known as Fritz because of his Germanic haircut, who was the epitome of the science teacher of school comics – domed forehead, round glasses, easily frayed temper and a tendency to create explosions in the lab. After one of these disasters, when there was not only a loud report and a flash but the room was suffused with the malodorous pong of sulphurated hydrogen, we all howled our approval. Mr Gardiner climbed on to a chair and addressed us: 'You think you are little gentlemen, but you're nothing but a crowd of Cabra gobshites.' We were absolutely thrilled by this; the idea that we had been able to provoke a teacher into the use of the word 'gobshite' was a significant achievement, although his assumption that Cabra produced more gobshites than any other suburb of Dublin appeared less than scientific.

Jack Cornish's old college friend Owen Sheehy-Skeffington chaired a schools debate in February 1963 at which I spoke on the motion 'that woman's place is in the kitchen'. I insisted that 'the prime purpose of the female is to feed the male. If I had my way she would be given a mat in the corner of the kitchen and chained to the stove.'

I was on the High School team with my good and, alas, recently deceased friend Paul Walsh, and the *Irish Times* reported my contribution thus: 'David Norris said "not only should women not receive equal pay, but their present activities should be drastically limited. It would be folly to cultivate an increased working class when unemployment existed."' Debate requires you to support or oppose a particular point of view, no matter what are your own feelings in the matter. It wasn't the last time that my sense of comic irony would be subject to misinterpretation.

Three days later the headmaster called me into his study to show me a letter he had received from Senator Sheehy-Skeffington, whose duties as chairman hadn't included acting as judge. He wrote, 'I just wanted to write to you to rectify an injustice. I was presiding at the schools debate in the Metropolitan Hall and there is no doubt that the most brilliant speaker was young Mr Norris from your school. It was a travesty that he did not win the award.'

The fact that somebody I admired and respected, and who was a close friend of Jack Cornish, would write such a letter meant more to me than winning the prize. I remembered that letter in the 1990s when I was down in University College Cork chairing a debate at the Philosoph, where I was honorary president. That night I saw a young man who was one of the finest speakers I have ever heard – he was brilliant, incisive and witty. Like me decades earlier he didn't win and he too was crestfallen. So I wrote to him, and told him my story from many years before, and hailed him as the outstanding speaker on that occasion. He responded immediately and I know that my letter meant as much to him as Sheehy-Skeffington's had to me. Generosity should not just be relished; it should also be passed on.

I come from an artistic family replete with painters, sculptors, writers and amateur musicians. Music has always enchanted me. My first efforts to play came in school on a primitive wooden recorder, but it did lead me to the piano, which I took up aged nine. I used to sit and listen to music on the old valve radio and my mother would take me up to recitals in the Royal Dublin Society library. I already loved Chopin, the haunting line of the melody bringing sadness, poignancy and longing in those flattened notes. I could imagine the Polish landscape in that music: the fields of snow, baroque palaces, fir trees and moonlight.

My mother never believed in going into debt, and the only time she made an exception to that was when she bought me a piano on an instalment plan. I attended the Reade Pianoforte School, over which Miss Reade presided in her severe Victorian attire. By a happy accident my piano teacher, who I adored, had a direct link with Chopin. Lily Huban was an ethereal kind of woman, thin and spiritual. She had been the demonstration pupil of Alfred Cortot at the Conservatoire in Paris in the 1920s. Cortot was the pupil of Émile Descombes, who was a pupil of Chopin. I felt a direct connection to the composer, and the first record I ever owned was of the complete Chopin waltzes played by Artur Rubinstein.

Another extra-curricular activity I enjoyed was the school magazine, which I edited for a time. It also saw the first of the many incidents where outspoken comments in the media got me into trouble. The reason was, of all things, an art review. The lavatories in High School were in a shed at the back of the schoolyard, with walls covered in clods of plaster and uneven brickwork. One of the pupils had incorporated these lumps and bumps into a creative, if mildly pornographic, depiction of the headmaster's wife. I saw the artistic merit, or at least the wit, and mischievously proceeded to review it in the pages of the school magazine as a piece of modern art in the manner of Henry Moore. This was not appreciated and my piece was suppressed: my first experience of censorship.

I was eleven years old when I first fell in love, with a fellow student at High School. He was a few years older than me, so I never got beyond the phase of idolatrous hero worship for this manly Greek-Cypriot youth. He played rugby on the school team, and had olive-brown skin, dazzling white teeth and jet-black hair, combined with the exotic air that comes from having roots in a sunny land. He was in the party when we went on a train excursion to Cork, and that rare chance to see him up close was the greatest day of my life thus far. I used to lurk around the school trying to catch a glimpse of him, but we had virtually no contact. Once or twice in his presence I deliberately made loud remarks of what I thought were a witty nature in an attempt to get his attention, and was once rewarded with a smile. Over fifty years later I still remember it.

For most people the teenage years are a nightmare, mainly caused by all those hormones whizzing around, looking for some kind of erotic stimulation. But if you were a gay teenager in Dublin in the 1950s, there was precious little outlet for these feelings. My mother had a subscription to *Paris-Match* magazine which I enjoyed reading, although her delight at my interest in extra-curricular French study was misplaced as I was far more fascinated by the handsome and athletic young men modelling underwear in the advertisements at the back.

Another diversion was to be found in a shop on Harcourt Street that sold outboard motors. There in the window stood a big cardboard cut-out of a rugged Australian waterskier, wearing Speedos as he skied along. I would pretend to be interested in the outboard motor while all the time gazing at the handsome athletic Aussie frame, snugly attired in what I much later discovered were nicknamed 'budgie-smugglers'.

On the corner of the same street was a little newsagent which sold pop music fanzines, of which *Pop Pics* was a favourite. It was essentially a fold-out poster with colour photographs of the stars, and I discovered one day that the current month's issue featured my favourite, Cliff Richard, in scenes from the movie *Summer Holiday*. The prized giant poster displayed Cliff stepping out of the shower, modestly wrapped in a bright white bath towel about his loins while displaying his generously furred and muscled chest. I hovered outside the shop for several days on my way home from school before I plucked up the courage to go in and buy it. I was joy personified as I travelled home on the bus with my purchase clutched in my hands, afraid to take it out of its thin brown-paper bag and open it up in case the other passengers saw. I liked Cliff's music too, and although he wasn't much older than me he was old enough to be a mature man. That he might have been gay never occurred to me, but it would have been my wildest dream.

Over the next few years I developed a general amorphous feeling about my own gender. I loved women, but there was something special about men. As a child I loved being hugged and having my hand held; perhaps it was just that I enjoyed being 'daddied' as a consequence of losing my own father so young. It gradually dawned on me that my friends were moving in a different – and to me disturbing – way as they started to display an interest in women. I warned them that they were playing with fire, reproving them, 'I don't think this is healthy, you'll get into trouble for this. It's *unnatural*.' We argued about it, but it never occurred to me that I was the odd man out.

My romantic feelings at the time were directed towards my best friend at school, David Miller. I spent a lot of time with him, and eventually explained that I loved him. He didn't show the slightest concern but made it clear that he wasn't interested in doing anything much about it. That passion carried on into

Trinity and into my twenties, when he married and emigrated to Canada. We are still in touch and I was honoured to be asked to stand as godfather for one of his children.

CHAPTER 3

In the College of the Sacred and Undivided Trinity

IALWAYS KNEW I WOULD GO ON TO TRINITY AFTER SCHOOL, BUT IT was Jack Cornish's guidance – and beyond-the-call-of-duty assistance – that made me opt to study English.

Fifty years ago Trinity College Dublin was much smaller than the modern educational giant – there were fewer than three thousand people on campus then, including staff and students. Nowadays that figure is over twenty thousand. For decades the Roman Catholic Archbishop of Dublin, John Charles McQuaid, had debarred his flock from entering the university, and the result was a student population profile unrepresentative of the national reality or the city outside its gates.

Dr McQuaid felt Trinity represented a corrupting influence on Catholics. And of course, from his own point of view, he was quite right. Trinity opened up the possibilities of questioning, and even of flinging a few particles of honest doubt in the face of dangerous and dishonest certainty.

Most of the Irish contingent were Protestants, and usually as poor as church mice like myself. But there was a strong international flavour given by a clatter of Hooray Henrys from the UK – usually Oxford or Cambridge rejects – who arrived complete with cravats, toney accents, sports cars and glamorous girlfriends with double-barrelled names.

IN THE COLLEGE OF THE SACRED AND UNDIVIDED TRINITY

I did the entrance scholarship in Classics and History, and won the Walter Wormser Harris Prize, which is given to the highest-scoring candidate who doesn't win a scholarship, a kind of consolation prize. That I didn't get a scholarship is unsurprising as I hadn't been studying the correct course for most of the preceding year. There was an initially daunting *viva voce* part to the exam, held in the vast Examination Hall with just one tiny table in the centre. Professor D. E. W. Wormell – who worked at the code-breaking operation in Bletchley Park during World War II – put me at my ease by speculating on how Falernian wine might have tasted in Ancient Rome. I read aloud one of Horace's odes about young lovers, one in which the way the lines of the poem broke on the page suggested to me that you could almost see them sneaking around a corner to kiss. I pointed this out and I think it helped me to a good mark.

It was a tactical decision on the basis of my results to take the entrance scholarship in Classics and History as you couldn't do it in English alone. As usual I wanted to do everything, but as soon as I got in I immediately changed to English.

I loved the atmosphere in Trinity, which was small enough that you got to know almost everyone if you drank coffee in a little coffee shop opposite the end of the Graduates Memorial Building in New Square. But the complete undergraduate experience passed me by, in a way, because it was a time of family difficulty and I was tormented by unrequited love. At this time, as throughout my early life, whenever I sought help from adults or the authorities of any kind, I was always met with the response 'It's terribly sad, but I'm reluctant to/can't/won't get involved.' This refusal of aid made me resolve to never say to another human being, 'I can't get involved.' From then on I vowed that I would always get involved.

I didn't take part in much extra-curricular activity while in college because my mother had a serious heart condition, but I did join both great debating societies – the Historical and the Philosophical – on my first day. My great-grandfather's cousin

Bram Stoker, incidentally, is the only person to have been president of the Phil *and* auditor of the Hist. This was a very remarkable achievement, because from their foundation right up to the present day the societies have made a fetish of despising and attempting to sabotage each other's meetings. I, however, had the slightly different distinction of being expelled from both societies by the end of my first term. I used to turn up from time to time like a type of intellectual flying column, and was always recognised by the chair and allowed to speak, which I did *ex tempore* and with extravagant gestures, which seemed to delight the audience.

The Hist threw me out for what they called 'academic nudity', which isn't anything nearly as exciting as it sounds but merely meant that I had spoken while not wearing a gown. The Phil expelled me for refusing to pay a fine which I regarded as capricious, arbitrary and unjust.

Neither seemed to hold it against me and I continued to attend and speak, and eventually won gold and silver medals for this, which I still prize, and over the years both awarded me honorary life memberships on several separate occasions, suggesting the cat-like nine lives I subsequently needed in political life. One medal was awarded for a paper I wrote on James Joyce, at which the guest of honour was the writer Anthony Burgess, famous for the novel and film *A Clockwork Orange*, who replied to my paper. After the meeting he presented me with a copy of his book on *Finnegans Wake*, inscribed to me with thanks for 'a most inspiring, ear- and mind-opening experience'.

I found a lot of the lectures on the English course enchanting, especially those of Robert Butler Digby French, whose entire contribution to scholarship was a monograph on the works of P. G. Wodehouse and writing some annual revues for the College Players. French, who was a grand-nephew of the lyricist Percy French, had lovely donnish, chintzy rooms with an open fire in the Rubrics (the oldest part of Trinity, whose name derives from the red Jacobean bricks of their construction) where he would welcome his students, sometimes proffering a glass of sherry. He had an endearingly urbane approach to teaching – one day he was striving to explain the heroic couplet when he got up from his armchair and, still puffing his pipe, walked to the window. He indicated the front square of the college and explained his point in terms of its architecture: 'Look out, dear boy. There is the concrete realisation of the Augustan age: delightful symmetry, a couplet wrought in stone in perfect balance and harmony.'

R.B.D., as we called him, allowed us to choose what we wanted to write about, so one day I announced I had written a paper on *A Portrait of the Artist as a Young Man* by James Joyce. He sniffed, and puffed on his pipe, before replying, 'Not really my sort of thing, dear boy, so don't expect much in the way of informed comment. But if you feel impelled I'm sure we'll all be interested.'

I had joined the staff by the time he died, and a group of us went to his funeral in Kilternan, in the Dublin Mountains. He was an extremely popular man, and when we arrived half an hour before the service the church was already full. Three o'clock came and there was no sign of the celebrant, so the organist continued to play. At 3.15 p.m. we still had no sign of any activity. However, at 3.30, by which stage the organist had exhausted his repertoire of sacred tunes and was showing a distinct tendency to wander into the world of popular songs, such as 'Would You Like to Swing on a Star' (catching himself just in time to modulate into a minor key), the vestry door opened and out came His Grace the Most Reverend George Otto Simms, Archbishop of Dublin.

'There will now be a short memorial service for R. B. D. French, whose funeral will take place in private at a later date,' he intoned.

It turned out that R.B.D.'s sister Nell had forgotten to notify the undertaker. The presence of a corpse is generally seen as a requirement for a successful funeral, but R.B.D. was still on a slab in the Adelaide Hospital, so, despite a punctilious attitude to life, he actually managed to miss his own funeral. After the service we went back to the Senior Common Room in Trinity where the college secretary, Gerry Giltrap, was reading the *Financial Times*. On being told the story, and without even lowering his newspaper, he murmured, 'Well, nothing should surprise one about the English Department, but it does seem somewhat appropriate in the circumstances . . . Tears without French.'

I hated examinations, and still get nightmares about them, but I usually did well, perhaps because of my unique approach to revision. I would close my bedroom door, switch my radio to the pirate pop station Radio Caroline, and put myself into a semi-hypnotic trance. I would have the text of *Beowulf* on the left side of the desk, and the modern English translation alongside, and I would chant aloud each in turn, in time with the music, memorising as I went. So when I was handed the exam paper, I would go, 'Ah yes, *Beowulf*: Grendel's mother . . . Let me see, that's The Tremeloes.' And off I would go, chanting the words to the tune to help me remember.

At the end of second year I won the First Foundation Scholarship in English language and literature, the premier academic award for undergraduates. That meant I did not have to pay fees as well as several other exotic perks, such as free accommodation in college, a free evening meal (called Commons, where we prayed in Latin for the foundress of the college, Queen Elizabeth I) and the right to shoot snipe in College Park (the snipe were long gone, sadly). As scholars we also had the right to keep a cat in our rooms, wear a sword into lectures and call for a pint of ale with our exam papers. The only privilege I remember exercising, however, was taking part in the annual marbles match between the scholars on the steps of the Dining Hall.

None of those delights appealed to me as much as the fact

that a first-class or upper-second-class result in the Schol exam allowed you to miss the end-of-year exams, which were then held in the autumn. This derogation meant I was able to pursue my primary aim, which was to go hitch-hiking on the continent. I wrote my papers from the heart, assessing the literature through the prism of the turbulent emotional life I was leading. I interpreted passionately and wrote passionately, with the result that my scripts went singing up to the top of the pile.

It was the first year that there was a single honours degree course in English, with language and literature combined, so it was quite a privilege to be the inaugural scholar. The best and most lasting memory about winning Schol was the look on my mother's face when I told her. She was very seriously ill and when I gave her the news as she lay in Sir Patrick Dun's Hospital the glow on her face made the whole thing worthwhile.

At the time I was truly tormented: family life was difficult and I was coming to realise what it meant to be gay in 1960s Ireland. I found solace by retreating into books. And my own anguish informed my love of literature. I didn't learn from the critics, but from my own intense feelings of exclusion. I found echoes of my own life in books such as *The Great Gatsby*. I could identify with Gatsby as he looked longingly at the 'single green light, minute and far away' which hung at the end of Daisy's dock and confirmed her magical, distant presence. I had a ritual at home in Ballsbridge whereby I would look out through the landing window at the red light flickering on the mast at RTÉ in Montrose, because it stood in a direct line with David Miller's house. It was a sacred thing to me. I certainly knew just how Gatsby felt, not just from reading but from the beating of my own heart.

I had already organised to spend third year in a single room when David Miller came up to ask me a favour. A friend in his year in medicine had contracted to go into a double set of rooms, but the other fellow had let him down. He didn't have a lot of money, so David asked me if I would mind going into the double set of rooms with his pal.

I thought that if he was a friend of David's he'd be all right, so I agreed after an initial meeting to give it a shot. Gabriel Slowey turned out to be the captain of the GAA club in Trinity, and as a result I got to know all the Gaelic football players and hurlers, and became a kind of mascot on their annual trips to play in the Sigerson Cup. A couple of them were doing art as a compulsory subsidiary subject, but hadn't a clue about it, so I would help them with their essays on Michelangelo or Renoir.

The GAA lads were a fascinating and totally different group of people to my usual circle of friends, and I had a great time with characters such as 'Jakes' Malone, Richie Copeland and Tony Hanahoe. They were much amused when I discovered that the Unionist icon Edward Carson was one of the founder members of the Trinity Hurling Club. Tony was a great friend and subsequently got me tickets for three of the epic battles between Dublin and Kerry in the 1970s, when he became a national hero as captain of the successful Dublin team.

I have always been keen on exercise myself, and use my small home gymnasium every day. I was a good rugby player when I was in school and continued for a while in college, and afterwards at Old Wesley, but gave it up when I got involved in the gay movement as I felt my openness about my sexuality might be embarrassing for the other players in the showers. On the school second XV I was a right-winger, which flattered my ego because the ball would be elegantly passed out along the line to me and as I had a good turn of speed, this allowed me to hare around like blazes to plant the leather egg between the posts to a burst of thunderous applause.

I ran my first Dublin City Marathon in 1988. It was a beautiful day and there was plenty of cheering from the crowd at St Stephen's Green, but I kept to the same moderate pace all the time and afterwards I went home and soaked myself in the bath. The next day I was lecturing in Trinity and could hardly make it down the stairs into the lecture hall. I did the marathon twice more but usually finished just as the workers were dismantling the clock. However, I showed that even in middle age I could find the determination and perseverance to complete the course. I treasure the medals and certificates I got and have them up on the wall of my gym at home.

During third year I moved home for a time as my mother hadn't been well. It was also a time of family trauma, which particularly affected her because of her heart condition. I was ill with pneumonia on the night she died, which was a couple of days after Christmas 1965. I got up in the middle of the night and put on an Original Dixieland Jazz Band record. That has haunted me since, because she hated jazz and I hope she didn't hear it in her last moments. I slept very late, and when I awoke the next morning I was struck by how quiet the house was. I went downstairs to find the post on the floor under the letterbox, which was odd because my mother was habitually an early riser. I went back upstairs, opened her door and found her dead in bed. She had had a heart attack during the night. It was my first direct experience of death and any notion of it being a romantic affair was shattered. Her skin was discoloured from the cessation of blood circulation and, as there was nobody else in the house, I had to help the doctor straighten her out because rigor mortis was setting in.

I couldn't believe that this woman I loved was there one day and gone the next, never again to share a chat, a summer evening's gardening or a story. It destroyed my already fragile sense of reality. What really shocked me was when I looked out the window I could see the number 52 bus was still running, oblivious to my personal catastrophe. I couldn't understand how such mundane realities continued in this devastating situation.

But life, and particularly life in Trinity, gradually reestablished itself. Even Dubliners who have never made their way in behind the walls of the university know of the famous Trinity Ball, an all-night affair which takes place towards the end of the academic year. It came at the end of Trinity Week, which was then the highlight of the Dublin social season.

One of the women I escorted was a dark-haired Irish beauty who had just got engaged but told me she would love to go because she knew I was 'safe'. I rather resented this assertion and littered the dashboard of the car with contraband condoms in order to make her nervous. But it was her mother who had a fit when she escorted her beloved daughter to my borrowed sports car and got an eyeful of the johnnies! Another was a wealthy American heiress who wore an original creation by Balenciaga. A third partner for the ball was a lively and entertaining young woman from one of the great landowning families. She told me, with unconscious irony, that it was a pleasure to be with a real man because all the partners her parents suggested 'turned out to be fairies'. I was envied by my friends for the beauty and sophistication of my female companions, but I would have preferred to have been with a man.

One year there was a rebellious rival event organised outside college by republican elements in concert with the Cumann Gaelach, Trinity's Irish-language society. I turned up at that attired in my uncle's court suit, with gold buttons, purple and yellow facings and a silk top hat. I was cheered as I sang 'Amhrán na bhFiann' in Irish, but they were less impressed by my encore of 'God Save the Queen'. I beat a retreat from that and tried to obtain access to the Trinity Ball via a side gate to the college. There I was met by the bouncers, who asked where I thought I was going. With considerable quantities of the Cumann Gaelach's wine inside, I raised myself up to my full five foot ten and a half and told them I was the Mongolian Ambassador, and an honoured guest at their university's celebrated social event. Perhaps the wine had caused my features to assume a Central Asian appearance, for I was surprised and delighted to be admitted.

Trinity in the sixties had something of the atmosphere of the roaring twenties. One fellow's father was so loaded that he bought him a house in Leeson Street where he could live while he was a student. He had one party for which he covered the entire back garden in striped silk and hired waiters to serve brandy, Lanson Black Label champagne and multi-coloured Balkan Sobranie cocktail cigarettes. Confronted with this Aladdin's cave of excess I got nicely addled and, visiting the bog, I found a huge Victorian bath filled to the brim with ice and packed with bottles of Lanson. Reckoning they wouldn't miss one, I stuck it under my oxter and exited. Having drunk the champagne, I bought a bulb, adaptor and shade in Woolworths and turned it into a lamp which still graces a Sheraton sideboard in my back drawing room.

In 1967 a group of us threw a party in Lisnabrucka, a beautiful fishing lodge near Ballynahinch, Co. Galway, owned by a friend of mine. I borrowed my brother's TR2 sports car to drive down and remember the feeling of freedom as we passed through towns such as Kilbeggan and Edgeworthstown with the car radio playing and the wind blowing through my hair, of which – unlike now – I had then quite an abundance. We had invited various county families, but one of our guests was a certain titled lady who was considered 'fast', and when she turned up some of the local gentry were scandalised and walked out.

I had many good friends in college, including Eiléan ní Chuilleanáin, Eavan Boland and Maria Taft, daughter of the US Ambassador and descendant of the former President William Taft. Dinah Stabb, whom I admired from afar, was in Players, had a successful acting career and still crops up on British TV dramas. Rosemary Gibson was a great character who once went to the Provost's garden party wearing nothing but a black plastic bag, accompanied by her future husband Andrew Gibb who in contrast wore a striped public-school blazer and boater hat. The Provost, Dr McConnell, who had already copiously enjoyed his own hospitality, was delighted and became our escort for the rest of the party. I was extremely fond of Rosy, who was a bundle of eccentricity, riding a motorcycle, smoking cigars and once jumping into the Liffey to save a drowning dog. It was entirely appropriate that, as Rosy Gibb, she went on to be Britain's most celebrated female clown.

There were a few very exotic creatures about the place, none more so than Constantin de Goguel de Toulouse-Lautrec, known as Gog, the great-grand-nephew of the Impressionist painter. For some reason we also had several sons of movie stars – Roc Brynner (son of Yul) and Chris Mitchum (son of Robert) – and musicians: Peter Adler (son of Larry). We had our own musical talents too, including Ian Whitcomb who had one hit, 'You Turn Me On', which reached number 8 in the American hit parade in 1965 while he was still at Trinity. He broke off from touring the US to come back to do his finals. Also there at that time was Chris Davison, later to receive international celebrity as the singer Chris de Burgh, Gate theatre director Michael Colgan, food critic Paolo Tullio, and the future U2 manager Paul McGuinness. At Trinity, however, I was very much a Rolling Stones fan. I saw them perform live in the Adelphi Cinema in Abbey Street, and thrilled to Mick Jagger skipping in the air, clicking his heels to 'It's All Over Now'.

My own brush with fame at Trinity was also one of the most truly mortifying episodes in my life. It occurred in the studios of Granada Television in Manchester, where I represented Trinity in the popular quiz *University Challenge*. There had been some controversy over the selection of the team, which was put together in a not entirely democratic fashion. The team was made up of mostly debating-society people, namely David Wagstaff, Michael Shiels, Mary Bourke and myself. Mary, of course, went on to marry Nick Robinson and become Ireland's first woman president.

In the dress-rehearsal run-through of the programme we trounced our opponents, Somerville College, Oxford. The result of this was a surfeit of confidence, and we relaxed during the break. I seem to remember a few of us downing a celebratory gin in the hospitality room.

By the time we got back to the studio we had lost the edge, and our expected victory march began to unravel. At one stage we had got so many questions wrong that our score threatened to go into the minus range. There was an awful stink when we came home, and *Trinity News* lambasted us for bringing 'shame' on the university after our 150–50 defeat. But the audience loved it as it was like a public execution, and it became so famous that it was repeated by ITV on several occasions. It is a horrible memory – I can never hear that awful jingle and Bamber Gascoigne prattling, 'Your starter for ten' without an involuntary regurgitation of the whole sorry episode.

My experience of quiz programmes has not been good. In fact, I featured in one of those British television run-downs of 'the top 100 worst TV programmes ever made'. It was the pilot for an RTÉ quiz show which I hosted and into which the station put no money at all. There was nothing as sophisticated as a computer to keep score – they just gave me a ring-bound flip-chart – and the rules were unbelievably convoluted. The whole episode was chaotic, with researchers still writing the questions out longhand after the filming had started, and they couldn't even get the questions and answers co-ordinated. So, if the question was 'What is the longest river in Brazil?' the contestant would answer, 'The Amazon.' And then I would say, 'Well, I thought so too, but apparently the answer is "Timbuktu".' We all corpsed with laughter, and happily the show never saw the light of day until it made that list of the worst programmes ever made.

I did well in my final exams, getting a double first, and just three days after getting my results I found myself in a job. I had taken an interest in areas of literature that were considered odd at the time, such as Joyce, and American literature, which was just opening up in Irish universities. I had got a first in my finals writing about the likes of Thomas Wolfe, Djuna Barnes and Scott Fitzgerald, and as nobody in Trinity taught the subject I was asked to give a series of lectures in the first term of the following academic year. At Christmas a permanent job came up and it was suggested that I apply. Nearly fifty people competed, but miraculously I got the job.

However, in a move that was entirely typical of Trinity administrators, the first course I was given to teach was a subject about which I knew almost nothing – poetry. But I was game, and took an unorthodox approach, going to the root of things and looking to the very nature of poetry itself. I scrutinized writers such as e. e. cummings, whose verse exists soundlessly on the page as a kind of concrete poetry, relying on typography and layout to make its point. In an age that did not place much value on metre, rhyme or form I was wrestling with the problem of where the dividing line between poetry and prose came, which kept bringing me back to Joyce and Anna Livia Plurabelle in *Finnegans Wake*.

I discussed my academic angst about this with Brendan Kennelly, and he told me the story of a similar discourse with Brendan Behan, who recited the following limerick to unravel the conundrum:

> *There was a young fellah named Rollocks,*
> *Who worked for Ferrier Pollocks.*
> *As he walked on the strand*
> *With his girl by the hand*
> *The tide came in up to his . . . knees.*

'Now,' said the playwright, '*that* is prose. But if the tide had come up another eighteen inches, it would've been poetry.' That story always went down well in lectures.

Like many Dubliners, I have my own story about Brendan Behan, although this one recalls an actual rather than fictional encounter. When I was about fifteen or sixteen, there was a public discussion on theatre with John B. Keane and Brendan, held in the Shelbourne Hotel as part of the Dublin Theatre Festival. We all went along expecting Brendan to be plastered, but his wife Beatrice had managed to impose some discipline so he entered the room looking a million dollars in a new tuxedo, white shirt and bow tie and smoking an enormous cigar.

The discussion between Brendan and John B. was fascinating, as at the beginning we had been asked to write down any questions we might wish to ask and submit them to the organisers. I wrote mine and handed it up; Brendan scrutinised it and in his lovely Dublin drawl said, 'Judging by the hand-writing I'd say this question comes from a well-educated young convent girl.' (Which showed his skills in both graphology and psychology!) 'Now, she's asked me what I think of the critics. I have only one thing to say, darling: the critic is like a eunuch in a harem. He sees the job done every night but he's unable to do it himself.'

When I started teaching I was nervous standing up in front of students, some of whom were older than me, but I soon settled and developed a certain style. In nearly thirty years' teaching I never wrote out lectures to read them to students. I would make a note of some ideas on index cards, which I used as a comfort blanket to put a sequence or structure to my thoughts, but I believed there was nothing more stultifying than watching a lecturer read from a prepared script.

Humour is a very powerful weapon, and one that can be used to make a serious point. I taught one year-long module on the theory of comedy, which went right back through philosophy from the ancients to the moderns. I decided as part of my course to recreate the lost Second Book of Aristotle's *Poetics*, which deals with comedy, and to reconstruct it by analogy with tech-niques he used in analysing tragedy. I felt that comedy had been undervalued by critics partly because of the loss of this book.

One of the things I said was that comedy relieved the tensions created when one set of messages is deliberately subverted by another simultaneous contradictory set of messages. I invented a series of terms, such as 'subversive juxtaposition', and showed, with illustrations from the various books, how these factors worked on the page. As the content of the lecture was philosophical and intellectual, it could have been academic in the worst sense, but I knew how to get around that. On the first morning I arrived riding my ancient bicycle along the corridor on the fourth floor of the Arts Block, wearing a three-piece suit and academic gown, a gold pocket watch and a clown's pate with a shock of red hair, a canary perched on top of my head and a rubber bulb in my pocket. When I squeezed the bulb the canary gave a little trill and water squirted from it. Throughout the lecture the bird would emit his little noise and the students in the front row would be soaked. They thought it was hilarious, although some thought I was being silly. What they didn't realise was that they were already experiencing directly the actual meat of the lecture – I was very clearly giving them several simultaneous contradictory messages, both physical and verbal, slapstick and intellectual, which invoked gusts of laughter.

Parallel to my early teaching career, I had embarked on a PhD thesis on James Joyce. He had the most varied linguistic palette of any author and said himself that he could make language do anything he wanted. Yet in *Dubliners* his use of language is deliberately restricted. The very first sentence of the book is a sequence of monosyllabic words: 'There was no hope for him this time: it was the third stroke.'

Joyce defined the style he used as 'scrupulous meanness', and he used it in order to give emphasis. *Dubliners* is a black-and-white series of one-dimensional silhouetted vignettes of Dublin, and that's what gives it its terrific power. I looked at the language and vocabulary Joyce used, and found words were repeated frequently and significantly. I analysed the linguistic patterns and recreated the vocabulary Joyce had assembled to form his so-called style of scrupulous meanness and demonstrated the effect that this had. For example, in every story bar one the word 'confused' is used, and in that other one it is implied. Its significance is that confusion is the response to life of the paralysed Dubliners in his stories.

There were several early drafts of *Dubliners*, which were kept in the Beinecke Rare Book and Manuscript Library in Yale. I wrote to ask would they send me copies of them, and as this was the first time anyone had ever asked to see them they had to have a board meeting. They eventually sent them on and I was able to examine the variant drafts and see that there were significant changes between them.

I also explored the humour in the book, about which nobody had ever written before. It is not a book that people usually think of in those terms, but every single story has an element of sometimes dark humour.

Trinity was in a state of transition and things sometimes got pretty heated, especially in the English department. There were rows, sometimes verging on the physical, about things such as methods of marking exam papers. There was considerable tension between various individuals, and factions developed in the department. The parents of Ireland might be surprised to learn that I seemed to be about the most balanced person in the place.

Some of my students' term essays on Joyce were given to a part-time teacher as part of this new system. One of the students, whom I knew as a good critic and imaginative essay writer, was marked as a 'fail' by this examiner, so I demanded to see the paper. The young woman had divided the essay into four parts, and wrote each in turn as a parody of *Dubliners*, *Portrait*, *Ulysses* and *Finnegans Wake*. But the examiner had failed her because she hadn't answered the question posed in the title of the essay in the formal way anticipated. I was outraged, because I had set the question myself and nothing could have illustrated better the student's understanding of Joyce's works. It was an absolutely superb essay and I felt that to punish creativity and imagination in that way was a sin against teaching. There was a lot of trouble about it, but I ensured she was given a first.

I also resented the way colleagues would colonise anything others had made successful. I had helped Brendan Kennelly to start the postgraduate diploma in Anglo-Irish literature, which was a great success for the university, and as it developed I prepared a year-long course on Joyce from *Dubliners* to *Finnegans Wake*. It became very popular but after a while I was surprised to find that my contribution had been pared down to two weeks and other lecturers were being moved in – so I said no thanks and withdrew from the course.

One morning I was cycling down to college when a country driver opened his car door and knocked me under a bus, whose wheels stopped about an inch from my head. The bicycle's wheel was buckled so I had to push it all the way down to Trinity to give my lecture. I had the presence of mind to take the reprobate's registration number and eventually extracted £700 from his insurance company. I was late, too, and at the end of the class I told the students, 'I know this lecture wasn't as good as it ought to be, and I'm sure you are all disappointed, but on my way here I was knocked off my bicycle . . .' And I burst into tears from the delayed shock.

Of course, the terror that you might lose the magic, or forget everything that you wanted to say, also gave an extra edge to the performance and ensured I never gave the same lecture twice. I would look straight into the eyes of students when teaching, because I knew they could always tell if a lecturer was telling them the truth, which I invariably did because literature was a great passion. I loved some writers with a great intensity, and questioned others, such as Ernest Hemingway, whom I would gleefully take to pieces in class – although I always respected their ability, and the fact that my students might take a different view.

I prepared meticulously the night before, and though I never wrote the lectures out in advance, I always had the points to hand so I could marshal my thoughts. I wouldn't just make points in a vacuum, but I would illustrate by performing from the work under discussion. I wanted to ignite the imagination of the students, so that they would go back and study the writer for themselves. It wasn't my job merely to parse and analyse, it was to get them excited, to explain to them what was being done and why it was so interesting.

I wasn't an academic snob, so I would happily introduce biographical details to our study of a writer, which would often be very important. I once got into trouble with this, after eventually discovering E. M. Forster's sexuality, so important to an understanding of his work. Academia had deliberately concealed the fact that Forster was gay, but I couldn't wait to tell my class the news and to discuss what it meant for our study of his work. One of my students was obviously enthralled by my thesis, for when he went home he told his parents, who complained to the Provost. Their complaint was not that I was a bad teacher, but that I was an outstanding teacher and therefore in a position to corrupt my students. I was summoned for a chat with the Provost, where I explained to him that I too had had many outstanding teachers, most of whom were heterosexual – and I hadn't caught anything off them. It was a silly complaint really, because I had to tell the truth about Forster and no lecturer could suppress this key to a most important aspect of his life and work.

There were all sorts of little personal rivalries, and examples of Henry Kissinger's truism that 'academic politics is the most bitter and vicious form of politics, because the stakes are so low'. Eventually the department split, acrimoniously. Towards the end of one particularly nasty meeting, I stood up and said, 'Ladies and gentlemen, you believe that you have divided yourselves into the Department of Early, Medieval and Renaissance English and the Department of Modern English. Well, you are wrong – because you have in fact been divided in three: the Department of Early, Medieval and Renaissance English, the Department of Modern English, and the Department of Norris Studies. It shall not be attending any further meetings of any of the other departments, but it shall do its best to maintain cordial relations with both. Thank you very much and good day.' And thereafter, besides examiners' meetings, I never attended a single meeting in the department.

I was not a conventional academic, and the art of lecturing at which I excelled was not recognised or valued. Maria Jolas, one of Joyce's closest friends, once said to me, 'Mr Norris, you are a true original.' Coming from her, that was some compliment. Certainly my lectures were anything but conventional.

Students came from all over college to attend my classes, but my refusal to play the politics of the department meant my life was made difficult. My growing profile internationally, and the many invitations to speak abroad, also irritated some colleagues. When I became a semi-official spokesman for the gay movement they really didn't like it. The more active politically I got, the more awkward the meetings in Trinity became, and my election to the Senate went largely unappreciated in the department. At the time the Upper House was quite widely reported in newspapers, and my frequent headline-grabbing speeches were used as another stick to beat me.

I felt there was an element of unconscious homophobia in some of this. I was well acquainted with the glass ceiling and the sticky floor. It didn't matter how brilliant my lectures were, and how widely they were appreciated abroad, or how generously the invitations flowed, it was always assumed that because of my work in the gay movement I was not giving a full commitment to the university. This attitude did not appear to affect my colleagues. Perhaps if I had engaged in the traditional hobbies of cricket, golf and adultery life would have been easier.

I did, however, receive the occasional pay rise. These were eagerly anticipated and when I examined my cheque after one,

I discovered there had been no change. I wrote indignantly to the college accountant and received a reply stating that I had indeed received an increase. He said this had had the effect of putting me into the next tax bracket, and that I had in fact received a negative increment and it was only due to the good will of the college that I had been rounded up to my original net pay. I wrote back, saying:

> Dear Mr Accountant,
> I am, I am glad to say, unfamiliar with the vulgarity of your trade.
> However I do have a nodding acquaintance with the English
> language. Let me assure you, there is no such animal as a negative
> increment. That of which you speak is excrement, and the next
> time I suggest you keep it to yourself.

I was chairman of the Friends of the Trinity Library for almost thirty years. We had an excellent little committee that worked together very well. For many years it included a delightful member of the library staff, Mr Mackie, and in the latter period I had the wonderful support of Aidan Heavey. Aidan used to draft and pass along notes at the annual general meeting which made things easier for me on these occasions. Under my determined leadership, we brought the Friends back into credit and as a result were able to redecorate a substantial room in the library and contribute to the purchase of some rare books.

I thoroughly enjoyed my time as chairman; I appear, however, to have blotted my copybook in some quarters by giving my papers to the National Library rather than Trinity. To be honest, Trinity never expressed any interest in them and it didn't occur to me.

The National Library invited me to lunch and Gerry Lyne, the keeper of manuscripts, offered to buy my papers. I told him he couldn't, at which his face dropped. I told him he could have them for nothing, on condition he took the whole bloody lot. All my papers on the gay movement, Senate campaigns, the North Great Georges Street Preservation Society and much more were handed over at a lovely ceremony presided over by Mary Robinson. This was great from my point of view as I could clear out masses of papers I had accumulated in my hoarding days. The room in which I had stored them was then freed up and became the last room in the house to be fully restored.

I left Trinity in 1994 after a debilitating bout of illness. I had been given a sabbatical and had been asked by the Department of Foreign Affairs to act for them as a kind of unpaid roving cultural ambassador across Eastern Europe and Scandinavia. I was delighted, as I got to meet some interesting people, such as Raoul Wallenberg's sister. About halfway through I started feeling rotten but soldiered on, and I eventually fell ill on a plane and ended up in hospital. It was determined that I had hepatitis non-A, non-B and non-C (they hadn't gone any further with classification at that stage). By analysing my schedule the medical people said I had probably contracted the disease from tainted water in Budapest. I used to describe this as my drink problem, maintaining that if I had stuck with whiskey I'd have been all right. It was the water that did me in.

After a year on sick leave Trinity appointed somebody else and told me to trigger the income guarantee scheme to which I had contributed for almost thirty years. It had nothing whatever to do with social welfare or state money, and it was a perfectly routine procedure available in many companies as part of the terms of employment. Hepatitis is well known to reduce energy levels, and as I worked full-time for the students of the university as well as the Senate, I certainly couldn't continue doing two full-time jobs although I might handle one. The university never asked me to return or offered me another job. I would have considered it, but it would have been a waste of taxpayers' money as I would have been hanging around doing supply teaching.

I didn't miss the interminable and rancorous department meetings, but I did miss the teaching, the atmosphere of the university and, of course, the students, who kept me young. As part of my severance I was forbidden to take up any other forms of lecturing, which I have always honoured, but happily there was no objection to me continuing to perform my one-man James Joyce show for charity.

CHAPTER 4

The Only Gay in the Village

I WAS BORN A CRIMINAL. FROM THE MOMENT OF MY ARRIVAL ON this planet, my essential nature defined me as such. There was simply nothing I could do about it, since homosexuality is a natural but minority variation of the sexual instinct. As the American author Wainwright Churchill points out, homosexual behaviour occurs 'throughout the mammalian order, occurring in frequency and complexity as one ascends the phylogenetic scale'. So if such activity is fully natural for a large minority of life on this planet, I sensed that there had to be some reason for the antagonism leading to historic human taboos. The source for this scapegoating of 10 per cent of the population, I discovered, was politico-religious, as it remains.

It starts in the Old Testament, hardly a compendium of morals that would be acceptable nowadays, with its endorsement of slavery, murder, rape and incest, its extraordinary bloodthirstiness and contempt for women. Through the ancient text, however, occasionally shine the voices of the prophets and psalmists, somehow evoking the real spirit of God. Nowadays all reputable scholars and most intelligent people accept the idea of historicity, or seeing things in their context. We can appreciate that to the Ancient Hebrews sperm was a national resource, not to be wasted in self-indulgence but to bring forth (preferably male) children in order to provide a fighting force to defend a beleaguered people in the desert. The problem now, however, is not under-population but the ever-increasing teeming millions. And the condemnation of same-sex behaviour in the Old Testament occurs within a code of living practices which also forbade interracial marriages, the eating of shellfish, the wearing of worsted cloth and women speaking in public – all of which have been modified in the light of our modern understanding. But we have clung on to the demonisation of gay people because it is a politically convenient source of power. Church or State, and sometimes both together, literally have their citizens by the balls if they can control their sexual lives through fear. This is understandable, but intolerable, and the irony of course is that the Jewish condemnation of homosexuality was incorporated into the Roman Empire at roughly the same time as hatred of the Jews.

Many years ago I did an examination of the parallel, from Roman times to the present day, between the persecution of the Jews and that of gay people, which was very illuminating. I was able to cite the creation of ghettos, outlawing of certain practices, stigmatisation, use of the Inquisition, burning and wearing of distinctive markings right up to the time of Hitler and Himmler. The latter wrote a code not only of racial hygiene, which condemned the Jews to obliteration, but of sexual hygiene, which did the same to gay people. It is thus doubly intolerable that the Spanish bishops were permitted to use the word 'virus' in their description of the gay community in Spain in the last decade. Such language comes directly from fascist ideology and is inappropriate in the twenty-first century.

At first it was just a matter for the Church and its obsession with sexual behaviour of all kinds. One need only look at the medieval penitentials, books where every sexual act and deviation is lovingly and meticulously recorded and the appropriate penances indicated. These include the ancient Gaelic penitentials of *Cummean Fada* in which various kinds of

75

homosexual behaviour are itemised. But it remained a matter for the Church alone until, by accident, the state took over certain of its functions in the English-speaking world. This happened in the 1530s when Henry VIII, in taking control of the monasteries, also took control of the ecclesiastical courts, which had previously tried the crimes of buggery and sodomy.

Interestingly, one of the greatest scholars of this era, Professor John McNeill SJ, wrote a superb book on biblical quotations concerning homosexual behaviour. He was given an *imprimi potest* (meaning it could be published) by the Church authorities, who expected it to be a damp squib. However, when it became an international academic and popular success the Vatican attempted to suppress it and silence McNeill. Courageously the publishers produced an Italian translation, including the correspondence with the Vatican. But McNeill was, and remains, silenced.

The law against buggery and sodomy did not extend to Ireland for technical reasons until the 1630s, when an Anglican bishop from the south of Ireland, John Atherton, spotted the opportunity for political advancement and launched the first Save Ireland from Sodomy campaign. He was ultimately successful, but as we are often warned, 'Be careful what you pray for', as Atherton became the first victim of his own law. Perhaps due to political rivalry, he was arrested on a charge of buggery with his servant and was executed near Smithfield Market in 1640, having been trundled in disgrace past Christ Church Cathedral. Ecclesiastical hypocrites note, and tremble.

Penalties ranged from life imprisonment to death by hanging, with the last execution for consensual sex between men taking place in Scotland in 1836, frighteningly close to our own times. The name given in law by the Church to sex between two men was '*crimen illud horribile, inter christianos non nominandum*' – 'that crime so horrible it is not to be spoken of among Christians' – and so a pall of silence descended which twisted and deformed so many lives and forced this behaviour underground.

The position was made even worse by the introduction in 1885 of the Labouchere Amendment, known as the 'blackmailer's charter', under which any act of 'gross indecency' was punishable by terms of imprisonment. Apart from its horrendously vindictive nature against a vulnerable minority, the principal difficulty with this law was that it did not define gross indecency, which led to some tragic, and some laughable, results. Two RAF men were convicted in the 1950s on the basis of having looked lewdly at each other in a pub. Lesbianism was not covered either, and when I argued later in court that this constituted discrimination based on gender alone, I was told that while women could be indecent, they could not be grossly so; that was apparently a privilege reserved for males alone. There is a myth that Queen Victoria opposed extending the law to include women because she could not imagine such things occurring between 'ladies'. But the Queen was in fact far too intelligent to entertain such nonsense. Nevertheless the Irish courts upheld the argument.

The ecclesiastic instruction that homosexuality was not to be mentioned was slavishly obeyed throughout society. It was a subject that was quite literally unmentionable, and throughout my youth was not referred to in newspapers, magazines or the broadcast media. The only hints one got were when a prominent personage such as Sir John Gielgud was arrested in a public lavatory, or aristocrats like Lord Montagu of Beaulieu were caught in compromising circumstances. Gradually the idiocy of this legislation began to dawn in Britain and a courageous group of MPs led by the late Dannie Abse campaigned to have the law changed. A committee was formed under Sir John Wolfenden that enquired into the questions of homosexuality and prostitution.

It is extraordinary how the prejudices of a small nomadic tribe in the Middle East spread first to the Roman Empire, then throughout Christendom and Islam, ending up finally in the British Empire, which spread it through the entire globe.

Tragically, in some African and Arab states homosexuality is still pursued with the utmost vigour. In the last two years, attending a meeting of Frontline, a group that helps human-rights defenders, I met a young African man called David Cato. I was not then to realise that, at the instigation of the Christian churches in Uganda, he was shortly to be butchered. It reminded me of Mahmoud Asgari and Ayaz Marhoni, the two lovely young Iranian men who were arrested because of their relation-ship, beaten and hanged from the back of a lorry. A married couple in Co. Cork who were revolted by this sent me a photo of their execution. There was a video too but I was unable to watch it. However, I forced an apology from the then Iranian Ambassador for the light manner in which he treated this barbarous incident during a private meeting of the Foreign Affairs Committee.

This was the background to the world into which I innocently emerged. In Ireland it was an austere era, and I was an outsider in every way. I was Anglican in a deeply Roman Catholic society; I was half English in a narrow and negatively republican state defined more by hatred of England than love of Ireland; and I was homosexual when you could be jailed for being so. I knew I was an outlaw, and that my life wasn't real, which was the reason I didn't get into politics until much later. Politics was for the real people, and real people went to dances in cricket and tennis clubs, got married, bought houses and ran for election while their wives sat on the platform beside them. Even as a child I was confronted with this unreality. All Irish schoolbooks concerned Daddy being at work and Mammy, as provided for in Mr de Valera's Constitution, in the kitchen; and in fiction, the lucky hero and heroine overcame all obstacles and ended happily at the altar. I had no external reality, it was all internal. Gay people were non-people who lived in a concealed and hidden world. We had to stay in the shadows, keeping our presence under the radar, because if we became real we would

My maternal grandmother, Margaret Fitz-Patrick, as a young woman.

Grandfather John Fitz-Patrick, Grandmother and their favourite dog Barney at home in Co. Laois.

ABOVE: Uncle Dick accompanying the young Queen Elizabeth II.

RIGHT: Uncle Dick welcomes Queen Mary to the Guards Chapel.

Above: My father John Bernard Norris as a young man.

Above right: My mother Aida Margaret Fitz-Patrick shortly after leaving Alexandra College, *c.*1920.

Right: My mother at the wheel outside Chief Justice Cherry's house in the Roaring Twenties.

Below: Mother, Father, John and pram in Africa, 1940.

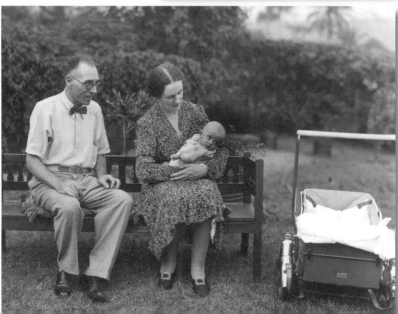

ABOVE LEFT: My Uncle Col. The Rev'd. Richard William Fitz-Patrick, MA., Q.H.C.

ABOVE: My parents at tea in Africa in the 1930s.

LEFT: The photograph of my mother's Bosman's Potto which appeared on the front page of the London evening papers in the 1930s.

BELOW LEFT: Uncle Max's wife Gabriella as a young woman in Transylvania.

BELOW: Dean Lamb, the dashing aviator who married my aunt Pauline.

Top Left: The once-elegant but now neglected Clinique Reine Elisabeth in Leopoldville where I was born.

Top Right: The SS *Copacabana*, the ship in which we made our wartime escape from Africa.

Middle Left: Uncle Dick, myself and my adored grandmother in the garden in Ballsbridge.

Middle Right: Mummy, myself and John at Killiney.

Left: John, Daddy and myself rock-pool fishing in the late 1940s.

ABOVE LEFT: John and myself sitting on the bumper of ZF 8.

RIGHT: John and myself, loving brothers.

LEFT: The last glimpse we ever had of my father (briefcase in hand) as he boarded an Aer Lingus plane at Collinstown Aerodrome, 1949.

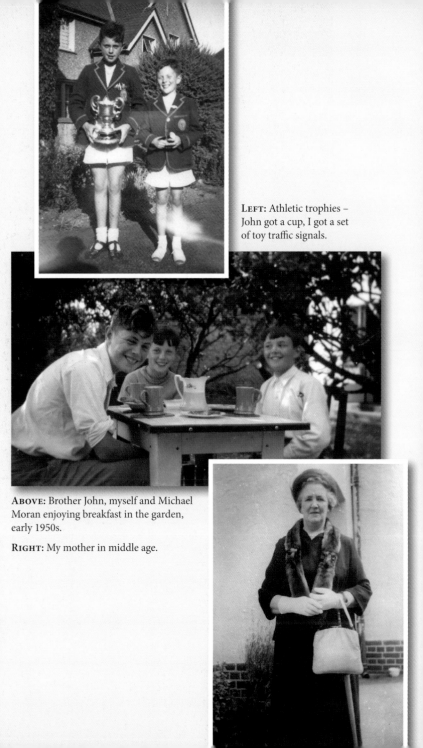

Left: Athletic trophies – John got a cup, I got a set of toy traffic signals.

Above: Brother John, myself and Michael Moran enjoying breakfast in the garden, early 1950s.

Right: My mother in middle age.

ABOVE: My graduation photo, 1968.

LEFT: David Miller and myself (snapped by a street photographer) crossing O'Connell Bridge, 1960s.

LEFT: My fiftieth birthday, with my Aunt Constance in her early nineties.

ABOVE: Nora and her dog Louis, snapped by me in the Troodos Mountains during one of our walks.

LEFT: My cat Buster and I at home in the Troodos.

be noticed, and that was dangerous. As a result my entire youth was stolen from me.

Towards the end of my schooldays I started to explore a little. I had a kindred spirit in school, and we occasionally visited a city centre bar called Bartley Dunne's which was a notorious haunt of the homosexual *demi-monde*. It was an Aladdin's cave to me, its wicker-clad Chianti bottles stiff with dribbled candle-wax, tea chests covered in red and white chequered cloths, heavy scarlet velvet drapes and an immense collection of multi-coloured liqueurs glinting away in their bottles. The place was peopled by lots of theatrical old queens, with the barmen clad in bum-freezer uniforms. While not being gay themselves, as far as I know, the Dunne brothers were quite theatrical in their own way. Barry would hand out little cards bearing the legend 'Bartley Dunne's, reminiscent of a left bank Paris bistro, haunt of aristocrats, poets and artists'. Whatever about that, Saturday night certainly resembled an amateur opera in full swing. There only ever seemed to be two records played over the sound system: 'Non, Je Ne Regrette Rien' by Edith Piaf, and Ray Charles's 'Take These Chains From My Heart'.

My friend and I were just flirting with the notion of being gay, and enjoyed the camp theatricality of this gloomy bar. We never really discussed our sexuality with any great seriousness but we both fancied the same rugby players and would spend our Friday nights traipsing across from Bartley Dunne's to Davy Byrne's and The Bailey in search of a glimpse of our latest out-half.

There were, of course, hundreds of thousands of other gay people in Ireland at the time, and if you accept Kinsey's reckoning of 10 per cent, then there were perhaps close to half a million. They were almost all in hiding, and as they didn't have blue ears or any other indicator, you wouldn't know one if you met him or her on the bus. There was no doubt about the man I met in the public lavatory in Capel Street on the way home from a social event, however. He flashed at me, and winked. I was in my early twenties and it was the first time I was confronted with the fact that I was not the only real gay in Ireland, and I was delighted. I was less delighted when he asked was it my first time, because when I said yes he dumped me. I call it my George Michael moment!

There was a hugely active sexual life in Dublin in the 1950s and 60s, but it was concentrated in public lavatories, because that was where society corralled gay people. I find it hard to imagine that nobody seemed to think it extraordinary to have a queue as long as you might see outside a cinema along Burgh Quay, and at the corner of Capel Street Bridge and Ormond Quay, every weekend evening. Every so often the guards would go in and fish an unfortunate pair out, but the general populace averted their gaze. Irish people just couldn't be gay, so what they could see with their own eyes could not actually be happening.

But there were intelligent people who had to have known that by making sexual relations between men a criminal offence they were just driving it underground. I've come across judges, doctors and clergy of all the churches who were queuing at the lavatories of Dublin in the 1950s and 60s. No one could afford to sustain a relationship, because if you were visible you were vulnerable, and the full force of public odium, police, courts, disgrace and joblessness would become a horrible reality. All society did was to deprive gay people of dignity and drive them into these situations. Most of my age cohort was psychologically damaged by the experience. Some became really neurotic and self-hating and, a bit like J. Edgar Hoover, they sometimes projected their hatred on to other gay people. But, astonishingly, amid all that hatred and oppression, love did survive. I am proud to know gay couples who met at this time, some of whom have stayed together for up to fifty-five years, a record that would put a lot of modern marriages to shame.

It was a shocking reflection on the Ireland of those days that a hurried encounter in a public lavatory was all that was offered to gay men. I was picked up on one occasion by a kerb crawler, a handsome young man who wore sunglasses even though it was evening, driving a fast car. He said he was an airline pilot, and took me to a hotel where I was effectively raped. I was so innocent that I wasn't sure if I could refuse or even protest: after all, he had paid for the room. It was horrible, but that is what that society did to people like me. The alternatives I was presented with were to be completely celibate, to rely on finding people for sex in lavatories, or to engage with strangers who might be physically violent. That was an appalling set of options, so when I read Plato's *Symposium* I realised there was a more civilised approach, albeit in a time and place far from Mr de Valera's Ireland. I felt very strongly that gay people were entitled to decent treatment like any ordinary citizen, not to be bought off by official Ireland occasionally turning a blind eye to the farmyard sexual activity that went on in public lavatories and parks.

I had learnt that being gay could be dangerous, so I internalised it for a time and it became a source of great difficulty. Then one Sunday in the late 1960s I noticed a small advertisement in the *Observer*, giving a box number for the Campaign for Homosexual Equality in Manchester. I agonised over replying to it, fearing it might be a blackmailer's ruse, but eventually sent off my postal order and SAE to the pagan land of England. Just in case there was something dodgy afoot, I called myself by the cunningly literary/Hibernian pseudonym of Alfred J. O'Neill. I was disappointed by the package which was sent back, being full of parochial English news and affairs and largely irrelevant to Ireland. I joined the organisation anyway, as its only Irish member, and thus rather timidly began my life as a gay-rights activist.

I next went to the founding meeting of the Southern Ireland Civil Rights Association in Regent House in Trinity in 1970. The group, headed up by Fr Enda McDonagh and Kader Asmal, had been formed to show solidarity with the beleaguered Catholic population of Northern Ireland, who were suffering discrimination in employment and housing. I listened as speaker after speaker castigated the Stormont Government for its repression of Roman Catholics in contrast with the favourable treatment of Protestant minorities in the Republic. The atmosphere was positively radioactive with self-congratulation. It was a mood I felt an inner compulsion to rupture.

I hadn't planned to speak, but the pent-up electricity of repression that I had carried discharged itself in a flash of anger. I rose to my feet and said that while I accepted what they said about the Republic being a safe place for Protestants, nevertheless as an Anglican I also knew that this was as much a matter of self-interest as altruism. We were as a community numerically small, financially powerful and politically almost masochistically mealy-mouthed in our toadying to the pseudo-Gaelic establishment. The smiles of sophisticated amusement at my remarks melted away when I continued by pointing out the hypocrisy of the speakers in not referring at all to the presence of a genuinely harassed minority to which I also belonged.

The initial response from the platform was rather patronising, and I vividly recall being told that the law that criminalised homosexuals was a dead letter and that if I minded my Ps and Qs and kept quiet, little harm was likely to come to me. However, I argued the point and one or two people, including that splendid champion of human rights the late Bridget Wilkinson, stood up and said, 'No, this is an injustice.' I am glad to say that the Southern Ireland Civil Rights Association thus became the first Irish organisation to include homosexual law reform on its agenda, although it was never a campaigning matter for the group.

It very much surprised me subsequently when Cardinal O'Connor of New York – who had been to the fore in passionately railing against the injustices inflicted on Catholics in Northern Ireland – turned around and took precisely the opposite approach towards gay people. He even went so far as to say that politicians had a duty to discriminate against gay people in employment and housing – the very things I had fought against alongside him for his flock. I was horrified that someone of such eminence in the major Christian denomination could take a view that went completely against the teachings of the gospel. That taught me that the real test of a proper commitment to human rights is to be prepared to defend the rights of people who are not like you, and who you might not like or of whom who might even disapprove.

The gay-rights movement in Ireland started in earnest in Trinity in 1973 after the students' union welfare officer attended a conference in the New University of Ulster at Coleraine about sexuality and sexual health. This was followed up by a conference which set up the Union for Sexual Freedom in Ireland, of which the Trinity branch was the Sexual Liberation Movement. That proved an interesting and illuminating experience. Of approximately fifteen slightly jittery people who turned up to its first session, all except one were homosexual and just a sprinkling were liberated enough to consider themselves 'gay'. The first major event we staged was a two-day Symposium on Homosexuality held in the Junior Common Room in Trinity.

However, it seemed to me absurdly quixotic for what I light-heartedly described as 'eleven poofs and a question mark' to spend their Monday evenings writing letters to the *Irish Times* demanding unrestricted access to contraception, so the first split in the movement resulted. I was, as was to become typical, the principal discordant element.

The last act of the Sexual Liberation Movement was a demonstration outside the British Embassy in June 1974, which was followed by a tiny march into the city centre and a picket on the Department of Justice in St Stephen's Green. We marched around for three-quarters of an hour, causing numerous couriers and messenger boys to fall, open-mouthed, off their bicycles.

CIÉ buses slowed so that the passengers and drivers could drink in our slogans, such as HOMOSEXUALS ARE REVOLTING, before a lorry pulled up in front of the department.

A large roll of carpet was flung out of the back of the lorry and a burly man descended. He took one look at us and shouted back to his colleague in the driving seat, 'Jesus, Mick, they're fuckin' queers!'

A head appeared at the window and took in the demonstration. Then a deep bass voice shouted back, 'Whorrabowra, sure I don't give a bollicks, a picket's a fuckin' picket, mate,' and with that an even larger and more muscular lorry driver jumped out of the cab and joined our picket for a quarter of an hour, leaving the minister's carpet stranded on the pavement. A splendid example of worker solidarity. The distinguished historian Diarmuid Ferriter included this story, my carefully crafted phonetic phrasing and all, in his excellent study of Irish social and sexual mores, but attributed it to the critic Quentin Fottrell, who was not even born when the march took place.

Eight or nine of us remained in the SLM and, after a long argument, my view that we should be completely honest and forthright about what we were prevailed, and we set up a group to campaign for gay rights. The Irish Gay Rights Movement (IGRM) was publicly launched at a meeting in the South County Hotel in June 1974, when thirty people turned up and we formed a steering committee. I helped to give the organisation its name, and argued strongly that we needed to make a bold statement by including the words 'Irish' and 'gay', which at the time was a shocking contradiction as society had decreed that you couldn't be both. It seemed to me the main arguments were: number one, we were Irish, number two, we were gay, number three, our mission was to demand recognition of our rights, and number four, we were a political movement. Prominent and talented members of that movement included Seán Connolly, who was to become general secretary, and Clement Clancy, Bernard Keogh and Edmund Lynch, all of whom in their different ways were deeply committed to the cause. I was elected first chairman.

Most people at that time refused to believe that Roger Casement or Padraig Pearse could be homosexual. Casement was a hero to me for his absolute commitment to human rights in Congo and again in South America for his work with the Putamayo Indians. The famous Black Diaries were no forgeries, and of course he was wildly promiscuous, but how could he be anything else? Society's strictures ensured he couldn't set up home with his true love, a bank official from Belfast who later married and lived on into the 1950s in retirement in Greystones, Co. Wicklow. There is no record of his attitude to Casement's life, execution or the subsequent debate about the diaries.

Other heroes of Irish nationalism were also less than 100 per cent heterosexual. Our landlord in the first IGRM building in Parnell Square was a grand-nephew of Michael Collins, and had the same name. I thought Mr Collins was a very caring landlord as he turned up at a lot of our functions. Reality only dawned on me when I saw him one night out on the dance floor, wrapped around another man. He was one of us, and as landlord had managed to get in free! I had a chat with him in the coffee bar and was greatly amused to hear that, according to him, he shared this trait with his great-uncle. I didn't know if he was teasing or not, but a subsequent event appeared to confirm it. An elderly man came in one night who had been visiting Sinn Féin's headquarters three doors down. He had fought in the Civil War more than half a century before and claimed to have been one of Michael Collins's principal boyfriends. I mentioned this to a well-known popular historian of the period, who confirmed that this was generally known in certain republican circles, who were deeply uncomfortable about it. Well, if Michael Collins was gay, or bisexual – so what? Who cares? It shouldn't matter as it is just a neutral fact. It certainly isn't a slur, and the vast majority of the Irish people no longer regard it as such. Anyway, this all lessened the surprise when it emerged recently that another absurdly macho figure, the leader of the Blueshirts, General Eoin O'Duffy, had been embroiled in a long affair with the great Irish actor Micheál Mac Liammóir.

The Irish nation had its first glimpse of a real live homosexual in July 1974, when I made an appearance on the summer magazine show *Last House*, presented by Áine O'Connor and John McColgan, which went out at 10.20 p.m. It was suggested that I do the interview in shadow, with my back to the camera and my voice disguised. I told them that if they did that they could do it without me, because the whole point I wanted to make was that I was a perfectly normal, ordinary person – and if I appeared on the air looking furtive then it would destroy the whole message. Áine was absolutely lovely. She was going out with the actor Gabriel Byrne at the time and I got to know him too. He is a remarkable man and a superb actor, as well as a fine writer. John McColgan, also a talented and generous man, has gone on to international celebrity with his partner Moya Doherty in the initiation of *Riverdance*.

I had never been in a TV studio before, and excitedly gazed around at the cameras and the make-up artists. It was a very simple interview, and Áine started it by asking me were homosexuals 'sick people'? So I said, 'Well, I had a cold last week the same as everyone else, but I don't feel otherwise sick at all.' One startled viewer complained to RTÉ that as some American group of psychiatrists had held it to be a disease, and it was still against the law in Ireland, I wasn't entitled to say that I *wasn't* sick, as I could be held to be thereby inciting criminal activity. The Broadcasting Complaints Commission bizarrely upheld his complaint.

Áine asked in what way Ireland had failed to cherish me. I replied:

'I was brought up in ignorance of the facts of my true nature. The word "homosexual" was barely known in Ireland, and not breathed in polite society, and I was allowed to grow up through my adolescence believing that I was possibly the only homosexual in Ireland, not knowing there were possibly thousands of other similarly isolated people here. I thought there might have been one or two in England because I had heard about the curious goings-on over there, but I did not realise that I was part of a very large but isolated community in this country.'

It was the second most watched programme on RTÉ that week – behind the detective series *Kojak* – and in its way was a significant event.

We had held a few dance hops in Trinity, for which we charged sixpence admission, so we were rather surprised when the first discos started bringing in serious money. Dublin's first proper gay disco was over a health-food store called Green Acres in Great Strand Street, and our first DJ was Hugo McManus, who wore a Carmen Miranda-style hat festooned with fruit, and flesh-coloured Speedos decorated with grapes and a banana. We soon realised that the discotheque was a very interesting machine we could harness as, besides a handful of pubs, nobody else was providing a social outlet for gay people in Dublin at the time. The disco crowd rapidly grew from dozens to hundreds, and we put on wine-and-cheese parties for the older set.

The disco continued to be a peripatetic thing until we found suitable premises on Parnell Square, and it occasionally was a troublesome responsibility. I've never believed in discrimination on the grounds of religion, sex, age, education, accent or anything else, but I do believe in discrimination on one count – behaviour. My attitude to those who came to the disco was all-inclusive, but if you didn't behave with respect for others you could just bugger off. We had problems with some young male tarts in the club and tried to clamp down on it. One particular lad, Goldie, was a frequent offender and often became threatening, and one night I asked him to leave. From his pocket he drew a metal comb sharpened into a point, and waved it at me, at which I slammed the door on him and called the police. The gardaí came and dragged him away, as he shouted, 'What are you takin' me away for? They're the fuckin' queers.' For all his faults, Goldie didn't deserve the end he eventually got: his body was found floating in the Liffey.

Even in those early days, the seeds of many future splits were becoming apparent. The movement was always divided between those who saw the organisation as one to provide gay people with a social life or access to like-minded sexual partners – a very reasonable approach, and one that addressed in a personal way how gay people were crippled by Irish society – and some other activists, including myself, who saw the possibility of harnessing that energy to create a political movement that would remove the stigma and destroy the discriminatory laws. Several people opposed this because of a fear that political action would draw down the wrath of the law upon us, which might lead to people losing their jobs or going to jail. That dichotomy was the cause of every split in the gay movement, and there were many. I was probably the cause of every single one of the splits, but I am unrepentant, because I felt the time was right to challenge the oppression of the law. I felt passionately with Edith Piaf, '*J'en ai le droit d'aimer*'. And not just in a public lavatory or a carefully constructed closet.

Edmund Lynch had a capacity for organising, but he also had a genius for getting up people's noses. There was a visceral antagonism between him and general secretary Seán Connolly, who was a civil servant and therefore constrained from being too publicly identified with the IGRM. Seán had a very low flashpoint and he and Edmund had frequent spats, in which I was usually caught in the middle.

In April 1977 there was a leadership election, and I topped the poll by some distance. However, an opposition had formed and within half an hour the result was overturned in a palace coup instigated by those elements more interested in the social side of gay life. I had been building up the IGRM for two years and had set up a structure of departments such as Publications,

THE ONLY GAY IN THE VILLAGE

Legal and Social, and many of these were headed by my lieutenants. The new regime abolished a lot of these posts and got rid of my co-workers, but they couldn't get rid of me because I had headed the poll. I was told I was rocking the boat, and drawing too much attention at a time when prosecutions had almost stopped and there seemed to be slightly more tolerance for gay people. But mere tolerance wasn't enough for me: I wanted to achieve full political, legal and civil rights.

I was presented with a blacklist of those with whom I was not to work or appoint to committees. I told them I wasn't battling one form of oppression just to join another, and I wanted no part in their Stalinist approach. An element of personal antagonism had crept in, and that bitterness even led to physical violence.

In many ways I was glad to be out of the IGRM, the time-consuming discos and hob-nobbing over cheese and wine. I threw myself wholeheartedly into the Campaign for Homosexual Law Reform – which I started as a political alternative – and its pursuit of the legal route to reforming the constitution. But it was a difficult time for the early pioneers of gay liberation as we watched from the sidelines while the Irish Gay Rights Movement fizzled away to nothing.

There was one last blessing for me before the IGRM dissolved in acrimony. One day shortly before Christmas 1975, I was wandering down Grafton Street. College was out of term and I was in no particular hurry when I saw a handsome, foreign-looking man coming towards me. I was immediately electrified by his attractiveness and physical presence, and turned as he passed to watch him walk away. Momentarily invigorated, I shrugged my shoulders and walked on.

I was working all day in Parnell Square on my own, and went down to Bartley Dunne's for one drink to wind down at the end of the evening. I spotted that a couple of my friends were sitting with some strangers so I sat drinking on my own. Someone came over and said they were a group over from the Middle East and they wanted to discuss gay politics with me, but I was tired and tetchy and told him that I had been working all day and wasn't in the mood for company. However, I reluctantly agreed to join them and when I did so I realised one of their number was the fellow I'd seen on Grafton Street. His name was Ezra.

I was excited by his presence, and although his English was poor at that stage, his eyes were just drinking me in. He was picking up only a small proportion of the chat, but I was in high gear and he enjoyed that and understood my expressions and dramatic gestures. We arranged to meet the following night at the disco, but my chances of further contact were reduced because I was on duty at the door. Ezra was inside dancing, but once two o'clock came I went up to him and said, 'I'm sorry, I'm very tired and I have to go home to Greystones, but I do hope we have another opportunity to meet.' He just excused himself from the man he was dancing with and said, 'I'm coming home with you.'

It was the first time I had woken up in the morning beside someone and thought, *Isn't this wonderful?* – every previous occasion it had been *How can I get him out of the house without being seen?* It was the Christmas holidays, so he was able to stay for a few weeks, and overnight my beautiful but sterile home was transformed. It was an Edwardian house with a large garden and a lovely new kitchen with all mod cons, but all that was ever prepared in it were boiled eggs and cups of tea. We went to the village and bought rice and spices and soon the wonderful smells of exotic Middle Eastern cuisine began emanating from my kitchen. It was a lovely romantic time, enjoying being in a relationship of what I believed was mutual love for the first time at thirty-one, as Christmas passed and the log fire crackled in the grate. I had my family at last.

Ezra returned to Israel and we began a long relationship which was mostly conducted by telephone and letter, interspersed with glorious periods when we could be together. At one stage he considered moving to Dublin, but immigration was difficult in those days and of course we had no legal status. Apparently the Aliens Office of the Department of Justice got wind of his presence here on one extended stay, and I was contacted by telephone.

'We understand you are harbouring an illegal alien, namely Miss Ezra Yitzhak,' the voice said.

I replied, 'With my hand on my heart I can assure you I am not harbouring a Miss Ezra Yitzhak. I have never met a Miss Ezra Yitzhak; in fact I have never even heard of a Miss Ezra Yitzhak.'

This, of course, was true. Ezra was many things, but he was no lady.

By the late 1970s we had prepared ourselves for the battle with the state, so I decided to take one last holiday in Israel, where the 'sexual healing' would be just what the doctor ordered. However, I arrived in Jerusalem to be given the devastating message: 'David, I'm sorry, we won't be sleeping together on this trip. I no longer find you physically attractive.' This was a mere three years after our first meeting, but it is the last time there was any attempt on either part at the physical expression of the love we still felt for each other. If one may dare use a classical distinction, it is that between *eros* and *agape*, physical and spiritual love, the very subject of Plato's *Symposium* that had so illuminated life for me. I felt that although I had lost the erotic content, I could be satisfied with the more lasting *agape*. I continued to visit, even though I now slept on a makeshift arrangement of blankets in the sitting room. I still loved him, of course, but as I would find during the presidential election campaign, the vulgar mind apparently cannot distinguish between the sexual and the spiritual.

Ezra had opened up a paradise of sexual pleasure to me, which I am profoundly glad to have experienced. It is such a significant aspect of the human personality that those who haven't experienced that collision of the erotic, the physical and the spiritual have missed something very rich. I was bitterly disappointed that he had cut that off from me, but I was glad I had experienced it. I understand the beauty and significance and sacredness of sexual relations, and always felt they are not the sort of thing to be frittered away on one-night stands. I am not standing in judgement of those who enjoy such things, but that was never for me, and never what I wanted.

I have never found the female body repulsive, and have experienced its beauty – indeed I have proved I am mechanically competent in that field – but it also wasn't what I wanted. There is something about the strength of masculinity that I find very reassuring, and the shared feeling of just the two of us against the world. It wasn't just a sexual thing, and that is what allowed me to continue to love Ezra.

I still considered I had a loving partnership with Ezra – he had many affairs but he assured me they were irrelevant – but my sexual relationship with him lasted just those three incomplete years. Ezra, like many Levantine people, was very practical. Sex was just another appetite to be satisfied, like hunger or thirst or sleep. And if I wasn't there to make him dinner, he would make himself a sandwich. Even during our first three years, I learnt later, he hadn't been faithful.

We held a party to mark the tenth anniversary of the start of our romance, although by that stage it was a *mariage blanc*. While we were washing up I lifted a glass to Ezra and said, 'Here's to the next ten years.' He said, 'David, why limit it to ten, why not for ever?' It seemed like a spiritual commitment and left open the possibility of us spending our lives together, whatever arrangement we decided to make. However, shortly after I returned home the voice on the answering machine I had given him as an anniversary present was not Ezra's, who refused to return my calls. It turned out that he had started a serious relationship with an Israeli javelin and discus champion, Isaac, which was devastating for me. I cannot describe the suffocating sense of isolation I experienced; I lay on the sofa in the drawing room at home, staring blindly at the bricks of the house opposite, trying desperately to cope with the weight of almost physical pain that swept over me.

I had already booked my ticket for the next trip to Jerusalem, but I didn't tell Ezra and went on my own to study Hebrew at the Hebrew University for six weeks. About two days before I was due to leave I was walking down Chopin Street, near the President's house, when I saw this tall man carrying a sports bag walking towards me. I had never met Isaac, seen a photograph of him, or even been given a description of what he looked like. But I knew instantly that man was Isaac; it was like an electric shock. I let him pass and turned to look, just as he was turning to look at me. That night I rang Ezra for a chat, not mentioning my location, and I asked what he was doing that evening. He said he had nothing planned, so I suggested we go for dinner. He then realised I was in Israel and was stunned: 'Isaac tell me you in Jerusalem, and I not believing him!'

Ezra and Isaac lived together for ten years, and I became great friends with Isaac. They came to stay with me in Dublin on several occasions and I stayed with them many times in Jerusalem. When they were broke I used to send them money in what I called the 'deserted wives' allowance'. I even acted as counsellor to reconcile them several times. I came to love Isaac – he is a wonderful man, and I was delighted and honoured to be best man at his wedding to Juan, a Spanish policeman, in Aranjuez, near Madrid in 2010.

I recently rediscovered the manuscript of a piece I wrote many years ago to help ameliorate the pain I felt when Ezra left me for Isaac. Re-reading it I experienced once more the exact feeling of that period of my life. I called it 'Places of the Heart', and it also explains my feelings for the golden city of Jerusalem:

This year I have not been to Jerusalem. It is the first time in many years that this has happened, and when I saw those sturdy travellers from the south, the swallows, wheel and swoop the other evening over the Vico Road, I felt a tug at my heart. Something in the movement of the birds suggested a very different scene; not the leaden waters of Killiney Bay but Jerusalem, City of Gold, with the silver and gilt domes of its mosques glistening in the Mediterranean heat.

A Sunday morning in the late '70s, walking on the ancient ramparts in the bright sunlight; but with a heavy heart because my bags were already packed for the return to Dublin. Suddenly there was a subtle change in the light. Interposed between the walls and rooves of the old city and the sun, a cloud of storks homing from Egypt, wings outstretched and motionless in the buoyant air, hung and glided in perfect formation, their feathers filtering the harsh light. We halted in wonder at the sight. The ancients would have forged a myth of the inter-connecting worlds of the human, the animal and the divine from that moment, but inevitably the blare of car horns dragged us back to everyday life.

For some reason the eve of departure frequently brought some such magical occurrence, perhaps due to the heightened nervous receptivity of anticipated leave-taking. (I remember for example a moonbow observed over Ramot one sleepless pre-flight midnight) but whatever the cause, even laying aside the fact that the three great monotheistic religions have their roots here, Jerusalem is a mystic place.

A special magic makes Jerusalem for me a place of the heart. For surely if this phrase means anything at all, it means a place where emotional adolescence ends in the exchange of love. And so it was with me. Through the friendship of one man I fell in love with the Levant and its peoples, and through him embraced its life and culture, the romantic lure of the East and even conquered my fear of flying. I remember clearly my first flight from London to Tel Aviv. We had to check in four or five hours before departure from Heathrow. I had a couple of pints to steady my nerves, and during the preceding hours every time I went to the lavatory I was re-frisked by the El-Al guard – tight was scarcely the word for security!

Everything was strange to me, the kosher in-flight meals, the sturdy, almost architectural character of the Hebrew language in contrast to the flowing Arabic script of English, and the gruff, guttural masculinity of its accent. And then the Hassidic Jews, incongruous in the sophisticated modernity of a great flying machine. I had never seen people like them before, dressed in black gabardine, fur caps, untidy and wispy, with straggling cummerbunds, frayed bits of leather and string wrapping their unathletic bodies, eyes alert for heresy, mouths suddenly popping into a gabble of religious or dietary dispute. Yet it was they who provided a focus for the pent-up emotion of us passengers. The sun was behind us, dipping toward the horizon like an angry orange thrown by one of the old Gods, when a vague rim of brown baked land became apparent. As if by instinct the Hassids flocked to the point in the plane closest to land – their land – Eretz Yisrael, from which they had been banished for perhaps two thousand years. Anachronistic they might be, but as they began to chant, they drew our sentiment towards them like scarecrow spirit-conductors.

A few minutes later we taxied to a halt and looking out of the window I could see the familiar international uniform of ground staff; overalls and ear-muffs. But the faces under the baseball-style caps were Phoenician, skin as brown as their brown eyes and hair as black as the runway tar. The cabin door opened and a soft gush of warm air flowed up the steps – a breath of enchantment and the first real whisper from the face of the East.

Dazed, exhausted and a little tipsy from the evening warmth, I emerged scanning the crowd outside the barrier anxiously. I needn't have worried. The face I wanted to see was there, trying to look solemn and composed but not even the hooded Iraqi lids could quench the delight in the eyes, and there was a smile that lit up the whole airport. We drove in a Sherut – the shared Mercedes limousine taxi service traditional between the larger cities of Israel – past shadowy palms and then onto a highway that curved gradually up towards the Jerusalem Hills.

My sole memory of that trip is the electric proximity of Ezra wedged in beside me in the back seat. Now, of course, the

Jerusalem–Tel Aviv Highway is as familiar to me as the Bray Road – the graceful white arches of the monastery at Latrun marking the start of the climb to the Holy City itself; the pathetic shells of military vehicles from 1948 abandoned at the side of the road like childhood's Dinky toys and preserved in the mountain air as a permanent memorial to those who died in the birth pangs of the Israeli nation; fields of sunflowers gone to seed standing with blackened disconsolate faces and stooped shoulders like some terrible photograph from Yad Vashem; or the arthritically twisted limbs of the vines on their ancient terraces.

The first address I lived at in Jerusalem was on the fringes of the fashionable embassy district. Ezra had taken the lease on a little 'house' behind one of the exclusive apartment blocks. The house itself was tiny, the former wash-house of the apartments, built in the 1930s from Jerusalem stone, and about the size of a comfortable bathroom in suburban Dublin. It consisted of one room into which you stepped immediately from the garden and in this restricted space we conducted every aspect of our lives both intimate and social, cooking, talking, sleeping, and entertaining friends. There was only one division of the space, a cubicle at the kitchen end of the room which contained a small hand basin and flushing lavatory above which a rickety shower attachment hung perilously. Here you could quite literally have the Dublin man's dream – a shower, a shite and a shave, and all simultaneously.

I was happy, for here at last after many years I belonged again to a social unit, even if our family consisted of only two members, and when the first invitation to the two of us as a couple arrived, my joy was complete. My duties consisted of hanging out the bedding to air under the pine trees in the morning, shaking the pine needles off them in the late afternoon, and making the bed, doing the washing up and organising the household. I was a curious mixture of Pasha and skivvy; for I also received my early morning coffee and copy of the Jerusalem Post out on the little terrace under the trees.

On my first visit I was timid about exploring on my own, particularly since I had no Hebrew, but at the confluence of Berlin

Street and Azza Street stood a lozenge-shaped kiosk strategically placed behind a bus-stop – Confiserie Marcelle. Here I could find a friendly refuge, exchanging memories of Paris in rusty French with Marcelle herself, a diminutive and twinkling exile from the Seine barricaded behind trays of Petits Fours, ranks of confectionery in jars, and boxes of exotic chocolates.

The suburbs of Jerusalem have their own beauty, elegant, clean buildings, leafy green gardens from which a sudden slash of colour shows red or purple from an exotic shrub, or higher up among the branches a yellow mist of mimosa spray, and overall the balm of evening bringing a scent of jasmine. Nevertheless, for me as I suspect for many, the real Jerusalem is the old city itself, for this is really the golden City of legend. Here the honey coloured stone has absorbed sunlight for centuries until it almost glows in the dark. A confusing network of alleys criss-crosses the quarters, Armenian, Jewish, Christian and Arab, allowing the unwary to get lost between the Jaffa Gate, breached to provide a ceremonial opening for the visit of pompous Kaiser Wilhelm the Second in 1911, and the Damascus gate where you can sit in an Arab café smoking a nargilah or hookah, and watch a gaggle of Hassids with long gandery strides make for the Kotel or Wailing Wall. We walked these alleyways many times, but seldom purchased anything except miniature cups of strong aromatic Turkish coffee or some pebbles of incense from an ancient relic of Ottoman days complete with red tarboosh, full of dusty courtesy in his cave near the Cardo. Our shopping we always did on Friday morning or early afternoon in the Mahane Yehuda, the ramshackle Jewish market behind Jaffa Street. What a confusion of vegetables, fruit and humans rioted along its narrow passages and stalls in preparation for every Sabbath! The visit to the Mahane Yehuda was a never-to-be-missed ritual even after our move away from damp dark Berlin Street to the bright well-aired flat in Ramot.

Where Berlin Street was satisfyingly bohemian, Ramot had all the comforts of suburbia, but most precious of all was the sense of light, for Jerusalem is above all a city of light. How many evenings have I stood at our window in Ramot watching the light change from blue to purple, and then the forest-clad hills across the valley darken and begin to shimmer with discreet light from paths and scattered houses. From the kitchen window I could catch a glimpse in the distance of the last few buses leaving by the highway for Tel Aviv as the traffic stopped to observe the holy day. Then after the meal and in the gentle light of candles, wearing the long flowing garments of the Hebron Arabs we would listen to songs of love from Oum Khalsoom, Fairuz or Farid Al Atrache. As the years went by, I found myself as much at home in Jerusalem as in Dublin. Even now when Ezra and I are apart, I find my thoughts returning and like a mirage the walls of the old city tufted with the mauve and white flowers of caper bushes rise before my eyes only to melt away again.

In my mind a pot-pourri of memories is stirred. Cool white rooms in Nachlaot with high-domed ceilings and tiled floors, little pads and pencils placed at the doorways of many Jerusalem dwellings, so messages can be left and no visit is totally in vain (would they survive in Dublin, even in the suburbs?), elaborate rituals of food and friendship, sturdy ice-cream vendors stamping across the roasting sand of Tel Aviv shouting 'arteek, arteek, leemone, vaneell, choco-choco' and stories, always stories, for the Jews like the Irish love a good tale. In a taxi, at a bus-stop, queuing in the cookie-shop, momentary intimacies are forged and life stories swapped.

I remember when three years into our friendship the physical side of my relationship with Ezra was abruptly and finally ended I went into exile in a little hotel in Hayarkon Street in Tel Aviv. Breakfast one morning was interrupted by the intrusion of a young American, brash and born-again, eager to share with us the gospel of his personal encounter with Christ. The only other people at breakfast were myself and an elderly Jewish couple. The couple were polite, non-committal, but as a Christian myself I felt deeply embarrassed and when the evangelist left I apologised to the old man. He smiled gently and said 'Thank you, but I have had worse. I was born in Germany. We lived in Munich. I lost my mother, my father, my brother, my sisters and my first wife. I survived myself only by accident. They came for us piecemeal and as I was the youngest I was nearly the last. It was amazing the way we lived. In the middle of madness we tried to live a normal life. The day that they came for my wife and myself I was out at the dentist for a long-standing appointment. My dentist was a Dr Goering, cousin of the Reichsmarschall. He continued treating Jews but they couldn't touch him. He told me to come back the next day for a filling. When I got home the Gestapo were waiting – they took me to the police compound where I was to be held awaiting transport to the camps. The next afternoon I was called out. I thought it was the end, but it was a messenger from the dentist. They gave me back my clothes. I was released for my appointment. The dentist said nothing. Once my filling was done I left the surgery and made straight for the station and got on the first train. I escaped. It was a miracle.'

An unbelievable tale, and yet looking at the old man and his second wife with their simple courtesy I knew it was true. Israel has many such stories and we are bound to listen. It is a place to which the heart is drawn inexorably.

Just a year ago I did go back. On my own. To be alone in Jerusalem was a strange, haunted feeling like coming out into the sunlight from a cinema, or waking from gas in an old-fashioned dentists. The buildings and people were familiar but both they and I, and the way I saw them, had changed in some irreversible, frightening way.

Since I was a child I have always when abroad scoured the night sky for the friendly, reassuring figure of Orion the Hunter. That visit he also had abandoned my sky which was now full of unfamiliar stars. I was sure it was an omen, and a black one at that. But I hadn't counted on the pre-departure miracles so often provided by Jerusalem, or perhaps I thought that my desolation had drained the magic from the entire city.

And then at 3.30am on the morning of my flight, as I left my bags at the gate for the taxi, suddenly low down on the horizon, sand-wiched between two tall buildings and lying on his side, one leg below the horizon as if he had just got up specially to say good-bye was my old friend, the hunter. So perhaps Isaac Singer was right when he wrote that no love of any kind is ever lost. Maybe the time will once more come when I will say to myself yet again, next year in Jerusalem. And mean it.

As the Irish Gay Rights Movement fell apart through the leadership cadre's own inefficiencies and in-fighting, people came to me and suggested we get some sort of group together again. The case was ongoing, and I had continued to be interested in gay politics, indeed had helped write one of the foundation documents for the International Gay Association in Coventry in 1978.

I initially resisted moves to start up another Irish gay organisation, but was persuaded that we could create a positive symbiosis between the personal and the political, and we could educate our own people about the advantages of the political fight for human rights. Others shared that view, and although I was the visible manifestation of the campaign, a lot of people who couldn't afford to be seen worked hard beneath the surface and deserve much of the credit.

Having formed the National Gay Federation, I tramped the streets of Dublin in search of suitable premises. One day I was on my way to visit Tony Hanahoe, my old college friend who was by then a solicitor, at his office on the corner of Parliament Street and Essex Quay. I was rambling through Temple Bar, an old part of the city which was mostly owned by CIÉ. The bus and train company had a plan to build a new transport hub there, so it was impossible to sell or rent property and the district had become largely derelict. I wandered up Fownes Street, where I saw a warehouse for rent which I thought might be suitable. On investigation, I found it was owned by John Cooke and Son, Jewellers. I knew John, who was a neighbour of mine in Greystones. He was a very decent man but he needed some convincing and two bottles of the best Madeira from the Trinity cellar to swing the deal.

The NGF was just starting, and had no money of its own, so I put every penny of my life savings of £12,000 into it, which covered the first year's rent and the cost of renovations. I later gave the banks a guarantee based on my home, which allowed us to get further funds released.

I set up Hirschfeld Enterprises Ltd to run the building and pay the wages and pension contributions of the one or two permanent employees, while the NGF ran the activities, and there was naturally a crossover of personnel. I distributed shares, although I retained 61 per cent because there was always a tendency in the gay movement to split, and as I had already been through several of those I had to protect the money I put in – and I had put in *all* the money.

I divided the rest of the shares up among the members of the board, for psychological reasons as much as anything else. I felt if people were on the board they were entitled to the respect of also being shareholders. They paid £1 for each share to make it legal, and none of us ever took a dividend, which meant the organisation had to pay a tax surcharge of 20 per cent on the fees that we didn't take out. Surely an irony, as we were doing the social and health work for the gay community that a caring government should have done. Not only were we working for nothing, we were actually expected to pay for the privilege.

Magnus Hirschfeld was a German pioneer of psychoanalysis of a similar calibre to Freud, Adler and Jung and a political campaigner for the removal of the penal code which dis-criminated against homosexuals. Hirschfeld almost succeeded under the Weimar Republic, but the arrival of the Nazis was devastating for him and his work. Among Adolf Hitler's first acts on seizing power was to send his bully boys to Hirschfeld's Institut für Sexualwissenschaft in Berlin, where he had recorded an enormous number of gay people's individual histories, and research into intersex and transsexuals. The Brownshirts ransacked his institute and burnt his library to the ground, and although Hirschfeld had been internationally renowned in the field of psychoanalysis, the Nazis almost succeeded in erasing his name from history.

I became very interested in Hirschfeld, his lover Karl Giese, and the gay people from the Third Reich who were forced to wear pink triangles and were butchered in Auschwitz. I started the Hirschfeld Foundation to raise funds for the cause, but people didn't want to be reminded of Nazi atrocities and it never took in any money. It is extraordinary how many 'liberal' people have a propensity to stick their heads in the sand when confronted by unpleasant realities.

I was even attacked for having 'extreme views' because I publicised the treatment of gay people in the camps. I was just telling the story of those men and their awful fate. I had met some concentration-camp survivors at an IGA conference, and asked them why they hadn't followed the Jewish victims in suing for restitution. They told me that some men had tried, but their action has just led to a reactivation of their convictions for homosexuality under the Nazis, and they were put back in prison to finish their sentences – without even getting any time off for the time they had already spent in the concentration camps.

I thought it was unjust that such a courageous man as Hirschfield was should be so obliterated, and started the process of reawakening the world to him by naming our gay community centre in his honour. The Hirschfeld Centre was opened in Fownes Street on St Patrick's Day 1979, and a year later Dr Noël Browne officially unveiled a brass plaque on the building. The plaque is now in the Little Museum of Dublin on St Stephen's Green. It was the first Hirschfeld Centre in the world, but it was followed by several more.

I spoke too, telling the assembled throng, 'The existence of the Hirschfeld Centre is living proof of gay people's new-found pride and testimony to the fact that we the gay citizens of Ireland need no longer fear to be openly ourselves . . .'

The Hirschfeld quickly became a unique community centre

with over a thousand members. Not only did we have offices for our political campaigns, but we were also able to house telephone helplines and counselling rooms, and a restaurant where people could meet for lunch. We had a library too, the basis of which was given to us by the novelist John Broderick. If ever there was an unsung hero of Gay Ireland it was John, who wrote very openly about being gay in the 1950s. He is a much underestimated man and a remarkable writer.

We had our own cinema, the Hirschfeld Biograph, which was run by Johnny McEvoy, the floor manager on *The Late Late Show* on RTÉ. Johnny was a perfectionist and a martinet, and always started his movies on the dot of 8 p.m., two or three nights a month for several years. It was a great place for gay people of all ages to meet, and even hosted European premières, while significant figures in the world of Irish film such as Liam O'Leary and Kieran Hickey would help put festivals together. The leading gay film historian Vito Russo came to give us a lecture on 'The Celluloid Closet' before he published his seminal book of the same name. I christened our cinema the Biograph because it reminded me of the hilarious Peter Sellers film *The Smallest Show on Earth*.

The most popular activity was the disco, Flikkers, which is Dutch for 'faggots'. Jim O'Hare, a brilliant art designer and both a real family man and good friend to the gay community, and Edmund Lynch, who worked in RTÉ, had spotted that Jim's set for a Eurovision Song Contest had been dumped in a back lot out in Montrose, so they rescued and restored it for the disco. A team of us went in and painted the walls ourselves and Jim organised a very sophisticated dance area. It was widely known as one of Dublin's leading dance clubs as, thanks to contacts in the airlines and the New York music industry, we were able to fly in the latest records. Elton John and Freddie Mercury came to visit when they were in town. One of our DJs was 'Fab' Vinnie, RTÉ's Vincent Hanley, and we held very successful themed discos on occasions such as Hallowe'en and

Valentine's Day. Tonie Walsh ran the discos at that stage and was a gifted designer who could create any sort of atmosphere. He worked his magic again, much later, on my sixtieth birthday party, when he turned the James Joyce Centre into a New Orleans sporting house with floral swags and oil-fired flambeaux.

We also started a youth group, which we kept isolated from older members to avoid any accusations of predatory behaviour. This happened after a young man visited the centre, said he was gay and wanted to join. Dermod Moore was in his early teens, so I had a cup of coffee with him and explained the delicacy of the situation. I asked him what his parents would think and he said they would have no problem with it. I told him I would need to discuss it with them. A week later, to my great surprise, he brought them in. It was Harry Moore of the well-known radio shop and his wife Phyl. We had a chat; they had known for some time that their son was gay and had accommodated themselves to it, and they were relieved there was a responsible place to which young people could come. As a result, a very carefully monitored group for young people was started. Phyl Moore was later to play a crucial role in the reform of the criminal law.

There were always two responsible adults in charge, to ensure that the young folk were never subjected to inappropriate attention. It became an important place for many young people coming to terms with their sexuality.

It was even suggested that I should add to the facilities by opening an all-male erotic sauna in the basement, which was a maze of tunnels. I was taken aback by the effrontery of this proposal and refused. To me money generated from running a volunteer brothel would have seemed tainted and run counter to everything for which I stood.

There was also an active publishing arm, which produced newsletters such as *In Touch* and a serious, high-quality magazine called *Identity* which was edited by Kieran Hickey, under the *nom de plume* Cissie Caffrey. Kieran also wrote the hilarious comedy revues that were put on at each year's end. One of our members, Philip Tyler, was a presenter on the RTÉ children's programme *Bosco*. He borrowed the puppet for the revue, and Kieran wrote a mildly obscene and terribly funny sketch. The curtains opened to reveal Bosco, who looked down and announced, 'I have a willy. Bet you didn't know that. They didn't tell you I was gay either!' It brought the house down but I doubt if RTÉ would have been so amused if they'd discovered what had been done to their prize puppet.

The first night the Hirschfeld Centre opened there were three or four hundred people in the place, and when I went to check downstairs I could see the floorboards were bouncing. A member who was also a structural engineer approached me to say it could be dangerous, so I had the music switched off. I addressed the throng and told them they could have a refund, or they could stay and chat to their friends and the coffee bar was free for the night, but there would be no more dancing that evening. I was booed and hissed at before one guy stood up and said, 'Hold on a minute. Isn't it just as well there is someone who *does* give a shit about our safety?' And the boos turned into cheers.

I worked hard for almost a decade, four nights a week, in that centre, and never asked anyone to do anything I wouldn't do. I worked as doorman, cashier, security, served in the coffee bar and unplugged the lavatories – I thought that if anyone saw me put my hand down the jacks then they wouldn't be offended by anything I might ask them to do.

This had always been my policy and once, in the earlier IGRM disco, when freeing the lavatory bowl, I took off a beautiful ring of my mother's – a set of diamonds enclosing an emerald in which was set a ruby. I set it on the washstand but when I turned around to dry my hands it was gone. Despite an appeal from the DJ it was never returned. I had my suspicions who took it and it rankled with me that people for whom I had given up so much would deprive me of a treasured memento of my mother.

The Hirschfeld also became the first nerve centre for the International Gay Association. Edmund and I argued at a conference that if the bureau was sited in Amsterdam the world in general would say, 'So what? Sure that's what you'd expect.' But opening the first HQ of an international gay organisation in holy Catholic Ireland would really create waves.

The most exciting thing about the IGA was what we called the Telephone Snowball, which was an idea from those innocent days before email or Twitter. We compiled and circulated a list of telephone numbers all over the world which we could ring in an emergency, and each person on that list had a list they were to ring too.

While I was the first openly gay man ever elected to a national parliament, there were two MPs who were unelected alternates in Italy, one of whom was Angelo Pezzana. He and some others flew to Ayatollah Khomeini's Iran to protest against the ill-treatment of gays. Naïvely, they started marching up and down outside a notorious prison waving placards, and were immediately yanked inside. Within an hour the Dublin office started the Telephone Snowball and shortly afterwards television cameras were pointing at the front door of the prison. We banged on diplomatic doors all over the world and government officials bombarded Iranian embassies until we got them out.

The Hirschfeld Centre played an important role in the campaign against AIDS as it tore its way through the community. I had a subscription to an American magazine called the *Advocate* and so became aware of a mysterious illness that began affecting gay people quite early in the 1980s. Although it had been endemic in central Africa for some time, it was introduced to North America by a Typhoid Mary-style air steward from Canada and spread rapidly, most noticeably within the gay community. It was originally called GRIDS – Gay-related immune deficiency syndrome. The gay community acted like the canary in the mine. They were health-conscious and immediately noted and reported symptoms.

Subsequent descriptions of the disease as 'the gay plague' were a complete misnomer. Global statistics demonstrate that even at that time 90 per cent of transmission was as a result of unprotected heterosexual activity or intravenous drug use. However, because many of the victims in the West were socially concealed, and in sub-Saharan Africa were black and did not show up in statistics, the existence of the disease was once again used to scapegoat the gay community.

As it progressed it became clear this was a very serious disease, and the Hirschfeld Centre invited two specialist doctors from San Francisco to come and give a series of talks to the gay community. We leafleted widely about the talks and about what individuals needed to do to avoid it. A group was formed called Gay Health Action, which did remarkable work for those members of the community living with AIDS. The centre sanctioned 250,000 leaflets which gave advice on safe sex and where people could turn to for help. I wrote to the Minister for Health, Barry Desmond, to advise him we were doing this, in full knowledge that we were breaking the Victorian Indecent Advertisement Act, which made it a criminal act to advertise VD clinics. The minister sent us a note back saying, 'Well done,' a truly Irish answer to an Irish problem but one that was both humane and welcome.

There was an ongoing debate about the use of condoms in safe sexual practices, with the Roman Catholic Church strongly opposed to their use. One mother wrote in to the newspapers to say that, as a devout Catholic, if she was presented with a choice between her son using a condom and getting AIDS, she would prefer he got AIDS. We challenged that kind of ignorance and extremism, and I was often angered by the rubbish talked by the usual suspects. As a political leader of the gay community I was often called upon to make a public stand.

*

One night in November 1985 I was working in my office on the top floor of the Hirschfeld Centre when I noticed some sparks coming from the perspex dome in the ceiling, and thought at first that the burglar alarm had short-circuited. I stuck two fire extinguishers under my arms and clambered on to the roof. It was a strange and horrifying sight to behold: the asphalt-coated felt was on fire, and there was a milk churn full of explosives sitting there, surrounded by firelighters and two barrels of petrol. It was as if the whole roof was a giant petrol bomb, just waiting to explode. I went on automatic pilot and blasted away with the fire extinguishers until all the flames were doused, and then shouted down for someone to call the police. A posse of gardaí arrived, stampeding up the stairs and terrifying the disco patrons, who had just started to arrive. The timing was obviously significant as, had the bombs exploded, the burning petrol would have landed on everyone on the street outside waiting to get in, and incinerated the 250 patrons already in Flikkers. Whoever was responsible for the averted massacre was never found.

The next day I was giving evidence to an inquiry on penal reform, and although I am nearly always punctual, that day I arrived a couple of minutes late. Later, during a coffee break, Mary McAleese, who was also there, sensed something was wrong and came over to me to ask, 'Are you all right?'

And I said, 'Yes. Why?'

She said, 'Well, you were a couple of minutes late, which is so unlike you, and you look like death on toast.'

So I told her, 'Well, I had to defuse a bomb on the roof of the centre last night.'

And it was only then reality hit me – and I realised I could have been blown to smithereens myself.

About two years later I got a phone call at three o'clock in the morning: as a key holder to the centre I needed to get there quickly, as fire had taken hold. Once the firemen had made sure there was no one in the place, the archive had been rescued and I knew the insurance was fully paid up, I relaxed. One disco bunny floated up to me and asked, 'How can you stand there with a smile on your face while our beautiful disco goes up in flames?' I could only quote him Dr Samuel Johnson when similarly reproached by James Boswell. When his house in London caught fire Johnson got his manservant to lay out a table and chair, and bring him a glass and a bottle of port, asking, 'Can a man not warm himself at his own fire?'

I still don't know if that fire was set maliciously, but there were a couple of earlier attempts at arson, and the bomb attack, so on the balance of probability it was malicious. I was relieved that no one had been hurt as, besides the human tragedy for the victim, my house was on the line if insurance did not cover any grievous injury. I had tired of the responsibility and wanted out of it, in order to concentrate on politics.

The history of the gay movement was like the development of the amoeba – a process of constantly dividing and renaming itself. That process of split and rancour continued and there was always a begrudging suspicion, too, that some of us on the board were making a fortune for ourselves. Some small splinter groups were critical of us, and even though we showed them the accounts of the centre and the federation, they couldn't get it out of their heads that we were in it for the cash. A number of entrepreneurs had targeted the gay scene and were making fortunes on the back of the pioneering work we had done. Nobody had any problem with that, while we were accused of having selfish and mercenary motives. It always seemed extraordinary to me that businessmen who were capitalising on our advances received no such criticism.

We investigated the possibility of resurrecting the Hirschfeld Centre. I had been given verbal assurances that in the redevelopment of Temple Bar due allowance would be made for the centre. The original plan for Temple Bar Square was that it would start at the Hirschfeld, which would have allowed us to erect fire escapes. But that did not happen and we became entombed in a concrete sarcophagus. Running a disco became impossible, but we were able to keep some of the activities going as the fire damage to the structure was not immediately apparent. The top floor was usable, so we allowed groups such as the FÁS group that produced the newspaper *Gay Community News* to use it.

However, after some time, at an AGM of the Hirschfeld company our accountants produced an engineer's report which said the building was becoming unsound and warned that board members would be jointly and severally responsible if it collapsed – which was very disturbing to me as I was the only member of the board who owned a house, which already had a lien on it for the earlier bank guarantee.

We were now in an impossible position and decided we had no choice but to sell the Hirschfeld Centre and relocate. I set off again on a frenetic search for new premises, including looking at the old Quaker meeting house – now the Irish Film Centre – but none proved suitable in the end. We sought help from the city and national authorities, but despite having been responsible for the renaissance of the area we were turned down many times and were the only group based in the area that was never given a grant. Dublin City Council recently promised to erect a blue plaque on the building marking its historic impact on the area and the nation, but to date has failed to do so.

Eventually the time came when we had to vacate the building. By that stage a group of people had constituted themselves as the Hirschfeld Research Group, with the aim of rebuilding a gay community centre. We had a series of meetings with this new committee, at the last of which I made them an offer of all my shares in the Hirschfeld Centre for nothing, and I told them that I expected the others on the board would do the same. We were prepared to hand over full ownership in return for taking on the surviving debt and releasing my home from the mortgage arrangement. (Most of the insurance money had been used up in the post-fire purchase of the building and we were slightly in debt.) I received the following letter:

> We regret to inform you that despite our best efforts to swing public interest in our favour, our efforts were in vain. We tried so hard to make people see the benefit of our plans, but they seem, despite the disadvantages, to want an alternative location.
>
> So it is with regret to have to thank you for all of the help and support given by you in the past. With many thanks you so kindly met, and an offer of all our support in any plans you should have in the future, I must say that we must drop our quest and go with the majority in their plans.
>
> I will say again that we all lend our support in anything you may plan for the future.
>
> The Hirschfeld Research Group – Outhouse

As the building deteriorated we were warned again we would be personally responsible for any injury to the occupants or passers-by, and told the various groups that they had to leave. We eventually had to take them to court, which absorbed significant amounts of the money, but led to a settlement in the end. The case was heard by Liam Devally, who was determined to 'see both sides', but it seemed perfectly obvious to me that we should have won outright. After all, it was I who located the premises, started the company and put in all the money. It was my house that was used as collateral, and in addition, I had offered the derelict premises to any group that would resurrect it.

The occupying group used my own words against me – I had said in interviews that my intention was not to make a profit, but to be of service to the gay community. They twisted that to mean that the Hirschfeld Centre had thereby become the property of the gay community, i.e. themselves. In the end we agreed to sell the building and give the majority of the surplus to Outhouse, the gay community's resource centre, and the remainder was to be divided proportionately among the shareholders. That led to quite a bit of bitterness, and I was spat at as I came out of the court, and told, 'You're not fit to call yourself a gay Senator,' a title I had always rejected anyway.

To me by far the most important organisation to be created since the demise of the Hirschfeld Centre is BeLonGTo. Michael Barron and his colleagues have created a vital, energetic and effective group for young people. It provides them with a community, lobbies against homophobic bullying in schools, has accreditation with various government and international bodies and has had a huge and positive impact on the well-being of young gay people. I was delighted to be invited by them as guest of honour to the first ever gay prom in Ireland a couple of years ago. I recalled for the audience my own feelings at being excluded in school from what was called the Sixth Form Dance. It just wouldn't have occurred to anyone in the 1960s that a boy in the sixth form might want to bring another young man as his escort. If it had been suggested it would have caused a national scandal.

I see great confidence in young gay people now, who can build lives around their gay identity and their gay friends without excluding heterosexual friends or family. Although there is still pain in growing up gay or lesbian, there is a lot less now, and I am happy to have helped to achieve that.

CHAPTER 5

Taking a Constitutional

ONE AFTERNOON SHORTLY AFTER MY MOTHER'S DEATH, I WENT for lunch with my aunt to Switzer's restaurant on Grafton Street. While there I suddenly got dizzy and started having palpitations, so an ambulance was called. I was taken to Baggot Street Hospital, where it was suspected I had suffered a heart attack, but on examination I was found to have had an anxiety attack, with some signs of arrhythmia. I was suffering great stress at the time, as I was still in mourning for my mother and the man I loved had just got engaged, but the anxiety attack was blamed on the fact that I was homosexual. I was sent to a psychiatrist, Dr McCracken, whose advice was that for the preservation of my health and to forestall a possible nervous collapse I should leave Ireland and go to live in the south of France, where these matters were better understood under the Code Napoléon.

This solution outraged me, as I had been brought up by the Irish side of my family and felt thoroughly Irish. My ancestors on my mother's side had been traced back to Aengus Óg in the second century, and I was well aware that the Danes, Normans, Cromwellians and English had tried to get us out for two thousand years and failed. I wasn't going to leave just because I was gay.

113

The injustice of the advice angered me, but it proved useful more than a decade later as it gave me purchase on the law. It meant I had *locus standi*; in other words I could show that the legislation had a direct quantifiable negative impact on me. Dr McCracken's report allowed me to stand up in court and say that the effect of the existence of the legislation on my psychological well-being was such that I had been professionally advised to leave my own country.

After the Irish Gay Rights Movement started to disintegrate, a group of us had set up the Campaign for Homosexual Law Reform. It was a tiny body, but we had gathered some important supporters such as the playwright Hugh Leonard, former minister Noel Browne TD and Dean Victor Griffin, one of the few prophetic voices in the Church of Ireland. My co-chair was a Trinity colleague called Mary McAleese, the future president. I listed all the patrons on our notepaper and began firing off letters to politicians, the newspapers, churches and anyone else we could think of. Our activity inspired the conservative opposition to denounce us as an international conspiracy to undermine Catholic values, funded by Jewish money from the United States, which gave us unexpected credibility. Suddenly our body, with four or five members and half a filing cabinet, was being attacked as a threat to the state.

In the IGRM we had had a panel of legal people, prime among whom was a wonderful man called Garrett Sheehan. Garrett was not gay, but he thought the law was unjust and he was happy to represent the people who came to us for help. What was interesting was that many of those people were eminently respectable – architects, clergy, teachers, lawyers and doctors, some of whom were married. They were the sort of people who wouldn't dream of coming to the disco because that wouldn't have been seen as respectable, but their sexual drives were still powerful and they had been caught with their pants down in the Phoenix Park or in the public lavatories on the quays.

Gay people were a soft target and if a garda knew where to find men engaged in sexual activity he could be sure they would go to any lengths to avoid public disgrace. The courts system was no better, and I saw people being humiliated for the entertainment of a court by being dragged through the minutiae of the acts they had performed, to the guffaws of everybody present. By our persistence, however, we eventually drove the conviction rate down to zero.

At that point I decided that what we were doing was not enough, that we should no longer meekly accept our role as victims but should take a more aggressive stance and put it up to the courts and government of a sovereign republic. Our first move was to try to get one of the accused men to take a stand and initiate a constitutional challenge to the law – but nobody wanted to put themselves out on that particular limb.

So our next move was obvious – I would take the case myself. By that stage both my parents were dead and I had a reasonably tolerant and liberal employer in Trinity College, so could not be pressured from those angles, and I had a passionate sense of the injustice of the law. But the most important advantage I had was that psychiatric report from 1966. I've never felt myself to be anything exceptional, but I was exceptional as a gay man in Ireland of the 1970s because I was able to speak out and put myself on the front line.

We sought an opinion from Donal Barrington SC, and he said we were morally and intellectually right but we would have to steel ourselves for a long battle because there were political, religious and social aspects to what we sought, and we would have to prepare Irish society for such a significant change. Shortly afterwards Donal was made a judge and had to bow out, so we turned to Garret Cooney. He was chosen because in addition to being a brilliant lawyer he was known to be a conservative Catholic and brother of a former Minister for Justice, Paddy Cooney. He brought in Paul Carney as his junior. It was felt we would need a second junior, so I turned to my old college friend Mary Robinson. As the case was going to focus on me and my experience under the law, she asked me early on to write down what it was like to grow up gay in Ireland.

I don't type and so wrote the essay out longhand in a school exercise book, in what I thought was a clinical, detached way. I told about my love for David Miller at school and how reassuring it was that I wasn't rejected. I told about how I would lie in bed in Wilfield Park listening to the bands playing at the cricket-club dances and how I knew this life was not for me. Mary said later that the essay had such an impact on her that she wept.

Our solicitor was John Jay, who was married to a Trinity colleague, Harden Rodgers. I was intimately involved in the case too, and insisted that it should not be run just as a dry, technical case. I wanted drama and I wanted the case to hit the headlines, to help sway the public to our side. I believed that one of the things that most crippled gay people in those days was the complete silence that obscured their existence. I resolved to produce a panel of international experts of the highest calibre to give evidence.

I travelled to America to research the archives of the National Gay Task Force in New York, having been in contact with its head, Bruce Voeller, who had agreed to help me research case precedents in his office. I was to stay at the New York apartment of two aides of the Borough President of Manhattan. Arriving at JFK Airport, I was puzzled that the lift I had been promised hadn't materialised, so I rang their office, to find that they had forgotten me in the pain and turmoil that followed the news that had just come in that Harvey Milk had been shot dead. Milk was the first openly gay man to be elected to office in California and is an icon to gay Americans. My visit was mostly hard work, researching legal cases involving gay people and finding precedents and experts that might help our battle.

Having begun proceedings in November 1977, we had more than two and a half years to wait before we were heard. On

24 June 1980 we presented our case to the High Court that the laws of 1861 and 1885 had not been in force since the enactment of the Irish Constitution, under Article 50 which provided that laws inconsistent with it would no longer be in force. The first contribution was from Garret Cooney, who stood up and said, 'My client is a congenital, irreversible homosexual.' That came as news to me but I felt, *If that's what it takes, that's what it takes.*

I had found several excellent expert witnesses to give evidence, one of whom was an American psychiatrist, Professor John P. Spiegel, who had never been in an Irish court before, and clearly didn't understand the arcane procedures. When the tipstaff comes in, he bows to the judge and the judge bows back. Professor Spiegel thought they were bowing to him, so he too bowed back. And then, out of politeness, they in turn bowed back, which set off a chain reaction where everyone in the place began nodding at each other like peacocks for several minutes.

The state's counsel then decided that my eminent psychiatric witness was gay, which he wasn't. He asked him, 'Do you have a personal animus in this case?'

'I don't know what you mean,' replied Spiegel.

Barrister: 'Well, I believe you have travelled here at your own expense?'

Spiegel: 'Yes, I have.'

Barrister: 'Can you explain that?'

Spiegel: 'Well, I believe in human rights.'

Barrister: 'What I'm asking, Professor Spiegel, is: are you a homosexual yourself?'

They certainly weren't anticipating the answer they got, which was an honest, blunt American one.

Spiegel: 'Well, I'm happily married but when I was in Harvard I would sometimes look at the other guys' cocks in the showers. So I suppose I'm a 1.7 on the Kinsey scale.'

We had some very courageous churchmen who also stood by us in Court Number 8, including Fr Joseph O'Leary, one of the most brilliant young Catholic theologians in the country, who has regrettably had to spend most of his life working outside Ireland because of the lack of intellectual freedom in the Irish Church, and the Jesuit Fr Micheál Mac Gréil who had written a marvellous book called *Prejudice and Tolerance in Ireland*. Fr Mac Gréil was not supporting one side or the other, but giving statistical and research-based evidence which showed that even before I took my case a plurality of the Irish people wanted the law changed.

I thought an official submission from the Roman Catholic hierarchy would be interesting, no matter what it said, as at least we would be flushing out opposing views. I wrote a letter to the Archbishop of Dublin asking for such a submission, but my request was ignored. So I sent a registered letter, which also was ignored. Then I telephoned to check what the problem was, and again nothing happened. In the end I popped around to the Archbishop's palace in Drumcondra and put another letter in the hand of his secretary. That at last provoked a response – which was that the Archbishop of Dublin did not get involved in individual cases.

During evidence the Attorney General's barrister, Aidan Browne, became quite irate with the Reverend Professor O'Leary, asking: 'Do you mean to stand there, Father, in your Roman collar, and tell me that you don't believe the act of buggery to be a crime?' The phrase exploded through the court like a cartoon balloon. He then asked me, 'Are you not aware that throughout history this form of activity has been universally despised, and condemned, and made illegal?' I told him he was incorrect, because the anthropologist Margaret Mead, supported by Clellan Ford and Frank Beach, had conclusively shown that over 60 per cent of primitive societies not only accepted homosexuality but institutionalised it.

Mr Browne asked me did I know of the Roman Emperor Justinian's condemnation of homosexuality, which I explained in the context of his time. Justinian had been advised by his principal soothsayer that there was a direct correlation between sex between men and earthquakes, so as a ruler who took the interests of his people to heart he felt that earthquakes should be avoided, but that our modern understanding of the relationship between sexual relations and seismic activity had advanced considerably in the intervening millennia. The next day's newspaper headline said, NO EARTHQUAKES IN IRELAND IF LAW REFORMED, SAYS NORRIS.

The government side did not produce any evidence of its own. Our opposition had tried to get expert witnesses, but no psychiatrist was willing to risk their reputation. The only Protestant judge on the High Court bench was appointed to hear the case, which obviated any risk of criticism on a sectarian basis. Judge Herbert McWilliam started off his judgement by conceding all the points we had made. It was like a manifesto of gay rights, and we began to think that miraculously we would win. But in a forty-minute address he suddenly changed direction and came down against us on the basis of the Christian and democratic nature of the Constitution which governed all our laws. We were shocked, but determined more than ever to smash the blatant injustice under which we had to live. The case had at least succeeded in having our grievances aired, and the reaction was positive and heartening. I was told that some Roman Catholic priests were holding up the judgement at Mass as an example of the lack of charity and understanding in Irish society. We were making progress.

Within seconds of Judge McWilliam finishing the reading of his judgement, I instructed our legal representatives to lodge an appeal to the Supreme Court. The state asked for and was awarded costs against me of £75,000. I had bought my house in North Great Georges Street shortly before for £25,000, so that might demonstrate the enormous debt with which I was confronted. It worried me for precisely one night, after which I thought, *What the hell, I haven't got the money anyway, so it's double or quits.*

Within a day or so, a letter addressed to me in shaky hand-writing arrived. It was from my dear old friend Desmond McCarthy. Inventor of genius, distiller of *poitín*, believer in fairies, he was the brother of Samuel Beckett's first girlfriend. He was a lover of women, but he understood humanity and his letter told me how he was sorry to have read in the papers that such a large sum had been awarded against me. But not to worry, he wrote, I was in the right and the right would prevail in the end. It was a short letter, with an even shorter postscript telling me he was in the Meath Hospital with incurable lung cancer. The next day I went to see him. He was propped up in bed, but still full of talk, brown eyes shining with fun. A day or two later he was dead. I think that showed the most extra-ordinary generosity of heart; for a man on what he knew to be his deathbed to bother about the day-to-day difficulties of an old friend seemed to me the highest form of decency.

The appeal was heard over four days in November 1982. Chief Justice Tom O'Higgins was supported by Judges Griffin and Finlay in rejecting our appeal. O'Higgins turned to the Bible for his justification for the Victorian law, concluding that all organised religions looked on homosexual acts with 'a deep revulsion as being contrary to the order of nature, a perversion of the biological functions of the sexual organs and an affront both to society and to God'.

The Chief Justice's judgement was lamentable, and he mis-directed himself in law, as Mr Henchy pointed out. Mr O'Higgins was only entitled to address matters presented to court in the first case, and any technical points that may have arisen from these. Since the state had signally failed to produce anything but a froth of argument from legal counsel, it was clear, Judge Henchy said, that in sporting terms I had won a walkover. Judge McCarthy discussed at length whether I had *locus standi*, or a right to take the case. These two aspects made it a case of some interest and it is still studied to this day. O'Higgins's judgement has been consigned to the dustbin of history, except when it is wheeled out to show how even a chief justice can get it spectacularly wrong.

It was sad that our own Supreme Court refused an opportunity to overturn a palpably unjust law, and delivered such an insulting and prejudiced judgement. I said afterwards that I thought it was strange that laws which Mr O'Higgins had judged to be constitutional had already been found to be in breach of fundamental human-rights legislation in Europe. On the steps of the court I said:

'What use is the Constitution to me? What use is the 1916 Declaration we hear so much about – to cherish all the children of the nation equally? I don't feel particularly cherished by the Supreme Court this afternoon.'

One major consolation was that because the judges decided my case was of constitutional significance, my costs in both cases should be paid by the state.

I appealed to the European Human Rights Commission, who found in my favour in May 1987, but Garret FitzGerald's Fine Gael–Labour government rejected its findings on the grounds that the state retained the right to legislate on moral affairs, and so we were forced to go to the European Court of Human Rights.

Mary Robinson was the leading counsel when the case was finally heard in Strasbourg in April 1988. I was put out to discover that even though I was the principal in the case, and in effect the employer of the lawyers, I wasn't allowed to open my mouth, and that all the submissions would be made by the legal teams. I was even more surprised to discover that my lawyers had been given generous expenses to stay at a five-star hotel, while mine barely covered the cost of a shebeen.

The solicitor John Jay was great fun, a lugubrious man with a face like a bloodhound, but with a mordant sense of humour. He spent some time in court drawing caricatures of the principals and writing slightly naughty limericks about them.

These he would pass to me with a very solemn expression as if they were important legal minutiae. I played the game by maintaining a serious demeanour too, which added to his amusement.

The ECHR's decision took a further six months to be handed down, and I heard the news early one morning when I took a telephone call from an RTÉ journalist. We had finally been vindicated, although the Irish judge, Brian Walsh, voted against us. I stressed that our win was not just for gay people but for the nation as a whole, as any extension of human rights was a boost to every citizen. My words were an echo of a speech by a man I have always admired, the great Liberator himself, Daniel O'Connell. During the acrimonious debates over Catholic Emancipation in the 1820s, he pointed out that values like dignity and freedom were not finite, and one lost nothing by granting them to other people. Rather, the dignity and freedom of everyone in society was enhanced.

Even with the prospect of full and equal status for gay people as Irish citizens, I was still called upon to fight battles against invincible ignorance. The Roman Catholic Archbishop of Dublin, Desmond Connell, had foolishly repeated some of the turgid drivel the Vatican periodically comes out with about human sexuality. I was at a concert for the Birmingham Six in the National Concert Hall in Earlsfort Terrace when the story broke, and an *Irish Times* reporter dragged me into a corner for a quote. I knew that Dr Connell had got his doctorate on the rather arcane topic of how God communicates with the angels, so I said, 'Dr Connell may very well know everything there is to know about angels, but you can take it from me he knows sweet fuck-all about fairies.' The *Times* bowdlerised it, printing it as 'sweet damn all', which tempered the riposte but ruined the alliteration.

Having won the legal battle, we were now in the realm of politics, and that was another shark-filled pond altogether.

History had shown we still had some way to go to change attitudes in Leinster House.

The political climate had changed with a new Fianna Fáil government, and when the Minister for Justice Ray Burke introduced the Video Bill, I insisted it include protection for gay people and Travellers. I had previously attempted to have these groups incorporated in a Senate amendment, only to meet strong resistance from his predecessor Mr Collins. But it was yet another Fianna Fáil Minister for Justice, Máire Geoghegan-Quinn, who finally introduced the Criminal Law (Sexual Offences) Bill in June 1993.

All in all it was probably just as well there was a four-year gap between winning in Strasbourg and the final Bill, as it gave the idea a chance to settle and become less disturbing to most elements in society. It also meant we had a new justice minister, who although, or perhaps because, she was a woman had more balls than all her colleagues put together. She was greatly influenced by Phyl Moore, a significant back-room figure in Fine Gael who spoke to the minister as the mother of a gay son, and crucially as one mother to another across the political divide.

One TD, Brendan McGahon, decried it at a parliamentary party meeting as 'a wankers' charter', a term I fail to understand. It would be a pretty peculiar situation if you had to apply for a charter to have a wank. Brendan, who had a great capacity for producing soundbites, came out with this:

'Homosexuality is a departure from normality and while homosexuals deserve our compassion they do not deserve our tolerance. That is how the man in the street thinks. The Lord provided us with sexual organs for a specific purpose. Homosexuals are like left-hand drivers driving on the right-hand side of the road.'

I suspect Brendan's right-wing views and half-baked theories on sexuality came out of his love of publicity, rather than any animosity towards gay people. I always had a soft spot for him

– he was extremely courageous in speaking out against the Provos in a constituency that was rife with them.

Many years later, I bumped into Brendan in the car park of Leinster House. He had been out of politics for a while, and he shook my hand. He told me his own son had recently told him he was gay himself. I asked Brendan what his response had been, and he told me he had given him a hug and told him he loved him. I thought this showed how everyone has the capacity for change once they realise how ordinary gay people really are.

Fine Gael put down a series of nasty amendments, including an attempt to add a discriminatory extra year to the age of consent to ensure gay people retained their second-class status. To her great credit Mrs Geoghegan-Quinn shot it down:

> I regret that Deputy Gay Mitchell and Fine Gael are proposing to end one form of inequality by introducing a different form of inequality.
>
> There is no logical reason for assuming that, while persons of 17 are capable of giving valid consent to heterosexual activity, persons of homosexual orientation do not acquire such capacity until they are older. Underlying any such proposition would be the idea that homosexual orientation carries with it the burdens of lack of maturity or lower intellect. There is no basis for any such assumption.

Mrs Geoghegan-Quinn told the Senate that as Minister for Justice she would need to be persuaded by clear factual evidence before she would bring in a measure of discrimination against an Irish citizen. And since none had been produced she was not accepting the amendments. I believe this was a very important enunciation of a golden rule as far as discrimination is concerned. It had nothing to do with homosexuality; it had everything to do with justice and equality.

I threatened to abstain on the Criminal Law (Sexual Offences) Bill in Seanad Éireann because it also introduced measures which discriminated against prostitutes. I wasn't going to take my liberty at the expense of another oppressed minority. That clause had been stuck in as a sop to the conservatives, which is typical of the level of pragmatism in politics. But the Bill went through without a vote on 24 June, so my principles were not put to the test on that occasion.

I was elated when I left Leinster House but I was surprised to find all the reporters, photographers and supporters had left. I slipped away quietly and went home alone. After a twenty-year battle nobody wanted my views on the momentous day. But I didn't care – for the first time, at forty-eight years of age, I felt almost a full citizen of my own country.

Not only did our legal battle span the devastating era of AIDS, but it also saw a shocking number of people become victims of anti-gay violence. I have known eight people who were murdered simply because they were gay – I doubt whether there is anyone who comes from my social and academic background but does not share my sexual orientation who can say that. Seven of them were in Dublin, including the RTÉ designer Charles Self, Frank McManus, and Declan Flynn, shockingly kicked to death in Fairview Park in 1982. His killers were convicted of manslaughter and given suspended sentences. Yet when one of them was convicted a little later for stealing a car he was jailed for six months. That was a vivid indication to gay people of how they were rated by society. Muggings and attacks by 'queer basher' gangs were routine, and I fell victim on a few occasions. In one instance I was attacked and beaten on Parnell Street, near my home, by people who recognised me from television, but I identified the culprits and got £1,000 compensation.

I set up a group to work towards a Civil Partnership Bill in 2004, and we held regular meetings in my home. In December that year I tabled a private member's Bill on civil partnerships, which would have recognised all unmarried partnerships homosexual or heterosexual, and specified that all the rights of marriage would apply to a civil partnership. After what had seemed to be positive discussions with the Justice Minister Michael McDowell and his senior staff, the government unexpectedly put down an amendment and indicated that it would vote the measure down. I threatened not to turn up to my own adjournment debate, which would have left an unexplained two-hour gap. I would have gone public on the fact that the Senate was suspended because of the government's sabotage. Eventually we got a compromise where we would adjourn with three minutes remaining, which would leave the Bill on the order paper at second stage. This, I believe, was the first time such a procedure had been adopted.

The government finally brought its own Bill to law, and civil partnerships were introduced on 1 January 2011. For me the Bill didn't go far enough because I felt it contained an abuse of children, as the children of a gay couple had no rights or connection to the surviving partner if the adopting parent died. This was madness. Gay people already had been legally able to adopt, but only as single individuals, which placed the children in a kind of limbo and at considerable risk. I openly attacked this as 'deliberate and knowing child abuse by the government'. It was for this reason that I opposed the Bill in the Seanad. But when a tiny conservative rump attempted a filibuster, and put down a series of what I regarded as nasty and unchristian amendments and an attempt to introduce a form of apartheid against gay people, I refused to go into the same division lobby with them. One of the amendments allowed for shopkeepers or providers of services to refuse the business of gay couples, while another would have allowed counsellors to refuse to counsel gay couples if the effect of their work would have kept the relationship intact. I thought nothing could more directly contravene the message of the gospels and Christ's parable of the Good Samaritan.

126

It was a relief when, after a marathon debate, the Bill finally went through, minus the amendments, which were overwhelmingly voted down, and I was able to give it a genuine if somewhat guarded welcome despite my earlier reservations:

'I am proud that this day has come . . . It is a victory, not for gay people, nor for Fianna Fáil, Fine Gael, the Green Party, the Labour Party or the Independents; it is a victory for decency, and for this country.'

One of the newspapers asked me was I going to take advantage of the law myself, but I told them quite accurately that I had been so busy pushing the boat out that I forgot to jump on board myself until it had cleared the harbour.

While I played a part in making Ireland safe for gay people, I was also interested in the way the word 'gay' made its way into general acceptance. I first heard the word used in that context in the late 1960s. Before that the word was 'queer', or 'ho-mo-sex-ual' – delivered in a clipped, surgical tone.

I have always hated the word 'queer', as it signalled that something was wrong with a person and I considered myself a perfectly normal ordinary person. There is a vogue in gay circles to 'reclaim' that ugly word, but it will never be reclaimed for anyone of my generation. Everything about the word connotes negative images of being different mentally and physically, and of being 'queer-bashed'. I accept that the English language is organic, but I will not allow myself to be called 'queer' by anyone.

'Gay' was good because it was the opposite of 'queer' – it was bright, assertive and positive, and it challenged people. It was astonishing to see the squeals of protest on the letters page of the *Irish Times* expressing a terrible angst that a gang of perverts had appropriated what was hitherto a good, wholesome word. Little did they know the etymological descent of the word from Shakespeare's time, when it was principally used in connection with prostitution of both sexes, although it had been sanitised by Victorian composers of sentimental verse. There was a lot of tripe from the middle classes, who protested that although, of course, they had lots of homosexual friends, they didn't want that word to be taken from them. Considering the suffering that gay people had gone through, leaving aside altogether the disproportionate contribution they made to English literature from Shakespeare to Wilde, one little word out of millions didn't seem much in the way of compensation. It became a kind of litmus test which you could use to find the real, concealed agenda.

Once we hit upon the word, the IGRM began promoting its use in reporting. From the late 1950s onwards I had compiled press cuttings of every reference to gay matters in the Irish press. Many of the early stories told of isolation, desperation and suicide, or gay men were featured in women's magazines as shadowy figures with their features blacked out. After the Stonewall Riots in New York, the word 'gay' arrived in Ireland and things started to change. Through the material that I had assembled it is possible to trace the change in the way the word entered the mainstream of the language. The first references came in capital letters, shrouded in inverted commas, and punctuated with a question mark – 'GAY?' Gradually the ornamentation was dropped, first the inverted commas, then the question mark, before finally it made its way into lower case. Now it sits unadorned on the page, three tiny letters that signify the final acceptance of a social revolution.

CHAPTER 6

Dusting the Aspidistras

. . . the aspidistra grows dusty in the window pane,
And the delicate tracery of the fanlight is obscured from light,
Yet, these, perchance, shall be dusted and shine brightly
  again . . .

'On North Great Georges Street' by Joyce's friend
and fellow writer Séumas O'Sullivan, written in the 1940s

THERE WEREN'T A LOT OF DISTRACTIONS GROWING UP IN Dublin in the early 1950s. It was an austere time and an austere place, as the country struggled to cope with the post-war economic hardship that forced many people to emigrate in search of work.

But on summer evenings and weekend afternoons my aunt would escort us on treasure hunts around the heart of the city. Of course the treasures we went in search of were not gems or precious metal, but the tarnished jewels of Georgian Dublin, an era when the city prospered and thousands of beautiful buildings were erected. Dublin was the first centrally planned city in Europe, a model of architectural order at a time when the centre of Paris was still a medieval warren.

Dublin's extraordinary elegance was in large part due to the establishment of the Wide Streets Commissioners in the mid-eighteenth century. They were given dictatorial powers and could control, down to the finest detail, not just the widths of the roads and pavements but the height, lighting and external appearance of the great houses and squares.

The Georgian era saw the focus of the city return to the river, and elegant homes grew up along the quays and into the more fashionable and prosperous Northside, where aristocrats and wealthy businessmen joined the development of the city. In 1748 the Duke of Leinster moved to the other side of the river, just south of Trinity, and built the most sumptuous private residence in the city. The FitzGerald family later sold their house to the Royal Dublin Society, a philanthropic body founded in 1739 to encourage the arts, sciences and agriculture. It maintained the building sensitively, while adding a lecture theatre and concert hall which have subsequently become the home of Dáil Eireann. They made the entire area a nucleus for intellectual and artistic activity. It was the RDS that built the four cultural institutions that surround it: the National Library, National Gallery, National Museum and Natural History Museum. It was also responsible for providing the Irish people with the College of Art, the Zoo and the Botanical Gardens, a positive residue of the sometimes despised Ascendancy. As a Laois man, I am proud that it was a fellow countyman, Thomas Prior, who was responsible for the foundation of the society, just as another Laois man, Bartholomew Mosse, created Europe's first purpose-built maternity hospital, the Rotunda, still in its original premises at the top of O'Connell Street.

The Senate meets in the duke's ballroom and picture gallery. When I was first elected the Senate met in the antechamber, as the central portion of the ceiling and part of the apse of the original chamber had started to collapse due to dry rot. I managed to get in during the restoration and recognised the work of one of the greatest of the Irish stuccodores of the eighteenth century, Michael Stapleton. It amuses me to hear tour groups, while looking up at the ceiling, say, 'They had great talent in them days but they couldn't do it now.' I take pleasure in telling them how a third of the ceiling has been replaced in the last few years by talented Irish craftsmen and not even I could tell the difference. So we *do* still have the talent.

This all meant nothing to a seven-year-old in short pants, however, when it was time for another Sunday-afternoon excursion from our home in Ballsbridge. There my aunt would delve into her dusty old treasure chest and retrieve one of the time-worn documents behind whose red wax seals lay part of our family history.

Most of these leases concerned our relatives the Stokers. From the mid-nineteenth century on, most of the Stokers lived in places such as Parnell Square, Mountjoy Square and York Street, which by the time we visited had become slum dwellings. One building, Ely House, survived in all its magnificence, facing down Hume Street towards St Stephen's Green, and is now ironically the headquarters of the Knights of Columbanus. This was the home of Sir Thornley Stoker, brother of Bram. Thornley was more highly regarded within the family, mainly because of his knighthood. Bram's connection with the theatre was regarded as 'unfortunate', but the writing of a sensational Gothic novel with an obvious sexual undercurrent was simply the last straw. The Stokers were greatly given to respectability but were often disappointed in its pursuit.

One of my relatives was the eighteenth-century portrait painter Bartholomew Stoker, a couple of whose works I have inherited. The National Gallery of Ireland also has several examples of his paintings, but when I enquired I was told they were in the 'reserve collection'. I also have a copy of un-published correspondence between Bram and Thornley about Bartholomew. The letters tell how he had contracted a fever, but when he appealed to his family for help they spurned him. He was found collapsed and dying, literally in the gutter, in Suffolk Street, Dublin. Only when he was safely dead did the family claim the body and give him a fashionable funeral, which Bram and Thornley agreed was classic Stoker behaviour.

My aunt had very good taste, and an appreciation of design. There was a glorious uniformity to the Georgian buildings, arranged in long terraces, but fascinating detail too, for which she had a keen eye. She would point out and explain the iron-work, the coalhole covers, the granite paving setts and the railings in extraordinary detail. She taught me about the tracery of the fanlights above the hall doors, the elegantly thin wood-work of the glazing bars in the now-dusty windows. She loved the elegant windows, and the way they were arranged to allow in maximum light.

By the 1950s these formerly palatial dwellings had declined and were now grim, unhealthy tenements where dozens of people were crammed into single-room flats. Most of the hall-ways were lit by one naked light bulb which, glimpsed through the bare-boned fanlight, would throw into relief the most wonderful plasterwork.

Those excursions gave me a great interest in the Georgian city, and when as a student in Trinity I heard about the Irish Georgian Society, set up by Desmond and Mariga Guinness, I joined. The foundation of the society had been almost accidental. Desmond had walked out of the side door of the Shelbourne Hotel one day, and seen workmen beginning to demolish a row of fine, large houses in Kildare Place. He did everything he could do to try to stop it, but came up against the ignorant attitude of people such as the Minister for Local Government, Kevin Boland, who derided the society as a collection of 'belted earls' and believed it was good to get rid of 'the last traces of the Ascendancy'.

I became friendly with both Desmond and Mariga, and she, being a member of the Bavarian royal family, was something out of the ordinary. She came to a dinner party given by two friends of mine. We were bidden for cocktails at 6.30 p.m., but when Mariga hadn't arrived by 7.30 we eventually sat down. About half an hour later there was a banging on the door and, after some muffled conversation, Mariga entered the dining room carrying what appeared to be a couple of wisps of hay. She presented them to her hosts, saying, 'Herbs, for the cook.' She was accompanied by two slightly embarrassed policemen who saw her safely to her seat and then withdrew.

What had happened was that Mariga, a somewhat eccentric driver even without the benefit of alcohol, had come flying up Christchurch Place in her battered old Citroën 2CV, banging into the side of an unmarked squad car. The young gardaí were unamused and a bit shaken until Mariga calmly wound the window down and enquired in her fluting voice, 'Are you the Pirates of Penzance?' This bizarre enquiry actually made sense, as the policemen had sung in the Gilbert and Sullivan production in Leixlip Castle the year before. They gallantly loaded Mariga into their car and brought her to the party.

I was sitting next to her and, searching for conversation, mentioned that I had just read a book about Mad King Ludwig of Bavaria, who was the patron of Wagner and builder of magnificent castles all over his kingdom. 'Do you approve of King Ludwig?' she asked, to which I replied that I most certainly did, not only on musical and architectural grounds but also because when they tried to have him declared mad he took the psychiatrist out for a row on the lake and drowned him. She laughed and said, 'I'm so glad you approve – he was my great-uncle.'

After my mother's death I resolved to buy a house in Mountjoy Square, but the trustees and solicitor to her estate wouldn't allow me to do so. I would have liked to, but I probably wasn't ready. I bought a four-bed semi-detached in Sweetmount Avenue, Dundrum, which was far too small for the old family furniture.

When I later bought my home on North Great Georges Street, its acquisition was yet another example of serendipity. In the late 1970s I was living in Greystones and was helping to run the successful gay disco at the IGRM building on Parnell Square. We used it as a way to fund our political, medical and social campaigns, but our success attracted other people who saw commercial opportunities, and the takings started to decline. One night a member of the committee suggested we go around to see what it was our rivals were doing that was taking away our clientele. He dragged me around the corner to the alternative disco, which was the first time I had ever consciously walked along North Great Georges Street. It was love at first sight.

Two-thirds of the way down the street there was one magnificent, beautifully maintained house. And there were obviously people living in it because there were crocuses growing in a window box, a polished knocker and a beautifully painted door. Of course, with my aunt's training, I looked through the fanlight to see an elegant eighteenth-century plasterwork ceiling.

At the time the only people who lived in the city centre were eccentrics or local-authority tenants. As I gazed at this lovely house, the person I was with said, 'That's Harold Clarke's home. He's a director of Eason's, the booksellers down in O'Connell Street.' I had met Harold at St Bartholomew's Church, where I sang in the choir; I didn't know him terribly well, but I knew who he was. He was a true pioneer of the restoration.

I resolved on the spot to buy a house on the street, and I kept my eye on the newspapers for several months before one eventually came up for sale at no. 18. My aunt was very discouraging, however. Although she loved the buildings, she knew what it was like to live in such a house. She warned me I would face enormous problems with maintenance, leaky roofs, rising damp and mountainous stairways.

I loved the atmosphere and decided to buy the house, but unfortunately I had to go abroad and missed the auction. I understood it had been sold, and it was not until months later that I discovered that it hadn't attracted a single bid but that the next-door neighbour had started the process of buying it. This turned out to be Harold Clarke, who was keen that the house didn't fall into unfriendly hands.

I approached him, and was interviewed by himself and a dowager from across the street to see if I was a suitable person to become their neighbour. It was agreed that Harold would continue to buy the house and then sell it on to me for the same sum. This proved very expensive as I had to pay two sets of solicitors' fees and stamp duty, but I was overjoyed that this house was mine and I moved in at the end of 1978.

A few months later I was walking up the street, and noticed that the lights were on in no. 9, by which I could see a man and woman, both up on ladders, scraping and painting a stunning rococo ceiling. They were picking out the flourishes in white and infilling the flat areas in red, which looked very dramatic.

The woman spotted me, opened the window and called out, 'Can I help you?'

And I said, 'I'm sorry, I don't mean to be intrusive, but I was just admiring your beautiful ceiling.'

She replied, 'Why don't you come in and have a good look. I know who you are, we're neighbours. My name is Josephine O'Connell and this is my husband Brendan.'

Josephine brought me through to the back of the house, into a comfortable, country-style kitchen, where happily she had just finished baking an apple tart. We sat down, demolished it and had a great chat. I told her I had noticed a number of people were restoring homes in the street, such as Harold Clarke and the architect Tom Kiernan, and suggested that we get together to form a political organisation. I felt there wasn't much point in each of us saving one house if the rest of the place collapsed around us.

In June 1979 I summoned a meeting in the drawing room of my home. There were about a dozen homeowners present, plus the rector of Belvedere College. The school, although technically in Great Denmark Street, dominates our street and can be seen from every doorway. And, of course, for me, it also had the James Joyce connection and some of the finest ceilings in Ireland.

I proposed we formalise our group and was duly elected chairman of the North Great Georges Street Preservation Society. We decided on a political programme and applied for grants to various people, including Lewis Clohessy of the Heritage Council, from which we got £3,000, a significant amount. Some thought the society should make little individual grants to restore their railings or repaint front doors, but I thought that would fritter away the money. I suggested we spend it all on one big project that would get the society's name out beyond our area, and make a statement of intent. We all felt passionately about Georgian Dublin and thought our own battle might inspire others.

We mounted an exhibition which compared North Great Georges Street to other nearby streets. The centrepiece was a diagrammatic map which told the story visually. In the middle was Parnell Square, with its two symmetrical sister streets North Great Georges Street and Dominick Street, and their attendant stable lanes, Rutland Place and Dominick Place. I had obtained some of the wonderful Lawrence Collection photographs to show how the streets had looked, intact, in 1911, and hired a professional photographer to show how both had changed by 1980. Almost all of Dominick Street had fallen to the wrecking ball since the 1950s and been replaced with the ugly egg-box style of Corporation flats. Our street was mostly in a bad state of repair and, ominously, gaps had started to appear as houses were demolished. This raised the question, in dramatic visual form, as to what the fate of North Great Georges Street would be.

The exhibition also showed how some houses had been restored and, with drawings by the architects living on the street

– Tom Kiernan, Josephine's husband Brendan, and John O'Connell, a celebrated conservation architect – we produced a booklet of our plans for the street, for which I wrote the text.

I arranged for display boards to be designed, mounted and lit professionally, and an impressive exhibition was staged in a very large room in the Loreto Convent, which was still owned by the nuns at the time. The Lord Mayor and all the local dignitaries came, and we received plenty of media coverage. The centre-piece was a suggestion as to what might be our fate, and how we could be helped to ensure the street was preserved for the people of Dublin.

We wanted more families to move in, because a street needs children if it is to be a vibrant, living community. The society started to research the ownership of the houses and actively seek out potential buyers. We would help them approach the owner, who in many cases was delighted to have someone take it off their hands. I checked a couple of years ago and found I had been personally involved in a positive change of ownership of twelve of the fifty houses in the street.

Our moves were treated with suspicion in some quarters, and I had an argument on RTÉ Radio with a local councillor, Michael O'Halloran. He had an initial resistance to what he saw as gentrification and challenged me, saying, 'That's all very fine but David Norris is only a blow-in. I was born in that street; I was born in one room.'

I countered this by saying, 'Well, Michael, how many rooms did you want to be born in? What did you think you were – a scrambled egg?'

The three of us in the studio dissolved into laughter and Michael became a good friend. He very graciously came down in his robes when he was Lord Mayor in 1984–5 and met some of his former neighbours. That was a day when all of us, land-lords, tenants, blow-ins and blue-blooded Northsiders, joined in celebration of our heritage. I always felt that was how it should be: forget about who paid for or even lived in the buildings in the eighteenth century, what was important was that it was a celebration of our native ingenuity, craftsmanship and artistry. The stuccodores, ironmongers and brickworkers, as well as those who lovingly crafted the hand-turned granite paving setts, were all Irishmen.

The Legion of Mary had its headquarters in a magnificent house at the top of the street, but the 'charitable' accommodation at the lower end was of a very different order. These five houses, 28 to 32, were full of little old ladies, most of whom had given birth as single mothers decades before, and had been placed there in the care of the legion, a Roman Catholic lay organisation. The legion did not appear to have the funds available for maintenance of the houses and they were in an appalling state. The corporation was in the process of rehousing the women, with the intention of demolishing the houses. In fact, the ultimate purpose of the city authorities was the demolition of the entire street, as it had done with Dominick Street.

I heard from Patty Duffy in the newsagent's on Parnell Street that one of the old ladies was unwell, so I went down to Dunnes Stores and bought her a roasted chicken. We had a great chat and it gave me an entry into the house to see the conditions, which were truly dreadful. There were leaks, sewage coming down the walls, rubbish bags stacked in corridors reeking with foul smells. But it was an interesting house to me because it was where Joyce's brother Charles had lived.

Shortly afterwards the corporation decided on immediate demolition and our society went into high gear. I came up with a plan to make the houses into student accommodation for Trinity, as numbers were increasing greatly at the time and there wasn't sufficient accommodation on or close to the campus. I went to the College Board with a proposal that they acquire them from the corporation for a nominal sum and renovate them as student dwellings. There was some enthusiasm at first, but it eventually fell foul of bureaucracy and lack of interest. I tried to organise a scheme myself, but I was warned by the corporation that if we used volunteer labour I would be personally liable for any injuries or industrial accidents. That scuppered that and the houses were pulled down. But not before, with the help of Tom Kiernan, I had acquired detailed drawings of the five buildings.

I also rescued the five doorcases before demolition, lugging them back and forth across the street in an old pram. I stored them in my basement and, some time later, a man from Dublin Corporation came to see them.

He shook his head and told me, 'Ah Jaysus, now, you'd need four or five men to lift one of them.' I told him that I had managed it on my own! I kept the doorcase of the house where Charles Joyce lived, and it now stands in a grotto in my back garden, with a life-size Buddha in the arch formed by the two limestone ionic columns and decorated lintels.

Having got hold of the architect's plan of the whole street, which showed the façades of the five houses that had been recently demolished (28–32) as well as 33 and 34 – two immensely grand houses which had been destroyed before my arrival on the street – we mounted a campaign to persuade the corporation to reinstate the buildings as local-authority housing. We wanted them to restore the façades and respect the Georgian integrity, with decent proportions to the rooms. Instead they unveiled an unpleasant, out-of-scale attempt to infill the gap. I got wind of what was happening and went around to the city manager, Frank Feely, and asked him could I see the plans. I ran them through a photocopier and leaked them to the *Irish Times*, which printed them prominently under the headline 'CORPORATION GEORGIAN?', and as a result the scheme was shelved.

Some people with an interest in preservation were very negative about Mr Feely, but I always found him approachable. You didn't always get what you wanted out of him but he was very fair, and open to persuasion. We still exchange Christmas cards every year, and Frank's is always a painting of the city he loves. I also enjoyed dealing with his assistant, Paddy Morrissey, a decent, practical Dubliner who was always as helpful as he could possibly be.

We then suggested to the corporation that they go to the open market and offer the ruins to developers of apartments, making reinstating the façade a condition of sale. A few developers were interested and the sites sold, but nothing happened. So I went back to Frank and reminded him that there was a time clause associated with the deal, and that the developers would lose the option if they didn't get a move on. I told him that if he didn't activate the clause immediately, I would make the position publicly known. Within a short time a scale model of the development was produced – which may or may not have been a holding exercise, but whatever was the case, to everyone's surprise the entire scheme sold out on the first day.

That was what kick-started the wholesale regeneration of the street and, arguably, significant parts of the north inner city. It was that development that proved to builders that you could sell urban apartments, and that people would come back to the city from the suburbs. The problem with this scheme, and several others in the area, was that there were too many one-bedroom apartments, which attracted the attention of investment property owners, leading to a transient element rather than a stable community, but I made sure that at least the façades were all restored exactly as they had been.

There was one other house I was passionately interested in saving, and not just because of my love of Georgian buildings – no. 35. The street had a reasonable Joycean connection, which I knew I could exploit to the benefit of the community. James Joyce lived around the corner in Fitzgibbon Street and went to school in Belvedere College; his brother Charles lived in no. 31; and he describes Stephen running down the street after the failure of a romance following the Easter play in *A Portrait of the Artist as a Young Man*.

His great friend Constantine Curran wrote in his memoir that, on the last day Joyce ever spent in Dublin, in 1912, the pair walked down North Great Georges Street listing all the people who lived there. They talked about the folklorist and poet Sir Samuel Ferguson, who wrote 'The Lark in the Clear Air', and who had a salon at no. 20 where W. B. Yeats was introduced to literary Dublin. They speculated whether no. 41 was where Arthur Guinness brewed the first glass of his famous stout, being at the time butler to the Church of Ireland Archbishop of Cashel.

I also discovered another connection, this time between Joyce and no. 35. It had originally been the home of the Earls of Kenmare, but they had left the street after the 1798 rebellion. The rebel Lord Edward Fitzgerald was shot and mortally wounded while being arrested by a party which included a man who lived across the street. Major William Swan, who himself was stabbed by Fitzgerald, was deputy to Major Sirr and lived in no. 22. Lady Kenmare had a soft spot for Lord Edward and couldn't bear to live in the same street as his assailant, so the house was sold. It was an educational establishment for a while, but by the time I came to the street it was in a bad state of repair. The house was divided up between various tenants, and I got to know Mr Regan, who had a little workshop making leather satchels. The Dublin Concert Band also used the building for rehearsals, but the roof was half off, which meant the rain would cascade down five storeys and the band's sheet music was mouldy from the damp. I discovered from going back through the leases that a previous occupier of the ground floor was a Mr Denis Maginnis, a name that rang a bell.

Mr Regan allowed me into the building, and when I entered the back parlour the hairs on the back of my neck stood up. It was a magnificent room in a terrible state of decay, with a filigree of delicate plasterwork Corinthian columns rising from floor to ceiling. In between were roundels which originally contained eighteenth-century paintings in the style of Fragonard –

but these had been replaced by vignetted pictures of various late-nineteenth- and early-twentieth-century styles of dancing.

I felt like Howard Carter must have done as he entered Tutankhamun's tomb. I was one of the few people in Dublin who could instantly decipher these hieroglyphics. For Denis Maginnis flitted in and out of *Ulysses* as the dancing master Professor Denis J. Maginni, and this was what remained of his dancing school.

He had the Irish inferiority complex, which led to him knocking the S off the end of his name and magically trans-forming himself into an Italian, which was suitably exotic for a dancing master. Then with that generosity for which we are renowned in Dublin, he awarded himself a professorship of Deportment and Dance. 'Professor' Maginni weaves his way very delicately, very primly in and out of the Wandering Rocks episode of Joyce's novel: 'in silk hat, slate frockcoat with silk facings, white kerchief tie, tight lavender trousers, canary gloves and pointed patent boots'. However, despite his effeminacy of dress, he managed to produce around nineteen children, although many died in infancy.

Armed with the connection to Joyce and the surviving evidence, I stormed around to Noel Carroll, who was spokesman for Dublin Corporation. I knew Noel because I had been a fan of athletics, and he was a former European champion who ran around College Park every day. Noel frequently got into trouble as he loved to shoot his mouth off. Once, after flooding on the Dodder, for which the corporation came under attack, he responded by saying that people who live beside a river should expect to get their feet wet once every fifty years. I recognised a kindred spirit.

There were just a few weeks to the scheduled demolition of the house, with the rubble already earmarked as infill for an extension to the Poolbeg generating station.

'If those savages knock that house down, I'll go on every television station in Europe and denounce them!' I railed.

Noel was very easygoing, however, and said, 'Now, David, that's a bit hard, would you not go the other route?'

'What is the other route?' I asked. 'I'll try anything.'

He suggested that I make a submission to the Cultural Committee of Dublin Corporation – an oxymoron if ever there was one.

I knew that group rather well. The previous year I'd seen a stunning dramatic production in England called *Mister X* and, being involved with the Project Theatre, suggested to the Sheridan brothers that they put the play on in Dublin. It was performed by the Gay Sweatshop Company, and once the Cultural Committee heard that, they demanded that their grant be removed. Of course they hadn't seen or read the play at this stage, or even read the reviews, but the mere name of the company was enough for them! One committee member said they 'didn't want any English funny bunnies coming over here'. They described what they *thought* was going to happen on stage, which consisted of every conceivable variety of analology, thimbleriggery and full-frontal nudity – none of which was in the play. However, the resulting publicity proved a great advantage as people queued around the block in the hope of seeing what they expected would be a truly shocking and obscene production. They were to be disappointed in this by what was universally described by the critics as a remarkably moving piece of theatre.

So, as far as the Cultural Committee was concerned there was still a bit of a whiff off me. When I went in to make my submission, two old lads sat up at the back, both ostentatiously reading their newspapers rather than look at me. One of them eventually lowered his *Evening Press* and asked a question.

'Mr Norris, supposing the corporation was to hand over this magnificent mansion to you and your friends to create a memorial to the late writer Mr James Joyce – about whom, I must say, there are still divided opinions in this town – I'd like to ask you what undertaking you can give to the Dublin

Corporation that you would not use it for your, ahem, *fringe* activities.'

I was able to persuade the gentlemen that I would confine my *fringe* activities behind the door of no. 18, and would leave no. 35 to be polluted exclusively by the shade of the late Mr James Joyce, of whom I was well aware there were still divided opinions in Dublin.

Despite this the society got the house at a peppercorn rent. The city authorities themselves had had possession of the building for forty years, but a mere six months later I was attacked at a meeting of the corporation because, it was said, I had done nothing at all to preserve the house. This was wrong, as we had undertaken a surveyor's report and had been beavering away, planning how to raise funds for what would be a very expensive project. I was also denounced as a wet, middle-class, gin-and-tonic-drinking liberal. They were wrong about the drink – I've never taken to the G&T – but at least I now knew my position in the social register.

The house was still semi-derelict, but by that stage we had an active, energetic committee which included Seán White of the School of Irish Studies and Godfrey Graham, the film cameraman whose grandparents had once lived in part of the house. Godfrey ran a film festival, which made some money, and I did my one-man show all over the world to raise funds. We also invited on to the committee Bob Joyce, grand-nephew of James and a financial consultant, and Michael Darcy, a prominent businessman, who were very important in keeping us on the straight and narrow. Pat McHugh, widow of the University College Dublin Professor of English Roger McHugh, was a key networker for us.

One day I was sweeping the steps outside my home when a car drew up and a familiar-looking man stepped out, carrying a box. He told me he had heard me on the BBC World Service the night before performing excerpts from *Finnegans Wake*.

'I was so proud . . .' he began, and I started to swell up, anticipating a compliment. Then he continued, 'of my uncle James Joyce.'

I recognised him then – he had been the principal mourner at the funeral of Florence, Joyce's last sister, ten years before. It was Ken Monaghan, the writer's nephew and closest Dublin relative.

'And I thought you should have these,' he said as he handed over a box of newspaper clippings, letters and photographs that his mother had collected over the years. His mother May Joyce Monaghan was the only one of the Dublin family who had followed James Joyce's career with pride.

Included were some handwritten postcards from Ken's Uncle Stanislaus, Joyce's brother, in Trieste and correspondence from his biographer Richard Ellmann. I said, 'That's extremely kind of you, but the best place for these is not with me, but across in no. 35 where we are starting the James Joyce Centre – would you come on the board?'

Ken became the genial and presiding spirit of the building, and over the years we raised €2 million and restored the house from top to bottom. We reinstated the great drawing-room ceilings after we found the original drawings. There's a photograph of me blithely signing a £250,000 contract with a builder, which I wasn't the slightest bit fazed about because I have no real notion of money.

Early on Trevor and Desirée Sullivan, a charming couple who were always a positive presence, ran a huge fundraising ball in the Shelbourne, at which the guest of honour was Eileen O'Casey, widow of the playwright Seán, who had given the centre the typewriter on which he wrote some of his great Dublin plays when he lived around the corner on the North Circular Road. The dinner was to be held on the sixtieth anniversary of her engagement, so I read back through the biographies and found that, as Seán had no money at the time, his present to her had been a box of six macaroons. I scoured

Dublin to get a box of the cakes, which we tied up with a red ribbon. I presented them to Eileen on the sixtieth anniversary of the day Seán had presented her with a similar present, which she found very moving. She gave me a big hug and insisted that I open the ball by dancing with her.

There was turbulence at times and we had to save the centre from the machinations of some people who wanted to close it down and sell it. I am still on the committee and the centre is a thriving enterprise run by Mark Traynor and James Quinn. It is the focus of a huge amount of activity around Bloomsday and all year round.

Some time in the late 1970s, numbers 5 and 6 North Great Georges Street came into the possession of the Revenue Commissioners Social Club. Now, if the entertainment that took place therein had been confined to austere tax officials then we might never have crossed swords, but after a while the club began renting out its rooms to punk-rock groups, discotheques and all sorts of people. The patrons drove around blowing car horns at 3 a.m., making indecent remarks through the letter-boxes, and puking on the cats.

This carry-on could not be tolerated, so the society went to court to object to its licence and to demand that all its planning permission requirements be upheld. The court was held in the former Dolphin Hotel in Temple Bar but, mysteriously, not one of the neighbours could come along – all had excuses, including even the nuns, who begged off by saying it was a holy day of obligation. It struck me later that I might have been one of the few residents of the street to be fully tax-compliant! Just one resident, a tenant, came along to support me and she certainly made an impact, by fainting in the dock. I was sworn in and gave the judge a highly colourful but accurate description of the various activities of the social club. Next in was a man from the club committee, who shrugged his shoulders and said something along the lines of 'Well it's all very well for Mr Norris down there in his Georgian house but what about me up there in the club floating around in the pools of puke and if I look sideways at one of them all I get is a poke in the snot.' It was a classic example of undermining your own case by the injudicious giving of evidence.

The judge found in our favour, fining the Revenue Club and insisting they implement all the planning clauses, such as only allowing people to exit in a residential area before midnight. I joked with the reporters as we left the court, suggesting some ribald headlines for what had been a very colourful case. The *Sunday World* printed the best one: PAYE – PUKE AS YOU EXIT.

As I made my way on to the street, one of those who had been in court sidled up to me and muttered, 'I sincerely hope, Mr fuckin' Norris, that you have your income tax affairs in order . . . ' Coincidence or not, two weeks later there was a sinister flutter through my letterbox as a manila envelope bearing a harp descended. The letter therein stated that I was thereby required to make a full declaration of all my assets held in the United Kingdom and continental Europe. I wrote back saying:

Dear Revenue Commissioners,

I am more excited than I can possibly express by your discovery of these previously unknown and strangely neglected assets. The only thing that disappoints me is your apparent diffidence – why, might I ask, do you cease your efforts at the borders of continental Europe? Why not conduct your pursuit beyond the Urals, indeed across the entire globe? Whatever spoils you turn-up I propose we divide 50–50, which I am sure you will agree is fair.

There was no reply.

Two further weeks passed and then another sinister letter arrived, telling me I was required to submit to a full Revenue examination of my tax affairs. I wasn't sure if it was an official letter or a leg-pull, but I decided a good dose of information overload was called for. Luckily I am by my nature a hoarder so I had the right reserves of ammunition. I replied again:

> Thank you for your letter. I am sure Seán and Máire Citizen can rest easy in their beds knowing that you are constantly on the prowl for financial malefactors. I would be delighted to be able to help you, but you must understand that since my recent elevation to the Bureau of the Oireachtas committee on Foreign Affairs I will not have the time I previously had to assist you so. I enclose my financial documents as requested, albeit in something of an unrefined state . . .

Then I summoned a taxi, loaded in three tea chests full of every conceivable item of financial transaction, including receipts for the skate straps bought for me in the harsh winter of 1947 in Miss Milligan's shop in Sandymount Green when I was three, and dispatched it to my correspondent. To my letter I added a sinister and threatening postscript: 'PS, there's plenty more where that came from.' Once again I was met by silence.

A few days later a little bird told me that I could pretty much do what I liked with my financial affairs as long as I never again communicated with the Revenue Commissioners by telephone, taxi cab or tea chest. Perhaps the whole thing was a hoax that backfired on the practical joker, but I used this story, with various embellishments, as part of my repertoire as an after-dinner speaker for many years.

The Labour Party MEP Brendan Halligan arranged introductions for me in Brussels, so I appointed myself as Envoy Extraordinary and Minister Plenipotentiary from North Great Georges Street to the European Community, flew to Brussels and managed to talk my way up to the eleventh floor of the Berlaymont building where the Commissioners were based. I told the officials about the 85 per cent unemployment rate in my area but they didn't believe me – 'That's worse than Naples,' they said – so they sent out some civil servants to check, and found I was right.

I learnt all kinds of interesting things there, especially from the Irish officials, who were most helpful and explained that the European Community was in essence a machine that didn't listen to emotional or aesthetic arguments; you just had to know which buttons to press. So, while there was no grant available for restoring eighteenth-century railings in Dublin, there was a grant for restoring eighteenth-century harpoons as used in the Scandinavian whaling industry. The machine didn't have any appreciation of the difference between these two types of eighteenth-century ironmongery, and so we qualified for a grant. I learnt a few more similar approaches and came back with a significant package, but one that required matching funding back in Ireland.

I was naïve, however, and soon discovered that the money was just evaporating, snaffled up by ministers for their own projects. North Great Georges Street was to get nothing. I rang the office of the relevant minister, a decent man called Séamus Brennan. It was about ten minutes to four and the secretary told me he had just left the office for the press conference.

So, doing a bit of Sherlock Holmesing, I asked was that the press conference about the European money?

Yes, it was, she confirmed. So I worked out that the most likely place for a press conference that he could get to in ten minutes was the Shelbourne Hotel.

'Ah yes,' I said, 'I should have seen that invitation. It's at four o'clock, in the Shelbourne Hotel, about the European money.'

'Yes,' she said.

So I got in to the press conference and stuck up my hand to ask a question.

'Could the minister explain how it is that money that was intended for the restoration of Georgian Dublin has been distrained away for other purposes, against the wishes and intention of the negotiators of this deal?'

Séamus said, 'Thank you. I know exactly what Senator Norris is talking about, and I don't think it should become controversial. Perhaps he could meet the secretary of my department after the conference.' And we eventually got an appropriate sum. I have to say that in the labyrinthine discussions, my good friend and fellow director Bob Joyce was a considerable help.

Saving the Joyce house was pivotal in our campaign to save the street. There was a laneway next to the building, and the two houses on the other side were gone, so the corporation would have had a stronger case for demolition if it had gone too. I was able to counter their plan to build those horrendous flats by drawing an analogy with the restoration of Rembrandt's *Night Watch* after it had been attacked by a lunatic with a knife. I pointed out that the Rijksmuseum didn't commission Picasso or Andy Warhol to complete the painting; they got a sympathetic craftsman to restore the masterpiece to its original glory by replicating what had been damaged. I believed North Great Georges Street was, architecturally speaking, an integral artistic composition, and that its problems were a mere rip in the canvas. And so after a long battle they agreed and restored the disputed buildings.

But we had to be eternally vigilant, and at one stage there was concern over the future of nos. 5 and 6, which were then in private hands and whose owners wanted to redevelop the site. The Building Control Bill had just been debated and I had raised the state of those two houses in the Senate. The Environment Minister, Padraig Flynn, said they would be protected by the legislation, but I was not so sure.

One day a convoy of heavy machinery arrived in the street to start the demolition, so I rang Mr Flynn's office, to be told he was in a meeting. I told the person answering the phone to get him out of the meeting, because, I said, 'If those houses are demolished there's going to be one hell of a row, and I'm going to be quoting back the guarantees that were given.' I got on to Dublin Corporation too, and the demolition was stopped.

We got into a few scrapes along the way, and a few heated arguments, but the most damaging row almost split the preservation society.

It came about because of a plan to close off the southern end of the street behind a set of gates. The street had become a rat-run for motorists trying to dodge the city's increasing traffic gridlock, as well as a racetrack for stolen cars, and all this was becoming a great concern to residents. One night I dreamed that we erected a set of gates at the bottom of the street. I got hold of a copy of Rocque's Map of Dublin from 1756 when the street was yet to be built, and the site was part of the Mount Eccles estate, owned by Nicholas Archdall. Where the street should be there was a tree-lined avenue which went up the hill and turned right, just past the Loreto Convent, leading into the courtyard of the manor house itself.

The entrance to the Archdall estate was at the bottom of the hill, where North Great Georges Street now meets Parnell Street, and there on Rocque's map was a massive set of gates. I took my dream to the society and, in the beginning, everyone agreed that the gates were a great idea. They told me I was a genius, but when I described in detail the gates that had featured in my dream they told me they were revolting Victorian monstrosities.

We brought our proposal to the city authorities, who were sympathetic, and our architects drew up a plan for closing the southern end of the street with a little bit of rebuilding on the car park. That end of the street was our main concern, as the houses opposite were also in a state of dereliction.

John O'Connell and I went on a tour of the derelict demesnes around Dublin, and struck oil out at Santry Court, which had been the home of the Domville family. It had been demolished in the 1940s but the very beautiful, late-eighteenth-century, French wrought-iron gates were still there, collapsed on the ground. The property now belonged to Pino Harris, an entrepreneur of genius who brought Hino trucks to Ireland in the 1960s. He lived near by on the canal bank in Phibsborough.

I called to his home, but he didn't seem too impressed by my pleas and started angling me down the garden path. With that his two little Jack Russell dogs came running into the garden and one squeezed out through the hedge. Outside lurked a large Alsatian, who grabbed the little dog in his jaws and looked like he was about to devour him. I had brought an old-fashioned brolly with me to protect me from the inclemency of the weather, and used the umbrella handle to catch Pino's dog under the oxter, pluck him from the Alsatian's mouth and lift him clean over the hedge to safety.

Pino was delighted and said, 'That was the neatest thing I've ever seen. Do come in and have a cup of tea. And what was that you were saying about those old gates?'

I explained again and he told me, 'They are the bane of my life, as I'm sure someone's going to fall over them and sue me. If you can get them out by Thursday they're yours. I don't want a price for them; you're doing me a favour.' I offered to call them the Pino Harris Gates and invited him to the opening, but he declined, and so we collected them and stored them in the Joyce Centre.

Typically of Dublin's begrudgery, a campaign against the gates was started, which turned very nasty and was targeted directly at me. Very dishonest material was distributed around the area saying we were snobs and wanted a gated community to keep out the lower orders. The *Irish Times* then got involved and printed copies of the plans, which for some reason were cropped and suggested – incorrectly – that there wouldn't even be pedestrian access through the gates. They also ran what purported to be an interview with me, but was actually a scissors-and-paste job as I hadn't spoken to the writer in over a year.

The truth was that the street would have been open

twenty-four hours a day to pedestrians – they weren't really gates, more like railings with four beautiful lantern posts. They didn't block the view of Belvedere College either, because the angle of the steep hill meant you could see the college over the top of them.

My good friend Desmond FitzGerald, the Knight of Glin, later president of the Irish Georgian Society, was then roped in and he wrote a completely idiotic letter saying that the ironwork was incompatible with the street, being of the wrong period, so I wrote a stinker back to him. I told him I had seen the letter he had sent to the corporation, and that it was of immense help to our side because it was so completely inaccurate. In return I got a lovely note confirming that he had indeed written the piece under pressure, without having any knowledge of the railings. He said he was now terrified to come down North Great Georges Street in case I stuck my head out of the window like Bessie Burgess and used my powerful vocal cords to sweep him off the pavement. At the bottom of the page, instead of the little happy face image, there was a circle with two eyes, a down-turned mouth and one little wisp of hair sticking up. It was so engaging and so typical of Desmond that I wrote him a warm letter and our friendship resumed.

I was very upset when I discovered the corporation had got a negative letter from the local chemist. I called down to see what was going on, and assured Mr Foley that I wouldn't be taking my business away but that I was surprised at what he had written. He explained that he had been asked to write a letter of objection, and did so, but that the person who asked him to write it had torn it up and demanded notepaper to write it themselves. I asked him to write a statement to that effect, which he did, and I gave it to my solicitor. A rather unpleasant atmosphere was created in the area and in the media.

We had the support of 98 per cent of owners and residents of the street, while the overwhelming number of objectors to the plan came from faraway places such as Surrey, Killarney and south Co. Dublin. Bertie Ahern had come to the Joyce Centre and made a promise that the gates would be up within the year, but the minute there was any trouble he turned tail and scarpered. The corporation was behind us too, and used a special section to accelerate the plan, but this was then used to portray the scheme as anti-democratic. That blazed up into another row and the proposal was shelved.

I have always believed that if you champion a policy that collapses, you should resign, so in the wake of the gates controversy I stepped down as chairman of the society. If the residents had any chance of the gates being restored, or fractures in the society being resolved in the future, I would have to get out of the way. I was happy with my contribution so far to the street's preservation. Our success has become a template for preservation groups all over the country, and we also had an important impact on the wider inner-city community. In the Joyce Centre we hired and trained young people as plaster-workers, who honed their skills in no. 35 and then went all over the country restoring plasterwork.

There were several capable chairpersons after me, and for the last eight years the society has been run by a distinguished barrister, Muireann Noonan, who has been very dynamic and organised things like a windowbox competition which brought great colour to the street. Under her leadership we won the All Ireland Pride of Place Award. The battle goes on, however – at one stage the city council wanted to lift the granite paving setts and replace them with modern concrete, a plan we luckily frustrated. North Great Georges Street is now largely residential and, with a couple of exceptions, lovingly restored.

Alongside the campaign for the street, I had my own little battle to preserve Georgian Dublin behind the doors of no. 18. It was a long and costly business but I succeeded in my plan to do one room per year over twenty-five years. When I moved in it was still full of tenants, but they gradually moved out. The previous owners had converted the building to apartments, which were superficially attractive, but the workmanship was very shoddy. I was confined to one floor, and had a lot of furniture in storage, but the two drawing rooms were vacated quite quickly so the eighteenth-century pieces found a suitable home.

The ground-floor tenants were the McGurk family, and I could sense Mrs McGurk was getting a bit uneasy about this new owner, so I went down to see her.

'Mrs McGurk,' I told her, 'I can understand that you might be feeling a little bit apprehensive, because other people are leaving. But they are just students and young doctors, and to them it is just a flat. You've been here all your life. This is your home and I respect that.'

The McGurks were devout Roman Catholics, daily communicants in Gardiner Street. They were a lovely couple: decent, refined Dublin people. Mrs McGurk thought Ezra was the greatest thing (apart from her pet dog Tiki), and one spring morning, as I headed off to Jerusalem, I tripped over a large Easter egg on the bottom stair. Out from her door popped Mrs McGurk, who said, 'I left that there so I'd hear you going out, because I know you're going over to see Ezra. And I just wanted you to know that I've made my special novena to the Sacred Heart for the intention that Ezra will come and live with you permanently, because I think you're such a lovely couple.' I was very touched by that.

One of my classic after-dinner stories involves Mrs McGurk, who used every so often to come up to the top of the house to pay the rent or to make sure I was all right. I had become a bit portly and decided to correct this by doing exercises. I purchased a book called *Fully Fit in Sixty Minutes a Week* by Todd Estabrook, United States Air Force (retired). In this, Monday, Wednesday and Saturday were divided into twenty-minute periods of exercise. There was a warm-up, main course and cool-down. Warm-up was all right. The main course contained some fairly gruelling exercises, lots of stomach crunches, press-ups and worst of all, a thing called back-overs. To accomplish this you lie flat on your back, fly your legs over your head, touch the ground behind your ears with your toes and count slowly to seven, expelling your breath as you do so. I performed these exercises neatly, perhaps a little skimpily but certainly modestly attired in the correct athletic underwear, although I was bare-chested. One fateful Wednesday I had just got to the count of four in the back-overs when there was a timid knock and the door opened. Mrs McGurk's head came around the door, took one look at a pair of naked shoulders with legs draped over them and said, 'Oh God, I'm terribly sorry, I'll come back when you're on your own.' I nearly suffered a rupture unravelling myself and chasing her down the stairs to prove that I was indeed on my own.

Mr McGurk died suddenly on his way to church one day, and I was honoured to be asked to help carry his coffin. And some years later, when Mrs McGurk died, it was an even greater honour to be asked to choose and deliver a reading at her funeral.

Not having the McGurks about was sad, but it meant I was able to rearrange the house and find a home for all the furniture. I did a lot of the donkey work, such as demolition, myself, and hired in craftsmen. I found out how to clean paint off the plasterwork, and tested a poultice made of various preparations which lifted the paint off but left the plaster intact.

The basement was in an appalling state, with a damp earthen floor which meant you could tell when the tide was in. Eighty tons of mass concrete had to be laid, so I renovated that last of all, and continue to have tenants there, one of whom was Sebastian Barry, the Booker Prize nominee. At one stage Anne Enright, who won the Booker in 2007, lived on the top floor – so it was quite a literary house at times. But the happiest arrangement of all was when a lovely couple, Gerry Rogers and Paul Berry, who owns the best flower shop in Dublin, Adonis Flower Designs in Patrick Street, moved in. Not a cross word passed between us in fourteen years, and when they left there were tears all round.

I am now more than three decades in the street, surrounded by wonderful neighbours, each of whose extraordinary homes has its own special flavour. But no. 18 belongs to me, and I belong to it. North Great Georges Street shines brightly again, and I am proud to have been part of that.

CHAPTER 7

Re-Joyce

IDISCOVERED JAMES JOYCE AT THE AGE OF NINE, BUT IT WASN'T AN altogether successful encounter. It occurred during one of Uncle Dick's periodic visits in the early 1950s, when I raided the small library that always travelled with him. He had been talking to us about a trip to the Phoenix Park more than forty years before when he had been chatting in schoolboy Italian with a cousin. They bumped into a tall, elegant but slightly seedy man who heard them talking Italian. He stopped and told them he had just opened a cinema in the city, called the Volta, and gave the boys complimentary tickets. It was, of course, James Joyce.

Though his name, like that of Oscar Wilde, was familiar to me from childhood, there was an intriguing whiff of sulphur about both writers. Adults always stopped talking about them when they noticed we children were listening.

I picked up a copy of *Dubliners* and a couple of my uncle's cigars and retired up a tree in the garden. The cigars were a great success; Joyce a terrible disappointment. I thought the book was a complete waste of time, and it was perfectly obvious to me that James Joyce hadn't the first idea how to tell a story. The one thing I did know about stories was that they should end with a bang, but these just seemed to evaporate and appeared to me the epitome of dullness.

But over the years I persevered, and became increasingly conscious that the writer had once walked down the same roads that I did. I remember the BBC broadcasting a section of *Ulysses* and being delighted to hear reference to *our* Sandymount Strand. I thought the idea that someone had turned the ordinary things I knew into world literature was wonderful. I also thought the fact that he had lived in Trieste, a placename printed on our ancient valve wireless along with the likes of Hilversum, Brno, Rome and Oslo, made him seem very exotic.

I identified with the fact that he was an outsider, rejected by polite Irish society. One might hear whispered references to Joyce and Wilde, but they were the unmentionables, challenging, anti-establishment and subversive. Joyce was absolutely anathema to official Ireland. When Charles Joyce died there were two and a half pages of obituary in the *Belvederian Annual* because he had founded the Legion of Mary in England. James wasn't even mentioned in his brother's obituary, let alone having his own death marked by a notice of any kind – and they died in the same week.

I was fortunate to develop my interest at a time when there were still some people around who had been at school with him and so had personal memories of the writer. Small meetings were organised where these people came to tell their stories about him. It was fascinating to hear them talk about Joyce as a real person, someone they had sat next to in class, or discuss how good he was at cricket or cross-country running. And even more intriguing, how his gift for mimicking the idiosyncrasies of the teachers kept the audiences in fits of laughter during the annual school play.

Michael Moran, John Doherty and I were still in our mid-teens when we started going to the theatre in town. I loved theatre, and the frisson you got from the creation of a reality in which you could be submerged. In September 1959, when I was just fifteen years old, we saw *The Voice of Shem* by Mary Manning in the Eblana Theatre, which was in the basement of

Busáras, the main Dublin bus station. This was Manning's dramatisation of *Finnegans Wake*, with Archie Sullivan as Earwicker and Patrick Bedford as Shem the Penman. I was both awestruck and exhilarated by May Cluskey and Marie Kean's portrayal of the two washerwomen from the Anna Livia Plurabelle scene. I had never experienced the electricity of language in that way. Joyce had completely captured and distilled the essence of the city: the voices of the street traders in Moore Street, the characters, the river, the geography, the laughter, the stories and the energy. I experienced what the critic Edmund Wilson called 'the shock of recognition'. Like all great art – whether poetry, painting, sculpture or literature – it opened my eyes to see reality in a totally different way.

Joyce had established a picture of early-twentieth-century Dublin so devastatingly accurate that to many the subject remains exhausted after his attentions. As an artist he possessed an enormous appetite, almost a greed, for the accent, nuance, phraseology, rhythm, lilt and anecdotal language of his native city.

After I heard *Finnegans Wake* being performed I went to the RDS Library to borrow the book and, yet again, I felt absolutely swindled. What was all this gibberish on the page? But gradually I started to realise it wasn't conventional writing; there were no propositional facts in it. It was a dream, and just like Dalí's paintings where time melts, time and language melt in *Finnegans Wake*. As Walter Pater said, 'All art aspires to music,' and this really was music. That is why it comes so alive on the stage but remains so exasperating on the page.

One of my few memories of my father is of him putting me in the child carrier on the back of his bicycle, and cycling up Sandymount Avenue across to Simmonscourt Road, up Anglesea Road and along the river at Beaver Row. And there, in Clonskeagh through a secret passageway, was the entrance to wild countryside along the banks of the Dodder. I can still see the sunlight poking through the leaves on that day over sixty years ago, and the wonderful feeling that we had discovered our own secret jungle. James Joyce was my own private jungle.

I loved him because I had discovered him for myself, like another great lifelong passion, the Original Dixieland Jazz Band. Michael and John were interested but not seized by Joyce – and when I read Richard Ellman's biography I discovered that he was also a fascinating man. I identified with his ruthless honesty about his sexuality, albeit a heterosexual truth. Joyce wrote about his first encounter with a prostitute and about storing erotic postcards up the chimney to be retrieved as required – but he did so while retaining human and moral values. He showed that it was possible to reject the platitudes of conventional morality and build for oneself a system of values and integrity. His name was mud in Dublin, and in my entire undergraduate career he was the subject of just one lecture, in which the Shakespearean scholar Professor J. K. Walton talked about textual aspects of *Ulysses*. This left me free to explore him by myself.

Quite different was the experience when the great short-story writer Frank O'Connor came to teach at Trinity for a year in the mid-1960s, and I took his creative-writing class. He had just come from teaching in the United States and wore a bolo instead of a tie, which gave him the look of a cowboy. He was tall with white hair and, like Joyce, Yeats and Dylan Thomas, possessed an absolutely distinctive voice, which came with a sonorous Cork accent.

Unlike the classic academic, O'Connor had the gift of making quite complex literary ideas accessible to his audience through illustrating his point with a story. One of my most abiding memories is of him explaining the essential element of the short-story form and the twist or change that must occur in the reader's mind. He told us how, as a boy, he had been brought by his mother to a carnival in Cork. The central attraction was a strongman wearing a leotard who flexed his muscles and exhibited to the audience a bar of iron. Then, with his muscles bulging and bringing his great strength to bear upon it, he bent it into the shape of a horseshoe and showed it again to the crowd, who gasped in admiration. After a pause, and once again straining every fibre, with beads of perspiration running down his forehead, he brought the bar of iron back again to its original shape, to renewed gasps from the crowd. O'Connor's point was that although it looked the same it could never be quite the same bar of iron in the imagination of those who had witnessed the feat. It had been used to demonstrate the miracle of human strength. That, he told us, was what should happen with a short story. At the end of a story the reader's mind should travel back over its incidents with a consciousness that had been subtly changed by the process of reading the story. This, in fact, is the universal rule by which all short stories operate, from the Christmas-cracker surprise endings of Maupassant to the apparent inconclusiveness of Joyce.

O'Connor – like Joyce's brother Stanislaus – never came to terms with *Ulysses*, and certainly not *Finnegans Wake*, because he thought Joyce was pushing the boundaries too far. He believed he had gone over to surrealism or Dadaism. To me, however, Joyce always remained the supreme classicist. He wasn't joking when he said his mind was schooled by old Aquinas, forged by the Jesuits. I think he must have been devastated when his former friend Oliver St John Gogarty dismissed *Finnegans Wake* as 'the biggest leg-pull in history'. Joyce spent seventeen years of his life writing that book, in extraordinarily difficult and turbulent circumstances, precisely quantifying and weighing every syllable to give the effect he wanted.

His great friend Frank Budgen told me of meeting Joyce one evening in a Zurich park. It is a story that has now been repeatedly published, but to hear it directly from Budgen himself was like being hit by a sledgehammer.

He asked Joyce how the writing was going, to be told it was going very well.

'How much did you get done today?' Frank asked. 'A chapter?'

Joyce shook his head.

'A couple of pages?'

No.

'A paragraph? A couple of sentences?'

'I completed one sentence,' Joyce replied. 'I had all the words yesterday, but today I got them in the right order.'

After that, how could anybody say that James Joyce's writing was chaotic?

The more you read Joyce, the greater the depth becomes apparent. The short stories in *Dubliners* continued to puzzle me – the first one, 'The Sisters', is so inconclusive that it doesn't even end in a full stop: 'So then, of course, when they saw that, that made them think that there was something gone wrong with him . . .' But the whole point of the story is that you have to go back, pick up the clues and join up the dots. The story is incomplete on the page and requires the reader's imagination to go back and re-read it.

The whole secret of *Dubliners* is in that first paragraph. It is written in a pallid, dreary style, which Joyce himself described as 'a style of scrupulous meanness' with lots of monosyllables – extraordinary for a writer with such an immense command of vocabulary – but there buried within are three key words which shine out like precious stones: 'gnomon', 'simony' and 'paralysis'. When I began a thesis on an analysis of *Dubliners* I found that when the critics had looked at 'gnomon' they found it was the indicator in a sundial, or in solid geometry the notional bit that you've left when you remove a smaller parallelogram from a larger one. For years they had been pursuing those dead-ends, but *gnomon* in Greek actually means 'interpreter'. And as Joyce had studied medicine, I reckoned he was examining the linguistic extrusions of the culture of Dublin like a doctor checking stool and urine samples from a patient and diagnosing the illness – a kind of literary scatoscopy. What Joyce diagnosed, characteristically with his innately theological Jesuit-trained mind, was simony.

'Simony' was named after Simon Magus, a biblical character who was jealous of the disciples' miracle-working and when told it was due to 'the holy spirit', tried to buy the secret of it from them. 'Simony' came to mean the notion that you could obtain spiritual things at a price. Joyce saw it as the disease, with its manifesting symptom 'paralysis'. Gnomon, or interpretation, was the cure – facing, accepting and taking control of one's own life.

Which is why, when every character in *Dubliners* is offered life, they become confused. In the story 'Eveline' the opening paragraph represents the quintessence of paralysis: 'She sat at the window watching the evening invade the avenue. Her head was leaned against the window curtains and in her nostrils was the odour of dusty cretonne.' It's a strange, reclusive life, where the most active element is evening, one of the most subtle of the day's happenings. Certainly not what any ordinary person would see as an 'invasion' – we think of *Blitzkrieg*, 'Shock and Awe' or 'Operation Cast Lead', not the fall of dusk in suburbia. She doesn't even seem to have leaned her own head, it is almost as if she is a mannequin in a shop window and someone has adjusted her posture. Her nose is open and contains dust particles but she doesn't even actively smell it. In fact, she is addicted to the dust that surrounds her, and when manly, open-hearted Frank enters her life she thinks he will give her life, perhaps love too. You would have to be pretty moribund to be presented with life. And Frank is going to take her to Buenos Aires, the city of fresh air. No wonder she stops halfway up the gangplank to the boat – the breeze of Buenos Aires will blow away her beloved dust. (On the other hand, luckily for Joyce, Nora had no such scruples.)

With most writers, once you've read a story and enjoyed it, going back to read it again is governed by the law of diminishing returns. But with Joyce the meaning is buried deep within the story and continues to develop further and deeper meanings every time you read it. This is just as true of the later books.

Joyce is an artist with a constantly developing style: *Dubliners* is a series of vignettes, one-dimensional silhouetted stories; *A Portrait of an Artist as a Young Man* is a portrait, so you get certain amounts of sunlight and shadow, *chiaroscuro* as the painters call it; but with *Ulysses* Joyce himself deliberately drew the parallel of a sculpture – a three-dimensional psychological counterpart – so the reader could walk around and see all sides of Bloom; and *Finnegans Wake* is Joyce, always ahead of his time, anticipating twenty-first-century multimedia.

The first member of Joyce's family I got to know was Ken Monaghan, who became a great friend, although he was ambivalent about his Uncle James. He recalled how Joyce borrowed a pound from his mother, who was then working for very small wages in Todd Burns department store in Henry Street, and despite several direct hints he never paid her back. Joyce was a blight on his children, too, as almost all famous fathers are. I will never forget Joyce's son Giorgio's comment about how uncomfortable it was to walk into a room full of American scholars, all of whom knew more about the intimate details of his parents' lives than he did.

In 1973 Joyce's sister Florence died. I had spotted the death notice in the paper, which noted that she was 'the last surviving sister of the late writer James Joyce'. I took that as an invitation to the literary community to attend, but as far as I could see I was the only one to do so. In the atmospheric Victorian cemetery of Mount Jerome, I noticed names on the gravestones that were the same as those in *Ulysses* or *Dubliners*. Florence was being buried right among the people that inhabited her brother's books. Afterwards, in typical Dublin fashion, the funeral party went for a drink in the pub across the road, although I kept to myself and had an orange juice. There was one man there, who may have been one of the cousins from England, who was the living image of Joyce – he had that full throat, electric-blue eyes, James's nose and a hat exactly like he used to wear. It was eerie, as if Joyce had come back from the dead for his sister's funeral.

Ken told me that he used to visit two old aunts at their home in Mountjoy Square, one of whom, Eva, had lived with James and Nora in Trieste. They were two young women born into respectable prosperity but who had seen their father drink his way through two substantial fortunes, commuting his pension and driving his family into a whirlpool of poverty in central Dublin. Stanislaus's diary records them chopping down banisters for firewood, drinking watery tea out of jam jars, and he himself having to stay in bed for days on end as his clothes and shoes had been pawned to buy food for the younger children. The sisters were very sensitive about having come from a particular social station that had been so rapidly and tragically lost. Further degradation was to follow in the 1920s when the pair got jobs, one in a bank and the other as a solicitor's secretary, and then *Ulysses* exploded from the Left Bank of Paris, revealing to the world the squalid reality of their family circumstances. Both were let go from their employment, and they were convinced it was because it had been discovered they were the sisters of the infamous writer.

Ken remembered that his aunts didn't have a clock in their apartment, but they had a telescope with which, by leaning out of a window, they would read the time off the clock on Findlater's Church. The women had the same type of curious encyclopaedic mind as James, and they used to buy the newspaper every day to read every single line of it from front to back, including the for-sale notices, births, deaths and marriages, and the racing programmes. They would then spend hours discussing the contents.

They also warned Ken never, under any circumstances, to

mention to anyone that he was the nephew of James Joyce. A lot of the family felt slighted because James had drawn pictures of their family life which they did not want to be placed on public view. In Edna O'Brien's wonderful 1999 biography, she asks, 'Was Joyce a monster?' – and concludes that he was, because all artists – particularly novelists – are. They have to be; like surgeons their compassion for the subject of their operations must never overcome their professional standards. Joyce's raw material was the life of his own family, friends and contemporaries. It was an act of great courage to use his genius to turn it into art, but it was also an act of heroic and intimate betrayal.

I nearly acquired an item of Joyce's correspondence myself about twenty-five years ago. I was contacted by a young lad who worked in a solicitor's office. He told me over the telephone that he had something I would be interested in and then revealed it was a letter written by Joyce to his father back in Dublin, who had evidently tried to put the bite on him financially. He sent me a photocopy. In the letter Joyce defended himself in the most labyrinthine way by pointing to the expensive tastes of his wife and daughter, the heating costs of his flat in Paris, the price of fur coats and dining at Fouquet's. He then suggested that his father should try to 'touch' his other son, Charles, instead, who was an easier mark as he was still in Dublin, living across the road from my house in North Great Georges Street.

Because of the local connection, I decided I would buy it. It was offered to me for £5; but I asked several people, including Ulick O'Connor, to give me an idea of the market value because I wanted to give a fair price. I rang the young lad back and offered him £75, which was a good deal of money in those days, and he agreed. We arranged to meet in a pub, but he failed to turn up. When I rang his office the next day, he calmly and cavalierly told me that his boss had overheard his conversation with me and, hearing my name and Joyce mentioned together, spotted a prize. His boss made an offer that he doubted I could match, so he sold him the letter. He didn't even have the manners to keep the appointment. The letter was eventually bought by Richard Ellman and published in the revised biography. I'm not a great collector of such items, however, so I quickly overcame my disappointment, and I eventually gave my considerable collection of Joyce books, many of them personally signed for me by the authors, to the Joyce Centre to help start its library.

One of the great problems Joyce presents to the reader is the grim and deadly earnestness of the Joycean critics. They reminded me of a convention of lunatic clockmakers, surrounded by cogs, wheels and springs yet scarcely one of them able to tell you the time. A special jargon grew up around Joyce, and the experimental nature of his later novels meant he became a sort of Rorschach blot on which critics could project their own lunacies. This all helped to distort the essential meaning. They were taken in by the appearance of the text and had little understanding of the way Joyce's mind worked. On the other hand there were some great critics, such as Ellman, Hugh Kenner and Harry Levine.

A major row blew up in 1984 over the publication of a revised edition of *Ulysses*. The original 1922 text had many errors, mostly of a slight typographical nature. A prominent German academic, Professor Hans-Walter Gabler, got the finance together to use computers to help produce a definitive version of *Ulysses*, which he called 'the critical and synoptic edition'. He corrected a lot of the obvious mistakes, but inevitably introduced a few more of his own.

Seán White, the Dean of the School of Irish Studies, asked me to have a look at what was going on, on behalf of a brilliant but eccentric American academic, Dr John Kidd. I found several examples of where the new edition was going wrong, such as correcting the well-known Irish measure of whiskey, the naggin, to a 'noggin'. Another occurs when Bloom is in the graveyard musing about the escape of corpse gas from the coffins: 'one whiff of that and you're a goner'. Joyce's manuscript wasn't clear, but it was obvious to anyone with any experience of Dublin parlance that it was as originally written. But the dons decided it was 'doner', like a kebab. There was another confusion of 'Thrift' and 'Shrift' in the bicycle race, but as I knew Mabel and Harry Thrift, descendants of the former Provost Thrift of Trinity, I was convinced that Thrift was the correct reading. I gave a paper at the Princess Grace Library in Monaco to a *colloque* of Joycean scholars lampooning the whole thing, which I called the 'Clinic for Textually Transmitted Diseases', where they gave 'short Shrift' to sufferers from 'Doner-rhea'. This went down like a lead balloon with the scholars, but in the end I was proved right by greater minds than my own.

After years of attending symposia and pursuing Joyce down all sorts of academic back alleys, I decided that the future, for me at least, lay in performance. I developed a stage show in which I strove to explain what Joyce was trying to do by dramatising and performing examples of his otherwise impenetrable writing.

I often got standing ovations from international audiences for performing passages from *Finnegans Wake*, which I had been told was only for the scholars – an opinion with which the scholars collaborated by erecting a fence around it. After a successful show, as the curtains parted for the last time I always felt I was merely taking a bow for Joyce himself, who desperately wanted *Finnegans Wake* to be enjoyed by the public. I recall coming across a quotation about Walton splitting the atom and Joyce splitting the word, which suggested that Joyce's literary experiments constituted a radioactive area which people should keep out of unless they were wearing protective clothing – available for purchase, naturally, from the academic establishment.

But I knew from my experience of hearing it performed in the Eblana that it wasn't like that, that *Finnegans Wake* was like music. Many people who, if asked, would say that, for example, the 'Blue Danube' was their favourite tune wouldn't be able to recognise it if you showed them the dots and dashes on the sheet music. So it is with the *Wake*: it's like a musical score – it needs to be read aloud, preferably performed by the equivalent of a professional musician. I don't think it's ever going to be popular reading, but performance gives it meaning to an audience and I think Joyce would have been delighted that his work is thus made accessible to the general public.

I had an argument on the French radio station RTF about just one word that appears on the first page of *Finnegans Wake*. The presenter got very animated about it, insisting it was rubbish, a jumble of meaningless characters.

I told him that he had to understand that Joyce was destroying the English language in non-violent compensation for 750 years of British colonisation, and reassembling it in the imagination of the Irish. And by so doing he had created one of the greatest works of literature, parts of which can only be understood when read in an Irish accent. I also pointed out that he had included elements of sixty other languages to add resonance. It is the greatest linguistic experiment ever in literature, as well as a celebration of the survival and triumph of the human spirit, within which every word has four or five levels of meaning.

As Joyce says himself in *Finnegans Wake*, 'It is not a misaffectual whyacinthinous riot of blots and blurs and bars and balls and hoops and wriggles and juxtaposed jottings linked by spurts of speed: it only looks as like it as damn it . . .' But he retained his loyalty to the basic rhythm of English, the iamb, the rhythm of heartbeat, which means you can scan the hundred-letter word 'bababadalgharaghtakamminarronnkonnbronn-tonnerronntuonnthunntrovarrhounawnskawntoohoohoorde-nenthur-nuk' despite the fact that it is visually intimidating, and means nothing to the reader: like a piece of music you can practise it and perform it. When you do it on stage people know exactly what it is – the first of a series of peals of thunder that Joyce echoes through the book.

And it is the same in *Ulysses*, where Joyce always leaves a clue for the ear – in 'Proteus' Stephen is walking on the shore: 'Listen: a fourworded wavespeech: seesoo, hrss, rsseeiss, ooos'. Most people pass it by, but by so doing they miss the moment the miracle happens: Stephen is trying to capture reality, and he does in that short sentence that replicates the sound of a wave breaking and ebbing on the shore.

People have often debated the closing passages of *Ulysses*, with its final whispered 'Yes', and I have sat through many hours listening to or reading the theories that it is an affirmation of life, or deeply cynical, or that Molly is thinking of and listing off her various real and imaginary lovers as she masturbates. But they all miss the point, which is that Joyce has already moved on.

In *Ulysses* Joyce is dealing with human relationships: communion, atonement, separation, division and reconciliation. Bloom, looking into the window of Yeates's the optician, thinks about the notion of parallax. This is an optical illusion created when you look at the stars and see two that appear to be the same size and close together. In reality they may be separated by millions of light-years but the effect of distance produces the illusion that they are in fact close to each other.

When Bloom masturbates looking at Gerty McDowell on Sandymount Strand it appears to be a sexual connection, but they are both projecting on to blank canvases. She sees him as the dark romantic hero of the book she's been reading, while he sees her as the equivalent of one of the nymphs over Molly's bed. But there's no meeting, she's just a catalyst for sexual release. That afternoon Molly has sex with Blazes Boylan, which causes Bloom intense, troubled emotions, but towards the end you realise that Boylan means absolutely nothing to her, he's merely an instrument of her pleasure.

In the middle of the book Bloom has his wine and gorgonzola, which sets up an effervescence on his palate. The effect of the wine and the flies buzzing on the glass bring to mind his first real physical encounter with Molly on Howth Head. And when she in turn thinks of Bloom almost her last thoughts are of that roll in the heather – and it is the only time in the book when the linguistic systems become exactly aligned and two people view the same experience in the same language. That is the clue that tells you that this is the moment when Joyce celebrates humanity being shared. And that is the true ending of the book – it's not the 'Yes, I said yes' passage. It's so typical of Joyce that the real ending of *Ulysses* is buried organically in a connection between the middle and the end.

As a boy, one of my most treasured books was *The Starry Heavens* by Professor A. M. Lowe, a present from my father, who was a friend of the author. It was a book about astronomy which explained the various constellations, of which my favourite was Orion, the hunter. I thought of how the Greek shepherds in ancient times had looked up to the stars and joined them together into figures like Orion, with his broad shoulders, belt and sheathed sword. That random series of stars has been formed into meaning by the human imagination and, now they've been connected, can never be unconnected. That is why art is immortal.

I gave a paper to one Joyce Symposium on the mystical aspects of *Finnegans Wake*. Joyce believed in magical books such as the Egyptian and Tibetan *Books of the Dead* and the Kabbalah, and thought that *Ulysses* foretold the death of several of his friends.

It struck me that *Finnegans Wake* was a bit like one of those old Hammer Horror films with Boris Karloff. I pictured some Transylvanian castle with a laboratory, bottles bubbling away and gigantic antennae like knitting needles on the roof conducting a bolt of lightning down to the basement, where a body made up of lots of different parts is consequently galvanised into life. In the *Wake* Joyce assembled the minute details of the elements of his experience. You have to know the contents of his pockets, his father's taste in opera, the sequence of events in his life and details of the Dublin streets he walked around. And while the reassembled elements of Joyce's mind that constitute the book lie inert on the operating table that is the *Wake*, it is as if the human mind and imagination of the reader, passing over the text by reading it, brings his consciousness momentarily back to life.

I spotted Richard Ellman sitting in the front row, his face remaining totally impassive, and I got the impression that he disapproved strongly of what I was saying. About six weeks later I met Seán Ó Mordha from RTÉ, who made a wonderful series of films about Joyce's life and, like myself, had become a friend of Ellman. He asked me had I seen Dick recently and I told him about the symposium and how I thought he wasn't a bit impressed by my talk. Ó Mordha said, 'Oh no, you are quite wrong, he told me about it and really enjoyed it. But you know he has motor neurone disease and it has completely immobilised his facial muscles.' That explained his frozen features, but I like to think that inside he was laughing away to himself.

I got to know the Cork writer Patricia Hutchins, who wrote the first biography of Joyce after his death, on which Ellman relied heavily. For the centenary in 1982 I had two gold medals struck, one for each of the two biographers. Patricia could be quite contrary and threw it back at me, saying, 'This bloody thing shows you how little you know about writers – a bit of money would have been a hell of a lot more practical.' But we remained friends and she showed me a remarkable document. She had gone to Switzerland to interview Carl Jung, who gave her a copy of his psychological profile of Joyce and his daughter Lucia. He said they were like two people in a river, but while Lucia was drowning James was diving.

Joyce was very wary of psychoanalysis. The wealthy

American Edith Rockefeller McCormack funded him and was keen that he be analysed by Freud, another of her stable of subsidised geniuses. But Joyce absolutely refused and their relationship broke down over it. He was right, of course: maybe he was mad, whatever that means, but who knows what would have happened if psychoanalysis had cured him? Perhaps he would have ended up as a bank clerk.

In the mid-1930s he wrote a series of letters in defence of his multifarious attempts to find a cure for Lucia's schizophrenia. No one with a human heart could fail to be touched by this obvious love of a parent for his damaged child and his urge to protect her at all costs, in a 1936 missive to Harriet Weaver.

> I am blamed by everybody for sacrificing that precious metal money to such an extent for such a purpose when it could be all done so cheaply and quietly by locking her up in an economical mental prison for the rest of her life.
>
> I will not do so as long as I see a single chance of hope for her recovery, nor blame her or punish her for the great crime she has committed in being a victim to one of the most elusive diseases known to man and unknown to medicine. And I imagine that if you were where she is and felt as she must you would perhaps feel some hope if you felt that you were neither abandoned nor forgotten.

The Irish Schizophrenia Society asked me to do a fundraiser for them around Bloomsday and wondered whether Joyce would have minded being associated with it. I told them that he would have been thrilled because of Lucia, a connection of which they weren't aware. And now, wonderfully, the day of awareness about schizophrenia is called Lucia Day in her honour.

If Beckett is the great Irish Protestant intellect, paring and constricting the human experience down to its very core as his later works become shorter and shorter, then Joyce is the great

Catholic mind, endlessly elaborating and decorating like the creator of a medieval manuscript. His whole life embodied the idea of a pilgrimage. He went into exile from Ireland, making a human, spiritual and at times animal connection with Nora Barnacle, disregarding all the social conventions of his time. He made his home in exotic places – the collapsing Austro-Hungarian Empire, the bohemian Paris of the 1920s, wartime Switzerland – challenging the whole establishment and setting up his own system of ethics and morality. And he let nothing – not world wars, millionaire heiresses, psychoanalysis, drunkenness, poverty, illness or blindness – deflect him from the joy of creation.

For his was indeed a heroic fight for artistic survival. Against all odds he constantly refused to do anything other than practise his vocation as a writer and as a forger of his country's conscience. And there was heroism in both. His single-minded devotion to his craft, his perseverance in the face of an almost universal lack of understanding or appreciation of his later work and the frequent attempts by fellow artists to divert him into more conventional ways, as well as his beloved daughter Lucia's descent into madness – nothing was allowed to derail him in his pursuit of the purity of his art.

Every morning he would go to his writing room, even when his eyes were so bad that he had to wear a white coat like a dentist to reflect the light on to the page. And there he would write in letters several inches high, carving out his masterpiece. And from time to time Nora would hear him laughing, indicative of his powerful spirit of defiance in the face of the inhumanity and the suffering around him.

Dubliners have an interesting relationship with Joyce. My friend and fellow Joycean Professor Morris Beja gave me a copy of a long-lost tape recording of a BBC programme made in 1951 to mark the tenth anniversary of Joyce's death. On that tape were the voices of Oliver St John Gogarty – the model for Buck

Mulligan – the publisher George Roberts, Joyce's brother Stanislaus and two of his sisters. Driving home I dropped into Arnotts, where I bought a new pair of shiny brown shoes, priced 37s. 6d. Fool that I was, I left the footwear and the tape on the back seat of the car and parked it outside my home. The next morning I emerged from the house to find the pavement lightly dusted with glass. The shoes were still there, but the tape was gone for ever. After the shock of loss, my first reaction was what a wonderful civilised city Dublin must be, where even car thieves would prefer a tape about an obscure writer to a pair of practical brogues.

CHAPTER 8

In Dublin Every Day is Bloomsday

I AM DELIGHTED THAT BLOOMSDAY IS THE NATIONAL LITERARY festival that it has become. It is the celebration of a book and a writer that have brought international recognition to our capital, and Joyce deserves to have one day a year when people can pay homage. He has put Dublin and Ireland on the global map in a way that many other countries envy. It wasn't always so, and I have been roundly criticised for my part in helping popularise both James Joyce and his special day. Some crabbed intellectuals have even accused me of 'vulgarising' Bloomsday.

Maria Jolas, a great friend and supporter of the writer, told me that once, when they were all discussing Bloomsday, Nora adopted an arch look and said, 'Sure that was the day I made a man out of Jim.'

James Joyce and Nora Barnacle first went out walking on the strand at Ringsend and Sandymount on the afternoon and early evening of Thursday, 16 June 1904. Nora's remark to Maria Jolas suggests that some form of sexual encounter took place that very evening. The specifics don't matter, because they really were in love.

They had no money, so there was no engagement, no exchange of rings and no official marriage until 1931, but James gave Nora the most wonderful wedding present of the twentieth century – the whole day enshrined for ever in the pages of *Ulysses*, which among other things was his tribute to his love for Nora.

Joyce himself celebrated Bloomsday in a typically raucous fashion at the Déjeuner Ulysse in 1929, marking twenty-five years since the day that he immortalised in *Ulysses*. It started as a very staid affair, with formal speeches, before things began to unravel in glorious fashion. The dinner was held in Les Vaux de Cernay, a village near Versailles, attended by about twenty supporters of the writer including Sylvia Beach, Adrienne Monnier and Samuel Beckett. Both Joyce and Beckett got totally paralytic, and on their way back to Paris they required several pit stops. Beckett was eventually abandoned in a public lavatory on the outskirts of Paris after he tested the charabanc driver's patience once too often.

Joyce and his friends continued to celebrate the day as a private joke, and dated letters with phrases such as 'Veille de la fête de la Madonne Bloom', which shows that he considered it was Molly's day as well as Leopold's. It is poignant to recall that, while in hospital for yet another eye operation, Joyce wrote in a notebook: 'Today 16 of June 1924 twenty years after. Will anybody remember this date?'

I had been wearing a straw boater for many years on 16 June. I concocted my own costume based on various elements of the book and photographs of Joyce himself taken on the beach in Torquay in the 1920s. The boater was taken from Blazes Boylan, the round dark spectacles from Joyce, a brocade waistcoat in honour of Buck Mulligan, plus blazer, white trousers, sailing plimsolls and an elegant cane. The costume evolved through the years and eventually became fixed. In its complete form it doesn't exist anywhere in *Ulysses*, but has now become the uniform for many Joyceans around the world on Bloomsday. I am immodestly pleased by my one international fashion statement!

Thus attired, I began my career as a performer of Joyce on Sandymount Strand in the 1960s. In those days Joyce was still in the air around the village, in an indefinable way. As children we played on the beach and saw the women with well-laden prams going into the Martello Tower to buy a kettle of boiling water for a penny to make tea. We walked our dogs along the strand that Gerty McDowell, Leopold Bloom, Cissy Caffrey and Edie Boardman still haunted.

As a student I would walk down to the seafront and read a piece from the Proteus or Nausicaa episode on Sandymount Strand, right at the place where the incidents had happened in the book. I thought there was a particular kind of sympathetic magic about performing in the places Joyce wrote about. And I would read in Gertie McDowell's simpering voice:

'The summer evening had begun to fold the world in its mysterious embrace. Far away in the west the sun was setting and the last glow of all too fleeting day lingered lovingly on sea and strand, on the proud promontory of dear old Howth guarding as ever the waters of the bay, on the weedgrown rocks along Sandymount shore and, last but not least, on the quiet church whence there streamed forth at times upon the stillness the voice of prayer to her who is in her pure radiance a beacon ever to the stormtossed heart of man, Mary, star of the sea.'

And to read it in full view of the actual Star of the Sea Church, and with Howth away in the distance and the pink blush of sunset on the sand, was magical. I was doing it purely as an act of homage and for my own enjoyment, but because Dubliners like eccentricity, small groups of people would gather around, and they would applaud.

The Americans were great supporters of Joyce through the years when he was anathema in Ireland, and many would visit Dublin around Bloomsday. The Irish newspapers had a field day with such frivolity, and savagely lampooned the likes of Professor Bernard Benstock, Tom Staley and Florence Walzl – a lovely lady who was an authority on *Dubliners* and who wandered around Ballsbridge trying to find where the 'Dublin by Lamplight laundry' had been. Across the Atlantic there were several Bloomsday celebrations in places such as the Gotham Book Mart in Manhattan. Ernest Hemingway, T. S. Eliot and Joyceans such as John Quinn frequented the place. They held readings at Gotham from the early 1950s, at which people like Joyce's old college friend Padraic Colum would read from the works. The owner of that celebrated bookshop, Frances Steloff, invited me to her 101st birthday party in 1987 at two days' notice – I think she thought I was part of the jet set and could drop everything to fly across the Atlantic!

The first Irish celebration was held in 1954, thirteen years after Joyce's death, in the wake of early moves to set up a Dublin Joyce Society. It is hard for people nowadays to imagine how courageous it was to be a supporter of Joyce then – he was the Antichrist to many in Irish society, including some of his own relatives, and his writings were widely condemned. I salute and cherish the courage shown by those people who spat in the eye of the establishment.

A group of literary bohemians including Tony Cronin, Myles na Gopaleen, Patrick Kavanagh and John Ryan resolved to mark the jubilee of the first Bloomsday. About twenty of them met up at the home of the celebrated architect Michael Scott, close to the tower in Sandycove where *Ulysses* opens.

They were all allotted roles parallel to those in the book, with Cronin acting as Stephen Dedalus while A. J. Leventhal, the registrar of Trinity – being the only Jew – stood in for Bloom. Myles was drunk before they started, and the day turned into an almighty booze-up. There was a plan to travel round the city through the day in horse-drawn carriages, visiting the scenes of the novel and ending in what Joyce called Nighttown, which had once been the brothel quarter of the city, but they stopped at so many pubs on the way that when they reached The Bailey in Duke Street, owned by John Ryan, their odyssey ended and the evening collapsed in a stew of inebriation and rancour.

John Ryan was the most charming, cultivated man you could

meet. He was a generous and kind benefactor of many artists and writers, and an excellent watercolour painter himself. John had a rackety life; he inherited a substantial amount of money through his family business, Monument Creameries, but the money was frittered away. He also founded the magazine *Envoy* and regularly broadcast on literary topics on RTÉ. He was totally lacking in literary jealousy and very generously handed on the Joycean torch that he and the others had kindled to my relatively young hands.

John showed me a film he made of that boozy Bloomsday, which demonstrated that, like the Déjeuner Ulysse, there was some controversy about their pit stops for bladder relief. He filmed Paddy Kavanagh and Myles na Gopaleen urinating up against a wall at Sandymount Strand, but when someone calls out to Kavanagh he turns and diverts his stream over Myles. So for anyone to tell me that I vulgarised Bloomsday . . .

There was nothing organised in Dublin for 16 June 1962, until the filmmaker John Huston made a generous donation so that the tower in Sandycove could open as a James Joyce museum. I was just seventeen years old and remained on the fringes of that Bloomsday, but I recall some of the distinguished visitors, including two of Joyce's sisters, Eileen Schaurek and May Monaghan. They were funny little women: both wore very respectable middle-class ladies' hats and their presence contributed to the special historic atmosphere.

Sylvia Beach, who published the first edition of *Ulysses* in 1922, came over from Paris for the opening, which took place four months before she died. That day she climbed up the rickety iron staircase which ran along the outside of the tower, and there was some concern that this dainty, bird-like woman might fall off. She raised a flag and complained that she never got any credit for inventing the name of 'Bloomsday'.

That was the year of the first Joyce Symposium too, at the Gresham Hotel, at which most of the speakers were American. I wasn't an official attendee, but managed to slither in at the back of the room. The organisers were a pair of American academics, Bernard Benstock and Tom Staley, and a Swiss photographer, Fritz Senn, who has probably the most encyclopaedic knowledge of Joyce of anyone on the planet. It is greatly to the credit of this small group that they kept Joyce's reputation alive when he was being so traduced in his homeland.

With just a series of speakers and a dinner, the Symposium wasn't the big event it is these days, and it wasn't much better two years later either, when the second Symposium was held in the Moyne Institute in Trinity overlooking College Park. The poet and lecturer Brendan Kennelly was one of the speakers, but apart from that there was little local interest in the event, and no Irish academics displayed any great passion for the writer. It was left to those who loved the works, such as John Ryan and Gerry O'Flaherty, to act as keepers of the flame. It was there that I first met Frank Budgen, a Cornish sculptor who was a great friend of Joyce in Zurich. I got on well with Frank, and liked him a lot, because he asked the important questions which sent the academics into a tizzy, always an entertaining sight.

He told the assembly: 'Talking with Joyce, I often wondered what his view was on whether the human spirit survived after death. I think this is the key to *Finnegans Wake*. Do you have any comments?' Frank's question was greeted with absolute silence. The academics were afraid of the question because it was a *human* question, but to my mind Budgen was 100 per cent right – this is the central question not only of *Finnegans Wake* but of life itself.

The Symposia were enormous fun. I travelled to Trieste in 1971, where I was virtually the only person from Ireland apart from a splendidly mischievous Cork man, Paddy Long of the Tourist Board. The organisers had invited the mayors of Trieste, Zurich, Paris and Dublin, and all except those from the author's native city turned up or sent officials. Joyce's niece Bozena

Delimata, daughter of his sister Eileen, suddenly materialised, in typical Joycean fashion quite penniless, and the hat had to be passed around to come up with her fare home. She had a great look of the writer, with her penetrating blue eyes, malicious wit and great sense of humour. She and I got on like a house on fire.

I always enjoyed visiting the cities associated with Joyce. In Trieste I went out to the Castle of Miramare, which James and Nora always regarded as a classic Triestean landmark, and to the opera house they attended. I went to the Orthodox Cathedral of St Spiridion to listen to a wonderful choir perform Russian liturgical music by Bortniansky and Tchaikovsky through clouds of incense. And it was there I discovered the solution to one of the many small but knotty problems in *Ulysses*.

In the Lotus Eaters episode, Leopold Bloom is in the Westland Row church watching the celebration of a morning Mass. He uses an irreverent phrase in describing the priest distributing the communion host: 'Hokypoky penny a lump', a completely inappropriate image for the Irish Catholic ritual, in which a thin wafer is used. But it was a completely appropriate image for the church Joyce was frequenting for aesthetic rather than religious reasons when he wrote that passage, the Cathedral of St Spiridion. I slowly realised this as I watched the priest come out to distribute communion with a big crusty loaf under his oxter, plucking a chunk off and handing it to each communicant. It was a lovely and appropriate moment of epiphany as I suddenly understood where Joyce got the idea for the 'lump'.

After one of the workshops in Trieste, at which I had spoken about *Finnegans Wake*, a woman came up to me and asked: 'You are Mr Norris from Dublin?'

'Yes.'

'I so much enjoyed your reading,' she said. 'It was very beautiful; when I closed my eyes you sounded just like Mr Joyce himself, except the rrrrrrrrrr.'

I must have looked puzzled.

'When Joyce read, he would roll the Rs,' she explained, introducing herself as Carola Giedion-Welcker, a friend of Joyce's from Zurich who had commissioned the sculptor Paul Speck to make his death mask in 1941.

Carola and I became close friends, and when she came to Dublin for a subsequent Bloomsday I gave her a little improvised Joycean tour. We went to Westland Row to buy a bar of lemon soap in Sweny's Chemist, just as Bloom does in the Calypso episode of *Ulysses*. She immediately understood the significance and said she never accepted a gift without giving one herself. With that she reached into her handbag and brought out an original photograph of herself and Joyce in Zurich in the 1930s. The back of the photo was signed by the two of them, and to my eternal regret I lent it to the *Irish Times* in 1982 when they were producing a supplement for the centenary. Not only did they fail to acknowledge the source of the photograph, but despite my asking them to treat it with care someone drew the printer's instructions through the signatures.

In 1975 I went to the Paris Symposium, which was run by Maria Jolas – a wonderful woman but sadly her committee made a complete bags of it. The Symposium was held in a converted shed in the Marais district of the city, and the enormous interior was partitioned by dropping a series of hessian curtains from the ceiling. The result was a Tower of Babel – as each of the papers was delivered you could hear fragments of the next one along, and when applause or laughter broke out in one it interrupted the discussions in the other.

I had been particularly looking forward to a slide show to be given by Giselle Freund, who took the famous photographs of Joyce for *Time* magazine in 1938. She took hundreds of photographs, including some very unusual pictures of him playing in the garden with Giorgio's dog. What made them extraordinary was that he was terrified of the animals, having been bitten by a dog when he was a child. The Paris Symposium organisers produced a projector for her to show them, but the slide carousel got stuck and resolutely refused to work – so to our great chagrin, and despite the Herculean efforts of a large number of technically incompetent Joycean scholars, we never did get to see Ms Freund's photos.

There was no hospitality at all at that Symposium, let alone a Bloomsday banquet. It was terrible, a missed opportunity as Joyce was well known at places like Fouquet's on the Champs-Elysées where, at that time, there was still an old waiter who remembered his visits. It was too much for me and I kicked up a fuss, pointing out that although it was the most expensive Symposium to date, we hadn't been given as much as a cocktail sausage.

'Well, if you think you can do it any better,' they told me, 'do it yourself.'

'Right,' I said, 'I will bring it back to Dublin.'

And I did.

Having been awarded the dubious distinction of organising the 1977 Symposium, I approached some of those involved in the early Dublin Symposia for help and advice. They wouldn't have anything to do with it: 'I'm not getting mixed up with that bunch again,' one of them told me. 'Those Americans would do you brain damage.'

I was soon to discover why. The clique who ran the international organisation had an infuriating tactic. Their technique was to set up a local committee who would do all the work on the ground and then, about three months out from the event, the unfortunate locals who had worked their arses off doing all the organisational drudgery would start to get letters and telegrams undermining them and the work they had done. The local committee would then resign, or dissolve in tears, and 'the permanent government' would step off the plane and take all the credit. They met tougher stuff in me. The American Bernard Benstock was the prime operator of that policy – he once sent around satirical minutes of our Dublin Joyce committee which suggested we were all drunk and talked in broad Oirish brogues. It was very funny, but certainly didn't help to foster cordial transatlantic relations.

I put together a committee which included the writers Seán White, John Ryan, Benedict Kiely and Ulick O'Connor. I wrote to UCD, successor to the old Royal University founded by Cardinal Newman where Joyce was a student, and asked them to put someone on the committee; but they weren't very interested in Joyce at the time. It seemed to me that Joyce was for all and his *alma mater* had a very good case to be centrally included.

True to the warnings, there was a late bid to undermine the committee. The issue they picked on was my insistence that I co-chair the Symposium, co-editing the proceedings, and that these be co-published in Ireland. I was adamant that the event enjoy the full participation of Irish writers, academics and intellectuals. The American academics were distinctly unamused and pointed out, with some justification, that they had kept the flame alive when Joyce was very unpopular in Dublin. They threatened to relocate the Symposium to Trieste, so I wrote back to Professor Benstock and thanked him for his note along the following lines:

I see with interest you propose spending Bloomsday in Trieste. I'm sure you'll enjoy that lovely city, but you may find yourself starved of Joycean company, as I now have 450 people registered – and I have their deposits. I imagine that Joyceans, being immensely practical people, will not want to forfeit their sizeable initial investment, because I won't be making any arrangements to transfer anything to Trieste. Perhaps you could let me know your final decision.

That ended all that nonsense, and they all duly arrived to spend Bloomsday in Dublin. We held a magnificent banquet, and I managed to excavate some fascinating characters with living, organic connections to Joyce. We invited Arthur Power, the painter who knew Joyce in Paris and shared an apartment with Modigliani, as well as Lennie Collinge, who had been the projectionist at the Volta Cinema, which was operated by James Joyce. Lennie, who was almost ninety years old, was learning Norwegian at the time to better understand *Finnegans Wake*. He was a most interesting man who remembered Joyce well. He told me: 'Poor Mr Joyce was a gentleman, he wasn't up to those Eye-talian electricians at all; they ran rings around him.' Lennie was convinced that the Italians were diddling Joyce, but in fact it was Joyce who was quite capable of diddling them, and his Italian investors had sent the workmen over to keep an eye on him.

Another significant figure we invited was Maria Jolas, originally from Louisville, Kentucky, but a great friend of Joyce in Paris. We had arranged for two Irish singers, Bill Golding and Anne Makower, to perform an entertainment at the banquet in the Dining Hall in Trinity during the coffee breaks. They sang songs associated with *Ulysses*, among them 'Love's Old Sweet Song' ('Just a song at twilight . . .'), but during the performance some of the academics started to titter and make disparaging remarks about Joyce's musical taste. Maria, who was sitting next to me, was livid. The sturdy white-haired old lady stood up, banged the table with her stick, and in a voice trembling with emotion said, 'You will not insult this beautiful music which Mr Joyce and I sang so often with pleasure in Paris in the 1930s. You will sing it again, and you will listen with due respect to the music he loved.' She led the singing herself, hand in hand with Anne Makower, and cowed the lot of them, with the result that the Joycean yellow-bellies did a U-turn and adopted it as the Joycean anthem, and it is now played to death at conferences and Bloomsday celebrations around the world.

*

The strain of running the Symposia was enormous – and they had never before made money – but in 1977 we made a profit of £800, which made the international symposiasts' eyes light up. They left £100 behind for the committee to have a party and took possession of the rest. But when Dublin was awarded the Centenary Symposium, I wasn't going to stand for mere crumbs from the table. I told the organisers that whatever profits were made in 1982 must be left behind for a permanent centre in Dublin which would celebrate the life and works of Joyce. What I had in mind, of course, was the James Joyce Cultural Centre in North Great Georges Street. There was a long debate but they eventually agreed and I set about organising a second Symposium.

Gus Martin of UCD and I sought and received sponsorship from, among others, American Express and Baileys Irish Cream. I recruited the poet and critic Anthony Cronin for the organising committee, but as I was a bit politically naïve at the time I didn't know that he was employed by the Taoiseach, Charles Haughey, as his cultural and artistic adviser. Tony had an office in Government Buildings right next door to Charlie, and when I rang him to ask for money for the Symposium, he asked me to hang on for a minute. When he returned he said, 'The man says we can have ten grand. You can do what you want with it, but he says you can then fuck off because you're not getting anything more.'

It was the first occasion anyone had been able to persuade Official Ireland to approve of the writer, and in many ways was the start of the indigenous Joyce industry. President Patrick Hillery came to open the event, which was quite a big deal because he was being associated with two people with questionable backgrounds – Mr Joyce and Mr Norris. But he came and greeted me warmly and sat beside me on the platform, although there was an undignified scuffle when a bigwig tried to muscle in and take one of the small number of seats on the platform, which meant the President's aide-de-camp had to stand.

Mr Haughey's subvention meant we could afford to invite distinguished literary figures from around the world such as the novelists Chinua Achebe, Jorge Luis Borges and Anthony Burgess, and the TV playwright Dennis Potter, with whom I became particularly friendly. The one disappointment was that Samuel Beckett was unable to travel. I wrote to him as chairman, and we received a beautiful reply, in scratchy hen's writing in black ink. He explained why he couldn't come, before closing with *I welcome this occasion to bow once again before I go, deep down, before his heroic work, heroic being.*

Some months before the centenary of Bloomsday in 2004, the Canadian critic Hugh Kenner had written to me and pointed out that while blue plaques had been erected all over Dublin in the places where Joyce lived, perhaps it was now time to mark the birthplace of Leopold Bloom. Hugh had worked out where he had been born, in a house on Clanbrassil Street in the south inner city. I thought that was a great idea, so we spoke to the old lady who lived there. She was amenable, I enlisted Dublin Tourism to make a plaque, and we invited Richard Ellman and Hugh Kenner to jointly perform the unveiling ceremony.

We all assembled at midday on 16 June in the front garden of this house where the great fictional hero was born. Hugh and Dick were just pulling the ribbon to unveil the plaque when I got a tap on the shoulder from this oul' lad, who was wheezily dismounting his bicycle.

'Excuse me,' he said, 'would you be Mr Norris, by any chance?'

'I do indeed have that signal honour,' I replied in my most freezing tone. 'Can I be of assistance to you?'

'Well, the boot is on the other foot now, sir, because I can be of assistance to *you* . . . I'm afraid I have a bit of bad news for you.' (That by the way is the defining characteristic of the Dubliner – the possession and the delighted delivery of the 'bad news'.) 'Well, youse are all scholars and professors, and don't get me wrong, I have the utmost regard for book learning. But what youse lack is what I do call the Local Knowledge.

'I've been around here all me life, and what you don't understand is that there are two Clanbrassil Streets, Upper and Lower. You're currently standing in Upper. There was never Jews in Upper Clanbrassil Street. Never! The Jews were all down there in Lower Clanbrassil Street. I didn't know Mr Leopold Bloom well myself, but I often seen him.

'There's something peculiar about them Jews – they aren't allowed to light their own fires of a Saturday. But Bloom was up to that dodge. Do you know what he used to do? He used to get my sister to go in and light the fire for his mother, and he'd give her a sixpence.

'You can say what you like about old Bloom, but he was very good to his old ma.'

I told him to get straight back to the hob of hell or wherever else he had emerged from, but when I got home that evening and opened the newspaper our shame was there for all to see: JOYCEANS GET THE WRONG HOUSE!

That is perhaps the greatest tribute that could ever be paid to Joyce – that this little old joxer, who had almost certainly never read *Ulysses*, was completely convinced that he had seen Leopold Bloom walk the streets of Dublin city. One of the dignitaries who was not there was Anthony Burgess, but I told him the story over a drink that night. Some time later I was horrified to see him on British television, retelling the story with himself as the centrepiece. But worst of all he got the punchline wrong, which seemed unforgivable at the time.

I ran the Symposium once more, in 1992, and remain as far as I know the only person to have organised three of these Joycean extravaganzas. It was an enormous logistical undertaking, booking hotels and venues, organising the academic side, and giving papers and performances myself. I don't go to them any more: I had attended every Symposium up to 1984, when I was forced to miss the Frankfurt event. It was as if I had 'collected' them: once my run was broken, I didn't feel any compulsion to attend any more.

What happened was that there were elements in the Trinity English Department that resented the fact that I had such a varied and public life, and attempts were made to 'put me in my box'. A departmental meeting was organised to deal with final examination results, and they insisted that I attend. I explained that I desperately wanted to attend the Frankfurt Symposium as it was to deal with the critical and synoptic edition, which was hugely controversial in Joycean circles at the time. I wasn't going on a golfing trip; I was going to the most important scholarly meeting in my subject. I had already submitted the marks, and all the Trinity meeting was concerned with was students on the borderline. I had already written up notes on each exam paper, and promised to be available on the telephone throughout the meeting. But they insisted on my physical presence and I had to stay in Dublin.

I should have told them to get lost, because someone told me afterwards that this was officialdom's attempt to clip Norris's wings. But as they discovered, they can clip away. I just grow new feathers.

Ending my run of Symposia was a blessing, however, because I wasn't enjoying them as much as I had. The papers were getting more abstract and dealing with notions such as post-structuralism and deconstruction. Some of the papers contained valuable insights, but most were complete drivel, a case of the emperor's new clothes.

I particularly hated all that nonsense about psychoanalysis that people such as Jacques Lacan tried to bring to the study of Joyce. I found him an appallingly dull old fraud. It was just an attempt to make the critic more important than the artist. The debate went on for several years, until it got to the point where Lacan, Derrida, Foucault and their acolytes were actually asserting that Joyce was not in control of meaning in his work, that the meaning was entirely resident in the imagination of the reader.

It all came to a head at a James Joyce conference at Coral Gables in Florida in 1989. Somebody gave a paper on what he called 'the intentionality of the text', which was too much for me. I became more and more annoyed at the discussion before finally I stood and addressed the attendance from the back of the hall.

'Thank you very much, ladies and gentlemen,' I began. 'You have been very kind to invite me here to Coral Gables, which is indeed a lovely place. I now propose to enjoy it all the more, although I am clearly unfit to share your exalted company. I've been listening here all morning to you suggesting that James Joyce was not in control of meaning, and that meaning was unstable in his works. And now I'm confronted with what you call "the intentionality of the text": that an inert piece of paper was capable of something that Joyce was not. This is a sophisticated notion far beyond my comprehension. I come from a strange little green island called Ireland that also produced Mr James Joyce, whose inadequacies you are now exposing. But just so you know you have not entirely wasted your hospitality; although I am not fit to share your company, I *do* enjoy sunbathing. And I now propose to go outside and sunbathe.'

And with that I left, taking my clothes off as I went back up the aisle, and I sat on a grassy knoll in my underpants, enjoying the warm Florida sun.

In recent years I have spent Bloomsday in Dublin, and watched it grow into an important festival that brings tourists and academics alike to the city of Joyce. Dubliners have grown to love the day, and I enjoy meeting old friends who come to pay homage to the writer. As Brendan Behan once said, 'In Dublin every day is Bloomsday.'

Forty years ago I tried to persuade Bord Fáilte, the Irish

tourist authority, that there was enormous potential in Bloomsday, that it could become an Irish Mardi Gras. At the time it was only marked privately by devotees, and they were very slow to wake up to it, but now there is plenty to engage the visitor who wishes to pay homage to the great writer.

In 1982 I enlisted the Horizon Theatre Company to re-enact the Wandering Rocks episode in costume, and we filmed the event. Some of the visiting scholars, such as Clive Hart, took part, and the citizens of Dublin were our unpaid extras. The costume idea took hold and now hundreds of people dress up in bowler hats and petticoats for the day, which always begins with a breakfast in the Joyce Centre or the Gresham Hotel and various locations across the city, including the Martello tower itself. For the centenary of Joyce's birth in 1982 we organised a free breakfast for ten thousand members of the public in the middle of O'Connell Street, which was closed for the event. One typical Dubliner was offended when told that, although it was free, she had to have a ticket. 'Youse can keep your shagging sausages. Do youse think I'm going to queue for James fuckin' Joyce?'

But the breakfast or the parade of Molly Blooms does not prevent the purists amusing themselves in their own way. There will still be the Joyce Symposium ringing with intellectual debate. I don't see any conflict between scholarship and fun – the Bloomsday celebrations have brought Joyce out of an ivory Martello tower.

While Bloomsday is a day for performing, I did have one private ritual which is now sadly gone for ever. After breakfasting on the inner organs of beasts and fowl, Ken Monaghan and I used to go off to the Cobalt Café across the street from the Joyce Centre for a quiet chuckle and our own satirical take on all the nonsense that was going on and what his uncle would have made of it. Bob Joyce and his wife Joyce would sometimes join us too, and it became a family event.

I dearly miss Ken, who became a great friend through all the years we worked on the Joyce Centre. He devised a marvellous walking tour of the north inner city which he gave every Bloomsday, and often gave a poignant talk on 'Joyce's Dublin family' which was published on his eightieth birthday in 2005. Ken, who died in 2010, was a great supporter of the writer, but less so of the man.

I am usually invited to read a passage from the book somewhere during the day, which I always enjoy. I don the boater and open the magical book, which throws me back to those warm summer evenings around Sandymount and a time, and a world, long departed.

CHAPTER 9

It's Showtime!

WHO COULD HAVE PREDICTED THAT THE SUPPOSEDLY ÉLITIST and impenetrable works of Joyce would provide the backdrop for a glorious tilt at showbiz, and a stage show that drew full houses from Rio to Beirut and Sligo to Sydney?

It all started in Trinity, and the Philosophical Society paper 'James Joyce: The Art of Chaos' that won me a gold medal in 1965. Part of the paper involved me reading excerpts aloud, which I did in various Dublin accents in a dramatic style. Anthony Burgess was the guest of honour and I had the pleasure of taking him to dinner before the event. The paper was very well received, and put the germ of an idea in my head. I assembled a selection of suitable passages and dressed in costume for a solo show in the Graduates Memorial Building. People came up to me afterwards saying what great acting ability I had shown and how I had encapsulated Joyce with the angle of my chin and turn of phrase, and how 'you would almost swear you, too, were blind'. But it wasn't acting at all – the man who did the lighting forgot to put filters in the lights and I *was* blind because the naked light bulbs ensured I couldn't see a bloody thing.

For Bloomsday 1968 I teamed up with Ronnie Drew, who I knew from Greystones. Ronnie was a big star because of his work with The Dubliners, and it was quite a coup to get him to join me on stage at the Players Theatre in Trinity. Ronnie had a unique voice, like a gravel pit in the Dublin Mountains bursting into song, but he suffered terribly from stage-fright and he almost had to be locked in his dressing room by his wife Deirdre before the show.

My performance of passages from Joyce was interspersed with Ronnie's wonderful rendition of Dublin street ballads. We almost came to blows over who would perform the opening – Joyce's satirical broadside 'Gas from a Burner' which both of us loved – but I prevailed. The stage was already set as the interior of a Dublin pub for another production so we just made some technical adjustments to turn it into a functioning bar. The Bailey pub provided stout and oysters, which were served from the stage in the interval, and the whole evening was a roaring success.

The idea lay dormant for some years until Michael O'Toole came to do the Anglo-Irish Literature diploma course as a mature student. Michael was a prominent journalist who wrote the Dubliner's Diary page in the *Evening Press* for years. We became firm friends. Michael suggested that I turn my lectures into a one-man show. He had been asked to organise a speaker for an Irish Countrywomen's Association fundraiser down the country, and he reckoned that if I could sell Joyce to that audience I could sell it anywhere. I didn't temper it any way, giving them the whole unexpurgated experience – and they loved it. Michael told me I was sitting on a goldmine.

He was right. I never made much money out of it, but it did take me all over the world. I performed it for many charities, raising funds for, among others, sufferers from arthritis, kidney disease and AIDS, and organisations supporting the homeless and victims of domestic abuse. I was a regular on the circuit and, thanks to Brendan Enright in the Westbury, Jimmy Dixon in the Shelbourne as well as the splendid Norah Lucey, one of the few people I have encountered either in theatrical or political life who is capable of delivering proper PR, the show could be relied upon to fill the ballrooms of any of the biggest hotels in Dublin.

The success of the fundraising also made me feel that I was having an impact in a direct way. One show helped to transform the life of a whole family, which was wonderful. Through Michael O'Toole and Aer Lingus I came across the story of a remarkable American woman who lived in Galway. She had been in an automobile smash in America in which her husband and children had all been killed. She came to Ireland to start a new life and began to foster children, most of whom had a disability of some kind. Out of her own tragedy she was able to give hope and help to more than twenty children, almost all of whom were able to leave the nest when the time came. Two of the foster children, however, had very serious problems and remained at home with her. There was P.P., a tiny, intelligent young man, who had a horrible disease which saw his bone structure shrink remorselessly, and his adopted sister, who had both spina bifida and Down's syndrome.

Aer Lingus adopted 'P.P.'s Wheel Appeal' to try to raise funds to help the family. I've always found that if it is a good cause lots of people are happy to offer help. The staff of the airline became involved too, and we secured the ballroom in Jury's Hotel free of charge from P. V. Doyle. Aer Lingus donated some splendid prizes, including two first-class transatlantic tickets, and we squeezed seven hundred people into Jury's for the show and auction. In that one night we raised enough to buy a specially adapted van. I thought it was marvellous that Joyce could be used to release the little trio who had hitherto been rendered captive by illness.

The next logical step was to raise funds for the Joyce Centre, the renovation of which was eating up money. There was a lot of interest in the United States, so we set up a tour, which proved to be an enormous success. We sold out a show on Broadway, at the 1,100-seater Symphony Space, but I was nearly late for the dress rehearsal because, I discovered, it is impossible to get a New York cab when it's raining. All Bob Joyce's efforts to flag down taxis failed so we decided to jump on the subway where, even in that extraordinary milieu, my stage costume of straw boater, dark glasses and elegant stick – which I had worn because I had also to carry a full costume change, make-up set, etc. – caused raised eyebrows.

I arrived in the nick of time, had a quick shower and, just pausing to put on a bathrobe, went out to the stage to do a sound and light check. We had just started when this officious squirt came into the auditorium and bawled, 'Clear the stage – I'm opening the doors to my public!'

I ignored him and went on with my sound check, and he came back in again and roared, 'Did you hear me? Clear the stage!'

I had had enough, so gave it back to him with gusto: 'Come here, you, let me tell you a few things. First, it's MY public, and second, you can let them in whenever you like.' And with that I opened my bathrobe, tossed it aside and stood there on stage bollock-naked to complete the sound check. And of course he couldn't let anyone in until I was finished. When I was satisfied all was ready I put back on the bathrobe and turned to him, saying, 'You may NOW admit MY public.'

Another night in New York we held an art exhibition before the show, but that dragged on and the show was delayed. The lights in my tiny dressing room failed and I was getting more and more stressed by the situation when the stage manager came in to say it was past the starting time. I told him my woes, to which he replied, 'I don't care, bud, this is New York City, the curtains fall at ten sharp.' I had to rush the show, and edit chunks from it as I went along. I was livid afterwards so Ken Monaghan and I decided to shun the first-night party and walk back to the Fitzpatrick Hotel.

We were crossing one of the seedy Manhattan side streets when a mugger grabbed Ken and said, 'Give me a twenny.' Ken only had two dollars, which he handed over, so then the man turned to me and demanded a twenty once more, screaming, 'Come on, come on, do you know what kind of day I've had?'

Something snapped and I came back with equal force.

'*Your* day! Do you know what kind of day *I've* had, you little shit? *I'm* an artist. I've had problems with make-up, and lighting, and the stage hands, and the audience turning up late and drunk. And YOU tell ME you've had a bad day!'

He stared at me for a second, wild-eyed, and then took off and ran!

Ken and I just sat down on the kerb and laughed.

While in New York I also took part in a variety show to raise funds for Irish cultural purposes. All the great and good were there, including Katharine Hepburn and Mia Farrow. Hepburn was there with her niece, and both were fascinated by Joyce, so Bob Joyce and I had a great conversation with them. At the end of the show Jim Sheridan said to me, 'David, will you take Mia round to Sardi's?' The stage door was opened for us and I emerged in full Joycean rig-out with boater, dark glasses and elegant cane, with Mia Farrow on my arm. The press corps was there and the flashbulbs popped, with journalists shouting, 'Who's the guy, Mia?' and 'Is there a new man in your life?' I was absolutely thrilled and scoured the next day's papers, but no photo had appeared. They had obviously discovered I was nobody of consequence.

As a result of the Joyce show I started getting requests to appear on TV and radio, which led to invitations to do after-dinner speeches for corporate entertainment. Thanks to my Rosie Probert syndrome – she was the character in *Under Milk Wood* who 'couldn't say no, even to midgets' – I accepted, and found I was doing a lot of entertainments for commercial bodies, which was taking up increasing amounts of my time. Miriam Smith, my valiant and loyal PA, suggested the only way to stop them was to charge them. So we set an exorbitant fee. To my astonishment they agreed, and I started getting contacted by agents. That helped with the restoration of my homes in North Great Georges Street and later in Cyprus, but the sting in the tail was that, as I try meticulously to record everything, I was hit with a big tax bill at the end of the year. By which time I had invariably spent the lot and had to borrow again.

Terry Wogan asked me to do my after-dinner entertainment for the Variety Club in the Savoy Hotel in London, and they would donate £5,000 to my favourite charity. There was a bit of anti-Irish feeling in Britain at the time, and to cap things off I was disconcerted by all the Paddy jokes at the pre-dinner reception. I started off speaking Irish as a deliberate gag which is one of my tricks, but the minute I started, this fellow sitting opposite took umbrage and then started muttering, 'Bloody Irish, coming over here, bloody IRA . . .' It was Denis Thatcher, consort of the prime minister of the day, and he turned the room against me. I unwound under the hostility and abandoned my efforts after eight minutes instead of the usual half an hour. Many of my heroes, like the Two Ronnies, were there and it was a truly grim and humiliating experience. However, I learnt something as a result: when you die on stage the corpse starts to stink immediately, and instead of coming over to the table to congratulate me, all the celebs made elaborate detours so they wouldn't have to confront me. All, that is, except Ned Sherrin, who with great kindness said, 'Don't worry, old boy, it's not your fault, you weren't quite what they were expecting. Your line was too sophisticated because your stories depended on elaboration. But what they wanted was the kind of classic English boom-boom one-liners in the manner of seaside post-cards, and they didn't know what to make of you.'

I went home crushed, but decided to turn this difficulty to my advantage. As I was still writing for the *Evening Herald* I penned my column that week on how I made a complete ass of myself in London, describing the circumstances of the dinner in a fairly heightened form. It was one of the most popular pieces I ever wrote, revealing to me that the public do quite like to see somebody up there taking a toss from time to time. People came up to me for weeks afterwards to say, 'That was the funniest piece you ever wrote. You made a right bollix of yourself in front of the English. I laughed till I cried.'

About six months later I was asked again to go to London, this time to propose a toast and tell some stories at a big dinner in the Palace of Whitehall. The first thing I saw when I arrived was a table of ten hosted by Terry Wogan, and I thought, *Oh God, it's going to happen all over again.*

The main speaker was the extremely popular Labour minister Mo Mowlam, but this time I found my wings and just took off. Having confessed my earlier failure, I think I am now allowed to say that I brought the room to its feet. A few days later there was a little article in one of the London papers saying that some unknown Irish politician had stolen the show and upstaged Mo Mowlam. I was delighted because it restored my confidence.

I loved doing the show, and had opportunities to perform it all over the world, which I did for the price of an airfare and a hotel. I did it in Rio de Janeiro, Buenos Aires, Sydney, Beijing, Paris, Geneva, London and all over the United States. In 1982 I was running the Symposium so couldn't take any Bloomsday invitations to foreign parts, but there was another cluster of events around Joyce's actual birthday on 2 February. I wanted to see Ezra so I took the sheaf of invites and plotted their origins on a big map of the world, and found that the nearest to Jerusalem was Beirut.

All the international Joyce community were invited but there was a civil war going on and there had been tensions along Lebanon's border with Israel since the previous summer. Three days before Joyce's birthday, the US Secretary of State, Alexander Haig, told President Ronald Reagan that Israel might, at any moment, invade Lebanon. The result was that only Gus Martin and I turned up. An old friend of mine, Suheil Bushrui of the American University in Beirut, was launching

Al-Dubliniyunn, his Arabic translation of *Dubliners*. We were the only guests in the Mayflower Hotel, so we had about eight people serving us breakfast every morning. There was an air of unreality to the trip, with Gus and myself looking out the windows at the bullets whizzing overhead.

I was performing my show in the concert hall of the American University when there was an almighty bang and all the lights went out. It turned out that a mortar had exploded near the building. I had the best sound effects of my life as it coincided with a moment when I was saying, 'And one moment tarabooming great blunderguns (poh!)'. I didn't know where to run, and was terrified I'd fall off the stage and literally break a leg, so I just kept going with the performance in the pitch darkness. After a while the lights came back up and the rest of the show passed without incident. At the end Suheil came rushing across the stage and embraced me, and presented me with a silk Charvet tie. He congratulated me on what he called 'a tour de force', and pointed out how the audience appreciated the show even though 85 per cent of them didn't have a word of English!

I went on that trip on the agreement that they would get me to Jerusalem afterwards, but because of the tensions on the border there were no transport links between the countries. I was advised the best route was via Amman in Jordan, but at the airport we were warned to duck down below the window on the bus out to the plane, so I wasn't convinced about its safety. My doubts weren't assuaged when the plane took off without warning as I was putting my bag on the rack, and then lifted practically vertically into the clouds.

After landing in Amman I went to book a ticket through to Israel, but was met with a quizzical look and the query, 'Where is that?' I told them it was next door, so then they said, 'Oh, perhaps you mean Palestine?' At that time, for Jordan, Israel didn't formally exist, and I was stranded for four days. I had to ring home to try to get a message out to Ezra, but the telephone line was bad and amid all the crackles I had to shout. The people in the office laughed like drains when they heard me saying, 'I'm stuck in Amman.'

'Really? All your Christmases must have come at once. But how is *he* feeling?'

I didn't get the *double entendre* immediately, but later in Jerusalem I was able to see the funny side.

When eventually arrangements were made, the Jordanians took me out to the Allenby Bridge, where they left me while they radioed the Israelis. It was like something out of John le Carré as I walked along the bridge towards the Israelis, who came out and picked me up. They opened my suitcase and came across some cassettes of what I thought was Arab music, which I had bought for Ezra in an Amman market, although since I had chosen them only by their covers they might easily have been the political speeches of George Habash. The soldier asked, 'Are you interested in this sort of material?' And I said, 'That's one of the things I admire so much about the Jewish people – their love of culture which transcends all boundaries.' That sorted that out, and I rang Ezra and spent a nice week in the YMCA in Jerusalem, seeing him during the day.

The biggest crowd I performed before was in a huge old Victorian theatre in Pittsburgh, where there were two thousand people, many of whom had been dragged there reluctantly by husbands and wives. The second half was largely composed of excerpts from *Finnegans Wake*, which most people regard as unreadable. I didn't mention that in the programme because I knew that if I did half the audience would stay in the bar after the interval, but within minutes the genius of Joyce had created a rapt audience. I revelled in the sense of electricity that performance brought me.

I also did the show, now called *Do You Hear What I'm Seeing?*, in the Everyman Palace Theatre in Cork for Gerald Goldberg, a former Lord Mayor of the city who wanted to raise money for the nursing home where his wife had been lovingly cared for in her final illness. We sold out all 650 seats and it went down so well that the manager of the theatre asked me to come back and do a week's run, which was the first commercial exploitation of the show. Over the years it has changed and it was drastically revised during the so-called window of opportunity of 1991–5.

In January 1991, fifty years after James Joyce's death, the copyright restrictions on the works were lifted. That meant that his estate could no longer prevent performance or quotation of the writings, or charge a royalty for doing so. However, four years later there was a harmonisation of laws throughout the European Union which had the effect of increasing copyright protection in Ireland from fifty years to seventy.

The result was that Joyce went back retrospectively into copyright, but I was able to prove that I had written and performed my show during that four-year window and so established copyright on that part of the works. I could do it wherever I wanted.

The last time I did the full show was in 2007, when I used it to raise funds for Ezra's charity to build a clean-water project in an impoverished village near Hebron in the West Bank. I got involved in that show from start to finish, which took four months of intense work to organise. I had immense help from Eddie Kenny, the indispensable Miriam Smith, and the James Joyce Centre. I wrote and helped design the programme, sold the advertising in it, and wrote to lots of wealthy businesspeople looking for contributions. The one person who really came through was the financier Dermot Desmond, who sent a cheque for €10,000. We had an auction too, to which various artists such as Louis le Brocquy, Aidan Bradley, Pauline Bewick, Patrick Scott, Anne Madden, Patrick Collins, Mick O'Dea, Mick Fitzharris and Willie Everson gave works. I had a well-known figure lined up to do the auction who pulled out at the last minute citing a commercial conflict. That meant that at the end of an exhausting two-hour show I had to do the auction myself. Some people said that it was even funnier than the show.

Nobody took a penny for their work, from the Clontarf Castle itself to volunteer front-of-house staff, and on that one night we raised €55,000. I paid for all the incidental expenses, postage, etc. myself, so that every single penny went directly to help suffering people. Our efforts put in clean water, helped to extend the school, installed a solar-power system and equipped the clinic.

Apart from my Joyce show I hadn't done much stage work since playing a newt in High School, but in 1993 I was asked to perform in *Side by Side by Sondheim*, a musical revue of Stephen Sondheim's songs, in Clontarf Castle. I had the part of the narrator, and we had a talented group of performers including Jim Doherty, Tony Kenny, Marian Duane and Joyce Teevan. I had to sing one song, 'Could I Leave You?', which I hated.

It was a cabaret venue, with dinner served before the show, and when the drink flowed it could be raucous. You had to keep your wits about you with the performers too. There was a door through which we all entered the stage, and where I would wait behind Tony, Joyce and Marian. The lights would come up and off they went to do the first number, closing the door behind them, and I would wait for my cue. On one particular night the three dashed off but I sensed something was up because their singing sounded nervous, and when I went to open the door I discovered why – Tony had pulled the handle off on his way out, and the door slammed behind him. I was trapped in a corridor with the only way out through the kitchen. Luckily there had been a Christmas function on during the day and they had a chimney rigged up for Santa Claus. With the spotlight on the door waiting for my entrance I came whizzing down the chimney on to the stage!

After the show transferred to the Olympia Theatre, my aunt became very ill. She was a very considerate woman who had never liked to disturb someone out of hours, but at six o'clock one morning she called me and asked me to ring for the doctor. It emerged that she had a tumour in her intestines. The doctors said they would not normally operate on someone in their nineties, but if they didn't in this case she would have exploded. She was on the operating table for five hours, during which I had to go on stage. People had paid money to see the show and I had to go on.

I was waiting for a telephone call, and would check every time I came off stage, and it eventually came at eleven o'clock to say the operation had been a success and the doctors were happy. When I called to visit her the next morning she was sitting up in bed demanding breakfast.

I took the role of narrator again for a show with Anne Bushnell which ran in the Helix Theatre and the National Concert Hall. It was a musical about Judy Garland, so I was required to sing and dance on one number, 'We're a Couple of Swells', despite the fact that I have no sense of rhythm and hate dancing. I always got the steps wrong, and as it was a high-kicking, arm-in-arm number, every night I got tangled up in Anne's legs and we ended up on the floor, to the consternation of the conductor, Proinnsias Ó Duinn. People got it into their heads that this was all a deliberate, sophisticated and funny piece of choreography and they came to expect it as one of the highlights of the show. But ironically when I got it right on the final night there was an audible sigh: the word had got around, and the audience was disgusted that we didn't take a tumble. One reviewer said, 'David Norris is the classic showbiz legend. Can't act, can't dance, can't sing, but he keeps the audience enthralled.'

In 1994 Kevin McHugh commissioned me to write a one-man play, *Oscar*, for the Dublin Theatre Festival. I wrote the play, with passages from the works of Oscar Wilde linked to the story of his life. I wanted other characters in it, but that wasn't possible so I added them with recorded voices. It started with

LEFT: Ezra as I first knew him.

BELOW: Ezra and I happily at ease in our djellabias.

Myself, Isaac and Nora's dog Louis in the snow, Troodos Mountains, Cyprus, 2008.

Two happy friends before the storm: Tevfik and myself in 2010.

ABOVE: First-ever Gay Pride march in Ireland, outside the Department of Justice in 1974.

ABOVE RIGHT: Ireland's first televised glimpse of a gay man on RTÉ's *Last House*, 1974, with Edmund Lynch (left), John McColgan and Áine O'Connor (both seated).

RIGHT: Trouble backstage. Myself, with Jim Sheridan on the right, and the cast of *Mister X* at the Project Theatre.

Gay politics. Just after presenting the foundation paper for the International Gay Association, Coventry, August 1978.

ABOVE: Love me, love my umbrella. Marshall of the Pride Parade, 2009.

ABOVE RIGHT: One of the crowd during a Gay Pride march, Parnell Square, 1990.

RIGHT: Acknowledging the crowd at Gay Pride, 2011.

Why I am still angry – two young men being publicly hanged in Iran for being gay.

Myself, Maria Jolas, playwright Denis Johnston and Bloom lookalike Gerry Davis, dedicating the Joyce seat in St Stephens Green, June 1982.

I play the Citizen as Ken Monaghan and Joyce Joyce look on.

ABOVE: Signing the first restoration contract for the Joyce Centre, with board member Michael Darcy and architect Jim O'Connor.

RIGHT: Ken Monaghan, his daughter Helen, wife Lucy and myself in the Joyce Centre on Ken's last Bloomsday.

BELOW: Visitors to the Joyce Centre included distinguished guests such as the late Gregory Peck (second from left) and Martin Scorsese (right).

ABOVE LEFT: My name in lights in Pittsburgh.

ABOVE: Bob Joyce and I post performance in New York, 1990s.

LEFT: Stately plump Buck Mulligan. During the Joyce show.

BELOW: PP's Wheel Appeal, with PP (front right) and his family.

LEFT: *James Joyce: The Musical* – with Ronnie Drew on stage in Trinity Players, 1968.

RIGHT: In Savona filming with Italian tenor Giuseppe di Stefano and his driver.

BELOW: Crossing the line. One of the three marathons I ran, all of which I finished.

the sound of boys in Portora, because he had been asked at school what his ambition was, and he said, 'To take a central role in a law case, "Regina v Oscar Wilde".' A classic case of answered prayers.

We started in the Taibhdhearc Theatre, and did several more around the country before we brought it to Andrew's Lane. The reviews were mixed, audiences loved it, but it hasn't been performed since.

I did another bit of creative drama, entirely on the hoof, for RTÉ. It was about ten o'clock on the morning of 1 April about twenty years ago, and Pat Kenny rang to say he had an idea and would I help. He was going to go on air in a minute or two and would like my permission to announce that David Norris was engaged to be married – and as this was long before the notion of civil partnership, the object of my affections was a woman. He asked was I on for it, and if so, I had ten minutes to dream up a story before he would bring me on air.

Of course I was up for such mischief, and when Pat called back to congratulate me over the airwaves, I played it very coy. I told him it was a private matter, known only to three people: my betrothed and I, and Dr Mary Henry, another Trinity Senator.

I reluctantly confirmed the story to Pat, revealing that my wife-to-be was a wonderful young woman I'd met at a Joyce conference in Miami. Her name was Colleen O'Donoghoe (the initials C.O.D. signalled a Dublin joke) and our relationship was very ecumenical. I explained that I was Church of Ireland, Colleen's father was Roman Catholic and her mother was Jewish. I made up a complete fantasy about meeting her through a discovery I had made of a cache of previously unknown letters in the Trinity Library in which Samuel Beckett applied for the job of James Joyce's secretary. I even 'read' excerpts from these imagined letters over the radio. (I was plagued for months afterwards by Joyce scholars from all over the place wanting access to the letters. Half of them didn't believe that I had invented them on the spot. They thought that I was just an academic dog-in-the-manger.)

I then told Pat that I was very upset that the story was now public, because it was a serious breach of patient confidentiality. Of course poor Dr Henry was totally innocent. I said that Colleen suffered from varicose veins and after Mary had very kindly offered to treat them Colleen must have inadvertently blabbed during a consultation.

Pat asked had we 'set the date', which I told him was being a bit premature. 'We're not quite sure whether there will be a wedding or not. It's not only the varicose veins Colleen is attending Dr Henry for, but also for a fertility examination to be sure she can have children.'

'Oh,' said Pat. 'You wouldn't marry her if she couldn't have children?'

'Come on, Pat,' I retorted, 'you and I are of an age when it's not all about sex. Children do come into it, and I'm not about to buy a pig in a poke.' That was guaranteed to tread on every feminist corn in the country, and it certainly melted the telephone switchboard.

Other radio stations picked it up as a real story, and one colleague rang me in tears to say she was delighted I had 'found happiness at last'. The lads in the gym gave me a bit of abuse over it, on the lines of 'Your own aren't enough for you, now you're raiding ours as well, you feckin' hypocrite!' A couple of days later I got a letter from two Cork engineers who congratulated me on my engagement and enclosed a packet of seeds which, they said, would 'be out in time for the wedding' – and of course they were a packet of mixed pansies! I wrote back saying, 'Dear Engineers, thank you so much for your generous gift which is greatly appreciated. Unfortunately, however, poor Colleen had to be sent to the vet to be put down as a result of her intransigent infertility and rampant varicose veins. However, as you might expect, the pansies are flourishing!'

*

I also did quite a lot of broadcasting with Newstalk radio, which was a wonderful learning experience. I firstly filled in on the Sean Moncrieff show, whose host is a delightful man with an individual, quirky style. I learnt to use the headphones, or cans, to read out emails from the screen, time myself to fade into the ads, read the weather forecast and give the station ID at the right time. I filled in a few times for George Hook and did battle with an American shock jock called Mikey Graham who, on several occasions, I left stunned because despite being what he called a 'Euroweenie', I rocked him with a few powerful hits. I was then given my own show on Sunday mornings, a type of *Desert Island Discs* interview-style show where interesting people chose three or four pieces of music and we had a relaxed chat. The producer was Sue Cahill, a bundle of energy and fun who taught me a lot.

My public profile has led to plenty of other opportunities. I was sent off on all sorts of assignments by broadcasters and newspapers, enjoying trips to China and up the Amazon. At one stage I even agreed to review restaurants. I got some mild criticism in one of the newspapers, which suggested that I didn't know anything about cooking, which of course was absolutely true. But I had invested in a copy of *Larousse Gastronomique* and any time my critics had a pop at me I was able to come back and splatter them all over the wall with my culinary knowledge. After all, to challenge the bible of cuisine would have been gastronomic blasphemy.

I pioneered the approach of writing in some detail about my guests in restaurant reviews. But when I had to keep repeating guests it looked rather shoddy, so I had to become a bit creative. One of my regulars was a prison officer, Patrick Landers, who had helped in my early Senate campaigns and was a tall, athletic, good-looking fellow with a big moustache. The first time I took him to dinner he was 'a senior official of the Department of Justice', becoming more exalted by the week. Eventually I changed his sex and called him Princess

Felicia Yusupova, a member of the White Russian aristocracy.

I took him to dinner in the Gresham, where a waitress approached:

'The Princess Felicia will have . . .' I started, before the woman burst out laughing.

I told her, 'You are most unkind. The Princess Felicia is a very old lady who has survived since the Russian Revolution of 1917 thanks to some radical hormone treatment, which explains her luxuriant moustache, deep voice and hairy legs.'

Keeping up the pretence, I mentioned Felicia in the review, but omitted reference to the hormones and hairy legs, and after it was printed any number of old snobs came up to me to ask after their great friend the princess.

At one stage the *Evening Herald* editor took me to lunch and suggested I write a column for his newspaper. I had just two questions – can I write what I like and will I get paid? He said yes to both and I wrote that column for three and a half years and never missed a deadline, although getting paid was like extracting teeth from a hen. Coincidence or not, I was let go eventually after a series of articles giving my trenchant views on George Bush junior and his war in Iraq.

In 2004 I was offered $50,000 for my life story by some Hollywood producers. Two friends of mine who work in the film business in LA, Scotty and Tegan, were centrally involved and came over to do a series of taped interviews. They were thinking in terms of Colin Farrell as the young David Norris, with Sir Anthony Hopkins taking over as I made my serene progress through middle age. I doubt if either Colin or Sir Anthony ever knew of the prestige that was being proffered to them! Anyway, a deal was struck with a production company in Los Angeles, who sent me a contract and told me, in the best Hollywood way, to get my lawyers to talk to their lawyers. I ambled across the road to my barrister friend Muireann, who told me not to touch it with a bargepole. The contract was hilarious – it reserved the right to alter my life story to suit the plot. They could have turned me into anything from Superman to a child molester. I trusted the original parties but it could have been sold on to another company, and who knows what would have happened then? One clause asked me to surrender my exclusive rights to the material in 'Ireland, Europe, the USA, the rest of the world, and the known and unknown universes'. I had visions of little green men on Mars or Pluto waiting with their tongues hanging out as *The Life of Norris* came rolling up on the big screen.

I did, however, have an opportunity in 1983 to celebrate the centenary of a great Irish artist, friend of Joyce and fellow tenor, the late John Count McCormack. I learnt a great deal about McCormack through making the film. Before the First World War, he was in Chicago when an American composer came and tried to tempt him to sing some of his songs. After an agreeable meeting they parted and McCormack took him to the lift. Embarrassed, his guest said, 'I am sorry, but I can't use this lift.' McCormack asked, 'Why not?' The composer replied, 'Because I am black.' McCormack was furious, summoned the manager and said, 'If the lift is not good enough for my guests, your hotel is not good enough for me,' which in the context of the period was pretty heroic.

I was also impressed by his moral courage at the time of the death of the composer Oscar Hammerstein I. Hammerstein being Jewish, McCormack applied for permission from the Roman Catholic Archbishop to attend his funeral. This was refused but, having thought it over, McCormack attended anyway.

As part of the film, I travelled to Savona, a small town on the borders of Italy and southern France, where McCormack had made his debut. There I was to meet with the celebrated Italian tenor and one-time lover of Maria Callas, Giuseppe Di Stefano. When he arrived in a white Rolls-Royce with his shirt slit down to his navel, exposing a chest covered in gold like the oldest swinger in town, I was not impressed. He caught me looking at the jewellery and asked, 'Admire my necklace? Callas, she gave it to me. She loved me very much.' This further alienated me, but the end came when I was compelled to accept an invitation to dinner that evening. I thought it would be in some ghastly pretentious restaurant.

I couldn't have been more wrong. We went to the equivalent of a fish and chip shop where a delicious concoction rather like Yorkshire pudding was made on a long spatula in an open oven. We sat at rough wooden tables and drank local wine out of carafes. Then a message was sent in. A crowd had gathered in the square, and they wanted to know if Giuseppe Di Stefano would honour them by singing. The table was pushed under the window, the casements flung wide and Di Stefano stood up on it and sang for fifteen minutes through the open window to an enraptured crowd below. I lost my heart to him completely. I knew I had misjudged him and the next day we did an excellent interview for the film.

I made several other films both for television and cinema over the years but the one that delighted me most was my collaboration with George Morrison. George is celebrated as the creator of a new film form with his epoch-making *cinema verité* epic *Mise Éire*, with music especially commissioned by him from the late Seán Ó Riada. I knew George and his wife Janet over a good number of years and used to go out for delightful dinner parties to their magical house hidden away in a wood at Shankill. We discussed all sorts of subjects, artistic, political and social, but found ourselves often concentrating on our mutual admiration for Joyce and the suppression by government sources decades earlier of his attempt to make a film in tribute to the great writer. Gradually, this idea came back to life and I collaborated with George in the making of his 2007 film *Dublin Day*, for which I assisted with the script and acted as narrator. It was the first film George had made in forty years and I am delighted to say has led to a rebirth of his creative genius.

*

About fifteen years ago RTÉ gave me a one-off television show, one of a six-part series featuring well-known people, including the wonderful comic Spike Milligan. As part of the deal I was allowed to invite my own guests, so I picked Agnes Bernelle. I was very fond of Agnes, a wonderful singer and actress. I once met her coming out of the Project Theatre and offered to walk her to her car. We were almost out at the Pigeon House in Ringsend, miles from the centre of Dublin, when I asked, 'Where exactly is your car?'

'Oh, it's in Dame Street. I hope you don't mind, but I was so enjoying the conversation . . .'

Agnes had the most extraordinary life. She grew up in Berlin, where her father, Rudolf Bernauer, owned the four biggest theatres and was a friend of Berthold Brecht and Kurt Weil. Agnes was half Jewish and fled Germany aged eighteen in 1939. She became part of the British black propaganda machine and worked as a presenter on a radio station under her codename of Miss Vicki. She used to undermine the Nazi regime with wicked hoaxes, the greatest of which was playing a request for a submarine commander by way of congratulation on the birth of his new twin daughters. She had found out that the submariner hadn't been on leave for eighteen months . . . he promptly sailed the U-boat into a British port and surrendered. She also concocted a scheme to get German women to send urine samples to the Nazi party HQ – they arrived by the million, most of them broken en route, so it was a wet day in Berlin!

On our walk to Sandymount she told me that her ex-husband Desmond Leslie had just left his Danish girlfriend, Drane, for a German lady called Seuer, and snorted, 'Typical of Desmond, out of the drain and into the sewer.'

Some years later she developed a brain tumour, and when surgery didn't work and the cancer returned, she went on a cucumber diet which she was convinced cured her – it certainly may have helped her because she lived on for another eleven years before, sadly, it recurred.

I always loved Aggie singing 'Lili Marlene' or 'Daddy's Lying Dead on the Ironing Board', but I knew she hadn't been at all well. I rang the hospital and asked her doctor would it be a cruelty to ask her to come on the show, but he said that it wasn't going to make a difference as there was no hope of recovery this time anyway, and it might even perk her up. So I asked her, and she was delighted.

The evening of the broadcast, she was collected and delivered to RTÉ, and it was sad to see how she had been affected by the illness. She sat waiting in the wings like a little crumpled doll, but the second she was brought to the microphone and the spotlight came on her she straightened up and started to shine. She sang wonderfully too, and there was magic in her eyes.

A few weeks later I was on my way home from Venice when there was a PA announcement at Marco Polo Airport: 'Would Senator David Norris please come to the desk for an urgent message.' I was sure it was bad news of my aunt, but it was the sad message that Aggie had died, and a request that I read at the funeral. It was a lovely ceremony, and as the coffin retreated, Gavin Friday sang 'Mack the Knife' from *The Threepenny Opera*. It was an electrifying performance, and at the very end he threw a rose on the coffin and shouted, 'Auf wiedersehen, Aggie.'

As a huge fan of old-time jazz, one of the greatest thrills of my life was being allowed to introduce the Original Dixieland Jazz Band on stage in Vicar Street. That happened because I was visiting some neighbours, John Hanley and John Aboud, who were surfing the internet. I was complaining about how it was destroying conversation when they told me how great it was, and how you could find absolutely anything on it. I didn't believe them, so they asked for a challenge and I said, 'The Original Dixieland Jazz Band.' Not only did they find masses of information, but they discovered that Jimmy La Rocca, son of the original cornet player Nick, had re-formed the band, and they were available for concerts in the US.

I first heard of the band back in Ballsbridge, where Michael Moran's father had a collection of ancient recordings; he had even seen the original group at the Hammersmith Palais de Dance in London in 1919. The Marquess of Donegall told me how he and the Prince of Wales arranged for them to play for George V at Windsor Castle, but the King nearly had a stroke. What a shame the performance and the King's reaction weren't filmed. They were formed in New Orleans in 1916 and their 'Livery Stable Blues' was the first 'jass' single ever issued. I was thrilled earlier this year to track down the final record I needed to complete my collection.

My sixtieth birthday was coming up, so with the help of Eddie Kenny from the Cobalt Café I got on to Harry Crosbie, who was an old pal, and Gerry Godley, who I had got to know through the Improvised Music Company. They really got enthused by my idea of bringing the band to Ireland to play for my sixtieth birthday party. The two of them took over the whole operation of flying the band over from New Orleans and organised a full European tour for them, so what should have cost $60,000 didn't cost me a penny.

Harry also offered to let me have Vicar Street for the night before the party, suggesting that I promote the Original Dixieland Jazz Band; the ticket sales would pay for the costs of my party. It was a wonderful gesture, and I thanked him for it, because it gave the people of Dublin a chance to hear one of the most historic jazz bands. But instead of pocketing the proceeds we gave all the money to cancer research and the De Paul trust for the homeless – which is how I got to be on stage at Vicar Street introducing the most remarkable jazz band in the world.

It also made us feel so virtuous that we were well able to let our hair down the next night for the birthday party. That was a marvellous night and at midnight they played 'Tiger Rag', with its lovely trombone growl, and I danced a solo Charleston. One of my most prized possessions is now the drumhead they presented to me, signed by the entire band. Because of fire regulations I had to restrict the numbers at the party in the Joyce Centre to three hundred, but even so, for weeks after I was blackguarded by people who had expected to be invited.

CHAPTER 10

Politics: A Vulgar Trade and My Part in It

I MAY HAVE STARTED MY POLITICAL CAREER BY FIGHTING FOR GAY rights, but I rapidly realised that the mechanism of discrimination used against people like me was exactly the same as that which operated against women, Travellers, religious minorities and other marginalised groups.

I found that if I was going to address injustice then I had to address inequality, and that meant I couldn't stay in the comfortable world of my parents, because once I understood the inequality I couldn't remain at ease. That's not necessarily a great moral attitude or fuelled by pure altruism, it is just that other people's suffering makes me miserable and uneasy. I'm one of life's picture straighteners – if I see something crooked or wrong I have to try my best to put it right. I'm a bit like my namesake Mr Norris in Christopher Isherwood's *Berlin Stories* who hated injustice because it disturbed his sense of the aesthetic. My entire political career has been about striving for internal and external equilibrium. I am not expecting any great credit or plaudits, but I do think it a bit thick to have my honour impugned by lies from people who have contributed nothing to public life except negative comment.

While some people will get involved in an exclusive fight for

Palestinian rights, some for Israeli rights, and others for Travellers' rights, that is too narrow a focus for me as a politician. For me it's all about human rights, whether the people involved are Palestinian, Israeli or gay – it's the principle I'm passionate about. You have to follow that principle wherever it takes you. But lots of people don't see that. The only way one can straighten all the pictures is by implementing the principle, not just what satisfies one's own needs or those of one's own group. It's an uncomfortable position to hold at times. When I criticised the blitzkrieg launched by Israel against the Palestinians in the so-called 'Operation Cast Lead', I was accused of anti-Semitism and reminded of the murderous homophobia of Islamic extremists. But two wrongs don't just not make a right; they actually have the effect of making a much bigger wrong.

The FitzPatricks had not been a political family since the turn of the eighteenth century. Like most southern unionists in the early years of the new state, they did not see a role for themselves at all. Some of them went as far as being 'cultural nationalists' and even rather liked the idea of speaking Irish, although they all supported the idea of being British and saw no conflict between that and also being Irish. But they definitely knew they were not *English*. They would have seen Grattan's Parliament as the ideal, and opposed the 1801 Act of Union because their loyalty was to the Crown, not to England. And although our branch of the family was Anglican, I am pleased by the fact that they actively supported Catholic emancipation.

Later, there may have been a sneaking admiration for Michael Collins, because he was such a handsome and dashing figure, although this probably ended when they learnt of his part in the murder of British officers during the War of Independence. My mother was a boarder in Alexandra College at the time, and told of some of the girls being woken to hear that one or both of their parents had been shot dead in their beds. I always found Collins an engaging figure, but this has also been tempered by my current understanding that his signature on the Anglo-Irish Treaty was just a ploy. He had every intention of fomenting a bloody civil war in the North of Ireland once he got the chance.

There was, however, no love at all for Mr de Valera, because many people they knew were ruined by his actions in the Economic War. But on the small number of occasions I found myself in his company I felt him to be a figure of considerable stature. He was very old and almost blind when I met him, but still a ramrod-straight figure, leaning on the arm of an aide-de-camp at the College Races. I thought his rejoinder to Churchill at the end of the war was masterly, although his reputation was damaged by publicly expressing sympathy to the German people on the death of Hitler. Lloyd George was right too when he said that dealing with Dev was like trying to pick up mercury on a fork. And let nobody think shady dealing in Irish politics commenced with Charlie Haughey, Ray Burke and Bertie Ahern. There was de Valera's skilful trousering of the pathetic dollar contributions of Irish-American skivvies with which he set up the *Irish Press*, and the milking of the Hospitals' Sweepstakes profits by those in charge.

The early 1920s was a time to keep the head down too, as atrocities were not unknown and my family would have heard about the incident just across the Slieve Bloom Mountains in Offaly, where the two Protestant Pearson brothers were shot and the rest of their family driven out to Australia. They had probably also heard rumours of the sectarian murder of seventy-three Protestants in Cork, who were captured, interrogated, in some cases tortured, and then shot by wildcat elements of the IRA. History, unfortunately, is ugly and complex. It is full of what Lord Denning described as 'appalling vistas'. However, if one chooses the Denning route of averting one's eyes from the truth simply because it is an appalling vista then one will never learn.

Being gay, I wasn't living in a real world anyway, but having a unionist background and an uncle who worked with royalty meant I did not feel at all welcome in the homogenous society that 1950s and 60s Ireland presented to itself. The fiftieth anniversary of the 1916 Easter Rising was the climax of that – I was appalled by the triumphalist celebration of blood sacrifice portrayed in what seemed to be an exclusively Catholic, Republican, white, heterosexual fest. The nose of anyone out-side the narrow definition of Irishness was being brutally rubbed in the dirt.

Like James Joyce, I find the blatant Anglophobia of people like Padraig Pearse repugnant – and also hypocritical as his father was, like my own, an English Protestant. The tribal hatred of England has always disgusted me. After all, we are two small islands inexorably linked, politically, culturally and genetically. Look at the signatories of the brave Proclamation of 1916, which was mercifully free of the usual xenophobia. Some of their names sound, as Pearse would have liked it, racially pure – but look a little closer and Cathal Brugha becomes Charlie Burgess, and Eamonn Ceannt becomes Edward Kent. And when one considers Countess Constance Markievicz, née Gore-Booth of Lissadell House, or Madame Maud Gonne McBride, who hadn't a single drop of Irish blood and whose first glimpse of the country was from the Curragh Camp where her father was a colonel in one of Queen Victoria's imperial regiments, one begins to see how complex the interrelations between our two peoples really are.

I had started to question the accepted verities at an early age. My mother had assured me that the British Empire was a wonderful institution, which conferred the benefits of civilis-ation on a generally ungrateful world, and I was happy to accept her word for that. But then I went to school, where I was forced to confront things such as the Penal Laws, the Great Famine and evictions. It was a truly horrible feeling to discover that all the things to which you have a sentimental attachment, such as the Church, the Empire and the royals, were capable of such dreadful things. Realising that was like finding that the nice old Santa Claus on whose knee you were sitting was a convicted paedophile. It was a good lesson though, for it taught me that you always have to question accepted truths and take nothing for granted. It didn't turn me into a mad republican, but it did make me grieve for the victims of injustice.

My family were very much political products of their period, and both parents were virulently anti-communist and confirmed unionists. My mother was always particularly delighted when the British team, led by Colonel Harry Llewellyn on Foxhunter, won the Aga Khan Cup at the RDS Horse Show and the entire members' stand rose to sing 'God Save the King'. My grandmother, who although due to the imprudence of her husband's family scarcely had an affluent lifestyle herself, believed strongly that with privilege there was also an obligation to look after those less well-off than oneself. However, they all believed in a hierarchical society where everyone had their place, and sang with gusto the verse now suppressed by the politically correct elements of Anglicanism from Mrs C. F. Alexander's hymn 'All Things Bright and Beautiful':

> *The rich man in his castle,*
> *the poor man at his gate,*
> *He made them, high or lowly,*
> *and ordered their estate.*

I can see the beauty and graciousness of their world, but it was a world founded on inequality.

My mother and aunt hadn't voted since the foundation of the Irish state, but in a general election in the 1950s I did persuade them to come out and give a no.1 preference to Noël Browne. I didn't have a great interest in politics, but was much taken by this independent-minded deputy who told the truth and got to the root of problems. He had an extraordinary way of speaking, which started off very low-key and steadily built in volume and power until he reached a passionate crescendo. I dragged the two ladies down to Lakelands Convent, where the polling station was situated, and their votes helped Noël get back to the Dáil.

Many years later I befriended Noël, and came to greatly admire his long and committed career, which saw him battling injustice at every turn. He had a terrible upbringing, with his family decimated by tuberculosis and the survivors packed off to England by his dying mother. Noël was well treated in England, but his brother, who was a hunchback, was put into an institution and used as a guinea pig to test out new treatments. The only time I ever saw Noël dissolve into tears was while talking about his brother, to whom they did the most terrible things, he said, simply because he was slow and ungainly while Noël was bright and handsome. After his brother died, Noël came back to Dublin, where he was spotted by a philanthropic medical family from Merrion Square called Chance, who put him through medical school at Trinity.

Over a long political career Noël was a member of virtually every party in the state, but because he stuck to his ideals – whereas parties by their nature are pragmatic animals – they would invariably kick him out. As Minister for Health from 1949 to 1951, he introduced various radical measures, including the tuberculosis-eradication scheme. By using funds from the Hospitals' Sweepstakes lottery, he built sanatoria, brought in the latest drugs and trained doctors. His next idea, the Mother and Child Scheme, brought the government down. He wanted to provide free medical services for nursing mothers, but the Roman Catholic Church objected to it, as did many of the medical establishment. They thought the family was their sacred province and saw the scheme as state interference. It was indefensible for them to reject it, but they were adamant. Noël dug his heels in and as a result the government collapsed in 1951. Noël never again held power, but he became the conscience of Ireland on all kinds of issues. He was vocal about contraception, and was the first to speak out against the

Magdalene laundries and about abortion information at a time when nobody would touch such issues.

At one stage my colleague Professor John Scattergood and I tried to get Noël an honorary degree, but I believe Trinity failed to live up to their vaunted liberal credentials and the proposal was turned down. I didn't want Noël to know, but I raised such a silent storm in the corridors of power that they were embarrassed into giving him an honorary fellowship, a much higher honour. Noël was thrilled and went to his grave not knowing how appallingly he had been treated by his old university.

Noël was one of the earliest supporters of the Campaign for Homosexual Law Reform and a great friend for thirty years. He nominated me at every election for the Seanad, and after he retired he moved to a little thatched cottage in the west. One morning, just before the 1997 election, I got my nomination papers back complete with his signature and a little note in his spindly hand wishing me well. And then I turned on the radio to hear he had just died. The saddest thing I've ever had to do in politics was to take up a bottle of Tipp-Ex and wipe Noël Browne's signature from that nomination paper.

As far as I am aware, Michael D. Higgins and I were, shamefully, the only two public representatives to attend his funeral in Ballinahown, Co. Galway. Some months later a memorial tribute was held in the Town Hall Theatre in Galway, attended by many of Noël's old friends including Dr Paddy Leahy, a courageous liberal doctor from Ballyfermot who was close to the end himself. The most electrifying moment was provided when a man from Connemara with a face like hewn granite in a tweed cap stood up and said, 'I have come this day from Connemara to speak of the *uaisleacht* of Noël Browne.' '*Uaisleacht*' was the perfect word, conveying much more than its approximate English synonym 'nobility'.

Another great hero of mine was Owen Sheehy-Skeffington, who, as I've already said, I first heard of through my old schoolmaster Jack Cornish, who was his great friend. 'Skeff' was a lecturer in French and a prime example of Trinity's dissenting tradition in the Senate for twenty years. A very stylish man about college, he was always immaculately turned out, with his hair Brylcreemed back and carrying a briefcase. For years he was the only radical voice in the Senate, and even his fellow Trinity Senators were wary of him. He lost his seat in 1961 to John Ross, a conservative candidate who was a prominent solicitor and who could afford a professional campaign. Something similar happened many years later when the liberal Senator Brendan Ryan from Cork was ousted by the well-funded campaign of Rónán Mullen, former spokesman for the Roman Catholic Archdiocese of Dublin. Charlie McDonald, a marvellous Cathaoirleach of the Seanad and a decent Laois man, many years later told me that although a conservative Catholic himself, he had deliberately befriended Owen because he was so isolated. Noël Browne paid him a superb tribute when he died in 1970, aged sixty-one:

'There were so few who dared to be different about the ugly inhumanity, hypocrisy and sectarian aspects of our society in the late thirties, forties, fifties and early sixties. Owen never failed and he suffered for it.

'He mocked the authoritarian, made fun of the arrogant, Owen the iconoclast, the gentle dissenter, the courteously humorous debunker of the pompous. He was as unpopular with those who liked to call themselves the extreme left as he was with the extreme right, since he hated cant and despised the bigot, whether religious or political.'

I had become exercised by the North in the early days of the civil-rights movement, when there was clearly serious injustice and discrimination. I couldn't understand why people were unable to get equal treatment in housing and employment just on the basis of their religion. Coming from a Southern unionist background, I was troubled by the early stages of the conflict in

Northern Ireland. Bloody Sunday was a key moment, when even RTÉ suggested that the first shots were fired by the IRA. However, the more that emerged about Bloody Sunday the more obvious it became it was a cover-up. The IRA had no mandate, but the British Army was an official organ of the state, which made its murders far worse. It wasn't easy for me to come to that conclusion.

Later that week I was on my way to a meeting about James Joyce when I came across a march to the British Embassy on Merrion Square. The Sinn Féin leader Daithí O'Connell was screeching from the back of a cart, coming out with inflammatory demagoguery including slogans along the lines of 'We are one race, one people, one nation.' I thought to myself, *I've heard that one before – wasn't it* 'Ein Volk, ein Reich, ein Führer'? Not, I suppose, surprising, when you consider that the Commander of the self-styled Irish Republican Army, Seán Russell, died in a U-boat on the way back from collaborating with the Nazis. Disgracefully, a plot of ground in Fairview was actually provided for the erection of a monument to that traitor to everything decent in Irish life.

As a conservationist I was disgusted that they burnt down the embassy, as we had already lost a dozen houses to the barbaric ESB head office on the same vista, which had been the longest continuous Georgian streetscape in the world. This was part of our Irish heritage, built by Irish craftsmen and even owned by Irish people, whatever about those who worked there. It was a repulsive and frightening occasion, the first time I had seen a mob under the control of fanatics.

I was appalled as the conflict went on and on, with terrible outrages on both sides. The nation that had given the world saints and scholars as well as great writers and scientists was now responsible for such innovations as car bombs and proxy suicide bombings. I knew the IRA weren't monsters, or stupid, but they suffered from a failure of imagination and had lost the capacity to put themselves in the place of their victims, perhaps because they had been themselves on the receiving end for so long, so I got involved in New Consensus, which was trying to bring people together from different perspectives. John Hume was 100 per cent right when he said the border wasn't on the map but in the mind.

At one stage the IRA was routinely blowing up the rail link between Dublin and Belfast, which was an absurd position – uniting Ireland by breaking a cross-border link which people used to visit their families and to shop. So in 1989 I got involved with the Peace Train, which was seen off from Connolly Station by the Lord Mayor of Dublin and met in Belfast by that city's mayor. On the way back we stopped in Portadown, where an announcement was made that the IRA had put a bomb on the track. After an hour's wait an official came to say that a bus was ready to take us the rest of the journey. We all trooped off, but as I was leaving I noticed Jack McQuillan was still in his seat. Jack had been a big GAA star and a great ally of Noël Browne in Clann na Poblachta who had gone so far as to leave the party in support of him after the Mother and Child controversy. He became an independent TD for Roscommon for years afterwards and a good and stalwart friend of mine.

I asked Jack was he OK, and he said he'd never felt better. 'But I'm not going to be forced off this Peace Train by a gang of thugs and bullies. I'm sitting here until we can travel back the way we came.'

I said, 'I wish I'd thought of that. I completely agree with you. I'm staying too.'

And with the bus ready to leave, the Fine Gael TD Monica Barnes came on to see what was up, and she agreed to stay too. The word went around and ninety of the campaigners got back on the train and stayed there overnight till it was safe to go on. People from both sides of the community came and gave us food, and the British Army gave us some of their rations.

We had to sleep on the floor, in the lavatories, in the corridors, and I was in one compartment next to the conservative Fine Gael TD Brendan McGahon. He got up the next morning, stretched, yawned and said, 'I had no idea it would be so much fun to sleep with David Norris!' to general laughter and applause.

About a week later Brendan was with a gaggle of ladies and I gave him a wave. He called me over and introduced me to the members of the Irish Countrywomen's Association from Termonfeckin, saying they didn't believe that he and I were friends. '*Friends?*' I said. 'That's a bit of a cooling-off, isn't it, after I slept with you in Portadown railway station last Saturday night?' Brendan became scarlet with embarrassment.

I picketed the Sinn Féin *ard-fheis* a few times, where I would recite Séamus Shields's passage from O'Casey's *Shadow of a Gunman* to the delegation: 'I'm a nationalist meself right enough – I believe in a United Ireland but I draw the line when I hear the gunmen blowin' about dyin' for the people, when it's the people that are dyin' for the gunmen!'

That was before the Shinners adopted a socially progressive stance, and for my pains I was routinely subjected to violently homophobic abuse from delegates as they entered the hall. I didn't care about the Shinners' theoretical stuff; all I saw was that people were being maimed and killed.

And then, as I predicted, they all kissed and made up. I once saw Marlene Dietrich at the Adelphi in Dublin, and she sang the marvellous Pete Seeger song 'Where Have All the Flowers Gone?' with its poignant line 'When will they ever learn?' It seems as if we're incapable of learning. It was sickening to see McGuinness and Paisley crowing like cocks on a dunghill after the misery they left behind. The real peacemakers like John Hume, the SDLP and some of the moderate unionists such as the McGimpsey brothers were sidelined, just a footnote in the history that they had helped to create. But on the other hand I'm genuinely pleased that Sinn Féin has given up the gun and entered democratic politics. I sat for several years beside Pearse Doherty in Seanad Éireann and found him both an agreeable companion and a highly intelligent political mind. There is now a small SF contingent in the Senate and I find myself frequently on the same side as they. Apart from me, they're the only decent pinkos left in the Upper House. You can certainly forget any connection between the modern Labour Party and socialism.

I was on the staff of Trinity when Mary Bourke, later President Mary Robinson, called by to tell me she was going to run for the Seanad in 1969 – and asked me to be part of her election team. I wasn't at all surprised at her plan – she had always had political ambitions – but I knew she had an enormous job to get elected. She was young, she was female, she was Roman Catholic – and none of those things would have favoured her with that electorate at that time. It was very unusual that any candidate would be elected at the first attempt, but sure enough Mary romped home with 1,100 votes.

When I finally made my own first foray into national politics it was in the immediate footsteps of Noël Browne. He had spent four years as a Trinity Senator alongside Mary Robinson, but in the 1977 general election he regained his seat in the Dáil. There was a feeling abroad that his Senate seat was up for grabs, so I decided to give it a whirl. There was an electorate of eleven thousand graduates at that stage, and I thought that the election was a marvellous way to propagandise some influential people who were the opinion formers in Irish society. I wanted to widen the discussion on gay rights, but also took the chance to raise other civil and human rights, as well as the preservation of Dublin's architectural heritage.

The candidates had a debate in Trinity, at which Catherine McGuinness said that I seemed to think I was going to be allowed to run the whole government on my own because I had such a wide range of issues – which was ironic given that I had to fight against the perception of me as a single-issue candidate. (I usually retorted that even if this were true it was still one more issue than the rest of the candidates put together.) Perhaps

Catherine was right, as I did have an exaggerated sense of my own importance, and I was completely convinced I was going to storm home atop the poll. I got 220 votes.

It was disappointing, but the campaign was an eye-opener and proved a useful part of the learning process as I was completely unfamiliar with the practical realities of Irish political battle.

There was, for example, the matter of collecting the ten signatures of those who would be your nominators and assentors. They had to be Trinity graduates, on the electoral register and Irish citizens. I realised that voters took certain messages from who you had got to sign, so I managed to get significant figures such as Noël Browne and Dean Victor Griffin to nominate me. Victor was a commanding and prophetic voice at a time when the Church of Ireland was generally pretty spineless, especially on controversial issues. He remains so to this day, and a good and valued friend who continues, every election, to sign my nomination papers. When assembling the nominators it was important also to be sensitive about things such as gender balance. And you had to be careful that your supporters weren't 'poached'– one year Shane Ross got Brendan Kennelly to nominate him, and as Brendan was head of the English Department at the time that sent out a particular message which wasn't of benefit to me. They were both friends of mine, so I thought it was a mistake, but I suspect it was Shane being mischievous.

I always tried to do something new every election, and one year I analysed the electorate and discovered there were high concentrations of graduates in the postal districts of Dublin 2, 4 and 6. I checked the addresses and if there were, say, eight graduates living on one road in Terenure I would call out and deliver material personally. It was very time-consuming, however, because you might have to spend an hour with one old dear who was delighted to have someone to talk to about Trinity. And then she would say she had already promised her no. 1 vote to someone else but would give me a no. 2, which was about as useful as the hundreds of thousands of Michael D.'s no. 2s I apparently got in the presidential election.

Another of my electioneering wheezes was to appeal to the high proportion of the Trinity electorate who went to international rugby matches. I had posters printed and hung on every lamppost for miles around on the approaches to Lansdowne Road for the Ireland v. France match. Lansdowne Road itself resembled the Führer Allee in Berlin, completely Norrisified by giant posters of me grinning down at the throng. I walked all the way to the stadium to observe the reaction and one Frenchman came up, pointed at a poster, then at me, and asked, 'C'est Monsieur le Président, n'est-ce pas?'

Those early days were great fun, but very labour-intensive. We had a production line on a series of trestle tables in my North Great Georges Street home, and lots of people would come in to stuff and lick envelopes. There was a great mixture of lefties, gays, conservationists and students, and the banter between the groups was hilarious. Every day we stopped at one o'clock, when Pat Landers would arrive with a vast cauldron of spaghetti bolognese. Pat was a great organiser, and we also had committed support from people like Ann Connolly, Sally and Séamus Shiels and their small daughter Aisling, John McBratney and Patrick Gageby, while Brian Murray has been my election agent since the start and was a pioneer of the use of computer analysis for elections.

It was a long haul to finally get elected. There was a flurry of three elections in eighteen months in the early 1980s, which almost bankrupted me. I increased my vote to 336, then 392 and in 1983 saw it rocket to 850. After that the graph rose perpendicularly.

I finally got elected in 1987, when there was a virtual dead-heat on first preferences between Ross (2,180), Robinson (2,123) and Norris (2,101). As the quota was 2,138 we all romped home. I was watching the count in the Exam Hall and when I knew I was certain to be elected I rang my aunt to tell her the news. Her reply expressed the classic FitzPatrick disdain for politics; she said, 'Oh dear, I suppose that means you'll be late for dinner. I have never understood why you want to mix with those appalling people.' She never seems to have considered what 'those appalling people' might make of me.

On that very subject, I heard later that the night I was elected the paint nearly came off the ceiling in the Dáil Bar, with scores of predictable jokes about keeping one's back to the wall when 'that bum boy' was about. When I was told of this my response was, 'What a cheek, have they ever looked in the mirror?' I was oblivious to all that fuss of course, as I had more important things to worry about, such as what I was going to wear for my maiden speech. I had everything laid out from the night before, but I was so nervous that I lost a button from my shirt. In the panic that followed my sewing it back on I broke both shoelaces, and wandered down to the Upper House decidedly lacking in elegance below the shins.

The Senate etiquette is that you say nothing on your first day, as your role as an apprentice requires you to simply listen and say nothing. As an independent, I had nobody to explain that to me – and I probably would have ignored such nonsense anyway. My election slogan had been 'Vote no. 1 Norris for an end to the quiet life in the Senate': I was there to cause waves, and I did so. The Senate rooms were being renovated at the time, and as the Dáil was in recess we held our session in that historic chamber. Far from being a shy debutant, on my first day I spoke on the order of business, on one of the pieces of legislation on which I was the only person in the chamber to have possession of a Supreme Court judgement handed down the previous day, and put in a motion to be discussed on the adjournment.

Most politicians, if they are honest, can't stand elections. To me, they are a wart on the face of democracy, but you can't have democracy without them. I particularly hate the period when an election is in the air but you don't know when it is going to be called and everything goes into suspended animation. It always reminds me of the tension coming up to exams. My back-room team has gradually dwindled as technological innovation means fewer foot-soldiers are required. Brian Murray is still my election agent, but the entire 2011 Senate campaign was run by my PA, friend and stalwart supporter Miriam Smith and myself, with the assistance of a professional mail marketing firm to handle the postage. I can never thank Miriam enough for her utter devotion and selfless capacity for hard work over the last seventeen years.

The Senate election coincided with the early stirrings of the presidential campaign and she came into the office many mornings at 8 a.m., had an apple for lunch and often didn't leave until after 8 p.m. Through our combined efforts I topped the poll with one-third of the first preferences, a historic achievement but one barely mentioned in the press. As a result of my electoral success I became Father of the House, the senior Senator. This entailed taking the chair on the opening day, making the opening speech and inviting the parties to nominate their candidates for leadership. Some officials tried to dissuade me from exercising my right to speak, but I insisted on doing so and made a vigorous rallying cry in favour of the preservation of the Senate. One of the officials passed me up a note saying, *Well done, I eat my words.*

There was always an edge against the university seats in the Seanad, because they were seen as representing an élite and were labelled undemocratic. If by an élite they mean the best, then I have no problem – why shouldn't we aim for that? But to question the democratic nature of those elections is outrageous, particularly when eleven of our sixty Senators are put there without any sort of election, at the whim of the Taoiseach, and the rest through a rigged system which ensures that only those affiliated to a party can be elected, and even that by a tiny electorate. The number of people who can vote is so small they have to multiply it by a thousand for public consumption – and the newspapers are complicit in this deception and dutifully print that so-and-so got 93,000 votes, when in fact he or she got 93 votes. There was a Senate by-election recently where the entire electoral register consisted of 227 voters. The political panels, controlled by the parties, are the real rotten boroughs and not the university seats. I have actually served in a Senate where every one of the named officers, the Cathaoirleach, the Leader of the House and the Leader of the Opposition had run, and lost, in the general election for the Dáil. One of them actually managed to fail in Dáil, European and Senate elections but still got his bum on a nice comfortable chair in the Upper House. I also remember in the old days seeing the party whips, appropriately so-called, herding the members into private rooms and giving them precise instructions on who they were to vote for and in what order. My mouth fell open when I first encountered this gross abuse of democracy, but nobody else seemed to bat an eyelid.

I'm not prepared to take lessons in democracy from someone who has a constituency of 227 when I have a constituency of 54,614, while my three colleagues who represent the National University of Ireland go before an electorate of 97,734. I got nearly 37 per cent of the poll last time, 5,600 first-preference votes, which is more than many TDs got. So, yes, the Senate is by its nature undemocratic and badly needs reform, but no one should lightly accuse the university seats of being undemocratic simply because they have been made an easy target.

The university Senators are usually the only ones whose names are recognised by the general public. In the past they have included figures such as Prof. John A. Murphy, Prof. Joe Lee, Mary Robinson and Noël Browne. The very nature of the university seats ensures that they produce strong Senators. During the election, instead of traipsing around the provinces sucking up to local councillors, NUI and Trinity candidates have to subject themselves to the scrutiny of a large, alert and

233

sometimes awkward group of voters who express a wide range of interests outside the narrow confines of partisan politics.

The representative element of the university seats needs to be strengthened by extending the franchise to other third-level institutions. I have long advocated this, but believe that the essential character of the two constituencies should be retained if possible. The Trinity constituency has traditionally been over-whelmingly a Dublin one, while NUI – representing the graduates of Cork, Galway, Maynooth and UCD – has, quite naturally, had a more national profile. I would like to see the Trinity constituency extended to include graduates of Dublin City University, Dublin Institute of Technology, the National College of Ireland and possibly also UCD. NUI should be similarly extended to include graduates of the University of Limerick and the various Institutes of Technology. This would keep these constituencies within manageable proportions while extending their representative capacity.

At the moment, elected on the university panels are the former owner and chief executive of a multi-million-pound supermarket business (Feargal Quinn), a prominent cancer specialist (Prof. John Crown), a leading economic thinker (Dr Seán Barrett), the Reid Professor of Criminal Law in Trinity College (Ivana Bacik), a former spokesman for the Roman Catholic Archdiocese of Dublin (Rónán Mullen) and myself. The range of expertise represented speaks for itself.

Like all institutions, the Senate is imperfect and should of course be subject to reform. Since 1937, despite a proliferation of reports recommending change, there has been no substantial attempt at reform. This was undoubtedly because it was, on the one hand, an intensive-care unit for those discarded from the Dáil and, on the other, a convenient launching pad for aspiring TDs.

The way to democratise the bulk of the Senate is to revise the nominating bodies and give the vote to ordinary members of these groups – which would mean all the doctors, nurses, dentists and other health professionals would vote on the medical panel, all the solicitors and bankers on the financial panel, all trade-union members on the trade-union panel, all the members of Macra, the ICMSA and the IFA on the agricultural panel and so on. That would mean you would get Senators who really know what they are talking about.

Several times I have tabled all-party-agreed reports that suggested reforms, but they have always been voted down on the instructions of the political parties. However, that never stopped them castigating the university Senators as élitist. There is a lot of hypocrisy and posturing in national politics, even at Senate level.

Despite the almost entire absence of media coverage, Seanad Éireann has consistently proved itself to be a seedbed of ideas which are subsequently taken up by the Dáil. I helped to pioneer the use of briefings in Buswell's, which has become a lucrative sideline for that hotel. For example, in the late 1980s the issue of AIDS was too hot for the parties and the Dáil was afraid to take it on. The atmosphere was toxic at the time, with much hostility towards those suffering from the illness, and talk of it being their own fault for everyone except children and haemophiliacs. I thought it was too important a debate to descend into acrimony so I hired a large room in Buswell's and invited along two people who were experts in the field. Fr Paul Lavelle worked with drug users in Dublin's inner city and he was able to talk about the heroin epidemic and how users' sharing of dirty needles was a major cause of infection. Dr Fiona Mulcahy was the first AIDS consultant and based in St James's Hospital. I chaired the meeting, but stayed neutral because I knew it was important to get the questions answered in a scientific way, and that the TDs and Senators would trust a priest and a doctor more than they would me.

The meeting proved extremely useful because it exposed the total ignorance of a lot of members, but helped them to understand the issue and helped to defuse their prejudices. I then put down a debate in Private Members Time, and the commentators were amazed at how mature and sensitive the debate was, with no hysteria or nonsense about gay plagues as might well have happened in the Dáil had the issue first emerged there. I also got speakers to come and inform the Senators on asylum and immigration legislation.

The problem with our political system is that it allows too much grandstanding and entrenched stances in debate. The whole idea of a parliament, and especially a senate, is to have informed discussion about topics and to educate each other and the public. We need to place the issues and viewpoints on the record to inform wider public discussion. Our speeches are rarely picked up by the media, but the full debates are now available online, which is some progress.

As far as I know I was the first person ever to put abortion in a political manifesto, in 1977, albeit a fairly neutral statement that the laws on abortion should be 'examined'. At the time it was a word you could barely mention. I knew a certain amount about it and thought it a very complex issue, and in itself a dreadful procedure. I had echoes in my mind of the Nurse Cadden case, which was widely reported on the radio when I was about ten years old. Mamie Cadden was an abortionist, one of whose procedures left a young woman bleeding to death down a lane off Hume Street. Abortion was something I was instinctively revolted by, but when I considered who were the victims I concluded that the principal victim was the woman. I have always tried to follow the principle of finding where the greatest pain and hurt is being suffered and addressing that, whatever the consequences. But I still recognise, and have publicly acknowledged, how complex this matter is.

The role of tutor in Trinity includes a counselling element, but when I applied to be one in the 1970s I was rejected, probably because I was gay. After I helped set up a counselling service for gay people I was asked to apply again, which I did, and was given a flock of about eighty students, all female. Apparently they didn't trust me with anything in trousers, which I thought partly insulting and partly hilarious.

In this role I was from time to time approached by young women who had unintentionally become pregnant. I would talk to the women and try to take the temperature down in what was inevitably a deeply emotional situation. Whatever decision these young women made would have consequences for their academic career, so I would encourage them to get the greatest support, if possible including their families and partner, and make a rational decision in the best circumstance. I also referred those who wanted it to a non-directive counselling agency. I hope I was able to help, and I only know of one woman who had an abortion; she remained perfectly content and completed her studies. Another eight or nine carried the pregnancy through to term. I believe that if these circumstances had been different most of these troubled young people would have gone, lonely and terrified, to the mailboat. You have got to be nuanced about abortion – it is a question of at what point human life begins. I do not believe that a fertilised egg the size of a pinhead is human, and I don't think you can call a foetus that has not developed a spinal cord, nervous system or brain fully human either. It is potentially human, but that potentiality can be interrupted, which may be sad but at times necessary.

I really object to the colonisation of language by right-wing fundamentalists who call themselves 'pro-life'. The actual terminology should be 'pro-choice' or 'anti-choice'. I'm 'pro-life' and besides figures like Pol Pot, Hitler or Mao Zedong I can't think of many people in the world who have not been 'pro-life'. I am a religious person, and I believe that if a foetus does have a soul, then God is perfectly capable of looking after it. Curiously, therefore, I can understand atheists being absolutist in opposition to abortion, but not so-called Christians.

I was brought up in a society where there was a certain position for women, as mothers and housewives, so I found the more raucous aspects of the feminist movement quite irritating. But I learnt a lot from women. At the 1979 IGA conference in Amsterdam I was pushing for a particular issue to be adopted as policy. I was gung-ho, demanding a vote, when a New Zealander called Sylvia Borren took me aside and started talking to me about finding consensus. I thought she was talking rubbish, but she patiently explained that even if it took all afternoon it could be, and often was, possible to arrive at something everyone could support. But if you shoved it through, as I was trying to do, by mere force of majority, a significant minority would have to put up with the result. They would soon be meeting in little groups and it would start festering away, leading to further time-wasting dissension. That was a very important lesson to learn.

I am prepared to take unpopular positions on a lot of things because of principle. Truth is a principle which I hold dear, although, as Bishop Berkeley remarked, 'Truth is the cry of all but the game of few.' My whole upbringing and nature means I would be deeply uncomfortable lying. Therefore I always told student leaders that third-level fees were coming back and I would support the government. They had been lulled by the extraordinary phrase 'free fees'. I pointed out that this was an ugly phrase as well as an oxymoron. There is no such thing as free fees. You either pay fees or you get free education. The government was aware of this contradiction because it was already charging substantial registration fees, and these would undoubtedly go up. I made it clear to the students that their battle should be in support of the Department of Education and against the Department of Finance, in order to make sure that the means test was set at an appropriate level. Many of the student leaders knew that I was right, and in fact told me so, but they lacked the courage to face their own electorate with the reality of the issue. In a situation where the economy is struggling, what resources the state possesses should be focused on the people who need them most. 'From each according to his capacity, to each according to his need' sums it up well. People who have plenty of money, or even adequate resources, should pay more, to give everyone an equal chance.

I believe in free universal education just as I believe in free universal access to healthcare. But unless you put the Scandinavian system of tax into operation you cannot have free education. I was appalled at the two-tier medical system which contributed to the death of Susie Long in Kilkenny because she was a mere public patient and didn't have access to private medicine. I said in the Senate, and I stand over the fact, that I felt ashamed as a legislator that we had allowed a situation where an Irish citizen could be sentenced to death for the crime of poverty.

The Cathaoirleach in my second term was Seán Doherty, who I found very engaging and good company, but who was an old-style Fianna Fáil rogue of whose actions I rarely approved. I had several serious clashes with him and once almost cost him his job.

There was an Oireachtas delegation going to Nicaragua, which was changed at the last minute to exclude Prof. John A. Murphy, who was representing the independents, and replace him with an FF man. It was suspected that Doherty had, at least, facilitated this switch so I felt something had to be done and the principle of the political neutrality of the Cathaoirleach defended. I made three specific charges against him on the Order of Business. Nothing happened for about three weeks, and Mr Doherty never challenged me in that time. However, on reflection all the parties eventually saw an opportunity to put an awkward young pup from the back benches in his proper place, ganged up on me and demanded I withdraw the remarks. I refused, so they brought it to the Committee on Procedures and Privileges, in front of which I was summoned to appear.

The hearing was held in the Cathaoirleach's office and I told them that I was very happy to co-operate, but only under adequate and proper provisions which would protect my civil and democratic rights: 'I want to be legally represented, I want the right to introduce witnesses, and I want the power to cross-examine. Most importantly, I want Mr Doherty to vacate the chair, as he cannot be the judge in his own case. And if you don't consent to my requirements I will not co-operate, and I will leave this room, seek out my colleague Mary Robinson, and we will get into a taxi and go down to the High Court where I will request a judicial review of your proceedings.' They rejected all my requests – it was a bit like Maggie Thatcher and her infamous 'Out, out, out' speech – and, after telling them they had brought whatever happened on themselves, I nearly took the door off its hinges on the way out.

At Mary's instigation I wrote a very full and detailed account of the whole affair. She told me I must not talk to the press and I observed her instruction to the letter. However, I made two copies and showed them to a couple of colleagues who supported me. I trusted them and one of them I still trust. However, somehow one of the newspapers got hold of the material and published it, accompanied by a photograph that had been taken of me unaware walking down Kildare Street with a briefcase. They also quite inaccurately suggested that I was doing this in order to get a place on the trip for myself, which would not have been technically possible even had I wanted it. I have always objected to the idea of patronage and the dispersal of positions on what are seen by some as 'junkets' as favours within the gift of political parties. They should be used, as I have always used them, to represent Ireland effectively and to stand up for the rights of oppressed people against injustice. Inevitably Mary Robinson saw the article and was furious. I had some difficulty in persuading her that I had not spoken to any newspaper people, but ultimately she accepted this and continued valiantly to fight my case – but it was a close call.

We got our review and it emerged that when Seán Doherty

had taken the matter to the legal officer of the Senate he had been advised that I was right. But he suppressed this advice, keeping it from the other members of the committee. When they found this out his former allies turned on him. It was a difficult time for me but it was a battle worth fighting, and I had marvellous support from Joe O'Toole and a tiny minority of others. There was a stormy confidence debate that went on for three hours, in which for legal reasons I was constrained to reading three carefully crafted paragraphs into the record, and the three Progressive Democrat Senators voted against him even though they were in government with Fianna Fáil. Mr Doherty survived, but by a very small margin.

Seán later had some trouble with the *Sunday Times*, and they asked me to give evidence against him on the basis that I could show he was corrupt because of the way he handled my case. No matter what my own personal reservations about him were, I refused, because I would not assist a Murdoch newspaper in doing down an Irish politician. It was the business of the Senate, not Rupert Murdoch, to deal with Mr Doherty, and we did so.

They tried to subpoena me, but as I knew they were after me I wasn't surprised when a knock came on my office door at Trinity while I was taking a tutorial with a small group of post-graduate students. I whispered a cunning plan to the students then disappeared under the table, and one wonderful American woman played a blinder.

'Have you come with the flowers?' she sobbed, dissolving in tears. 'You must have heard that Mr Norris had a heart attack in the lecture hall a short while ago and has just died,' she wailed. That got rid of the process server, if only temporarily.

They got me in the end and I had to turn up in court, but they knew I was a hostile witness and they did not call me.

Seán was a complex man with sharp intelligence and a keen wit. He had a unique way of talking, using very convoluted, high-sounding sentences in an unsuccessful bid to appear sophisticated. He also had the habit, shared with several Fianna Fáil men of that era, of talking about himself in the third person. I liked his devotion to his family, and late in his life he had a sincere conversion to religion and gave up drink. He and Trevor Sargent organised a series of prayer breakfasts, to which I refused to go as even though I'm a regular churchgoer I cannot bear these kinds of religious huddles.

The Senate had been mathematically constructed by Mr de Valera in such a way as to ensure that it would be virtually impossible to defeat the government. I regarded this as an intellectual challenge and perfected a mechanism to achieve the apparently impossible task. But it would need a particular constellation of events to occur in order to be successful.

My opportunity came on the Larceny Bill. Whenever the legislators were extending protections or privileges to marginalised groups I ensured they included provisions for sexual orientation and membership of the Traveller community. One of my colleagues had put down a well-meaning amendment along these lines to the Larceny Bill but he didn't completely understand the way it worked and, as he worded it, it would have actually boomeranged to penalise gay people more severely. I have a TV monitor in my office to follow proceedings, and on this I spotted a tactical opportunity as there was nobody else from the government side in the chamber.

I ran over to the chamber and started talking about misprision of felony, a technical legal notion that I knew something about, but the Cathaoirleach wouldn't let me speak because the Justice Minister, Ray Burke, had already stood up to reply. So I called for a voice vote, and the Cathaoirleach called for my supporters to say *tá* (yes), which we did, but as the system has an automatic assumption of victory for the government side, he declared the vote defeated. I protested, saying that he had to have heard someone say *níl* (no) for it to be defeated and that wasn't possible because as he could plainly see there wasn't a single person on the government benches.

The Senate clerks started rushing around looking for the books on procedure, and there was an almighty row out in the lobby, before the white-faced Cathaoirleach had to announce we were successful. I then called for a roll-call walk-through vote on the amendment, and they still hadn't sorted it out so I won again. It showed the Senate still had some teeth and taught the government that we couldn't be taken for granted. Mr Haughey was livid and sacked the Fianna Fáil chief whip and the whole Senate front bench. It caused some discomfort to those who had previously dismissed me as an effete academic walkover in political terms.

Although I never had an official meeting with Charles J. Haughey in Government Buildings, we had other encounters. He had turned the sod for the Financial Services Centre using a quote from the Nighttown episode of *Ulysses*, where Bloom imagines he's Lord Mayor of Dublin and says, 'Yea, on the word of a Bloom, ye shall ere long enter into the golden city which is to be, the new Bloomusalem in the Nova Hibernia of the future.'

The *Irish Times* environment correspondent objected to this so I wrote to the *Times*, pointing out that 'the quotation indeed may be appropriate. I recall pointing out at the time that Mr Haughey in his speech appeared to be unaware of the literary significance of context. After all, Bloom was hallucinating when he made this speech, his audience was a collection of whores and drunkards, the location was a brothel and none of the prophecies ever came true.'

About a week later I was up at the conferring of the first degrees at Dublin City University and watched the procession as Charlie marched up wearing a crushed-velvet hat and what looked like the Kinsealy curtains wrapped around him. I gave my neighbour a dig in the ribs and said, in a broad Dublin accent, pointing at Haughey, 'I don't know who SHE is, but I DO love the hat!' The woman squawked with laughter and Charlie stared across and caught me with his gimlet eyes.

Once the ceremony ended I reckoned it was time to beat a hasty retreat, but I didn't realise how fast the Taoiseach could be. He darted across and caught me, growling, 'Senator, I want you to know that, despite what you wrote in the *Irish Times*, I have a deep and abiding love for the works of James Joyce.' We had a mutual friend in Anthony Cronin, who was one of the earliest, finest and most courageous celebrators of Joyce's genius, so I told Charlie that I didn't doubt him, but at least I now knew that whenever I wanted him to get the message I should write to the *Irish Times* and not the Department of the Taoiseach. I had been writing to him over funding the rebuilding of the Hirschfeld Centre and had never got as much as an acknowledgement. He laughed uproariously, and I was on his Christmas-card list thereafter. There was no doubt he was a rogue, but I have always found a sense of humour an engaging quality.

The last time I saw him was at a dinner hosted by John Bruton in honour of Séamus Heaney, who had just been awarded the Nobel Prize for Literature. He was out of politics and wasn't very well, and when he took me aside he said, 'Will you keep an eye on the young lad for me?' I told him that I thought Seán was well able to look after himself, but I think it showed there was a decent, human side to Mr Haughey.

Haughey's great rival in that era was Garret FitzGerald, and I got the chance to compare the two during the preparations for the 1982 International James Joyce Symposium. I found Mr Haughey to be clear and decisive, and whilst FitzGerald was well intentioned and had a genuine interest in Joyce (his father had tried to get him the Nobel Prize), he was fussy and I never quite knew where I was with him. The two portraits hanging on the landing between the Senate and the Dáil capture the two men accurately. Garret is presented in an Impressionistic style, looking fuzzy, his hair resembling a well-used Brillo pad, whereas Charlie has a realistic, almost photographic quality and an imperial pose.

One of my pet projects was the Dublin metro, which I was the first parliamentarian to propose more than twenty years ago. I was passionate about the idea and spoke about it to the *Sunday Tribune*, which got the attention of Cormac Rabbitte and Rudy Monaghan, who had their own plan for a metro. We got together and they briefed me on all the technicalities and became my unpaid specialist advisers. I had been pushing it for some time when the government changed without an election, which produced a very interesting situation in the Seanad. Instead of the automatic government majority there was now a minority there, with the six university Senators holding the balance of power.

I tabled amendments to the Dublin Transport Bill to make provision for the metro, which had the astonishing effect of cabinet ministers phoning me several times a day, putting me under intense pressure to remove the amendments. They came out with the usual line, 'We're going to do this anyway, you're just getting in the way,' but as I knew they had no intention of doing so I insisted on pushing my amendments through.

We enlisted the help of Garret FitzGerald, who had worked as a transport economist, and he did the calculations, which proved that the on-surface Luas tram would not meet the traffic requirements of the city because of its inability to increase the frequency or length of trams, not to mention the visual intrusion of power lines and disruption of traffic. With our underground system you had none of these problems.

On one occasion when Cormac, Rudy and I called up to his house in Palmerston Road for a meeting we discovered that his wife Joan had died that morning. We were shocked, and apologised for intruding, but Garret insisted we come in because he said he wanted to have something else to think about. He made us tea and we sat down and worked out all the calculations, which I think acted as a salve to his grief for a while.

I fought for the metro for many years and enlisted some

powerful allies. Eoin Ryan was a Fianna Fáil junior minister who became convinced of its merits when I got him to meet Professor Manuel Melis Maynar, the man who had driven the building of the Barcelona and Madrid undergrounds at a fraction of the cost and much more quickly than was envisaged for Dublin. Eoin brought it to the cabinet subcommittee.

The mandarins were set against the plan and brought up all sorts of nonsense to stall it. At one stage they said an underground was impossible because of the river running through Dublin. I hit back: 'Imagine, our little Liffey causing so many problems when they could manage to build under far bigger rivers such as the Hudson, the Thames and the Seine.' Then they told me there was something peculiar about the geology of the city, so I told them there was more likely to be something peculiar about their geologists.

Unfortunately we hit the economic downturn before the metro got going, and it has now been 'deferred'. They've spent quite a bit on planning it, though, so I hope it will be returned to at some stage.

The major political figure in my part of the city for many years was Tony Gregory, an independent member of Dáil Éireann from 1982 until his death in 2009, aged just sixty-one. He was a socialist, and his main concern was the living conditions of the people, drugs, housing and employment, and we became great allies. I always said that I had started with an appreciation of architectural values and through that developed a realisation of people's needs. Tony's motivation was the people, but through that he came to appreciate the architecture. He would tease me about being part of 'the gin-and-tonic brigade', but grew to appreciate what we were doing on North Great Georges Street, both in aesthetic and practical terms, with our employment of twenty people to work in the Joyce Centre on a FÁS community employment scheme.

Tony did extraordinary work in the area, and hasn't been

given enough credit for coming up with the idea for the Criminal Assets Bureau. He saw that the only way to catch the drug dealers was to look at their tax, social security and police records together. I pushed it in the Senate and made sure the part that he played was acknowledged in the official account of the proceedings.

He also had a lighter side. He and Mick Rafferty would come up to the Joyce Centre every Bloomsday and have the crowd in stitches of laughter with their performance of passages from *Ulysses*. They later organised their own Bloomsday festival in the neighbouring area, where they would re-enact Nighttown with the local women dressed up as tarts.

When Tony was first elected he held the balance of power and saw his chance to do a deal to benefit his long-neglected constituents. He summoned Haughey and FitzGerald up to his office in Ballybough, a poor neighbourhood in the north inner city, and played them off against each other. He ended up delivering schools, playgrounds and employment to his margin-alised people in the most deprived part of Dublin. Mr Haughey was a dealmaker and, in the case of the 'Gregory Deal', he kept his word and a serious intervention was made in return for Tony's support. However, the agreement collapsed when Dr FitzGerald took over. The further implementation of measures to relieve the poverty and distress of the inner city were aban-doned in favour of right-wing policies, despite all Dr FitzGerald's personal charm and decency.

Tony and I battled in the Oireachtas against the scourge of the drugs trade, which decimated our neighbourhood for years. The war on drugs is nonsense in my opinion, a waste of time and already lost in any case. The amount of drugs seized by the gardaí is minimal and represents a small percentage of the true movement of drugs through this country. The only solution is to legalise, regulate and monitor, but this is not a problem that can be solved by Ireland alone – it has to be done at a global level. The drugs trade can be destroyed only if it is attacked at its root, which is financial reward. All that previous policies have done is help enormous profits accrue to criminals. The result is the drug-crazed arrogance of gangsters and the horrific grief of so many families, many of them innocent victims caught in the brutal crossfire.

I was privileged to do Tony's last interview. I was presenting a show on Newstalk and when he came into the studio straight from his cancer therapy it was obvious he could barely walk. He told me straight, 'I don't know if I can do this,' but I told him not to worry, that there was no pressure. If he liked he could just come in and have a cup of coffee and see how he felt, we could stop the interview any time he wanted. We started talking about the usual subjects, but the minute Tony got on to ideas his eyes lit up, and he became very animated. I couldn't stop him talking. He was terribly frail but mentally he was still radiant and his spirit was transcendent.

Albert Reynolds was another politician I liked personally, and he once showed me considerable generosity. One of the restrictions placed on the Senate is that anything it proposes cannot create a cost on the exchequer. That means you cannot really bring in amendments on the Budget, but you can make recommendations, or *molltaí*.

I was exercised by the preservation of Dublin's inner city and I drafted a series of proposals giving tax relief to individual owners who were preserving listed buildings. I went to meet people in the Department of Finance but made the terrible mistake of going in on my own, and as I am useless at arithmetic the civil servants tied me in knots. I gave up after half an hour, saying, 'You have conclusively proved me wrong here, but I still know I'm right and so if you will indulge me I will be back with someone who can explain my ideas in your language.' I got hold of the economist Paul Tansey and he argued my case brilliantly.

On Budget day I was having lunch in the canteen when the Cathaoirleach, Senator Tras Honan, came over, grabbed me by the arm and said, 'David, you've missed your moment of glory.

It's a great day for the Seanad! Albert is after accepting three and a half pages of your amendments; it has never been done before and he's named you as the originator.' That was extraordinarily generous of Albert, as the usual way governments adopted ideas was to reject the amendment and then come up with their own similar wording, as they never want to give credit to anyone else.

I got a chance to return the favour in a small way some years later, at a conference about Northern Ireland in Merton College, Oxford. At one session a group of English politicians were sneering at Albert because he had started off as a railway porter in Longford. It's a vulgar trait one finds in certain sections of English 'society' – some Tory MPs used to heckle the deputy PM John Prescott by shouting, 'Two gin and tonics, please' because he had been a steward on a cruise liner. I was furious, and knew that Albert had risen to lead our country by hard work and intelligence, making his fortune as a music promoter, showband impresario and pet-food manufacturer. I told them, 'I'm half English but it disgusts me to hear this kind of thing. You look down on the Jews, the Chinese and the Irish, who are infinitely more aristocratic than you are. You have an armorial orgasm if you can go back as far as the Battle of Waterloo, whereas there are people in Ireland, China and Israel who can trace themselves back to the birth of history.' They would have done better to listen to the simple wisdom of a man like Albert Reynolds who, whatever else one might say about him, certainly had his finger on the pulse of the Irish people.

It is dangerous to generalise, but having ancestors in both lands I feel I can say that the English as a group are infinitely less sophisticated than the Irish. The English idea of humour is a one-liner with sexual innuendo. They don't understand the storytelling of the Irish. Their cartoonists, as far back as James Gillray, are crude, depicting the Irish as apes, and newspaper headlines use infantile language to abuse people with lines such as 'FROG OFF'. Their press is the reason why they got disastrous leaders like Margaret Thatcher and Tony Blair and got rid of people like Edward Heath, who was a very good leader but widely lampooned over his heaving-shoulder laugh and limp handshake.

Even in Ireland, John Bruton's distinctive braying laugh made people discount him. That was a mistake, because he was a highly intelligent man, if not nearly as gifted as his brother Richard. Mr Bruton always seemed to me to be prone to conservative views and in his job as EU Ambassador to the United Nations he was far too close to the Bush regime.

Bruton was succeeded as Taoiseach by my local TD, Bertie Ahern, but any dream his constituents might have had that this would herald a golden age for Dublin Central was sadly to prove fruitless. He did very little for the north inner city – Parnell Street was a total disgrace and remains so, with only the arrival of the Asian and African entrepreneurs, who have set up shops and restaurants on short leases, giving it a new energy. The roads are potholed, the pavements are dangerous and from the Rotunda Hospital down to Capel Street there's nothing left of a glorious stretch of Georgian Dublin. Several of the façades on that street were protected, but were allowed to decay and then demolished. It was such a betrayal of the city by Mr Ahern to allow that to go unchecked, despite plenty of lobbying and pressure from myself and others.

With Bertie, you always departed his office feeling you had got the sun, the moon and the stars. But as the door closed the sun went into an eclipse, the moon went in behind a cloud, and the stars twinkled out one by one. By the time you got to the end of the corridor all you had left was a nice, fuzzy feeling.

Brian Cowen, who succeeded him, sometimes appeared ungainly and even boorish, but behind that there was a very sharp intellect and a considerable sense of humour. When he was Foreign Minister I approached him over individual human-rights cases, and there was none of his usual bluster – I found him open and sensitive, a side the public never saw.

He and Brian Lenihan made dreadful decisions, but very few people understand what it is like to be in such a position as they found themselves. Politicians are much more timorous than they're given credit for. Noël Browne had the courage to take on the system – but all the *taoisigh* I've known were *part* of the system, and an expression of it. And when the system turned against them, they buckled. So when the banks called them to that fateful midnight meeting of 29/30 September 2008, Mr Cowen and Mr Lenihan gave in immediately, because they had nothing to protect them against that particular threat. They had the armour to protect themselves against individual attacks from within or without their own or other parties, but when the *system* itself put them under pressure they just didn't know what to do.

But I have always been fighting against the system, so that inside I developed the steel and determination that few of the politicians could afford to show. I knew the mistakes that were being made, and they were the same all over Europe. The preservation of the system was put before the welfare of the people, which was completely the wrong priority. In good government, whether at national or European level, priority should be given to the welfare of the people, then the effect on the system assessed and the system recalibrated to cater for the well-being of the people. Unfortunately, there appear to be no political leaders in Europe with a sense of vision. They tend to think in parochial terms of their own, or party political, advantage. When I think of this I am reminded of the greatest Roman emperor, Marcus Aurelius, whose *Meditations* form part of my favourite reading. The eighteenth-century historian Edward Gibbon is scathing about all the other emperors, but of Marcus Aurelius he says that he was unique because he put the welfare of his people above everything else. Would that some of our own leaders could share that epitaph.

Margaret Thatcher introduced a very nasty clause into British legislation, banning what she described as the 'promotion' of homosexuality. This was after her attention was drawn to a little booklet published in Denmark called *Jenny Lives with Eric and Martin*. I was curious and secured a copy. It was a little illustrated pamphlet which described a weekend in Copenhagen where two gay men were living together. One of them had previously been married and had a daughter. He maintained good relations with his former wife and the little girl used to come and spend weekends with the two men. One section illustrated an incident when the three of them were out on the street and a neighbour started shouting abuse. The child was frightened but the men explained to her that this was just an elderly neighbour who was confused. They told her that the majority of people find their life partner to be a person of the opposite sex but a small number find that they want to share their life with someone of the same sex. Since this was something that hadn't been discussed openly until recently, people of their neighbour's age were frightened of this apparently new idea and this was what had led to the insults. It seemed to me to be a perfectly wholesome and reasonable attitude to take, and I felt that young people could only benefit from such good common sense. I tried to table a motion about it in the Senate. However, I found to my amazement that not one of the fifty-nine other Senators in the house was prepared to sign my motion in order to allow it to be discussed. Apparently it was the mere existence of a child in the story that had imposed this *fatwa* upon open discussion. As someone who has always fought not only for the rights of gay people but for children, I was very saddened by this.

Indeed, one of my proudest achievements was the passing of the 'guardian *ad litem*' amendment in 1996. I had been briefed by the children's charity Barnardo's about the case of a seven-year-old in Britain called Maria Colwell who had been abused by her stepfather, but after intervention by the local authorities she was returned to him and subsequently murdered. It led to a change in the law there with the introduction of the guardian *ad litem*, an officer appointed by the court to represent exclusively the welfare of the child.

I put that down on the order paper, seconded by Senator Brendan Ryan, and although I argued for several weeks with the Junior Minister, Noel Treacy, he was under constant pressure not to accept my amendment. In the end I wore him down and Mr Treacy said he would take the risk because it was in the interest of children. And I know that it has saved children, which is why it really hurt when I was portrayed during the presidential election as in some way disposed to the abuse of children. Nothing could have been further from the truth and the record shows that. I feel that I have at least as great a practical track record for protecting children as any other parliamentarian in this country.

I have monitored the use of guardian *ad litem* since, but it hasn't been adequately resourced. In awful instances like the Roscommon incest case it was found that the system was not operated effectively and horrendous crimes were committed. That is the most frustrating and heartbreaking thing of all: I did my work as a legislator on behalf of children, but the state failed them.

The state has also failed the people at large, in the matter of the financial crisis. In some ways I would have loved to have been involved in politics at the higher level, but the least attractive job to me would have been minister for finance. I have difficulty with numbers but I am good with ideas.

I was able to see what was happening as our economy un-ravelled in the late 2000s. I spoke five times in the Senate, warning about the dangerous bubble, and questioning the role of the ratings agencies, Lehman Brothers and Goldman Sachs – and was one of only five Senators to vote against the suicidal bank guarantee. I also put the names of the hitherto secret bondholders on the record of the Senate, to ensure the Irish people knew to whom they were beholden, despite the fact that the Cathaoirleach became apoplectic and nearly cracked the

Senate bell with his gong trying to silence me. Eventually, because I refused to be intimidated, he had to suspend the Senate for half an hour and move to the next business.

The level of ignorance in some of the financial debates was astounding. When we were coming to the first bank guarantee, I asked what I thought was the crucial question: 'What exactly is the size of the guarantee?' The answer was €400 billion. I next asked what was our gross national product. There was confusion among the advisers and a telephone call had to be made to discover that the GNP for the previous year was €200 billion. I pointed out that we were giving an undertaking that could cost us a minimum of twice our entire GNP. This seemed to me to be insanity, but I was the only one who asked such a question. I could see that there would be a mortgage crisis in which people's very homes would be threatened. I proposed the creation of a department of home security to protect citizens in this area, but regrettably this was ignored. In fact I realised subsequently that what I was witnessing was the greatest transfer of wealth from the poor to the rich in human history.

Behind the concept of the state lies the reality of the people. The experience and suffering of ordinary citizens has been completely ignored.

In my contributions in the Senate I mined back through the Phil Monaghan lecture that I had given in Cork University some years before. In particular I thought we should be going to the root of the whole problem within the financial system, and I gave a definition of money which I have never seen anywhere else. I described money as 'the symbolic representation of energy'. In the old days you worked for the farmer, and in reward for your day's work he gave you a sack of potatoes which was practical, tangible and realistic and which you could use to feed your family. The next stage was that the farmer gave you half a sack of potatoes and a gold mark. The potatoes now represented a diminishing asset and the gold mark, although it had a degree of intrinsic value because of the precious metal involved, was moving inexorably towards the merely symbolic. Then came the development of paper money, and I well remember on top of the old banknotes the words 'The Governor of the Bank of Ireland promises to pay the bearer on demand the sum of £20 or its equivalent' – presumably in gold. Fat chance!

With the Industrial Revolution and the mechanisation of industry, people wanted to expand their factories and so the Stock Exchange developed so that factory owners and industrialists could float loans in return for dividends to be paid to those who had invested. To that you can add the development of wireless telegraphy and the so-called futures markets, in which next year's crops could be traded, and you have a situation in which notional money could be transmitted transcontinentally by electronic means to purchase things that didn't even exist. It was becoming a mixture of madhouse and casino.

This effect was greatly magnified in recent years by the use of computers and the cocaine-fuelled energies of some participants in the big stock markets. It was not long before inexperienced young dealers were gambling away incalculable amounts of money and when their gambles did not succeed venerable institutions which had successfully traded for centuries were brought to their knees, pensions lost and people left un-employed. In many sections of the international stock market the human element appears to have been deleted altogether and replaced by mathematical algorithms stored on computers that automatically instruct when to purchase or sell shares, regard-less of a wider understanding of prevailing conditions. Most horribly, a series of academic articles have suggested recently that a number of the major investment houses have used their financial might deliberately to help instigate food shortages through the buying of futures in order to make a profit. The much-vaunted market is completely indifferent to the misery and destruction of people.

I recall the collapse of Communism, when there was a certain amount of gloating in political circles, and warning that the next obsequies might be for Capitalism. It was so obviously based on a flawed premise: that of the infinitely expanding market. The markets, and even the production of goods, cannot expand infinitely when confronted by the finite resources of a small planet.

In the Senate I pointed to the historical precedent of how the German Reich was constructed by Bismarck from the raw material of Prussia and an assortment of small kingdoms, princedoms and dukedoms. They first of all created a customs union, the Zollverein, and this released centrifugal and centripetal forces that led almost inevitably to the unification of Germany.

I repeatedly stated my belief that these same forces had been released by a series of EU treaties, making it more and more inescapable that Europe would either federalise or burst apart as a result of the ability or inability of its leaders to control the fiscal destiny of the continent.

Of course, some financial institutions prospered during all this mess. Goldman Sachs, who helped to massage the Greek government's accounts and continually sailed very close to the wind, was among these. But perhaps most noxious were the ratings agencies who had already been involved in the Enron collapse and the production of the so-called 'toxic bundles' in which unsustainable subprime mortgages were given a coating of acceptable products. It seems now as if a small number of enormous financial institutions and ratings agencies, which grew fat on conflicts of interest, have greater powers than government; as a result people all over the world are driven into penury and misery. I have several times called for the creation of an international financial court, before which individuals and companies could be tried for economic crimes against humanity, as in the Nuremberg trials, where major companies such as I. G. Farben, Thyssen and Krupp were indicted and senior executives were tried and convicted.

I made the point that the financial crisis wasn't a tsunami, earthquake or any other sort of natural disaster – it was a man-made one and must therefore be susceptible to a man-made solution. I then asked them to look at which financial institution had actually worked in the interests of the Irish people, and the obvious one was the National Treasury Management Agency, so I suggested we have a National Property Management Agency. This was a full three months before the government came up with its idea of the National Asset Management Agency. This seemed to me, when it eventually emerged, like a toxic, bastardised version of my original notion and, as I pointed out in the Senate, the title itself was rubbish because what they were managing were not assets – there were virtually no assets left within Anglo Irish Bank – but liabilities.

My solution was to first nationalise the banks and amalgamate them into a single entity called the Bank of Ireland, strain out all the septic elements into a 'bad bank' and then metaphorically tow Anglo Irish Bank out and sink it in the Atlantic. My NPMA would then manage the assets, principally property, in the interest of the Irish people.

One idea I put forward was to take a portion of the land banks around the major population centres and parcel the land into allotments for the four hundred thousand un-employed, which they would get on application, and subject to review. They would then be issued with seeds, tools and a manual. This plan would have got people off the couch to become active and in contact with living things. It would help their diet, their budget and their mood. It was a simple idea which I brought up several times without anyone reporting it. I complained that the media only allowed me to be heard by the people when I talked about buggery or Joyce, so of course the next day's newspaper headline was NORRIS COMPLAINS ABOUT BUGGERY AND JOYCE, with virtually nothing about my financial proposals.

The Oireachtas sat into the early hours of the morning for a week to get through the NAMA legislation – though it was interesting how some high-profile members didn't bother to show unless there were media opportunities. Joe O'Toole and I worked hard to get several amendments into the Bill, which made NAMA accountable to the Oireachtas. This was a very important part of the legislation but not a single word was written in the media about it.

In the Senate Joe was a great strategist and fantastic for doing deals, as well as a terrific speaker in both Irish and English. He is also the most loyal friend you could have. He was very wise, and wily, instantly spotting the reason why particular moves were being made. He was pretty fearless too, and well respected as he had been a national figure as president of the Irish Congress of Trade Unions. Joe had a roguish sense of humour, which had outward expression in never wearing his tie straight, but flicked over his shoulder. He worked hard in the Senate and was steadfast in supporting me in the traumas of the Doherty case, as well as on East Timor and gay rights.

During the Senate debate I told Brian Lenihan that I had analysed what he had meant when he used phrases like 'Anglo Irish Bank is of systemic importance' and therefore had to be rescued regardless of the consequences. Essentially – whether he knew it or not – what he was saying was that the preservation of the system was of greater importance than the welfare of the people, which I told him was a catastrophic error which would come back to haunt the country. Good government must always put the welfare of the people above the preservation of the system, but they were preserving a system that was rotten and should have been allowed to collapse. This, it turned out, was not just an Irish but an international problem. The politicians' response to the economic crisis was indecisive and dithering. What we needed was clear thinking and decisions in the interest of the people, but they allowed themselves to be bullied by the bankers.

What was appalling about the crisis was the way certain

elements of the establishment used it to silence their opponents and settle old scores. In full knowledge of what was coming down the tracks, the government and civil servants abolished the Combat Poverty Agency, and then went after the Equality Authority and the Human Rights Commission. The Equality Authority's budget was slashed and a new board installed. I was astonished at the way some people were complicit in this, and went on the attack. I secured a two-hour debate in my Private Members Time and said that we were facing a financial disaster and the government was deliberately silencing or neutering all the bodies charged with defending the vulnerable people who were going to bear the brunt of the pain. I thought it was so important to warn the people and send a shot across the bows of government that uncharacteristically I wrote the speech out and issued it to every newspaper and radio and TV station. I needn't have bothered, because once again an important issue that affected every citizen was left totally unreported by the media.

The Senate still plays a vital role in public life. A lot of the criticism of it is based on ignorance and misinformation. The reason why the government wants to abolish the Seanad is not financial or democratic, but because there are still a few dissenting voices there that cause them trouble. The Seanad has a role as the conscience of the Oireachtas and I see myself as part of a line that stretches from Sheehy-Skeffington, through Browne, Robinson, Higgins and O'Toole – Senators who have stood up on behalf of people who would never have their interests represented otherwise, and certainly not by government.

CHAPTER 11

Foreign Affairs

BACK IN THE 1980S, I WAS ONE OF THE FEW PEOPLE IN IRISH public life to criticise Saddam Hussein and voted against our export deals with him because of his treatment of various minorities, including the Kurds. An army marches on its stomach, and the fact that his Iraqi revolutionary guards were marching with stomachs full of prime Irish beef didn't sit well with me.

In the Senate I proposed cancelling the contracts, to which the government spokesman replied that whilst I may have articulated a moral view, was it one Ireland could afford? He was a decent man who I always liked, but I rounded on him, asking was Ireland unable to afford a moral foreign policy? If so, why did we have a Christian constitution? I called for a vote, but only a handful backed me. There is no doubt that our constitution is a Christian one. This was the fundamental legal concept quoted against me in his negative judgement by Justice McWilliam in the High Court. What I wanted the government spokesman to tell me was why the Christian morality of our constitution wasn't extended to foreign policy. In the end we had the worst of both worlds – we sold the beef, Saddam's government defaulted on the payments, and the export credit-guarantee system which was invoked by the beef barons actually cost the Irish people over £100 million. If they'd taken my advice they would not only have done the decent thing but they would have saved a hell of a lot of money as well.

It was always difficult to get accountability in issues of foreign policy because the minister would hide behind the mandarins in Iveagh House, and they would hide behind the minister. It irritated me that we were unique as a parliament in Europe in not having a foreign affairs committee. Although it had been proposed several times, it had always been shot down at the insistence of Iveagh House, who didn't want ordinary public representatives sticking their noses into such elevated areas of policy.

I raised the notion of a joint Oireachtas foreign affairs committee in my Private Members Time several times in succession. I researched the record and found that Senators always voted in favour of it when they were in opposition, and against it when they were in government. On my third attempt to raise the issue, I was able to produce a list which demonstrated that at one stage or another every single Senator had voted in its favour. I announced that 'There is clearly unanimity about the question, as everyone is on the record in acknowledging we need a foreign affairs committee. And while the government is having a technical difficulty in implementing the wishes of Parliament, I am happy to step into the breach and provide a Framework Foreign Affairs Committee, the first meeting of which will be held on Wednesday at two p.m. in Kildare House.'

I met Michael D. Higgins for coffee and told him that a committee with him at its head would have a greater chance of being taken seriously, so he consented to become chair, with me as secretary. Obstacles were raised and I had great difficulty getting a committee room, but I threatened I would go public if they persisted. To the great alarm of the government and Iveagh House, prominent members of all parties – including Fianna Fáil TDs such as David Andrews and Tom Kitt – turned up and put themselves forward for the committee.

I wrote to announce our formation to all the other foreign affairs committees in Europe, and some of them wrote back, which gave us a degree of recognition. I announced this *de facto* situation in the Senate. The idea of a foreign affairs committee headed by Messrs Higgins and Norris was not the kind of thing that appealed to either Mr Haughey or the mandarins. All kinds of attempts were made to block it, such as not being permitted to circulate information to the members about meetings. I got around that by putting down motions which said that 'Seanad Éireann takes notice of the fact that there will be a meeting of the Foreign Affairs Committee in room eleven at 2 p.m. on Thursday.' I would then read this out perfectly legally on the order paper at the start of the day's business, which meant everyone got the message.

Eventually the Higgins/Norris nightmare was sufficient catalyst to prompt the government into establishing an official Joint Oireachtas Foreign Affairs Committee, and I have been on it since the start, the only member to have served without a break.

Our first chairman was Brian Lenihan Sr, who proved excellent as not only was he a former foreign minister but as a decent man he was impartial and gave everyone a chance to contribute. He was succeeded as chair by Dessie O'Malley, who was prepared to allow the committee to take challenging positions. For instance, Ireland had stayed neutral at the United Nations with regard to the imposition of sanctions on Cuba by the United States of America. An attempt was made to slide us unobtrusively into the American camp and change our neutral position to a yes vote. This was spotted by our committee, and a fairly tense exchange of messages occurred with our representatives in New York which ensured we did not, on that occasion at least, become yes-men. I approached Mr O'Malley and suggested we establish a small bureau of five to set the agenda, which became a very powerful group. Naturally I made sure I was a member of this élite grouping, which meant I could raise issues like Tibet and East Timor.

*

The Foreign Affairs Committee had a budget which could be used to organise fact-finding missions abroad, which led to us being called 'the Trips Committee'. I never regarded it as such, and on numerous occasions I turned down trips or passed them on to people who I knew had a particular interest in the subject. One trip I was invited on was to Israel, but because I thought it was important other people got the chance to see the situation I got someone else to take my place. I knew the country and the issues very well, so taking a free trip would be a waste of the taxpayers' money. I made sure I was there for all the meetings, however, by joining the travelling party at my own expense.

Some of the trips were to attend the Assembly of the Inter Parliamentary Union. Some parliamentarians go through their entire career without attending even a single assembly, but I was lucky enough to attend four. The IPU is a gathering of elected representatives of virtually all the parliaments of the world, and does much good work fostering understanding between politicians and promoting human rights.

I had developed what the Irish call 'a devotion' to a remarkable man called Raoul Wallenberg, a Swedish diplomat who had saved tens of thousands of Jews during the Second World War as a special representative in Budapest. At risk of his own life, he went unarmed on to the cattle trains taking the despised Jews to Auschwitz, and rescued them by issuing Swedish passports. When Budapest fell to the Red Army he was arrested on suspicion of espionage, 'disappeared', and after the war was shamefully abandoned to his fate. The Russians originally claimed that he had been shot by Hungarian fascists. In fact what happened was he was arrested and interrogated by the Soviets, who didn't believe his story about trying to save the lives of Jews. They decided he was a spy and arrested him. I was subsequently told that unfortunately a KGB officer – later to rise dizzyingly through the ranks of the Kremlin – stole his car and some valuable items. This was one of the elements that later complicated Wallenberg's fate.

In recent years the Russians have admitted that they had originally lied about his death in 1945, and that he had still been alive in the Lubyanka until 1947, when he allegedly died of a heart attack. But for many years there was a belief that he was still alive, strongly supported by circumstantial evidence, which I assiduously gathered, and I became part of an international campaign that was waged to secure his release. I am convinced that he survived for at least thirty years after his capture. It is astonishing that such a noble man was abandoned to his fate by the Allies, his own government and even some members of his own family.

One interesting aspect of the story emerged when the Department of Foreign Affairs asked me to entertain a delightful visitor called Alvar Alsterdal, the Swedish cultural attaché in London who was interested in Joyce. I agreed to do so on condition he told me in return what he knew about Wallenberg. When I had sated his taste for Joyce, he asked me what I had thought of the recent film about Wallenberg that had been made starring Richard Chamberlain. I told him it was rather chocolate-boxy, especially the scene where Chamberlain jumps on board a moving train with a bottle of champagne and two glasses in a romantic gesture aimed at a Hungarian countess. Alsterdal told me that was just Hollywood, because Wallenberg wasn't interested in women; he was gay. It was an important moment for me to discover that someone I enormously admired was also a member of my slim pantheon of gay heroes. I never used this information publicly, as I thought it might discredit my efforts on his behalf by suggesting I had an ulterior motive for pushing the Wallenberg case.

There was an IPU meeting in Budapest and as it was being held around the anniversary of Wallenberg's disappearance I secured a speaking slot in advance from the organisers. On the plane over I was told the leader of our delegation had commandeered my slot, which led to a huge row. Eventually we agreed to split the time, but my antagonist spoke first and because his speaking style was tedious, flatulent and cliché-ridden, he went way over time and had to be 'gonged' three times. That meant there was no possibility whatever of my speaking in any slot.

Afterwards I went to the platform secretary to discuss my difficulty, explaining that I had a gentleman's agreement, but how of course they only work when *both* parties are gentlemen. I explained my passionate commitment to Raoul Wallenberg and asked could he help me to secure another slot. His reply wasn't what I expected.

'Is that a *Trinity* tie?' he asked.

'It is,' I replied.

'How *is* R. B. D. French?'

It turned out that R.B.D. had been his tutor. He went on to explain to me that if I was to vote against any of the plenary votes at the full session, he would have to call on me to explain my dissenting vote. So, in the interests of justice I voted against whatever was proposed, and therefore got the chance to speak, which I used to highlight Raoul Wallenberg. Afterwards one of the interpreters came to me in tears because her father had been one of those saved by Wallenberg.

When I got the itinerary for the IPU meeting in Canberra in 1993, I saw that we were travelling first-class. I wasn't a member of the government so didn't need to travel first-class, so I asked the office could I use the fare to make some travel arrangements of my own to do some work on the way.

They agreed to that, so as both Trinity and the Senate were out of term I travelled Dublin–London–Singapore–Hong Kong–Beijing–Canberra, staying two or three days in each. In Beijing I got in touch with the Irish Ambassador, who invited me to dinner with a charming couple called Wen Jieruo and Xiao Qian. Xiao was a celebrated Chinese writer and journalist who had decided to translate *Ulysses* – 'In old age one should do something monumental,' he said – and I can't imagine anything more monumental at eighty-five years of age.

We discussed how the Oxen of the Sun episode could be represented in Chinese, with its hotchpotch of styles and pastiches up to modern American slang. It would not make sense to a reader unfamiliar with the development of English literature, so he decided to base it on the development of Chinese from ancient scripts up to modern Beijing slang. Xiao was educated in England and had known many important literary figures. He had letters from E. M. Forster which the Red Guards forced him to burn during the Cultural Revolution. Such almost accidental cultural exchanges can bear significant fruit, and I was delighted that as a result of this meeting I and a couple of others were invited back for the launch of the translation. Such developments can lead to greater understanding between peoples.

At the IPU meeting itself I raised a series of issues and took the opportunity of being in the Australian Parliament to denounce Australian policy on East Timor in the presence of the Foreign Minister. I named ten Timorese people who were being illegally detained by the Indonesians. Some time later they sent me a colourful traditional robe to thank me, saying I had saved their lives by naming them. I made a fraternal visit to the East Timor Embassy, which was an old freight container painted with the black and red colours of the Timorese flag, and got on Australian television news and in all the newspapers. It was a significant contribution and was widely covered all over the world, but strangely not mentioned at all in the Irish media. I asked one newspaper executive when I got home why that was and I was told, 'An Irish politician on a junket is a story; an Irish politician working is not sexy. It's just not a story at all.'

At the end of the conference I flew on to Fiji, via New Zealand, and spent a week there visiting some of the uninhabited islands and attracting some marriage proposals. Alas, they came from a pair of dusky maidens and I could not bring myself to commit to a mixed marriage. They were cuddly and good-humoured, but they *were* women. I spent the weekend with friends in Los Angeles before flying home via London. On my round-the-world trip I had worked harder than anyone else, *and* enjoyed myself, and it cost the taxpayer less than if I had taken the first-class trip.

A year later there was an invitation on the mat from the Chinese government along the lines: 'Dear Mr Norris, please you will attend the translate of your book *Ulysses*, you will arrive on Friday. We will pay nothing; your government will pay everything. Please confirm your attendance.' I was touched, and amused as well as flattered to have been suspected of having perpetrated *Ulysses* among my other crimes – and to further extend the fun I sent it on to Iveagh House for a view. They decided to send me, as well as Bob Joyce from the Joyce Centre, and Declan Kiberd from UCD.

I gave a paper which referred to the Cyclops episode, in which Leopold Bloom is attacked over his race, and he gets into a definition of what is a nation. So after a brief disquisition on the text, I told them that it is important that we don't leave these as mere academic ideas; the real test is to apply them to one's own situation. 'Yes,' they cried, 'we must learn.' OK, I said, let's take the example of Tibet – it is geographically separate, had its independence for hundreds of years, has a different language, religion, ethnicity and geography. So is Tibet a nation? There was what could truly be described as a free and frank exchange of views, which was such a success that I did it everywhere I went in China. When I got home I was astonished to read a piece in the *Irish Times* about the trip which suggested that I had never once mentioned Tibet!

I experienced further excitement in Baghdad in December 2000, when I joined an Oireachtas delegation made up of David Andrews, Michael D. Higgins, John Gormley and Senator Mick Lanigan. Because of the sanctions we were unable to fly into

Iraq, so instead we were met by a relative of Saddam Hussein in Amman in Jordan and brought in a convoy across the desert. That was a nightmare journey of 1,100 kilometres, as everyone was carsick at speeds of over 150 kph. The other side of the road was filled with convoys of sanctions-busting oil tankers, and because the surface was littered with oil slicks we kept swerving on to the sand. They were reluctant to stop even for a pee because, as we found out afterwards, there were armed insurgent groups along the route who frequently took hostages, especially well-fed Westerners.

Besides our work for the Oireachtas, I had another mission in Baghdad. Just before the trip I had been asked by an American pharmaceutical company to do a big after-dinner speech-cum-entertainment at a major conference in Powerscourt, for which they offered me several thousand pounds. I was aware that the United Nations sanctions were having a devastating effect on the Iraqi health service, so I contacted some of the aid agencies and asked them to find out what was needed at the children's hospital in Baghdad. They got me a list, of penicillin and painkillers etc., and I punted my fee on acquiring the required items. I brought two suitcases to Baghdad, one with my pyjamas and the other packed tight with medicines, syringes and God knows what. I was terrified it would be opened at one of the airports through which we passed on our way to the Middle East. That would have given the papers headlines about 'Drug Smuggler Norris', as it was contrary to UN sanctions, although I felt justified in sanctions-busting in the face of the suffering of innocent children. I arranged to meet someone in the car park of the hotel, where I handed the contraband over, and later on during the trip we visited the children's hospital, where we saw the terrible sight of mothers nursing children who were suffering from enriched-uranium poisoning, as they were later to suffer the effects of white phosphorous illegally used against the civilian population of Fallujah.

Of all our meetings there, the most impressive was with a

young doctor who was also Minister for Health. You could see he was agonised by the lack of instruments and drugs deliberately withheld under sanctions. He may have been a member of the Ba'ath Party but he wasn't kowtowing, he had no respect for the officials and only cared about the staff and patients. I saw him as a Noël Browne type of doctor – a man who identified with the people.

We met the Foreign Minister, Tariq Aziz, who was quite a small man and dressed in military fatigues. These occasions are usually highly choreographed and not entirely realistic. There will be an exchange of pleasantries by the senior figures, then everyone else gets their chance down the line. Our delegation was led by David Andrews, who was a recent Foreign Affairs minister and chairman of the Irish Red Cross. During his speech he mentioned the phrase 'humanitarian values', at which Tariq Aziz exploded and told him that Iraq was not a Third World country, to be lectured to about human rights by the likes of Ireland. He told us forcefully that his country was the cradle of civilisation, and condemned Anglo-American-Israeli aggression.

I was a lowly member of the delegation and had to wait a while before I had a chance to speak, but by the time it arrived I was ready to give it to him right between the eyes. I said, 'As regards Anglo-American-Israeli aggression, you're not exactly virgins on that score but luckily most of the things you fired over at Israel weren't fired straight so they landed in the sand. And as far as humanitarian issues are concerned, I expect you to be on my side, Dr Aziz. The principal reason I'm here is to look at the impact of United Nations sanctions on hospitals and on the women and children treated there. And I support your government and others in the rejection of these sanctions. But I'm also interested in the impact of your government's policies on your own people . . .'

'Such as what?' he demanded.

'Well, how about intimidation, arbitrary arrest, illegal detention, torture, imprisonment, and murder, for a start?'

'None of that is true,' he said.

I contradicted him, and told him I was a patron of a group in Ireland who dealt with victims of torture by the regime he represented. I had met them and seen their scars. He demanded their names, and I told him he must be joking: these people still had families in Iraq who might be endangered by my doing so. He said that it was a lie, and that the tortured people were CIA agents, at which I exploded and started shouting at him.

'How dare you make this accusation against these people who've already suffered enough? I demand you withdraw that disgraceful remark and apologise.'

We had to be hauled apart by uniformed staff before David Andrews stepped in and mollified the situation and the meeting continued. I remembered that Dr Aziz was Christian, so when we were leaving, as it was nearly Christmas, I wished him the compliments of the season and we shook hands.

As he left the room the former Foreign Minister said to me out of the side of his mouth, 'I sincerely hope, Norris, that we get out of this fucking country alive after what you just said to him!'

Months later I received an invitation to the sixtieth birthday party of Saddam Hussein and an offer to fly me to Baghdad. I didn't know whether this was a salute to my bravery or a ploy to get me there so I could be assassinated with the prod of a poisoned umbrella in my behind. I told my PA to reply: 'Mr Norris regrets he is unable to dine tonight.'

As a result of my vocal support of the Tibetan people, I was asked by the Unrepresented Nations and Peoples Organisation to be part of their delegation to visit Lhasa. UNPO represents lots of peoples without an independent state such as Kosovans, Assyrians, Kurds and Tibetans. The delegation also included two Dutch people, Cees Flinterman, a professor of human-rights law, and Josephine Verspaget, a Member of Parliament.

We flew to Beijing first, then to the western Chinese city of

Xi'an, where the famous Terracotta Army was discovered. We had a day to kill in the hotel, which I decided to fill by seeing these extraordinary statues. The organisers wanted us to lie low by staying in the hotel, but I thought that would make us look even more suspicious as we were supposed to be tourists, so off we went to find the soldiers. Our taxi-man misunderstood our wish to see ancient sites and brought us to an appalling theme park where the Seven Wonders of the World had all been rebuilt – the Hanging Gardens of Babylon, the pyramids and the rest, all lovingly recreated in plastic – but we did ultimately find the emperor's warriors.

It was difficult at the time to get into Tibet, but we eventually flew to Lhasa. As soon as we got there we felt the pressure from the altitude – Lhasa is 11,500 feet above sea level – and we all got headaches. Josephine Verspaget was the worst affected and had to have treatment and use an oxygen pillow.

The first thing we saw when we left the airport was the largest cement factory in the world, which we later visited. There was a complete city built inside that factory, with entire blocks of apartments, shops and restaurants. We also came across the odd sight of people in traditional costume crawling along on their hands and knees – they were on an ancient pilgrimage from the provinces to Lhasa via the most direct route, and the factory was just another inconvenience in the way.

We visited the Barkor market, and the enormous Potala Palace where the Dalai Lama had lived. There we saw the total rape of a culture in the empty shelves where the great Buddhist books and manuscripts had been stored, but had been taken to Beijing for what the Chinese called 'safe keeping'.

We met a group of monks in the palace, one of whom surreptitiously passed us a message written in pencil on pieces of cigarette paper. It read, *Tell the world we are not Chinese; we are Tibetans. We love and respect the Dalai Lama and he represents Tibet for us*. He was taking a great personal risk as there were closed-circuit cameras everywhere.

Wandering through the temples off Jokhang Square I heard an outbreak of shouting, so I climbed on a roof to see into what looked like a school. What I witnessed appeared to be a re-education class, with Chinese officials shouting at the young monks and getting them to repeat things. I didn't know either language but the atmosphere was certainly one of coercion.

Everywhere there were pictures of the bogus Panchen Lama (the next most important spiritual and political leader after the Dalai Lama) installed by the Chinese. I would perform a little one-act play of making a huge fuss at these photos of what I called the 'Dalai Lama' and being very surprised at how much he had changed and how ill he looked. That drove the Chinese officials mad – the mere mention of the Dalai Lama was forbidden. I would annoy them further by insisting on Tibetan stamps in the post office, not the Chinese ones they tried to sell me.

The Chinese had flattened 95 per cent of Tibetan monasteries during and after the Cultural Revolution, so we drove to see the rebuilding work on one of the most famous, the Ganden Monastery. That was another three thousand feet up, and the route involved speeding up the side of mountains without guardrails, being driven by a jolly driver who kept turning around to laugh and joke with us while holding the steering wheel with one hand. I eventually asked to be let out, but when I said I would walk the rest of the way he thought it was hilarious. I just lay in terror on the floor in the back between the seats.

The monastery was fascinating, except for the loo, which was only flushed once a year when the snow melted. The tea they served us was foul – instead of milk they would melt rancid yak butter into it. I thought the best thing would be to get rid of it in one swallow, which was the biggest mistake of my life as that only convinced them that I wanted more. When our time came to leave I wanted to walk down, but they told me it would take seven hours on foot so I had another grim trip back to Lhasa. Next day, on the way to another city, we had a blow-out but luckily on flat ground – twenty-four hours earlier and that could have meant the end of us.

We flew from Lhasa to Kathmandu, passing Mount Everest en route. We flew at about thirty thousand feet so were parallel to the mountain range, with spectacular views of this vast white desert and Everest's serene peak. In a lush green bowl we landed in the magical city of Kathmandu, a name that had entranced me since I was a child. There we met and listened to the moving stories of refugees who had walked across the Himalayas from Tibet. After a day there we flew to Delhi and travelled by train on to Dharamsala for an audience with the Dalai Lama.

I've met His Holiness three or four times, but being in his presence is still an extraordinary experience. The first time I met him I was one of about a dozen who were given an audience in a Dublin hotel. Halfway through his speech he stopped, smiled, and said, 'Now I forget what I say. I very silly old man. I must ask Mr Secretary what comes next.' Our hearts went out to him for his honesty. Most political leaders would stumble on and try to cover up the fact that they'd had such a lapse.

He was a man who could giggle and be serious at the same time, but on our visit to Dharamsala he was hungry for information about Lhasa, where he hadn't been allowed visit for forty years. He enjoyed the stories we told him about our trip, and he especially liked the one about trying to buy Tibetan stamps – he told me, 'Mr Norris, you should be an actor.' He is a most extraordinary man; the last thing he told me was that he was praying for the Chinese because they were doing so much damage to their souls by their behaviour in Tibet.

He also told me the real story behind the drama surrounding the Panchen Lama. Apparently Beijing had ordered the senior lamas in Tibet to go formally through the ritual but pick a particular boy whom they had selected. They did go through the ritual, and found to their surprise that they selected the Chinese candidate as the reincarnation anyway. This news was transmitted to the Dalai Lama in Dharamsala, who told me that he

273

himself had then conducted the divination rituals and was astonished to come up with the same name. He repeated the process with the same result, and so confirmed the Panchen Lama as the boy who had been selected by Beijing. However, the minute the Chinese heard that, they kidnapped their original choice and he has never been seen since. They installed another candidate who they are grooming as the successor to the Dalai Lama.

The first time I ever heard of East Timor was when Mary Robinson asked me to second a Senate motion about it. But I trusted Mary's judgement and agreed.

I later looked through the briefing material she sent me and discovered she was absolutely right about the injustices that were going on there. East Timor was a former Dutch colony which was invaded by the brutal Indonesian regime in 1975. Through the reign of terror, 200,000 of the population of 660,000 were massacred.

When my friend Tom Hyland started telling me about the campaign I got involved too, helping organise debates in the Senate and introducing Tom to the Foreign Affairs Committee. I boycotted Tony Blair's address to the Oireachtas as a protest against British arms sales to Indonesia. Tom was a bus driver who used to park his no. 79 bus in Parnell Square and come around for chats and cups of tea. He was a natural *seanchaí* whose stories would have me rolling around the floor.

One evening in 1991 he and some friends were watching a television programme made by John Pilger about the massacre of civilian protesters in a graveyard in Dili, the capital of East Timor, by Indonesian troops. Horrified by the images, Tom had had difficulty in sleeping. The next day he and his friends had gone into the city and approached businesses to donate office supplies, and with that they set up the embryo East Timor Ireland Solidarity Campaign in Tom's home in Ballyfermot. Tom quit his job in CIÉ and through the sheer power of his personality turned East Timor into the best-known foreign issue in Ireland, cajoling the government to take an active role in supporting the independence movement.

In 1995, I and a small group of civil-rights activists were arrested on the way to a peaceful commemoration of the fourth anniversary of the Dili massacre. We were spotted in Dempasar Airport in Bali, and as the Indonesian police circled us, I noticed that most of the people in the departure hall were Westerners heading for Sydney and Los Angeles.

I hopped up on a suitcase and asked the crowd if they were interested in U2, and if so would they like to see a handwritten poem by Bono in support of the people of East Timor. Tom Hyland had got this poem and given it to me to read at the ceremony in Dili. As a crowd gathered the cops backed off, and I began to read aloud:

'"To the good people of East Timor. On behalf of myself, Bono, and the band U2, on behalf of most scribes and poets, most music, film and object makers, both here in Ireland and around the world, please be sure that we know of your strife and that even if we are not allowed to see, you know that we hear of you, and that when we don't hear from you we think of you . . . all the more.

' *"LOVE FROM A SHORT DISTANCE" by Bono*

> 'There is no silence deep enough
> No blackout dark enough
> No corruption thick enough
> No business deal big enough
> No politicians bent enough
> No heart hollow enough
> No grave wide enough
> To bury your story
> And keep it from us.'

275

When I was finished I announced, 'My name is David Norris, and I'm here with Patricia McKenna MEP and Nobua Soma, the Roman Catholic Bishop of Nagoya in Japan. We are about to be kidnapped by the Indonesian secret police, so when you get to Sydney or Los Angeles could you please let the wire services know what's happening.'

We were then seized, which became a bit farcical as they were convinced I was married to a large Maori lady and Patricia McKenna was our daughter. I demanded they serve us tea and biscuits before they deported us.

When we got to Singapore the stunt with the poem had obviously worked as there were dozens of reporters around the plane. I never did get to Dili, but the Indonesians got much more bad publicity than if they'd let us in to light a candle and read a poem.

As an Irishman, a Dubliner and a human being I swelled with pride when I heard a BBC broadcast at the time of the downfall of the Suharto regime in Indonesia. Dr Peter Carey, lecturer in Oriental Studies in Oxford University, announced, 'Of course in the downfall of Suharto one must acknowledge the significant role played by Tom Hyland of Ballyfermot in Dublin.' If ever there was a David and Goliath story, that was it.

I was a vigorous Irish representative on the trip to Iran in 1996 too, when we were received by President Rafsanjani and his foreign minister, Ali Akbar Velayati. When it was my turn to speak I raised the matter of religious discrimination, citing a town that had a tiny Jewish population where all the men had been arrested, and the treatment of the Baha'is. I also brought up a story of two young women who had recently been split with an axe after being accused of being lesbian. By that stage I could see the Irish Ambassador was in silent hysterics.

Rafsanjani told me that I didn't understand because I was in a Muslim country, but I was able to tell them I had read the Koran, and indeed had done so the previous evening in my hotel. I showed them where the holy prophet Muhammad, blessed be his name, describes the story of Sodom and Gomorrah, but nowhere did he say that homosexuals should be chopped in pieces. So I asked them did they presume to make themselves a higher moral authority than the Holy Prophet himself? There was an awkward silence before someone produced pistachios and fizzy water so I never got the answer.

I decided I wanted a Persian carpet as I always try to bring home something characteristic of the places I visit. It was a journey cloaked in mystery, with a James Bond-like change of cars on the way. In the carpet store there was a whole ceremony involving tea and philosophical discussions, little of which concerned carpets. I chose one, which we packed into the car, and bought a huge canvas sixteen-wheeler suitcase to carry it in. I made sure it was stowed in Tehran Airport, but by the time we got to Schiphol there was no sign of it. I got into a serious row with the airport staff, demanded to be let into the luggage area, and missed my onward flight to Dublin. When they finally let me in I spotted it immediately and they became very apologetic. They offered me a free flight to anywhere in the world or $500, so I said, 'Send me home on economy and I'll take the five hundred dollars.' The fact that the carpet cost me precisely the same amount only added to my pleasure, and it now adorns my dining room.

The leader of our delegation was Liam Naughten, a decent, honourable and good-humoured man who was Cathaoirleach of the Senate. I had a little soirée at home to baptise the carpet, but sadly two days later Liam was killed in a car crash. My last memory of him was laughing and singing in the dining room where I had installed the famous carpet.

I also raised the treatment of gay people in India. The night before the Inter Parliamentary Union conference in New Delhi in 1993 the Irish Ambassador gave a dinner for us. She offered to help us at the conference, so I asked her for a list of organisations that dealt with AIDS – there were seventy, of which only one mentioned gay men. Homosexuality and AIDS were taboo subjects, but I raised them forcefully in the main public session and electrified the audience. I concluded by saying, 'I speak from a particular viewpoint, because as a gay man myself I have seen too many of my friends and colleagues die unnecessarily because of the ignorance that has been allowed to spread about this disease. And I say to this host country of India, you have an unexploded bomb in your midst and by driving it underground you are going to make it a hell of a lot worse.'

When I got back to my desk my colleagues congratulated me, but said that I had blown it at the end, pointing to our stony-faced, alphabetically-arranged neighbours – Iran, Iraq, and Israel. Seemingly, the Iraqi and Iranian delegates had lifted eighteen inches off their seats when I 'came out'. But in the interval many delegates discreetly approached me to say they were gay too and thanked me for saying it.

Homosexuality was still illegal in India, which ensured the radio and newspapers covered my speech widely. I kicked up another fuss when I found out that Indian gay men and female sex workers had held a meeting on AIDS in the same hotel the previous year but the authorities had thrown them out. I was able to be blunt, but it was a privilege to be able to be so – because I was independent I was able to represent Ireland in an extraordinary way. Those tours most certainly were not junkets.

I raised the AIDS issue again with Kader Asmal, who was a Trinity law lecturer for more than twenty years before he returned to his native South Africa on the dismantling of apartheid. Kader became a minister in Nelson Mandela's government but frequently returned to Dublin. On one of his last trips he came to talk to the Foreign Affairs Committee. He was in a very relaxed mood, and asked that the meeting be informal, as he had great friends there. He pointed out two old comrades and academic colleagues, and recounted the days he fought alongside them against apartheid, and for civil and human rights in Ireland too. Kader requested the chairman that these two old warhorses be allowed to ask him the first questions. So I asked him how he could possibly put up with the dangerous rubbish that Thabo Mbeki was coming out with about AIDS, suggesting it could be cured by eating cucumbers and having sex with virgins. And I followed that up by demanding he explain why the South African government had never intervened with Robert Mugabe, who was completely out of control in Zimbabwe. And then Michael D. Higgins stepped forward to give him a few more slaps.

In an exasperated tone Kader threw up his hands and said, 'I should have known better than to leave myself open to a pair of left-wing loonies like Michael D. and David Norris.' From Kader, that was a real compliment.

Another issue on which I campaigned was the use of cluster bombs and other illegal munitions. I always thought they were a filthy weapon, and particularly as, when the bombs break up, the 'droplets' look like soft-drink cans. The result has been an enormous number of casualties, especially among children. These and other weapons, such as flechette shells, are obviously directed at civilians.

I was briefed by Tony da Costa of Pax Christi and I put motions through the Senate and the Foreign Affairs Committee. This is where the Roman Catholic Church has done such wonderful and unrecognised work – in organisations like Trocaire, Afri and Pax Christi there are people who take the Christian message seriously and try to implement it to make a difference to the lives of ordinary people.

I was very heavily involved in persuading the government to campaign against the bombs, and in a great compliment to Ireland it became known as the Dublin Initiative. A convention banning the manufacture, sale and use of cluster weapons was signed here in 2008 and more than half the countries in the world have signed it since.

The most recent IPU meeting I attended was in Kenya, where, among other things, I was able to persuade the Swedish delegation not to withdraw their amendment to a motion protecting women against violence, which would have extended such protection specifically to lesbian women. They had been given the impression that it would cause damage by being heavily defeated, but I made a powerful and impassioned speech. Unfortunately, however, because of the early hour of the morning, by no means were all of the delegates there. When we voted in the afternoon it only lost by a very narrow majority, so we did at least score a moral victory, and it was widely said that if more of the delegates had heard my speech in the morning, we would have won.

I found the poverty, dirt and corruption revolting, but I left with a tremendous admiration for the Kenyan people. We visited some of the shanty towns and slums and it was quite extraordinary to see how families who lived in one-room shacks with sewage running through their homes still managed to send their children out to school looking immaculate. Another thing that heartened me enormously was when we visited some of these schools in co-operation with organisations like GOAL and Trocaire. They were often run by Irish orders of nuns and priests. Their selfless dedication must be remembered in an age when all the headlines highlight the appalling depravity of a minority of abusive priests. I've always been against labelling of any kind, and I believe these selfless men and women are a credit to Ireland.

There were other times when I just took off on my own. One example of this was when I heard on the BBC World Service the Norwegian Foreign Minister expressing concern about climate change and saying that any politician who was seriously interested should come and visit the northern part of his country within the Arctic Circle and witness for themselves the impact it was having. The Norwegian Ambassador to Ireland was very helpful in making arrangements, though I paid for the trip myself. I went to Svalbard and visited the most northerly place of human habitation on the planet, Longyearbyen. There, deep in disused mine shafts, they had a repository of seeds from all over the world, safely protected in case of some cataclysmic global event. Even from the plane, as we approached the Arctic region it was perfectly clear looking out of the window that the glaciers were shrinking dramatically. The ice floes were also becoming less predictable, making it difficult for polar bears. The day before I arrived a polar bear crazed with hunger had entered the village and been shot.

As a member of the Foreign Affairs Committee, I naturally took part domestically in debates on subjects of international significance such as the various EU treaties which, with reservations, I always supported. Until it came to the first Lisbon Treaty.

I was concerned that the treaty could be manipulated to assist in the creation of a European munitions industry for export at the instigation of the French and British. I felt that there were quite enough armaments without us formally joining this bloody trade. I campaigned on this basis against the treaty until at the last minute I succeeded in extracting from the Cabinet a written commitment that they would use their veto to prevent this. That allowed me honourably to change sides and vote yes in the referendum.

CHAPTER 12

A Shot at the Park

THE INAUGURATION OF MARY ROBINSON AS THE SEVENTH President of Ireland on 3 December 1990 was a glorious occasion which confirmed the extraordinary changes that had begun to happen in our nation. Not only was she the first woman president, but Mary's election was a vindication by the Irish people of the way the country was altering and their thorough approval of that process. Our new president had been at the heart of the battle to liberalise our laws, and her work had been vital in the successes to date. Not only had Ireland begun to move towards the twenty-first century, but Mary Robinson was one of those who had led it there.

Young people find it difficult to believe that forty years ago our politicians could be so idiotic as to make it a criminal offence to buy or possess a piece of rubber or other forms of contraception. A wife and mother called Mary McGee took a legal action against the state, and won. Her lawyer was Mary Robinson.

Young people find it difficult to believe that thirty years ago Irish women were judged as unfit to sit on juries. Two activists called Máirín de Burca and Mary Anderson took a legal action against the state, and won. Their lawyer was Mary Robinson.

And young people find it difficult to believe that twenty years ago two men could go to jail or be subjected to electric shocks, simply for the physical expression of love between them in private. I took an action against the state, and won. My lawyer was Mary Robinson.

When Mary was putting together her bid for the presidency in 1990, she asked me again to be on her team. I'm particularly proud to have been one of the twenty signatures on her nomination papers. To be honest I didn't think she was going to win – I expected it was going to be another glorious left-wing defeat. Mary is quite a shy person, and can come across as aloof. But she herself was transformed by starting to campaign early and then experiencing the overwhelming wave of affection and support towards her. That gave her confidence and made her realise that people liked and respected her.

At one stage Mary was interviewed by *Hot Press*, a music magazine which also covered politics, and she used the opportunity to revisit some of her old foes. The forces of reaction were in her sights, and she made some bold statements about contraception and gay rights. ROBINSON WOULD PROMOTE GAY RIGHTS ran the headline in the *Irish Times* the next day.

With the whole kerfuffle threatening to derail the campaign, some of her back-room handlers took fright. They were terrified that her opponents would hang 'abortion' and 'homosexuality' around her neck, which could have been the kiss of death. I was contacted and asked to 'disappear'. I said of course, because too often people in politics, particularly on the left, think they are more important than the cause. To me the most important thing was to get Mary elected, and if that meant me keeping quiet then I was happy to do so. I continued to help out discreetly with fundraising and getting people out to vote, but I was no longer part of the team.

On the day after the poll I was out in the RDS count centre when the first boxes were being opened. The ballots came from the Aran Islands, which had consistently voted Fianna Fáil since the beginning of the state. As they were opened, out tumbled all these votes with '1' written beside Mary Robinson's name. And as box after box went for her, I knew she had done it.

She was a remarkable president in the way she started to bring people in from the margins of society. She also did Ireland great honour as a speaker who had international stature, clearly the equal of any world figure. That was wonderful for a small country like Ireland, then still sometimes portrayed in the international media as backward.

Mary McAleese commands similar international respect, and while many have compared and contrasted them in bold terms, I see the differences much more subtly. They both have a passionate commitment to human rights and both made important contributions to the struggle for gay rights at crucial points in the long campaign. I knew Mary McAleese from Trinity, where she had succeeded Mary Robinson as Reid Professor of Criminal Law, and always found her to be outspoken and courageous. She certainly showed that in 1976 when she agreed to co-chair the Campaign for Homosexual Law Reform with me.

As a politician she could be a shrewd, and even ruthless, person, but she can be warm too. And just as President Robinson was the perfect president to crown a time of great social change, so was President McAleese the right president to be in office as momentous changes were happening in the north of the island. She had the grace – as someone who was bombed out of her home in Ardoyne – to go building bridges between the loyalists and people of her own background. That took remarkable imagination and generosity and greatly enhanced the presidency.

The thing all three of us have in common, of course, is that we all once worked in Trinity. That is a remarkable tribute to a remarkable university. Many more of our colleagues have made their own mark in extraordinary ways, and I believe the reason is that the atmosphere in the college allows everything to be questioned. It encourages you to hold up an idea and examine it from every angle. That was especially true of the ground-breaking work on gay rights. Back in the 1970s and 1980s Trinity was the only intellectual environment in Ireland where that was possible.

I was first sounded out about a possible run for the presidency in September 1997. A group of Greens and independents rang to ask could they meet me, and I invited them around to the house. John Gormley and Tony Gregory wanted permission to throw my hat in the ring, and said that they already had some independent backers. I told them they would find it difficult to get the required support, but if they did so I would give it everything I had. I never thought it realistic, but rather a very interesting marker as to how well an outsider – indeed, a pariah to many – would fare.

I never really thought it was a runner, as there were only ten or twelve independent and Green members of the Oireachtas we could rely on, which meant we needed the support of the Labour Party to get to the required twenty nominations. There were several people in Labour who wanted me to run, and we discussed it with them in general terms. They were all set to propose me when Dick Spring arrived at the selection convention and announced that the party's candidate would be Adi Roche.

Someone produced an antagonistic button and others started making cracks about me being gay, so I launched a pre-emptive strike with my own slogan – 'Vote no. 1 Norris and put a queen back in the Vice-Regal Lodge' – which stepped on plenty of staid, traditionalist corns. I did it to take the sting out of the homophobia and only when my nomination was no longer realistic.

As Mary McAleese's first term was drawing to a close in 2003–4 there was a lot of speculation about whether she would be re-elected unopposed. There was a brief attempt to give the public a choice in the matter, but the parties weren't interested and were all determined to have an agreed candidate to save the cost of having an election. Some members of the public approached me and asked me to stand, but when the Labour Party made it clear they weren't going to offer support, either to me or more significantly to their own Michael D. Higgins, it fizzled out quickly.

That party arrogance about the presidency has always seemed grossly undemocratic to me. They regard it, like the position of Lord Mayor of Dublin, as a numbers game. Indeed in the course of the 2011 presidential race one of the leading members of Fine Gael actually said to me, 'We've never had the Park. It's our turn now.' As far as I was concerned it was never the turn of any party: it was always the people's turn, and I said so. From 1973 to 1990 the establishment colluded to deny the people a vote on three occasions, and again in 2004. There was another attempt at foisting an agreed candidate in 2011, and if they had got away with it that would have meant the Irish people wouldn't have had a say in electing its first citizen for more than two decades. By the time the next one came along only people over forty years of age would have ever voted in a presidential election, and there would have been only two chances to vote in nearly half a century.

After the general election in February 2011, none of the parties had the money to spend and were quite happy to do the Irish people out of their choice yet again. Fine Gael tried to persuade Séamus Heaney to be an agreed candidate, and very nearly succeeded. However, the whole thing was handled badly and I think the Heaneys realised they were being used. Séamus is not just a great poet, he is universally loved for his talent and his innate modesty, while Marie has her own distinctive qualities. I've no doubt they would have been a remarkable presidential couple.

When I put my name forward, and when the early opinion polls showed I could get into the race – and might even win – that put the kibosh on the carve-up. Thus I delivered item no. 1 of my agenda for the Irish people – a genuine, if (as it turned out) a particularly filthy, presidential election campaign.

While the groundwork had been done by my having been mentioned twice previously as a potential candidate, the eureka moment arose in a very unconventional fashion.

In the spring of 2010 I was a team leader on *Operation Transformation*, an RTÉ television programme that encourages people to get active and lose weight. For that series they pitted a group of politicians against teams made up of Dublin housewives and Galway taxi drivers. I was made leader and was determined we were going to win, as I thought it was time we politicos were at last associated with something positive. I organised our efforts systematically, with Miriam emailing the team all the time to remind them about weigh-ins and generally geeing them along.

The contest was fun, but it was a serious issue too because of the growth of obesity and type-2 diabetes. (In fact, I kept the *Operation Transformation* team together afterwards as an all-party group to look into the whole question of obesity and related illness. We made recommendations to government concerning calorie identification in restaurants, which are currently being seriously examined. So what started as fun had a serious and practical effect.) I lost more than two and a half stones, while others including Paul Gogarty, Fergus O'Dowd, Tom Sheehan and Seán Connick also lost significant amounts, and we won the whole competition.

A few weeks later I organised a lunch for all the contestants, to which I invited Gerry Ryan and the show's producer Gary Flood. Miriam and I mocked up some certificates and got Gerry to sign and present them to each member of the team. The Dáil restaurant was packed with TDs and their constituents that day, and as we walked through to leave, I was mobbed by women,

men and children of all ages. I was surprised to see they didn't seem as interested in Gerry.

I walked Gerry out to the gate and he said, 'Jaysis, Norris, I think you could do it.'

'What do you mean?'

'I think you could take the Park.'

A week or two later I was supposed to be on *The Late Late Show*, and on the Friday afternoon I got a call from Miriam saying that her sister had read on the internet that Gerry Ryan had just died. I told her it was probably a joke; just the sort of leg-pull Gerry was fond of playing. But she then got a call from the producer to confirm the terrible and unexpected news and to say that nevertheless I was still required out in Montrose that night.

On the show I told Ryan Tubridy the story of Gerry's very last words to me, and went on to say I was seriously considering what he had said. That brought an immense response, and Miriam was snowed under with people offering encouragement and help. Among those who got in touch was Liam McCabe, a golf-course entrepreneur from Co. Kilkenny, who asked to meet me to discuss the campaign.

We met for coffee, and I was immediately impressed. Liam is a small, wiry, thin-faced man with intense eyes, a clipped delivery and a genius for planning, honed in his work as a mountain rescue co-ordinator. He had done meticulous research and presented me with an outline of how the election could be won. The folder was stuffed with detailed diagrams of how the team and campaign could be organised, with sections on the nomination system, and the legalities, practicalities and politics of what lay ahead. It was a stunning document. Ultimately, however, the problem turned out not to be the thought behind it, but its implementation. There hadn't been a presidential election for so long that the game had changed. The parties had their long-established, full-time nationwide organisations, but independents like myself found it difficult to produce a professional machine. And the problem with my team was that a section of it disintegrated under the first significant stress. As an old friend and savvy political observer said, 'They ran off at the first whiff of cordite.'

From my first meeting with Liam, I felt I had been extremely lucky to meet him. He was steady as a rock, a man of clear mind, absolute integrity and total loyalty, qualities that remained true throughout the campaign and beyond. Like all of us, of course, his judgement could be faulty on occasions.

We started having meetings to develop the plan, and settled on twelve or thirteen areas of responsibility. We went about finding people to fill them, which is when I made my first crucial mistake. I was told to stay out of the interview process, so decisions were made to appoint senior staff without consulting me.

Miriam and I had been deluged with offers from people who were willing to work for free, which is why it was a drawback for our small campaign that others required payment for their services. A small number became paid employees as the campaign intensified; some were well worth it, and the ones that charged the least were the best, such as Maurice O'Donoghue and David McCarthy, of both of whom I cannot speak highly enough. Liam McCabe himself took a year off his business and refused to accept even one cent – he was generous, and rarely even took money for petrol when we were on the road. I had to practically physically force money on him on the few occasions I did manage to persuade him to do so.

I accept full responsibility for the mistakes made because I was the chief executive of the campaign and failed to exert my authority. The only two people on the team whom I knew before the campaign were my assistant Miriam and my good neighbour and friend Muireann Noonan. Miriam in particular worked around the clock for months, barely taking time to rest or even eat properly. Muireann also gave me good advice, some of which I took, and tirelessly drove me around the country.

The team and I discussed the vital issue of financing and I explained I had very little money. We were going to have to work hard at fundraising, but I think we started too late and never appointed anyone who was capable of raising sufficient funds. That was a desolation to me because I have personally raised millions, perhaps tens of millions, for worthy causes, but again I was told to stay away because interference would undermine the team. I should have had the confidence to override that – after all, the buck stopped with me and I was going to be picking up the bill at the end anyway.

The myth that I am a wealthy man and have had a cushy life has always puzzled me, but people don't realise I came from almost nothing in financial terms and have had to work hard for what I have. It's a capacity for lateral thinking, rather than wealth, that gives me a comfortable life. I do own a lovely car, a Jaguar XJ6, but it cost me just €6,000 because it's over fifteen years old and third-hand, and is probably the cheapest car in the Leinster House car park. I have a beautiful home, but I bought it for £25,000 thirty-five years ago when it was partly derelict in what was sometimes described as a slum, and did it up at the rate of one room per year. My furniture was inherited. All that might give the impression I have money but it isn't true, and it is sad that some people resent the mirage of my supposed moneyed status.

I certainly didn't have my tongue hanging out for the presidency – I was just prepared to serve the people at the expense of my own personal fulfilment, which has been the story of my life. Every night I would have gone back to the empty Áras, whereas in my own street and locale I have many great friends. Let no one think I was doing it for the money. I announced right at the start that I would put most of the presidential income aside to make the office more efficient and accessible to the people. I would not let it be absorbed back into the general exchequer to be wasted. I was the first person in the campaign to make this commitment.

Very early on, Tom Hyland came in to visit me on a trip home from East Timor. He urged me not to stand, warning me that I would be taken apart. I told him I thought that was actually a good reason for standing, because you can't be frightened off by bullies; someone has to stand up to them. We knew from early on that mud was going to be thrown, so Liam suggested we open what he called a 'skeleton' file where controversies could be placed to allow the team to develop defensive strategies. Miriam trawled back ten years and various skeletons in my closet were thrown into it, including an article in *Magill* magazine by a woman called Helen Lucy Burke.

We considered launching the presidential election campaign in my ancestral homeland of Laois, but there were several practical reasons why that wasn't feasible. Instead we kicked it off in the Science Gallery in Trinity on 14 March 2011. It was a fitting venue as it was in the heart of Dublin, part of my university, and signalled my commitment to innovation and celebrating our great scientists.

We prepared for the launch by making a one-minute video showing me striding confidently down O'Connell Street. The video makers had previously walked along the street with me and noticed how the general public kept coming up to say hello, and the taxi drivers were always waving and shouting support. So we recorded that journey, which helped show that I was confident and that people warmed to me. The film started with me coming out of my home, walking down O'Connell Street, turning on to Pearse Street and ending at the door of the Science Gallery. It was shown to the audience there and as the film ended I walked through the door, creating a satisfactorily dramatic effect. Launching in Trinity was also a useful signal that I was still committed to representing the university, as the Senate election was about to get under way.

I threw myself into campaigning for the presidency in whatever time I had left after my Senate work. I had always worked a twelve- to sixteen-hour day, but as the campaign progressed I was getting by on four hours' sleep.

On 24 June I was invited as guest of honour to give the keynote address for the Ireland–US Council Dinner at Dublin Castle. The arrangement had been finalised many weeks earlier but on the day I was contacted by the organisers to say that government officials had called to find out if I was the main speaker, and when that was confirmed the organisers were rather embarrassed to discover that Lucinda Creighton, a Fine Gael junior minister, was to be parachuted in to gazump me.

Lucinda Creighton arrived slightly dishevelled and apologised that she had come straight from the airport. That didn't stop her dislodging one of the prominent guests from his seat at the table, and standing up unexpectedly to make a long rambling speech which seemed to have been written by advisers on the plane home. She had apparently been flown back to ensure that I did not achieve any prominence. Throughout her speech she referred to me condescendingly and told the audience that although she had to deal with serious matters, 'David', as she called me, would provide plenty of entertainment later. It was a classic attempt to cast me as a buffoon. However, her dull speech received its due reward, and mine received a satisfyingly different response.

The first signs of how dirty the election was going to be emerged with the launch of the website davidnorris4president. com. It was designed so that on first sight it looked like my own website, but once you read on, it was a vicious mixture of abuse and juvenile homophobia. We discovered that behind it was a fundamentalist group. I had come across them before at the time of the Civil Partnership Bill, when they were picketing Leinster House. One morning, on my way into the Senate, I was being interviewed by the BBC about a completely different subject when these protesters kept shouting and pushing in and nearly put my eye out with a placard. In the end the TV crew had had to give up – how's that for freedom of speech?

One of the ways the election differed from previous ones was the way much of the battling was done online. Twitter and Facebook hadn't been thought of when Mary McAleese was elected, and the election of Barack Obama in 2008 had shown how social media could be harnessed to great effect. Dónal Mulligan, who had come to see me with a former Trinity student of mine, was exceptionally good as the social media campaign director, and we secured an online presence bigger than that of all the other parties put together. By early summer we had thirty thousand signatures of people demanding I be nominated. It was a very effective method of campaigning, but unfortunately it faltered when Dónal left the campaign in July.

While social media was an efficient way of spreading our message and contacting supporters, it also became a feeding pool for some of the nastiest abuse. We were able to track how some antagonists stayed up all night planting lies about me around the various internet sites. This brought back memories of the early days of my political life when I regularly attracted hate mail, some of which was violently obscene. But even cranks can be dangerous, and some of the calls that Miriam had to take were disturbing. One anonymous man said that he knew where I lived and was organising a gang of toughs to intercept me, hold me down on the pavement and castrate me.

As the campaign progressed I raced to the top of the opinion polls and stayed there for months. I always recognised that the opinion polls are will-o'-the-wisps and have the effect of putting a target on your back if you are the early front runner. It was nevertheless a pleasure to read them. I had started at the margins of Irish society and was now in with a chance of being at the centre of Irish life. I had identified three areas that I wanted to campaign on, and made them the three pillars of my campaign – mental health, enterprise and culture.

I picked mental health even though I didn't think it would win me any votes. I was wrong, as the public support for my stand was absolutely overwhelming. Everywhere I went people came up to me to say, 'Thank God someone is taking on this issue.' I believed it was vital to take away the stigma that surrounds depression – a stigma which goes back to the days of the mental hospital and the workhouse. I also felt it was important that someone at last made a major public issue of the plague of suicide.

With regard to the second pillar, as someone who had started and managed two commercially successful enterprises, one of which led to the development of Temple Bar and the other played a pivotal role in the revival of North Great Georges Street, I had hands-on experience of business life. I saw the encouragement of enterprise as a way of giving people hope.

As far as the third pillar was concerned, while I had always been associated in the public mind with culture through my championing of writers, I wanted to expand the definition of 'culture' by celebrating our scientists too, whom I felt had never got their due recognition. I kept hammering the point that Irishmen had split the atom, built the White House and invented the basis for our modern computerised world. A nineteenth-century Earl of Rosse had developed the world's largest telescope at Birr Castle, and his successor invented the steam turbine, which revolutionised transatlantic travel. While we know about Joyce and Yeats, and how the Irish have written three-quarters of English literature, why does nobody talk about science, which is also part of the imagination? I wanted to sing about the Beaufort scale, Boyle's law and George Boole's pioneering work on computer language. I talked about all these ideas on local radio, but when the campaign went national I was never again given the chance to put them forward.

All three pillars were linked by that creative imagination that distinguishes the Irish.

Out on the road, I was enjoying myself and being immensely moved by the unquenchable spirit of the Irish people. I visited

Clonmel as guest at a lunch in aid of a drop-in centre for people with cancer. The event usually attracted 250 people, but the organisers told me that as soon as my name went on the ticket they got 500. After the lunch and speeches I went around visiting the tables. I told my handlers that I wasn't leaving the room until every single person who wanted to talk to me or have a photograph taken was happy, and it took two hours to see everyone. These were people who had faced real difficulties, including one woman who I was told had just had 'bad news', which I took to mean she hadn't long left to live. The organisers rang afterwards to thank us and said that I had lifted them with laughter. The whole energy of the afternoon gave me a wonderful positive feeling.

Another event that ran over time was organised by a splendid and admirable group of young people who were raising funds for Nepal. It was out in the wilds of Clare and they also had The Chieftains playing, but though they meant well they hadn't organised anything on such a scale before and it was a bit chaotic, with everything running considerably over time. They asked me at the last minute to do the auction, which was totally unorganised so I had to take it in hand and improvise. The whole evening went on for hours and by eleven o'clock my handlers were trying to drag me out before I was belatedly called on to speak. I insisted we stay, as there was no point putting in all that effort only to alienate the several hundred people who were there by walking out before the end. I eventually got home at the bright light of dawn and the start of another day.

A visit to a mental-health drop-in centre in Tralee was an enrichment and a joy. They presented me with a decorated slate, which I see every night when I'm getting ready for bed. It shows a bright moon surrounded by stars and the words read MAY YOU HAVE A FULL MOON ON A DARK NIGHT AND THE ROAD DOWNHILL ALL THE WAY TO YOUR DOOR. After we left they rang Miriam to say thanks and mentioned in passing that I was the first 'important person', as they described it, to visit them in eleven and a half years. That told me something significant – they didn't say I was the first to visit them 'for years', or 'many years' or even 'eleven years'. They had been counting the months since anyone 'important' had visited.

At a splendid drop-in centre in Portarlington I bought a painting, *The Moon over Cliffs and Sea*, by a gifted artist called Fiona Fitzpatrick, as companion piece for the slate from Tralee.

I went to other facilities that had never been visited by politicians, and my admiration and love for my fellow Irish men and women increased. These were homes, hospitals and care centres that had already been hit by serious cuts in funding, which was noticeable in the threadbare sheets on many beds. But those sheets were always spotlessly clean and never once did I see anyone with bedsores, which was a sign of the dedication of the overstretched staff. Irish people are second to none in the commitment they show to those in their care – they far exceed what is expected of them in their jobs. It convinced me that the key to solving the healthcare crisis was matching judicious use of scarce state resources with the spirit of the volunteer movement.

I was campaigning three or four days a week all over the country as well as fulfilling my Senate role, and had the benefit of enjoying the beauty of the Irish landscapes for once from the passenger seat. My good neighbour Morgan Pillay drove me for most of the campaign, until the final phase when we hired two very decent ex-army drivers.

When we visited Castlerea, Co. Roscommon, I was delighted to see the local TD, Luke 'Ming' Flanagan, turn up to welcome me – and even more so when he produced a huge sack of turf. He had heard me talking about my open fire at home and my love of real turf, so his seventy-eight-year-old father had gone out that morning and produced a sackful just for me.

A lovely woman on the main street of Castlerea invited me in for tea. She was very welcoming, but explained that she couldn't go to the supporters' meeting that night as she had to take a neighbour to Mass. However, she suggested that if I went into the supermarket next door they would announce it over the tannoy. Two young men came up to me in the supermarket and asked could they have their photo taken with me. I could see they were very fit and they modestly admitted to being successful athletes in tennis and swimming. As they walked away an elderly lady whispered to me, 'Aren't they lovely? Do you know, they're a couple and we all adore them,' and the shop manager said the same. I thought to myself that if these lovely young lads are accepted for what they are in the heart of Roscommon then we really have changed as a nation. The fact that I was part of making that change lifted my heart.

I was getting votes hand over fist when another daft decision was taken, to outlaw the word 'fun'. Elements of the team wanted to package me so I would appear more statesmanlike and suited to the dignity of the office, to which I reluctantly agreed. Two of the people I most admire in the world, the Dalai Lama and Archbishop Desmond Tutu, have never felt the need to be deadly serious at all times. They are men who deal with the gravest issues, and yet can often be seen smiling, laughing and performing for the camera. I have always found humour to be a powerful weapon in getting people on your side – but now it was to be taken away.

I was invited to give the Bartholomew Mosse lecture, which commemorates the founder of the Rotunda maternity hospital. My speech was submitted for scrutiny to senior members of the team, who thought that a whole series of passages – on issues such as pre- and post-natal health and the world population crisis – were dynamite. To win meant I should be safe (and therefore bland) and they larded my script with more anodyne comments. However, I improvised from the written text and, interestingly, got a positive response that was a very great surprise to members of the team who had come to observe. Their fears proved groundless anyway, as no one from the media showed the slightest interest. I noticed a troika developing between my election agent, director of elections and PR representative. I was sometimes given a good scolding by one or all of them, either before or after interviews, public speeches or presentations to councils. It was no doubt a well-intentioned attempt to manage my excesses, but I didn't find it helpful. I surprised myself by my fortitude in those difficult circumstances; but then I have always tried to be a professional.

On another occasion I had to talk to a very powerful audience of TV and radio station owners and was given a prepared script that was the dullest I have ever delivered. The argument I was presented with was that I could either get a standing ovation or win the Park, but not both. I delivered the platitudes with as much panache as I could and, as I anticipated, the result was muted applause. I told Liam afterwards that I would not be doing that again if I could possibly help it. At around this time I was rather pained to discover that some of those who accompanied me were writing reports for the troika, without my knowledge, on my demeanour and political attitudes. Once again I should have put my foot down, but I didn't.

Our trips around Ireland were organised so I could highlight each pillar of my campaign, but as the campaign developed they coincided with county-council meetings, which were to be a vital component of the nomination strategy. One of the very special back-room people was Trish McNamara, who organised complex schedules for me every day. I was deadly serious about my objectives and the three pillars of my campaign, and met with leading figures in Irish life including the head of the Industrial Development Agency, the Irish Countrywomen's Association, the Arts Council, mental-health organisations including Pieta House, Headstrong, Jigsaw and Cregg House, and various other significant groups, with a view to informing myself fully.

To be nominated to run, a candidate must have the signatures of twenty members of the Oireachtas, or the support of four local authorities. I had previously raised the grossly undemocratic nature of this system when I made a submission to the All-Party Commission for Constitutional Reform.

In fact, as far back as 1998 an all-party commission had acknowledged the fundamental lack of democracy in the nomination process. It recommended that the number of Oireachtas members' signatures required be reduced to ten, and that the validated signatures of ten thousand citizens should also allow entry to the contest. Catherine Murphy TD reintroduced the proposals in February 2012, but they were again shot down by the government. Had the establishment parties not ignored the proposals for fifteen years I would have been the first person to be nominated, because I had already thirty thousand online signatures and wouldn't have had any difficulty getting ten Oireachtas members.

At the end of April I spoke to Finian McGrath TD about supporting my nomination. He wanted to know what my policies were, which, I explained to him, showed a misunderstanding of the role of the office because a president doesn't have policies. The office bearer articulates a vision of what they want to contribute; policies just bring you into conflict with the executive. That said, I wanted to expand the role so that, for example, when the German chancellor or French president was invited over they wouldn't just get a banquet in Dublin Castle. I wanted to take them to see the consequences of their governments' economic policies and the way they were blighting the lives of Irish people.

After this explanation he agreed to support me, but I asked him to hold off announcing this until I had put together a group of signatories. However, before I could do so he announced his support. He was joined within days by Catherine Murphy, Mick Wallace, Ming Flanagan, Joan Collins, Stephen Donnelly and Maureen O'Sullivan and Senators Seán Barrett, Marie-Louise O'Donnell, Mary Jane O'Brien and Professor John Crown among others, who remained supportive to the very end. I found an extraordinary degree of treachery among some old political friends and loyalty among some new ones. There were others again whose support was half-hearted and insultingly conditional, but in the end I didn't need any of them, because against all odds I succeeded in getting a local-authority nomination.

I was getting a good reaction in the councils, but they could not officially nominate me until the election was called, a three-week window in September. Team member Stephen Boyle, a man of clear intellect, produced a magic formula of words which would allow the councils to commit to supporting me before then, which although not legally enforceable had a very strong obligation built in. The independent councillor David O'Connor proposed such a motion in Fingal, and when it was passed we had the first of the four councils we needed.

I had an early inkling of what I was up against when I visited Longford. I was well received, but a decent Fine Gael councillor called Louis Belton, who I remembered from his time in the Senate, told me that he was very sorry but they had been ordered by Fine Gael head office not to support me. I suggested that they abstain, which meant I could still get the nomination, but he said that the instruction was to vote *against* me. It was the first time I had been told I was being deliberately blocked by Fine Gael.

Helen Lucy Burke was a waspish little woman. She had never been in any sense a friend or colleague of mine, indeed scarcely even an acquaintance; but I was aware of her reputation. She seemed to encourage controversy, appearing on a *Late Late Show* debate on contraception, during which one woman mentioned that she had eight children. According to an interview article by Kim Bielenberg in the weekend supplement to the *Irish Independent* in the autumn of 2011, Miss Burke replied, 'Any Alsatian bitch could say that.'

She had been an official in Dublin County Council but also contributed restaurant reviews to various publications. In the pages of the *Sunday Tribune* she wrote in a coruscating fashion about food, and later turned her forensic approach to hotel reviews.

She parted company with Vincent Browne quite suddenly, leading to a midnight phone call to me from Mr Browne asking me to take over her restaurant column. I did it for six months before I started getting hate mail from people who said they objected to me eating while people were starving in Ethiopia. It was becoming a chore and I was keen to get out of it when I discovered Vincent had beaten me to it. One day I sauntered into the office to collect my post when I found a note in my pigeon-hole which went something along these lines:

Dear David,
When I gave you the job of restaurant critic six months ago you
protested that you knew nothing about food and wine, and I
didn't believe you then; I do now.
Goodbye, Vincent

I elaborated on some of these details and turned it into a kind of shaggy-dog story, which was very popular with my after-dinner audiences, but which I realise may not have endeared me to the acerbic Miss Burke.

She returned to the post on my departure, and the next I heard of her was before Christmas 2001 when she rang to request an interview for *Magill* magazine. It was the run-up to an election and at first I refused to meet her but she perse-vered. I was tired of being endlessly interrogated about sexual matters and having everything I said distorted and sensation-alised, so I put it to her that she could not ask me questions of a sexual nature and she agreed.

A week or two later she rang me while I was getting ready to go abroad to report on the incidence of sexual abuse in

Thailand for the UN. She read me two or three paragraphs from her piece, where I spotted that she had blurred the distinction I had made between paedophilia and classic Greek pederasty. It's quite easy to mix these two phrases up and I think that I did so myself, but they have got different meanings. I asked her to change paedophilia to pederasty. It emerged in 2011 that the editor had also instructed that the article should be typed up and the full transcript shown to me. This was never done.

In the *Magill* article, headlined THE FREE RADICAL, our wide-ranging discussion was distilled down to the controversial parts where I examined Plato's *Symposium*.

I flew off to do my work, but when I got back I was confronted with a front-page story in *Ireland on Sunday* headlined SENATOR BACKS SEX WITH CHILDREN, and FURY AT GAY'S 'PAEDOPHILIA IS OK' MESSAGE. I was dumbstruck, but immediately went on RTÉ Radio to explain.

I did an interview with Joe Jackson in the *Sunday Independent* within the next few days to make it plain how I abhorred child abuse and had a track record in battling it. To this day I am very grateful to him for what he did at that stage. In the Jackson interview I pointed out how I had asked for corrections that weren't made, which provoked a phone call from Miss Burke. She told me, 'I take great offence at your impugning of my professional standards,' but without a word of sympathy for the hell she had put me through. I told her to listen to the tapes and if I wasn't correct in what I said to call me back. I never heard from her again.

On 30 May 2011 I was in the car driving to the Phoenix Park, where I was due to do a photo shoot for the Bloom floral festival, when we got a call saying Helen Lucy Burke was going to be on *Liveline* to talk about the *Magill* article and the producer wanted to know would I go on too. She was astonishingly cruel and negative – calling what she presented as my views 'astounding' and 'evil' – and left dangling the slur 'He was going

Welcoming President Hillery to the opening of the 1982 Joyce International Symposium.

Launching my election campaign with old friends Dean Victor Griffin and the late Dr Noël Browne.

ABOVE: Election manifesto, 1983.

RIGHT: A confident candidate, Front Square, Trinity College Dublin.

LEFT: A brooding Parnell-like figure, at home, 1989.

ABOVE: Backstage at the National Concert Hall with President Daniel Ortega. I was compère of a benefit concert for Nicaragua.

ABOVE: Meeting with Yasser Arafat in Gaza.

RIGHT: The full cast of my explosive meeting with Tariq Aziz, Baghdad, 2000.

LEFT: Meeting Ban Ki-moon in Dublin Castle, 2010.

BELOW: Visiting an AIDS project in Chiang Mai, Thailand, on behalf of the United Nations.

ABOVE: Discussing strategy with Tom Hyland and East Timorese refugee José Lopes.

RIGHT: With His Holiness the Dalai Lama in Dharamsala.

LEFT: Receiving the Lord Mayor's Award from Lord Mayor of Dublin Eibhlin Byrne at the Mansion House, 2007.

BELOW: In the front line as Father of the House at the convening of the Senate, 2011.

With Mary Robinson at the handing over of papers to the National Library, 2007.

Two old friends. Michael D. Higgins signing a book of essays for me at the National Library, 2007.

Above: Helping cancer awareness, Daffodil Day, Herbert Park, 2010.

Left: With a group of schoolgirls in the early stages of the 2011 presidential election.

Below: Under siege at home. My forced withdrawal from the presidential race.

Watching the count at the presidential election, RDS, October 2011.

A gracious host. My family and friends were early guests of new President Michael D. Higgins and his wife Sabina, Áras an Uachtaráin, December 2011. From left to right: Muireann Noonan, Miriam Gordon Smith, John Norris, Sabina Higgins, President Michael D. Higgins, myself, Mary Norris, Michael Moran, Abigail Moran and Eddie Kenny.

Relaxing at home in North Great Georges Street.

off on his holidays to Thailand,' although I had told her the purpose of my mission – which was, ironically, to investigate trafficking in women and children for sex, and the AIDS situation in that country.

She openly stated that her intention was to stop me getting a nomination, thereby depriving the Irish people of their right to choose, a curious view of democracy, but we were expecting the issue to come up and we released a statement:

> During the course of a comprehensive conversation, Miss Burke and I engaged in an academic discussion about classical Greece and sexual activity in a historical context; it was a hypothetical, intellectual conversation which should not have been seen as a considered representation of my views on some of the issues discussed over dinner. The article did contain other valid comments from me on human rights and equality issues but the references to sexual activity were what were emphasised and subsequently picked up and taken out of context in other media outlets.

> The presentation of references to sexuality in the article attributed to me were misleading in that they do not convey the context in which they were made. People should judge me on my record and actions as a public servant, over the last 35 years and on the causes and campaigns, for which I have fought, and not on an academic conversation with a journalist over dinner. I did not ever and would not approve of the finished article as it appeared.

That unpleasant controversy blew over quickly, but there was one nasty sting in the tail which showed me what I could expect for the rest of the campaign.

Morning Ireland had recently marked its twenty-fifth anniversary, and everyone in Leinster House was tripping over themselves to congratulate it. I was a lone voice in refusing to do so. I criticised its self-regarding anniversary show, which I pointed out was full of technical mistakes, and had over recent months featured some of its regular presenters whinnying and giggling at their own jokes. I felt it was forfeiting its reputation as a serious current-affairs show in favour of what the Americans call 'factoids' and 'infotainment'.

I was invited on to talk about my campaign with Áine Lawlor, who swiftly gutted me. I was trying to put my interview with Helen Lucy Burke in context by explaining the significance of Plato's *Symposium* – I was just about to explain that the whole book is a hymn of praise for spiritual, not physical, love when she butted in with the cheap line 'But Senator Norris, you are not running for President in Ancient Greece.'

Ms Lawlor was lauded for that by some commentators, who called it the 'killer blow'. If it was such a thing then that is a reproach to our whole society, because it suggests that the Irish people have sunk to the level of intellectual vacuity that is represented by the tabloid press. This is a country that preserved classical learning throughout the Middle Ages; this is a country that during the Famine impressed French travellers that even the raggedest starving children were still learning Latin and Greek. To have a powerful interviewer sneer at me as if we had no right to tap into the wisdom of Ancient Greece was greatly offensive. After the programme was over Ms Lawlor professed sympathy and suggested I get good PR advice.

Politicians are just ordinary people who accept a different level of responsibility from the community. That shouldn't expose them automatically to contempt. But if they do something wrong, or their private behaviour contradicts their public utterances, then they are fair game. Ordinary decent, hard-working politicians should not be subject to ill-informed abuse. There is also a serious issue with the manners of broadcasters these days – people with no knowledge or background in politics and who have never had the critical responsibility for taking a decision frequently interrupt, heckle and abuse even cabinet ministers. In my own case, reporters who had never even set foot in the Senate or had any acquaintance with my record presumed to act in a rude, aggressive or hectoring manner.

The newspapers rang some survivors of sexual abuse and read them selected extracts of what I was supposed to have said, allowing them to concoct headlines like FURY OF ABUSE SURVIVORS AT NORRIS. I was heartened to see that Michael O'Brien didn't fall into their trap. A year before I had spoken passionately about abuse at the launch of Karen Coleman's book on the subject. I met Michael there and we had a good chat and he impressed me with his courage. The viewing public had been riveted when he spoke on television about his experience in Catholic institutions. I will never forget his eyes blazing as he said, 'They beat the shite out of me, they raped me, they buggered me and then the next morning they put the holy host in me mouth.' I used his words verbatim during the debate on the Blasphemy Bill. I said that if ever there was a definition of blasphemy this was it. I was grateful that when the newspapers rang him he was judicious and said, 'If David Norris said that . . .'

I was one of the few politicians to have studied the various reports on state and clerical abuse of children forensically, and did the most detailed analysis looking at the principles behind it, but no one bothered to check my record. I was outraged by the behaviour of the Catholic Church, but I don't believe I was unfairly critical. Indeed, I publicly defended Archbishop Desmond Connell in 2002 when a newspaper headline announced CONNELL VISITS PERVERT PRIEST IN PRISON. First of all I thought he was entitled to his correct form of address, and second I asked where precisely did the author of the headline imagine that Christ himself would be except visiting sinners in jail?

After the *Magill* article there was a small sectarian element who sent abusive emails, but that was overwhelmed by the number of clergy of all denominations and also devout Catholics who supported me – many of whom sent me prayers and said they were lighting candles for me.

*

In the last week of July Miriam took a call from someone who said he worked for a Sunday newspaper. He claimed to have letters which showed I had asked for clemency in some kind of legal case involving Ezra and sex with a minor in Israel, and did I want to make a comment as they proposed to publish the correspondence?

Miriam rang me, and once she mentioned the correspondence I remembered the incident. She went back through the files again and found eight letters which had gone back and forth to various lawyers in Israel in 1997. We had earlier presumed that ten years was far enough back to go to compile the skeleton file, but this had happened long before that point. To be honest, I had forgotten all about it; I was always getting Ezra out of trouble – on one occasion I gave him a sum of money so large I would be embarrassed to mention it, to get him out of a tight spot with his finances – and also helped pay for his house. It had never occurred to me, or even to Miriam, who had actually typed the letters.

When we dug them out of the archive I was prepared to stand by them. I believe in loyalty and if a friend is in trouble that is when you are called upon to help them. I have no time for fair-weather friends. I also have no apology to make to anyone over the letters I sent. I knew Ezra's vulnerability and emotional volatility. He told me that as a young man he had shot part of his leg off because he didn't want to serve in the army; of course I was going to write a letter to help him when confronted with prison.

He had concealed the whole story from me at the time the offence was committed, and indeed five years later, when he was tried and convicted. I knew nothing about what had happened until the stage when he was appealing the severity of the sentence. I wrote several letters asking for clemency and explaining Ezra's fragile state. Ironically, I was the only person who showed any interest in the welfare of the young man – the

prosecution never did and the judge ignored the recommendations of the two welfare officers appointed by the courts.

I brought the matter to Liam's attention, and he called a meeting of the most senior members of the team. I sat and waited
while Derek Murphy, director of elections, Jane Cregan, my
PR agent, Liam and Muireann read the letters. At one stage
I saw Jane grimace, and I asked her, 'Can I take it you're staying with the campaign?' She told me, 'Now is not the time to
discuss that,' but a couple of days later I was to see on the nine
o'clock news a picture of a telephone and hear her taped
message telling callers she no longer worked for the Norris
campaign.

The following evening, Wednesday, there was a meeting of the
wider committee of fifteen in my basement, which I very much
wanted to attend. I told Liam I had a responsibility to put the
letters in context as I was the only person who knew the background to it all. There had been a suggestion that I had
deliberately concealed the letters from the team, which I
absolutely had not, and I wanted to nail that lie too.

But I was told that I could not go downstairs, that people
were hysterical with rage. Liam told me, 'I don't want you in
this house. Take yourself away from here and I'll telephone you
when the meeting's over.' I believe now that that was a
disastrous move.

The meeting was due to start at 5.30 p.m., so about an hour
before, I drove out on my own to Howth Head and parked in
the car park overlooking the sea. I was going back over it all in
my head, walking around in circles, barely taking in the beautiful scenery. What was most difficult was the people coming up
to say hello and telling me I was doing well in the election when
I knew exactly what was happening just a few miles away.

It had an echo for me of the early days of my relationship
with Ezra. I had helped him to buy an apartment in Ramot and
one afternoon his family rang to say they were on the way over.
Ezra got into a panic and told me to get out of the house. I was

forced to clamber through the back window while they were coming through the front door. I will never forget the humiliation of climbing out the window of a house for which I had helped to pay. When they had left I told Ezra that I would never do that again – and if that was what he expected of me then it was over for me.

That summer's evening in Howth I found myself thrown out of my own home by people who had misunderstood the essential loyalty and decency of both my nature and my acts. That was the nadir for me. I had violated one of my own principles, which was never to allow anyone to take control of my life. The HQ was the HQ, but my house was my home and I should never have allowed myself to be evicted from it, for no matter how short a time. But I was under so much pressure I agreed to go.

I was in Howth for hour after hour, waiting for the phone to ring, so at 9.30 I called Liam and said, 'What on earth is happening? Don't tell me the meeting is still going on?'

And Liam said, 'I'm sorry, I forgot to ring you, I'm on my way home to Kilkenny.'

When I asked him whether the team had resigned, he equivocated and told me it was up to me to make the decision. It was a very unhappy night. It turned out that three or four relatively significant members of the team had indeed walked away. I first had confirmation of the desertion of some senior members of my team in the pages of a Sunday newspaper. They had, of course, the right to resign, but I felt I was entitled to the courtesy of being directly informed of their decision. What I did not know at that time was the intense pressure, amounting in some cases to blackmail, exerted on members of my team by the media and in particular the print press.

The following morning I was in the kitchen washing the vessels while listening to Newstalk. John Drennan from the *Sunday Independent* and Ming Flanagan were on, discussing the latest developments. Ming told how he and his

wife had agreed the night before that they would have no problem having David Norris babysit their children. John Drennan
came in with 'Well I wouldn't let him within an ass's roar of
mine.'

My heart lurched and I nearly dropped the cup I was drying.
'Why?' he was asked.

'Because he'd bore the bejaysus out of them talking about
Plato and Joyce,' he replied.

And I thought to myself, *That is one great lad, because that's
the right answer.*

So when we were discussing a media strategy I insisted I
would only talk to Mr Drennan. I knew him from around
Leinster House and was never particularly close to him – I even
used to tease him that he came across as a sour-faced tit who
was a disgrace to the midland bogs we both came from. He was
the last person I expected to give me a fair hearing but at least
on this occasion my misjudgement was a positive one. Eoghan
Harris and the *Sunday Indo* had been supportive all along
too, and Anne Harris and Aengus Fanning really got behind me
– and for that I am deeply grateful. In the last week or so of the
campaign this support seemed to cease, possibly because I
refused to get up close and personal with Martin McGuinness
of Sinn Féin, but neither they nor their newspaper ever attacked
me which provided some respite.

Because the man who called Miriam had said he was going to
publish the letters, we decided to release the longest and most
detailed one to the *Sunday Independent* to accompany the interview. But as it turned out, none of the other Sunday papers
printed the letters. It was a lie all the time. They never had the
letters. It was a classic and mean-minded journalistic 'sting', but
thanks to my naïvety and the lack of political experience of
some of my team, it worked.

I invited John over on Friday morning, and we did the
interview in the kitchen. He had barely sat down when there
was a knock on the door, which turned out to be someone from

the *Sun*. The playwright Dennis Potter once warned me about Rupert Murdoch, and I was on the record saying that the proper place for the *Sun* was cut into squares and hanging on a rusty nail in an outside lavatory in the rainforest.

I told her I wasn't talking to her, or anyone else. But from then on there was a constant ringing, banging and hammering at the door. It got so bad that at one stage we were forced to move out to the garden. The interview took several hours, and by the time John left there were several vans and cars double-parked outside.

I couldn't move out of my house, and I was alone, and I thought, *I'll never be able to sleep and I may start to act irrationally, so I've got to get out of here.* I rang Michael Moran, who I hadn't seen in months, and told him I was asking for a real favour: could I come and stay with him and his wife Abigail for a few days? Like true friends they immediately said yes.

Because the media were at the front door, the only way out was across the roof; so I rang Eddie Kenny in the Cobalt Café two doors up and asked for his help. I told him I was going to climb over the parapet on the roof, along a ledge and then over another parapet to his house. I asked him to leave his skylight open. But, after talking with Muireann, Eddie firmly told me not to do that because I was so distraught that I could have easily fallen – and then the press would have said I'd jumped. Muireann came up with a brilliant strategy, and Eddie told me to pack my bags and go up to the roof where his sons Jamie and Adam would collect them from me. He then told me to saunter across the road to Muireann's house as if I was going for tea.

As I crossed the street about eight o'clock I was accosted by two young women who said they were from the *Sun* and, to its eternal disgrace if true, the *Irish Times*. I didn't know either of them. They came out with the usual line 'We want to tell your side of the story,' to which I gave a wintry acknowledgement. Muireann's son, Faoláin Collins, who had been included in all the plans, opened the door, and I walked through their house, out the back, down the garden and into the lane at the rear, where Eddie had the engine running in his classic green Mercedes. I leaned down below the window so I wouldn't be seen and we zoomed across the top of North Great Georges Street, down the lane behind the houses where Eddie's lads were waiting, and collected my bags.

On the way out to Monkstown I got a call from Finian McGrath. I told him we were in crisis mode but asked for three days while I saw how it developed. I suspected from his tone that he was jumping, and I told Eddie that was probably me out of the race, at which he burst into tears. But Finian couldn't wait and yet again went to the media. He really dropped me in the manure by talking about the protection of children, which sounded to me as if I was a threat instead of one of the staunchest defenders of the rights of children and young people. Finian had been first in, and now he was first out.

The controversy raged over the weekend, when it emerged that a number of the other candidates had written similar letters too, some indeed for convicted murderers. Professor William Schabas, of the Irish Centre for Human Rights in the National University of Ireland, Galway, a noted world authority, wrote a powerful letter to the newspapers:

Elected Irish politicians, especially those in Government, shouldn't contact Irish judges to influence Irish cases. But it's an entirely different thing when the politician and the judge are from different systems. In that case, there is no fouling of the separation of powers and no reason for the influence, if any, to be based on improper considerations.

When former Bosnian Serb politician Biljana Plavsic was sentenced for crimes against humanity by the International Criminal Tribunal for the former Yugoslavia, prominent international personalities, including former US secretary of state Madeleine Albright and Swedish prime minister Carl Bildt, argued for mitigation. Nobody thought that was unacceptable. Nor should they deprecate

311

David Norris's noble effort to ensure that an old friend wasn't punished too harshly.

Indeed, among those who also wrote clemency letters for Ezra at that time were several distinguished Israeli artists and human-rights activists, as well as a former Israeli deputy attorney general. Some commentators made a meal about official Senate notepaper being used, but that was my business notepaper as an elected member. A member of the public later wrote in to complain to the parliamentary body, an inquiry was held, and he was told that, after official examination of the complaint, it was clear I had done nothing wrong.

Michael and Abby had a comfortable room ready for me in their home, and I spent a lovely bank-holiday weekend with them catching up on old memories. It was my sixty-seventh birthday on the Sunday and we had a small party, with delicious roast lamb for dinner, and cake and balloons sent out by Muireann and her family. What I thought was going to be the worst birthday of my life instead turned out to be one of the best.

Over the weekend I was in constant touch with Muireann, who told me she was greatly amused at the press pack camped outside my door with their flasks and sandwiches. I took malicious pleasure in knowing they were hanging around or trying to sleep in the back of their jeeps for nearly four days while across the other side of the bay I was comforted by the love of my friends. They started ringing Muireann's bell too, and even tried to interview her six-year-old daughter Déidinn. She's a feisty little thing and just said, 'You know already Mr Norris is not here,' and closed the door.

With Jane Cregan out of the picture, there was general agreement that what we needed was a 'rottweiler' who would be tough and capable of dealing with the press. Eddie suggested the PR man Paul Allen, who had known his brother since schooldays. Mr Allen had offered help to me earlier in the campaign when I bumped into him in Leinster House, so we got in touch with him.

Liam and the others thought my bid was probably finished, while I oscillated between optimism and despair, but Muireann and Miriam were encouraging me to hang in. I now think they were right, but in the circumstances of that weekend I was under enormous pressure because the media just would not let up. I don't think people realise what it is like to be under siege in your own home with the door being banged relentlessly, even after having said explicitly and repeatedly that you would not be giving interviews.

There was huge pressure on me to say I was wrong, which is why there is a nod in that direction in the withdrawal speech. I said then that I didn't think I was sufficiently sympathetic to the young man – but in fact I was the only one who was in any way sympathetic. I am proud of those letters and if they ever emerge I hope the moralisers cringe with shame. I will not be publishing them; I stand by my principles on that matter.

I always adhere to what Joyce wrote in *A Portrait of the Artist* where Stephen's father tells him, 'never peach on a fellow'. I felt that if I released the letters it would stir it up further and the media would be out in Israel looking for the man at the centre of the original case, who is now in his thirties and has settled down. I didn't think it was right for me to visit that upon an innocent civilian.

Israel is a complex and sophisticated country, with many differing points of view. But I have no doubt that, among other sources, there was some Israeli involvement in the whole smear. Ezra has been a dogged campaigner for the rights of Palestinians for many years, and stories about his trial are regularly fed to the press there in a deliberate attempt to hinder his humanitarian work. I have no idea at what level the smear was sanctioned, but it was clear that some people in Israel, especially in the settler movement, were quite happy to have a malign influence on the democratic processes in a friendly state.

This matter was thrown into sharp focus by the revelations in June 2012 about the Deputy Israeli Ambassador, Mrs Nurit Tinari-Modai, who is married to the Ambassador himself. A cable she sent to Jerusalem, in which she suggested undermining Israeli advocates of Palestinian human rights by printing their photographs and implying that they are double agents collaborating with Mossad, and in particular drawing attention to supposed psychological difficulties and 'problems of sexual identity', was revealed. I raised this matter in Seanad Éireann and asked if it could be determined whether this undermining was confined to Israel or extended to Ireland.

On the Tuesday morning Eddie came out to Michael and Abby's and we drove back into town. I had decided to withdraw, and had been discussing the exit with Liam, Muireann and Paul Allen. We went around the back of Muireann and Tony's house and worked on the speech in the kitchen. Mr Allen suggested I finish with a quote from Joyce, but I thought that was too predictable and went for a line that had come to me as Eddie and I crossed the Samuel Beckett Bridge that morning.

The press pack was still outside no. 18, and a news release was issued to the media that I would be making an announcement at 2 p.m. The speech was still being finalised at 1.50, and at 1.55 Tony Collins and Ger Siggins were still wrestling with a recalcitrant printer as they hurriedly collated and stapled copies of the speech.

My own car was parked around the back of Muireann's, and Morgan Pillay drove me up the lane and down the street to my house, where I got out. An enormous throng of media people had gathered outside my front door and were gazing steadfastly at it. They assumed I was inside the house and so hadn't expected me to be driven up the street in my own car. None of them noticed what was going on until I got out of the car and made my way through the crowd to my doorway, saying, 'I have something to say which you may wish to hear.' That gave them a shock as they had been waiting for the front door to open.

I had specifically insisted that my speech be taped to the podium so I could go straight to reading it. I was assured by the PR team that this would be taken care of, but when I got to the steps there was no sign of it. Luckily I had put a spare copy in my pocket, but I was flustered as I retrieved and opened it.

When it was finished, I turned and walked into my home, where Michael and Abby had tea and biscuits ready, and we just sat around going through old photo albums and talking about our parents until the reporters cleared off. Eddie and Morgan's wives, Dorothy and Katiani, had made some food and we had a delicious buffet as Muireann, Miriam and her husband Noel joined us for the post-mortem.

I decided I didn't want to hang around Dublin any longer, and the following afternoon I flew to Cyprus for a break. I now think that if I had stayed and battled on I might have been in with a chance of winning the presidency, or at least reaching the quota for state support, but every single commentator said I had to go, the pressure was immense, and some of my team had buckled.

Even after I pulled out the public remained loyal – and in one opinion poll I was still the most popular choice as the next President of Ireland, even though I was no longer in the race.

CHAPTER 13

The Meeja and Politics

Yet let me flap this Bug with gilded wings,
This painted Child of Dirt that stinks and stings;
Whose Buzz the Witty and the Fair annoys,
Yet Wit ne'er tastes, and Beauty ne'er enjoys,
. . .
Whether in florid Impotence he speaks,
And, as the Prompter breathes, the Puppet squeaks;
Or at the Ear of Eve, familiar Toad,
Half Froth, half Venom, spits himself abroad,
In Puns, or Politicks, or Tales, or Lyes,
Or Spite, or Smut, or Rymes, or Blasphemies.

Alexander Pope, 'An Epistle to Dr Arbuthnot'

THE MEEJA, AS THE MEDIA IS OFTEN CALLED IN IRELAND, IS IN
danger of becoming – under the influence of the press
barons of our neighbouring island – an amorphous and sometimes corrosive sludge in which complex ideas are bowdlerised
by those who are at best semi-literate. And just as in the neighbouring island, despite the evidence of the Leveson Inquiry,
which should have galvanised them into action, the
pusillanimous nature of most politicians reinforces this degradation. There are often no particular likes or dislikes. It's usually

316

not paying off grudges (although in some cases such as my own it can be), just a commercial matter of selling newspapers. Life is full of ups and downs, and I've experienced this syndrome all my life. Even in the gay movement: one moment I was a little tin god, the next the greatest shit on earth. Neither extreme was true. However, one of the great advantages of increasing age is that one develops the equivalent of stabiliser fins so, although rocked by abuse, one rarely suffers the full *Titanic* moment.

I have never sought the attention of the broadcast or print media for myself in any aspect of my public life, although some might find that hard to believe. I was, for many years, top of the pops with the press, because I would talk about subjects no other politician would touch, such as the fight to preserve Georgian Dublin, gay rights and the start of the AIDS epidemic, and I had a quotable turn of phrase. It was this very openness that led them consistently to court me. Even after the presidential election was over, and I spoke out in the Senate about what I felt was an exploitative and vulgar television show called *Tallafornia*, I received fourteen requests from newspapers, radio and TV stations in the space of twelve hours. This time I ignored all of them.

There were, of course, other factors, such as the PR train crash that I believe was my presidential election bid. Sinister forces were undoubtedly at work, but I scrupulously avoided either being fooled by the initial favourable poll results or falling prey to the various conspiracy theories fed to me by a press corps eager for an answer that would give them a sensational headline along the lines of 'Vatican/Mossad/KGB/Mafia/Opus Dei/Sinn Féin/Labour/Fine Gael infiltrate Norris campaign'. Whatever the intriguing hints dangled in front of me, it would have been quite inappropriate for me at that stage as a presidential candidate to stir up difficulties between states with which this country wished to maintain good diplomatic relations. I am, however, aware of the various sinister forces ranged against me. There may well have been international or party connections involved, but it would have been injudicious to make accusations without very specific proof.

This is all by way of context for what is the $64,000 question of the campaign for the position of ninth President of Ireland: would you vote for a blind, alcoholic, cocaine-sniffing promoter of paedophilia, a homosexually promiscuous social-welfare fraudster and occasional rapist who corruptly used his position in the Upper House to obtain passports for his lovers, and encouraged parents to have sex with their own children? And, to cap it all, was a pompous Protestant with a posh accent and a Trinity tie?

None of those accusations, each of which was made against me in one media organ or another during the campaign, had a scintilla of truth about it apart from my religious affiliation (of which I'm unashamed), my accent (of which I'm unaware), my Trinity degree (of which I'm proud) and the question of pomposity (of which I would be an inappropriate judge).

So would any sane person vote for such a candidate? I wouldn't have thought so, but strangely enough, despite the intensely negative media barrage, 110,000 Irish people gave me their first preference, 60 per cent of the second preferences going to my good friend Michael D. Higgins and, according to unofficial tallies, I got at least 60 per cent of his second preferences in return. That suggests that right up to the last minute I was a serious candidate who had to be undermined by the establishment, which set about it in a single-minded way.

It also illustrates that while a lot of decent people may still indulge the lower end of Grub Street by buying trashy newspapers, many do so for a laugh, the sports page, or the page 3 tits and bums, and don't believe a word that they read. And in my opinion – and I'm a fully paid-up member of the National Union of Journalists – they're quite right too, but maybe they should think before they buy. You've only got to take a glance across to Britain and the Leveson Inquiry to see that this is not just a personal belief. The general secretary of the National

Union of Journalists, Michelle Stanistreet, told the Leveson Inquiry:

> We want to show how the culture in a workplace is led from the top; how bullying and pressure from editors, coupled with staff shortages and dwindling resources, puts journalists under huge pressure to deliver – a context where shortcuts become inevitable. We have long been campaigning for a conscience clause in contracts, so when journalists stand up for an ethical principle they have protection against being dismissed.

The *Irish Times*, in an editorial on 7 February 2012, came out very clearly on the issue:

> All bounds of decency have been broken, not to mention criminality and mendacity on a breathtaking scale. Rights, dignity, trampled on. Privacy, be damned. And not alone by the late unlamented *News of the World*. A culture of anything-goes was pervasive, justified on the basis of a spurious 'public interest', an attitude reflected most crassly last week by former *NoW* hack Paul McMullen at the hearing: 'Privacy is the space bad people need to do bad things in. Privacy is for paedos . . .'

The magazine *Hot Press* pointed out that, just as in banking, press barons and their minions felt that they were above the rules:

> A central theme among these submissions to Leveson is that there was a cavalier disregard for old-fashioned journalistic virtues, like methodical research, solid evidence, careful analysis . . .
>
> The same might be said in Ireland, but for quite different reasons. Here too a culture has grown where there is scant regard for privacy or principle, for deep research or time-consuming trawls for evidence. Media here have moved well beyond reportage too, and are now engaged in news making.

In his evidence to Leveson on 28 May 2012, the former British Prime Minister Tony Blair spoke about the intense power of the press and his decision to 'manage, not confront' it. He admitted that he 'certainly did fear the power' being directed at him, and told the inquiry, 'Once they're against you, that's it. It's full on, full frontal, day in, day out.' He instanced a newspaper which attacked himself, his family, his children and people associated with him even when he was out of office. He most significantly said, 'With any of these big media groups you fall out with them and you watch out, because it's literally relentless and unremitting when that happens . . . but the power of it is indisputable.' So he chose management rather than confrontation.

The response the next day of the Irish press ombudsman, Professor John Horgan, was to say, 'None the less Leveson is saying to editors particularly, "Look, I feel the present situation isn't quite up to scratch."'

I have always felt that the Press Council was not really independent, and had little or no power to sanction or compel its membership; these conditions, I feel, must create a difficulty in their task of vindicating the rights of the citizen. Most especially myself, since for many years I have consistently championed the rights of those ordinary citizens who have been unjustly vilified and had their privacy invaded by the press. Unlike Mr Blair, I *did* confront the press with their misdeeds.

People have taken their own lives after seeing their reputations wrongly traduced, employees have been terrified and a considerable number of people arrested, some convicted, and police and politics corrupted – and the public has no effective defence. Politicians as a group, and those in charge of press regulation, seem to me to have just about the same by way of guts as a burst gooseberry.

My campaign was in ruins, but a few days after I arrived in Cyprus one of my neighbours noticed there was an unfamiliar vehicle concealed in bushes near my holiday home in the

Troodos Mountains. Tim had been a colonel in the British special services so took it on himself to check it out, and discovered that there was a photographer lurking inside. He was presumably the one who covertly used a telephoto lens to take a shot of me wearing shorts as I got out of the car in my garage.

That photograph appeared a day or two later in the *Sun* beside a story headlined NORRIS FLEES TO EZRA LOVE NEST. In fact Ezra has only been to visit fewer than a dozen times in the decade since I bought and restored the house, and on his brief visits always kept strictly to his own sleeping quarters. That was followed by a whole screed of garbage over the next few days, some of which was written by a woman who was by-lined as the newspaper's 'crime editor'. That attribution was significant because apparently I was now being presented as a fully fledged criminal! The stories were along the lines of 'failed gay presidential candidate flees to mountainside love nest he shared with child-rapist lover'. Curiously, one piece was largely bowdlerised from an article I had myself written about Cyprus – it was easy to spot my contributions as they were by far the best-written paragraphs in the whole newspaper. The *Sun* had the cheek to say not only that the articles were 'exclusive', but that the newspaper held the copyright. Apparently they believe they have the right to claim copyright over my original work without consultation or attribution. In literary terms this is usually called plagiarism.

Once the photographer had been got rid of (I ditched him after he followed us in a James Bond-style chase around the hairpin bends of the mountains, during which we dodged into a vineyard and watched him sail fruitlessly past), I relaxed and enjoyed my break.

I first discovered Cyprus about fifteen years ago, when Ezra showed me an advertisement in an Israeli newspaper offering a four-day holiday on the island for the bargain price of $99. I thought it was a fantastic offer but Ezra chickened out, so I eventually went on my own and had a great time. I hired a car and drove over the mountains and, my personal situation in Jerusalem having become at last intolerable even to me, resolved to buy a place there. It took me almost a month of searching to find what I wanted, but in the end I hit upon a curious, oddly shaped, derelict house with its courtyard overgrown with caper bushes and littered inside with cobwebs, old clothes and broken furniture. I fell in love at once with its unspoilt nature and the stunning views. I spent years restoring it carefully in the traditional Cypriot manner, in particular one enormously long room with a beautiful coffered cedarwood ceiling, which has at its centre a magnificent Ottoman stone arch opening on to a wooden balcony.

It's situated at the top of the village, and I can look out over the terracotta roofs, the Byzantine tower of the church and then across the vineyards to the sea at Paphos thirty miles away. I like the location because it's away from the tourist trail, and there I relax and go for long walks with my friend Nora. My Cypriot neighbours regard me as a kind of St Francis because I have tamed a family of feral cats and made friends with a small Cypriot owl whose call I can imitate so perfectly that it lands on the telephone wire outside my window and answers. I love being in Cyprus; I am happy there because of the sun, the ancient tradition of agriculture, and because I am accorded the status of villager – an ordinary person at peace with the world.

I spent six weeks in the Troodos Mountains, but halfway through that period I started getting calls from Ireland saying that the campaign office, which was in the process of being wound down, had received three thousand emails pleading with me to rejoin the race. Muireann, Miriam and Liam kept me in the picture.

I flew home in the first week in September with my mind made up to give it another go. There had been several more opinion polls. No one was forging ahead – and the polls that included me showed that I retained a high level of support.

Nominations were due to close in little more than three

weeks, on 28 September, so we set about trying to rustle up Oireachtas support once more. Stories started to appear in the Sunday papers on the weekend of 11 September, and speculation was rife all week when it was announced I was to appear on *The Late Late Show* the following Friday. On the programme I told Ryan Tubridy that I was actively seeking a nomination, and that it would be the biggest comeback in Irish political history if I got one. With twelve days left to go, I was facing an uphill battle.

I met nearly all of the independent TDs and Senators, and a significant number agreed to support me. Professor John Crown, despite reservations about the wisdom of my running, maintained steadfast support. Richard Boyd-Barrett was helpful, but he kept his powder dry because he wasn't sure I was left-wing enough. I see myself as more left-wing than even Richard is, as I regard myself as essentially a communist. People see the suit and hear the accent, know I go to Communion every Sunday in St Patrick's Cathedral and am a member of the Kildare Street Club, so they make assumptions. But I absolutely believe that we should run the planet on the basis of Marx's line 'From each according to his ability, to each according to his needs.' Which is also, incidentally, the basis of the Christian message in the gospels.

As Sinn Féin had more than twenty Oireachtas members they would have had no difficulty in nominating their own candidate without outside support, but they had also started securing others outside the party when I was out of the race, presumably to deliberately narrow the field and increase their own chances. One such was Ming Flanagan, who later asked Sinn Féin to release him to reactivate his nomination of myself, which they wouldn't. He was very upset and went with me to face down Mary Lou McDonald, telling her that if he had to go down to the Custom House and physically scrape his name off McGuinness's nomination paper in order to get me into the race he would. That took balls. What I love about Ming is that he is 100 per cent honest, no matter where that takes him.

Miriam worked away on the Oireachtas members, but it proved difficult to pull in the last few votes. It was like watching a slow bicycle race as they all manoeuvered to be the kingmaker who provided signature number twenty. The signing session with Shane Ross was short and lacking in the warmth one would expect between two people who had been colleagues and friends for over twenty years. He was number eighteen, but I never did get the final two. Further scrapings of the bottom of the barrel proved futile, as Mattie McGrath backed out under pressure from his constituency workers while Michael Lowry said he would only support me if I needed just one more.

I had also been pursuing the local-authority route, but had come up against a serious problem. There were now three other independent candidates who were fishing in the same pond. We had Fingal in the bag, the first council to come out in support of my candidacy, but it became increasingly difficult to add to that number.

It was a fraught fortnight as we criss-crossed Ireland by car, fighting the press all the way. From then on I never did an interview in which all the old controversies weren't raised. Facebook and Twitter were full of anonymous rumours of scandal concerning all the other candidates, but I seemed to be the only one to have these taken up and treated as 'facts' in the mainstream media.

Another problem to emerge was that Mary Davis was going around hoovering up far more than the four nominations that she needed – she ended up with no fewer than thirteen councils. Her oft-repeated council speech seemed to turn the nomination process into a referendum on the Special Olympics.

In addition, every single council had been anonymously circulated with very questionable and sometimes downright defamatory material about me, so they naturally went for the safe option. To be fair to Seán Gallagher, he picked up his four councils very quickly and then withdrew honourably.

I spent a lot of time and energy chasing the councils, and with less than a week to go until nominations closed, I was being written off by the commentariat. Despite their unremitting negativity, an opinion poll in the *Sunday Business Post* showed me still leading the field with 21 per cent, followed by Higgins on 18 per cent, McGuinness with 16 per cent, Mitchell and Davis with 13 per cent, Gallagher with 11 per cent and Dana on 6 per cent. My ancestral homeland of Laois gave me another marvellous boost by nominating me, and then with two days to go I made a hurried dash to Waterford and delivered an impassioned speech to the council. That gallant city, which had given me such a welcome during the Tall Ships Race, stood firm and agreed to support me. As we approached the deadline, things were becoming dramatic, and in Kilkenny a special meeting was organised for the final day to decide on a nomination, with a garda escort on standby to race the official papers up to Dublin. In the end this was not needed.

With time running out, my best hope was Dublin City Council, which met the night before nominations closed, but had a strong Labour Party representation. Michael D. Higgins had always said that he believed councillors should be free to vote for whoever they wanted, which was generous but no more than I expected from a decent and democratic man. Early on the day of the Dublin meeting he reiterated that view and asked Labour councillors not to obstruct my entry to the race. I arrived in City Hall just as he was leaving and we had a warm chat in the rotunda and were photographed together by the huge press contingent.

I was nominated by one of the most courageous victims of institutional and child sex abuse, Mannix Flynn. If that isn't good enough for the people who falsely accused me of being soft on child abuse then I don't know what is. I have respected Mannix for over twenty years. He was one of the first people to tell the truth about the abuse that went on in the industrial schools when he blew the whistle on Letterfrack industrial school. He made a fantastic, courageous speech, and I was warmly received by most of the councillors. In the end the representatives of the people of the city I love granted me the nomination by thirty votes to six. I was in the race at last.

At eleven o'clock the following morning I made the short journey from my home to the Custom House, where I lodged my papers before the noon deadline. It was an enormous relief to have finally joined the contest proper and now, still atop the opinion polls, I had just under a month to persuade the Irish people I was what they wanted in the race to be the ninth President of Ireland.

We drove straight to RTÉ for the first of the election debates. The seven candidates posed outside for the first group photocall of the campaign, which were always a bit of a scrum. The *News at One* radio debate was moderated by Seán O'Rourke, and it was there that one of the chief structural difficulties of the campaign became apparent – the field of seven was the largest ever in a presidential election. Broadcasting rules meant that everyone was supposed to have a fair share of coverage, which meant at times a ludicrously brief run-through of each candidate on news programmes. The broadcasters were not going to lengthen the debate just because there were extra participants. That meant that while an hour-long debate between three candidates would give them up to twenty minutes each – plenty of time to expound on their ideas – dividing up sixty minutes, including intro, ad breaks etc. between seven candidates was completely unwieldy and ensured soundbites were the norm. And once you got the set-pieces and the moderators' grandstanding out of the way there was no room at all for real debate.

Despite this, we were required to attend no fewer than fourteen debates over the course of the four weeks. Generally nothing was agreed in advance, so the broadcasting fraternity kept clicking its fingers and summoning the candidates at short notice for their ritual grilling. The election resembled a reality TV show at times, with the massaging of the egos of the pre-senters the most important element. I am known as a good and effective debater, but never once got an opportunity to show those skills, let alone outline my vision or explain my ideas.

Our media overlords bleat everlastingly about the freedom of the press, but what about freedom of expression? Or freedom to discuss controversial ideas? These are freedoms they *won't* allow. I sparked off the very election itself, and well before any of the other candidates had declared themselves had targeted the three principal issues (culture, enterprise and mental health) – but I was the only one who was not allowed to speak on them. I have always found it regrettable that I'm pigeonholed and that a large swathe of my views are not permitted to be heard. My contribution to Irish life outside Joyce, gay rights and Georgian architecture has been systematically suppressed, but I live in hope that it may eventually be unearthed by some scholar who combines an interest in history and politics with a capacity for politico-literary archaeology.

The television campaign had opened with a tedious *Late Late Show* debate, from which I was mostly excluded when agents of some of the other candidates objected that I had been on the show a fortnight before, although that was prior to my being an official candidate and technically shouldn't have counted. But at least it showed that the political establishment still thought I was a real threat. As a result I was yet again forbidden from making my pitch and merely subjected to the routine negative grilling.

Ryan Tubridy, a very decent man, was visibly uncomfortable and expressed his unease to me afterwards in the hospitality room. I knew he was just doing his job, as he had been given a battering by the critics as a result of a slight fall in his ratings and for being too polite to his guests, and he was under internal pressure to rectify this. I presented the perfect opportunity.

Vincent Browne now fronts a political chat show on TV3, on

which he hosted the candidates a few days later at the station's studios. Vincent has a reputation as a contrarian, and felt the need to live up to that on the debate. He tackled most – but not all – of the candidates in turn, grilling them on one entirely predictable subject, such as Martin McGuinness's past as an IRA commander. I noticed that we had run over time and that someone from the production team was waving at Vincent to tell him to wind up the programme. Apart from the general questions addressed to all the candidates, he hadn't got around to throwing his anticipated hand grenade in my direction, and I relaxed.

But Vincent ignored the production team and started asking me questions about the Ezra letters. We had earlier explained that we had legal advice from both Israeli and Irish lawyers that we couldn't release the other letters, but Vincent came out with the classic stunt of 'revealing' that he had had contact with some Israeli academic who had given contrary advice. He waved around a letter which he claimed contradicted the advice I had received, and which came from an eminent Israeli legal authority. The next day I looked up this eminent authority and discovered his principal contributions were on Jewish marriage and dietary laws. He did not seem to have published anything at all on the relevant issues of privacy, *in camera* trials or criminal law generally. I have since wondered whether this incident was initiated by TV3 or suggested by some external source.

Vincent put me on the spot by demanding the name of my Israeli and Irish lawyers, but I had not been given full information by my PR team. As Vincent growled his way to a conclusion I thanked him for signing the petition demanding that I be allowed to run, which he didn't like at all. With typical disregard for the electorate, the media reports of the event concentrated on the fact that Michael D. was standing on a box, but they also gave me a few belts.

Bizarrely, at Christmas Vincent and representatives of two of the papers that had attacked me with the greatest astringency gave me an award as Political Survivor of the Year. He wanted me to go out to the studio in Ballymount to take part in the programme and collect the award, but I declined the honour. I was quite surprised when a small glass trophy was delivered to Leinster House.

When I look back on the sorry mess of the resurrection of unpleasant and prurient articles, and the whole vitiated process in the media, the words of James Joyce come to mind: 'Sniffer of carrion, premature gravedigger, seeker of the nest of evil in the bosom of a good word'.

When I returned to the race on an apparent wave of public good will, it was clear that I was going to be undermined. The people had taken me to their heart and there is nothing more dangerous to the political and media establishment – so they sent in the carrion sniffers.

Every conceivable dirty trick was used in a bid to derail my campaign. There was scarcely a radio station or publication that didn't vilify, ridicule or defame me – it was like trying to deal with every individual snowflake in a blizzard. I have signed documentary evidence that in at least one tabloid newspaper a vocabulary was suggested to journalists to be used when writing about me. This included words such as 'effeminate', 'fey', 'camp', 'gay' and 'flamboyant'. In a situation reminiscent in every detail of evidence supplied through the National Union of Journalists to the Leveson Inquiry, my correspondents almost instantly regretted having contacted me and I was besieged by letters and emails begging me not to reveal their identities because of the level of bullying and dismissal that obtained in tabloid newspaper offices in Ireland. In the respectable newspapers there was also a lot of concealed homophobia, often camouflaged despite the shrill denials of the critics who usually prefaced their spite with phrases of the 'Some of my best friends are gay' type.

*

Language is a very significant determinant in politics. In the Senate I have several times called for a scholarly examination of the language system employed by the allies in the Iraq War. Victor Klemperer, a German Jewish academic married to a Christian, who survived the Second World War in hiding, wrote a fascinating book which analysed how the shift into fascism in Germany was preceded by a shift in language which made it culturally acceptable to do what the Reich did to the Jews and other minorities. Christopher Isherwood had noted the same change in his Berlin stories when he said that language had 'gone off the gold standard'. It happened again in the Iraq War, when euphemisms like 'shake and bake' or 'bunker busters' were used for weapons of mass murder. Phrases like 'extra-ordinary rendition' and 'collateral damage' were used to gull the public in precisely the same way Joseph Goebbels did. (Indeed, I led the exposure in the Oireachtas of the infamous 'extra-ordinary rendition' flights through Shannon and spearheaded opposition in the Seanad to the Iraq War.)

I repeatedly suggested that it would be a practical, and not merely theoretical, role for the world of academia to examine the way in which language is used to corrupt political systems, but then of course I suppose it is a vain hope. In the groves of Academe few are prepared to risk their positions. Indeed, as has been made clear by analyses of the relationship between pro-fessors in the Ivy League universities and the corrupt world of the great financial institutions and ratings agencies, some of these people have no principles at all.

Of those involved in smearing me, some were either open or closeted gays themselves. But then many of the worst homo-phobes in history were gay, like J. Edgar Hoover and Roy Cohn. On RTÉ television and radio there were jokes about me 'taking it up the Áras' or 'feeling the flagpole', and how you wouldn't want to be in front of me in a rugby scrum etc. If that had been said about any of the female candidates the sisterhood would at the very least have picketed RTÉ, but there was a strangely subdued silence from the liberals. One hears a lot from the predictable group of conservative reactionary hacks in the press about the so-called 'liberal agenda', and the clique who are supposed to run the media from Dublin 4. Maybe they do, but there wasn't much sign of them around when I was being so dishonestly done in. Of course the usual claque of self-promoting and self-proclaimed 'Christians' showed no such restraint in the Pharisaical virulence of their attacks which were strangely at variance with their alleged devotion to Jesus, 'the King of Love'.

I believe that one of the reasons why I was vilified was because I had been critical of the media at various stages over the past thirty years and have been vocal about their declining standards. There were powerful forces waiting in the long grass, and out they came. Some in the media decided that I was 'fair game', as though I were some form of 'legitimate target' to be pursued.

People in politics invariably have strong egos and would do anything to see their name in the newspaper. I am not without ego myself, but as I have pointed out already, I never courted the media. I was always good copy because I told the truth about my sexuality, religion, politics, etc. The fact that I so frequently agreed to co-operate with PR for charities – and that I made light-hearted after-dinner speeches and took part in photo stunts to attract publicity and funding for charities working with cancer, women and children in slavery, arthritis and many more – probably didn't help. Photos were trawled up by picture editors to degrade my contribution on serious issues. Charity photos of me with a bucket and spade were used to illustrate my departure to Cyprus, while a shot of me with green balloons publicising an ecological group was used to associate me with a transvestite party which I hadn't even attended. Pictures were taken to serve their agenda – at one meeting a photo of me waiting to meet a mayor was cropped to get across the idea that I was isolated. Another trick was for the photographer to whisper to me so I would cup my ear to hear, and could be snapped looking deaf and old. Some picture desks seemed to have an obsession with such shots, and photographers did everything to catch me in awkward positions such as changing jackets while on the move or clumsily clambering out of a campaign car. One photographer actually had the gall to call me a spoilsport for successfully derailing some of her attempts.

There rarely has been a more systematic campaign of personal vilification of any individual in Irish politics with so little justification. Very few people could understand what I was put through. When the controversy arose over Plato's *Symposium* I wasn't talking about molesting children, but my enemies linked it to the abuse of children by priests. Many of the people who used my attempts to consider and understand the complex issues around the subject of consent as an excuse to defame me all had one thing in common. Many were homophobic, some were prejudiced, some were religiously or politically motivated, but what united them all was their smugness.

A couple of years ago I chanced upon an archive programme in which I appeared. It was a political discussion several decades old in which I was speaking in favour of the decriminalisation of homosexuality and being roundly berated for this by a sanctimonious priest from the back row. At the time I had no idea who he was, but when I saw the repeat, I instantly recognised his face. It was the late Fr Seán Fortune, who concurrently with verbally abusing me on television was raping altar boys in the diocese of Ferns. He also epitomised self-satisfied smugness.

One of the most disgusting examples of double standard was when the tabloid press attacked RTÉ over the Fr Kevin Reynolds case. Of course the libel of Fr Reynolds was an appalling thing to happen but for the *canaille* to spout a lot of indignation about the evils of doorstepping, about promulgating lies and not properly researching facts is an extraordinary example of a projection of their own flaws. What they correctly accuse RTÉ of is no less than the same practices in which they were systematically involved themselves, as I know to my cost.

Even an *Irish Times* columnist, David Adams, remarked on how many of the smears were motivated by homophobia: 'Imagine for a second how it must feel to be publicly smeared in the way that Norris has. The treatment of this Joycean scholar is somewhat blackly analogous with the calculated destruction of Oscar Wilde. I have never met Norris, but he strikes me as a fundamentally decent person – his major weakness, it appears, is to presume that everyone is as fair-minded and decent as himself.'

My contempt for the industry and most of its practitioners doesn't prevent me continuing my membership of the National Union of Journalists, however. I do have respect for a minority of real reporters, decent, sometimes heroic and brave people. It would be invidious to name a random selection, but they *are* there. Many have been critical of me, but at least they have treated some of my ideas as worthy of consideration even when they didn't agree with them.

Nevertheless, proportionately there are not very many of intellectual substance in the Irish media; most deal in second-hand ideas. I was amused to hear one commentator say there wasn't enough intellectual power in Leinster House to fuel one light bulb. Yet when I used the Senate to expose a huge financial scandal involving one of the largest European banks at the Financial Services Centre, my adjournment debate was raided by one of the 'serious' papers. The story occupied nearly a full page of the newspaper but neglected to mention either myself or the Senate. I could multiply such instances almost endlessly.

I am not over-impressed by the self-importance and self-righteous pontificating of many of our political correspondents. One of those I *do* have time for wrote that part of my problem was that I dealt in ideas – and, as he said, you can't deal with ideas in a bearpit. The election had turned into a reality/talent contest, run by and for the media. Its ringmasters, whether they wished it or not, were media celebrities like Miriam O'Callaghan, Vincent Browne, Pat Kenny and Seán O'Rourke, and after every single debate their colleagues in print predictably said that it had been won by whichever media celebrity had chaired the debate.

I was railroaded into appearing on the Ivan Yates show on Newstalk. I hadn't been told by my handlers that Ivan had a back problem which required him to do the whole interview either lying on the floor or standing towering over me. It was quite disconcerting to have him hectoring me from on high one moment, and then disappearing inexplicably from sight. There was another fellow in the studio called Chris, who started chipping in with questions instead of twiddling the knobs. I thought he was the sound operator and couldn't work out why he kept asking questions, but as I have learnt since, he was actually part of the interview team.

The media, and in particular the tabloid press, have become an unelected, uncontrolled and unaccountable tyranny. It is very telling that virtually every newspaper in the country, having called for the fully independent regulation of every single other profession, absolutely refuse to take this medicine themselves. They have apparently replaced the Catholic hierarchy as the bully boys of Irish political life. Tony Blair flying off to Australia to do obeisance to Rupert Murdoch is a direct parallel to the various *taoisigh* who submitted legislation for approval to Archbishop John Charles McQuaid, and I have no doubt a similar situation applies here now with regard to the media.

One of the most damaging stories was about my departure from Trinity. A reporter asked me a question about my 'pension', which completely wrongfooted me, as I didn't know what he was talking about. It turned out they were asking me about a perfectly standard income-protection scheme of which I had availed myself. What I did was perfectly appropriate, on instruction from my employers, and precisely what anyone would have done in my position, and in fact an identical scheme was in place in some of the newspapers that attacked me, which made it a bit of a farce.

The story was distorted by the media, which presented it as social-welfare fraud, which I then got hit with everywhere I went. Even Dublin taxi drivers, who in the main had backed me all the way, started attacking me over it. I have never got a penny from the social-welfare system in my life, let alone defrauded it. I am actually entitled to a small contributory pension from the state but I have never claimed it because I reckon there are people who need it more than I. The only thing I have ever taken is the free travel pass, because I am mechanically incompetent and was forever missing the Luas when I couldn't get the ticket machine to work, and even that I use at most a couple of times a month.

However, even some of the tabloids gave me credit for the debate on TG4, which was partly conducted in Irish – one of the papers judged I had won the debate while most of the others ranked me second. People seemed to be astonished I had reasonable Irish. One debate commentator said I had very good Irish 'but he spoke it in the accent of the Irish R.M.', which I don't think is true, but who am I to judge?

On the campaign trail, among the people, things were happier. I had to be disciplined on my forays around the country because I could have completely reversed the weight losses I made on *Operation Transformation*. Everywhere I went I was offered generous slices of apple tart and chocolate cake, along with the inevitable welcoming cup of tea. Happily, any excesses could be sorted out by my new friend and personal trainer Carl Coultry, who never charged me a penny and even got his wife and daughter involved in helping the campaign. Across the road, all of Muireann's family got characteristically stuck in: the youngest, Déidinn, organised a stall selling cupcakes at the street's open day, which raised the enormous sum of €200. With the support of a dynamic six-year-old like that, who also canvassed her schoolmates, how could I go wrong?

I enjoyed visiting the farmers' markets to buy real honey and marmalade to go with the lovely home-made brown bread, and where I could see the way people were battling the recession in their own ways. Rather than sit around waiting for the tide to turn, people were putting their skills to making products that they could sell for a few bob. There is an enormous vitality in Ireland, and a genius for innovation. I visited enterprise centres in virtually every county, and again I saw a pattern emerge. The successful centres were those where the local authority had provided modular units at fair rents and experienced mentoring. The most innovative enterprises were those producing goods that sprang from the local area and weren't just dumped on them from Dublin.

It wasn't just adults that were showing innovation. Even before the election started I was invited down to the Sacred Heart School in Clonakilty to be guest of honour at a transition-year class. The whole notion of transition year had been criticised by some parents, who wanted it dropped, but the school had decided to keep it going. There was quite a number of fascinating projects, some of which showed real commercial potential, but the one that most excited me was the brainchild of six girls. There was a local problem caused by the run-off of nutrients from fertiliser into the sea, which created a bloom of a kind of seaweed on the seashore. This sea lettuce rotted and made swimming unpleasant, and both locals and tourists hated the foul smell. The girls took samples and demonstrated in the laboratory that the seaweed could be harvested and compressed into briquettes, which produced just as much heat as turf and burned for twice as long. I thought it was superb that these young women had taken a problem and turned it into something positive and productive. I walked away, saying, 'There's hope for this country.'

I was inspired by a woman called Sheila Byrne who had

developed a remarkable and essentially simple method of helping to ease the burden of dyslexia called Readassist. She
organised a petition that got up to twenty thousand signatures
in favour of my candidacy, which was presented to me at
Leinster House. People like herself, Clive Salter and Leanne
Doyle put every ounce of energy at my disposal and never once
faltered. I had many wonderful volunteers all over the country,
among whom was one who came from the United States. Carlos
Clark was a very gifted young man who saved the day on
several occasions with his technical wizardry and willingness to
turn his hand to anything.

I saw more of Ireland in 2011 than I'd seen in all my life – I
visited every single county at least twice. We did enormous
mileage, up to three hundred miles a day. As the campaign
heated up, reporters and TV crews would tag along on these
trips. They witnessed and even filmed me being mobbed on the
streets – it took me four hours to do one side of the quays in
Waterford at the Tall Ships Race – and not once was that ever
reported or shown on television. But as soon as one heckler
came along, that would be covered.

I found 99.9 per cent of the people I met to be warm and
friendly, but I did have a small number of unpleasant
experiences. Once, at the very outset of the campaign, I was
chatting to a woman on Grafton Street when a respectable-
looking man came along with a little girl perched on his
shoulders. He interrupted us and began venomously attacking
me over Christian values and his perception of my views on
child abuse. He said, 'If you allow your name to go forward we
will make sure you are destroyed.'

The woman turned on him and said, 'Why are you being so
obnoxious to this decent man?'

Just then the former Progressive Democrat Senator John
Minihan materialised, and when he heard what this man was
saying he told him, 'You don't know what you are talking
about. I worked for many years in Seanad Éireann with this

337

man, and he's one of the finest people I know. He has a record that cannot be equalled in the protection of children.'

I never raised my voice and kept in total control, while the man was loud-voiced and I sensed that this was upsetting his daughter. I was shaken at his outburst, but I was also astonished at the lack of respect he showed to his child, who couldn't have been more than four years of age.

There was another, scarier encounter on Talbot Street in Dublin. I had been invited to visit a crèche around the corner, but was followed in by a pair of strange young women. They started haranguing me so we left immediately, to avoid any trauma for the children. Outside one of them made a phone call and began following me, until they were joined by a wild-eyed man who I subsequently discovered had rather obscure political connections. He physically threatened me and started pushing and shoving me and members of my team. He was literally frothing at the mouth. Eventually he was subdued by security personnel at Connolly Station where I was to take a train to Drogheda.

On the other hand, I was always buoyed up when I attended Communion, which I insisted I did every Sunday on the campaign trail just as I would have at home. I think it was this spiritual enrichment that kept me sane during the difficult times. Just as when you're in love every pop song on the radio seems directed personally at you, the psalms, canticles, prayers and hymns all seemed to carry a message of comfort and reassurance.

On one trip we stayed overnight after visiting the Ballinasloe Horse Fair. On the next morning, which was Sunday, I found the nearest Anglican church miles out in the countryside, where we heard a wonderful sermon and the parson introduced me to the oldest member of the congregation, who happened to be a cousin of a relative of mine.

I enjoyed visiting cultural sites of all kinds around the country. I have always maintained that heritage tourism is an important economic engine, but I also believe it is important that Irish people themselves learn about our rich culture and history. I was greatly heartened that so much work had been done in developing cultural and historical centres around the country, and that so many new theatres had been opened since my own days on the road.

Towards the end of the campaign I knew it was now just a matter of salvaging my reputation while fighting as bravely as I could to make the quarter-quota which would mitigate my losses, made more difficult by the size of the field and a hostile press. The media were just as determined that I wouldn't, which was an act of extraordinary spite because they knew that at that stage all my life savings were gone. But still they wouldn't stop. Articles that were plainly false were published, apologised for, then published again.

Five days before the election Helen Lucy Burke's tapes were broadcast on *Liveline*. She later admitted that she had had them for some time but deliberately waited to release them when they would have maximum 'impact'. Despite her attacks on me, I had immediately after the first volley put out messages on Twitter and Facebook urging supporters not to return insult for insult. I didn't receive any warning about the broadcast until thirty minutes before the show, when I was driving at high speed from addressing Cork County Council to do the same in Waterford. I was right up against the deadline and could have missed the vital nomination from Waterford if I had done what RTÉ wanted and pulled in to the side of the road to take the interview. The tapes as broadcast were indistinct and in parts sounded to me, at least, doctored, my voice slowed down from its usual rapid high pitch to an uncharacteristic indistinct bass, sounding like Barry White on a night out.

The final debate of the fractious campaign coincided with Dublin's worst rainstorm in years. We were in danger of not being able to reach Montrose, as many of the roads around Dublin 4 were flooded, but I would have got there by hook or by crook, even if I had to swim. I was delighted it was the last debate, and I was much more relaxed. The advisers had finally agreed to give me the names of who it was in Israel that had given us the legal advice which had caused Vincent Browne such consternation, but now nobody bothered to ask.

I had always maintained civilised relations with Martin McGuinness, as with the other candidates, having said at the outset that I would run a clean campaign and rely on my strengths, not any perceived weaknesses of others. But there's a ruthlessness about him that you can see in his eyes. He came out with a lot of blather about how he would only accept the average industrial wage, which is a regular Sinn Féin mantra. What they don't tell you is that the taxpayer still pays exactly the same amount of money; the excess goes to the party, so their TDs get the benefit of it anyway. I was the first to be asked about presidential pay, and I said I wouldn't forgo the salary as it would be unfair to tie the hands of the next person to assume office. I repeated what I said at the very beginning of the campaign, that I would live frugally and put the majority of my salary into a fund to improve the access of people to the presidency. On the final *Frontline* debate I suggested to Mr McGuinness, 'You didn't get that fancy bus you have parked outside on the average industrial wage, did you, Martin?'

My heart went out to Seán Gallagher when the fake tweet was read out and his face went deathly white. I felt sorry for him because at core he's a decent man. However, it was a debate and it was I who instantly picked up on his slips of the tongue such as the unfortunate use of the word 'envelope', which harked back to the days of Charlie Haughey and Bertie Ahern. The whole way that issue was handled was very shoddy, but then all RTÉ was interested in was dramatic television.

Mary Davis was allowed the last word at the end of that final debate – or at least she thought she was. She came out with the predictable stuff about what the country needed being someone wholesome and hard-working who would tell the truth and inspire the people, so I dramatically opened my arms to capture the cameras and said, 'And here I am!' So I did, after all, get the last word.

On polling day, Thursday 27 October, I went down early with Muireann to the Central Model Schools on Marlborough Street where I always vote. The last couple of opinion polls had been promising and I hoped the *Frontline* debate would have turned things around for me, but the media had succeeded, in their own phraseology, in 'monstering' me.

After a hearty breakfast the following morning I went out to the Ballsbridge count centre, where it was soon clear that Michael D. was going to win. I was glad to be the first to congratulate him but I didn't want to hang around the RDS as media fodder so came home and spent the day working while listening to the radio. Eddie brought me back into Dublin Castle for the official announcement, where we all lined up on the stage.

Michael D. and Sabina were radiant and their children naturally overjoyed. A very nice man came towards the front of the stage and leaned up to shake my hand and asked was I very disappointed? I told him, 'Well, I wouldn't be human if I wasn't disappointed, but I tell you something, we've got a bloody good man as President.' And he said, 'I'm delighted to hear you say that – I'm his brother.' I made a short speech of congratulations in which I told Michael D. that as he was finally elected with 1,007,104 votes he was Ireland's first 'political millionaire'.

I had got just short of 110,000 votes, less than half the threshold for getting the €200,000 payment towards expenses. This highlighted the inequity of the whole system. If you accept that Seán Gallagher was a species of unofficial Fianna Fáil candidate – and he was on their national executive until a short time before he went forward, and had canvassed for the party in the general election – every single genuine independent (as well as the candidate of the largest party in the state) failed to make the quota. Having seven candidates distorted the whole process and it was simple mathematics that most would not receive funding. I believe that passing the arduous test of getting a nomination should be sufficient to qualify for some funding, perhaps on a graduated basis. In the event it was only the party candidates that qualified for state assistance.

I had warned my team that I had very little money to spend, and my life savings ran out very quickly. At the point I left the campaign in August, we had spent €70,000, but costs ran out of control on my return and the total bill came to well over €350,000, which I may well be paying off for the rest of my days. But the majority of my supporters, both at HQ in Dublin and around the country, were an inspiration.

As one of the unsuccessful candidates I was invited to President Higgins's inauguration, where I sat between Gerry Adams and Cardinal Seán Brady. I had to be careful which way I turned so I didn't confuse my conversations – armalites on one hand and Carmelites on the other. Just as at Mary Robinson's inauguration, I looked up at the FitzPatrick banner hanging proudly among the standards of the knights of St Patrick and thought of the family crest with the motto in Irish: *Ceart laidir abú* (and in Latin *Fortis sub forte fatiscet*) – Right will prevail. I brought along my cousin Jennifer Gill, who with extraordinary generosity had offered me financial assistance from her savings at a time when things were painfully tight. We had pleasant chats with Maeve Hillery and Mary Robinson, and I met lots of old friends. In the circumstances it was an enjoyable and positive occasion, and a few weeks after his inauguration, President Higgins graciously invited me and seven members of my family and friends for lunch in Áras an Uachtaráin.

I was still deeply disappointed, but that all ended within a week when I got to Cyprus and was reunited with Nora and

Tim. However, one night I woke up with tears streaming down my face and my heart thumping against my ribcage so hard I thought it was going to burst. I had been dreaming about the way people who were close to me were taken out and destroyed by sections of the press. That was what the Gestapo did. If they couldn't break you, they tortured people close to you in front of your very eyes.

Since the election I have had no contact with Ezra. When the storm about the letters broke I'd rung him in Sweden, where he was receiving some accolade for his human-rights work. I told him that the story of his conviction was about to come out and that the media would undoubtedly be on to him, so I asked him not to talk to them, to which he agreed. To my dismay he then talked to one of the tabloid newspapers, so I rang and asked him what he was doing and he said, 'What difference could it make?' I told him it was the only time in my life I had ever asked him to do something for me and I was sorry that he wouldn't do it and I begged him not to do it again. A couple of days later he did a live interview on the one o'clock RTÉ news. So I rang him again and begged he remain silent, but again he did another major interview, with the *Irish Times*.

The sad thing is that while I had come to an accommodation with all of Ezra's faults, the media couldn't leave it alone. What they have succeeded in doing is make me numb. I now neither love nor hate Ezra, I am simply indifferent. I respect his wonderful work, but I am completely, at least for the time being, frozen to him as a friend. I doubt this is an achievement of which any decent journalist could feel proud: the final destruction of forty years of love and friendship which I had worked desperately to preserve in its various forms.

However, what the press has also succeeded in doing is removing the last possible gag; I will continue to speak out even more fearlessly against the decline in standards in the media, despite the fact that I know well how vengeful they are and how they will attempt to exact retribution. The media has become an apparently untouchable dictatorship. Although nobody else in public life appears to have the guts to take this on, I will certainly do my best to clear out that Augean stable.

The Communications Minister, Pat Rabbitte, came to the Senate in February 2012 to talk about media standards and I told him about how an editor of one of the tabloids told me that what was happening to me during the campaign was 'payback' for standing up for the victims of the invasion of privacy and, more particularly, for what I had done in respect of the Defamation Bill 2006, the first version of which I forced to be withdrawn, to the fury of the press. I thought this an astonishing demonstration of the intention of sections of the media to interfere with the democratic process by intimidating politicians. This particular gentleman then had the impertinence to attribute the situation to what he called the 'spinelessness' of politicians. Perhaps he had a point. During the debate in the Senate, I asked Minister Rabbitte a number of questions. In the light of references at the Leveson Inquiry by witnesses who clearly stated that the practices described extended to Ireland, would he appoint a representative to attend the inquiry? The answer was no. Would he move the Privacy Bill which was promised and was on the order paper in the government's name? The answer was no. Would he establish an Irish inquiry to parallel Leveson? The answer was no.

When I finished speaking I received a round of applause from my colleagues, but as I looked around the Senate chamber I noticed that most of them were clapping silently below the level of the desktop, careful to avoid the cameras and microphones, and those from the new tyranny who would be studying the film. That was a truly Orwellian experience.

As this book goes to print, the press apologies have started rolling in. However, after being vilified in front pages, centrefold spreads and editorials, upon which 'kind and concerned friends' could not forego comment, it seems little recompense to receive a couple of paragraphs on the fold inside the newspaper, unremarked upon so far by anyone of my acquaintance.

Michael D. Higgins is a remarkable and gifted man, and he has my continued friendship, loyalty and complete support. If I had been elected, however, it would have represented a tectonic shift in Irish politics, public life and society. It would have been global news, and I regret that didn't happen because it would have advanced things for minorities the world over, particularly gay people.

I had worried that Michael D.'s election would mean that every lever of power in the land would be in the hands of the government, but while it might appear to be so, he has proved himself to be strongly independent and I have no doubt he will continue to speak out when he sees fit. He has already shown himself to be a great president and a worthy successor to the two Marys in the short time he has been in office. Yes, indeed, the forces of reaction did succeed in getting rid of one liberal, but their underhanded tactics have blown up in their faces and brought in a gallant, courageous and thoroughly liberal man in Michael D. Higgins.

In retrospect, the whole thing has shaken out beautifully, because we have got a superb president: an honourable man who will put his neck on the line for the marginalised and the vulnerable. And I'm where I should be also, on the back benches of Seanad Éireann, saying the things that nobody else in this country is prepared to say.

Over the years, as I have said, many of my ideas have been lifted as people leapt on board various bandwagons and pushed me off. But the important thing is that these ideas benefit the Irish people and that they arrive at their destination, not who is on board when they arrive there. Bandwagon jumpers are always very quickly forgotten. All through my life I have told the truth and it has got me into trouble. The mass of people seem to prefer half-truths or comforting lies; but I will continue to give them the full truth as I see it, right between the eyes. And, as I have shown with many of the causes for which I have worked, the establishment sometimes catches up, even if it takes five, ten, fifteen years or more.

Enoch Powell came out with that line that all political careers end in failure – but he was wrong – they don't. All political careers simply end, just as all lives end. You achieve what you can in your career, or life, if you have the courage to do so. I got a few knocks along the way, but I certainly don't feel that I'm a failure. You've got to dream the world as it should be, and then do your best to make it happen.

As I approach seventy, with plenty of vitality, I can still look forward to going to Cyprus several times a year. On the other hand, if I had won I would have had to ask the permission of the government to go to my own house there. I could have lost dear friends like Isaac and Nora. I've always been a servant of the public, but now I feel entitled to be a little more self-indulgent with the last phase of my life, and spend more of it with my friends.

CHAPTER 14

Laughter and the Love of Friends

O, all the money e'er I had,
I spent it in good company.
And all the harm that e'er I've done,
alas it was to none but me.
And all I've done for want of wit
to mem'ry now I can't recall;
So fill to me the parting glass,
Good night and joy be with you all.

'The Parting Glass', traditional Scottish ballad

I AM A MAN OF STRONG BELIEF AND PRACTICAL FAITH, AN attendee every Sunday at St Patrick's Cathedral, whose most famous dean was the eighteenth-century writer Jonathan Swift. I would not presume to compare myself to the great satirist and author of *Gulliver's Travels*, but I do share something of his *saeva indignatio* at the prospect of human injustice. I have been going there for sixty years and for a number of years have been a member of its board, but my religious beliefs are governed by the theological principle of positive doubt, which requires you to acknowledge with humility your own ignorance of divinity. I do not know the answer to the riddle of the universe, what God thinks or whether the soul survives death, but I *believe* it does.

No one knows these things in the way you know the colour of your front door, be he the Pope of Rome, Grand Ayatollah, Archbishop of Canterbury, Chief Rabbi or Grand Mufti of Jerusalem. Nor do I think you can persuade someone logically of the existence of God, but I am grateful that as I grow older my faith becomes stronger day by day.

During one of our campaign car journeys, I told Liam that I was thinking of giving a lecture beginning 'Let us imagine a universe in which the laws are all either random, chaotic or absent.' His reply was, 'I can't imagine anybody else coming up with something like that. You are either mad or a genius. How many people would start a sentence with "Let us imagine a universe"? At the moment getting to the next village is as much as most people could imagine.'

But there is no reason why such cosmic randomness should not have happened. All we can be certain of is the existence of our own consciousness. René Descartes said, '*Cogito ergo sum*' – I think, therefore I am. Everything else, the basis of science, logic and mathematics, everything that we believe we know about the physical world comes simply from the human observation of recurring events. When I was a student in Trinity, undergraduates were required to take a subsidiary subject. If you did arts it had to be a science subject, and vice versa. Philosophy was then regarded as a science and so I chose it. I didn't care for the logical calculus but I fell in love with the spirit of Bishop Berkeley.

He attacked the idea of materialism and the idea that there was anything that could be described as essential matter. As an illustration he took an apple: 'How do you know it's there? You can smell it, taste it, see it, feel it.' In other words your perception, and your awareness of the existence of the apple, is dependent on the senses, and from this he coined the phrase '*Esse est percipi*' – To be is to be perceived. This raised the question, if you were alone in the countryside observing a field of cows, did they evaporate if you turned your back on them?

Berkeley's answer was superb: of course they didn't. Into the equation he introduced God as the subtending agent within the universe. It is God's duty and role in the universe to keep us in existence by perceiving us.

There is some general truth in this, as one can conclude from the experience of human love. We become more alive as we are perceived more lovingly, more intensely, by a particular person, and our life is magically enriched by our increased perception of them. This is a truth that all of us experience in our lives and is true also of religion.

I have never warmed to St Paul, it is St John who speaks to me. Particularly when he talks of love: 'He that loveth not knoweth not God; for God is love'; 'If a man say, I love God, and hateth his brother, he is a liar: for he that loveth not his brother whom he hath seen, how can he love God whom he hath not seen?'

Belief comes from a combination of tradition, experience and the opening of oneself to the experience of God through the sacraments and prayer. As an Anglican I find the question of miracles interesting. In our church they appear to have stopped at the time of the Reformation, which is a bit odd if we are prepared to believe in them at all. But full belief does lead to the possibility of commercial hoax. I do not believe that the Virgin Mary goes on a tour of pilgrimage sites every so often, from Lourdes to Knock to Medjugorje. Her appearance in these places would suggest a certain narrow social selectivity and limited conversational capacity. She only ever turns up in places where she is guaranteed a warm welcome from her fellow Roman Catholics and rarely seems to have anything interesting to say. I would be more impressed if she were to appear in the pulpit of Ian Paisley's church during a service and deliver a sermon on the evils of bigotry. After all, she's had two thousand years to prepare such a message.

However, although I treat these things with a certain lightness, I also do entertain a respect for the various Marian shrines.

I recognise that they have become holy places, not by any mysterious appearance of the Blessed Virgin but by the devotion, grief, prayers and exhortations of the pilgrims who visit and almost universally return refreshed, whether they have received a cure or not. So I agree with my Roman Catholic friends that these are places to be revered, but the origin of my reverence is in the humanity of the pilgrims rather than divine visitation.

Nor do I doubt that one can have access to extraordinary spiritual feelings. At a crucial time in our relationship I was confronted with a situation when it appeared that I might never again set eyes on Ezra. I was stricken with grief. For the first time I realised that the heart actually can break. It is a physical effect which almost stops one's breathing. You eventually lose consciousness for a moment through exhaustion and then, after the momentary peace, a terrible awareness of what has happened re-emerges.

I was lying on the couch in the front drawing room when suddenly I felt a presence as if there was someone in the room with me; when I looked around there was just an open door which reminded me of that extraordinary picture of David Hockney's – an open Californian window, clothes tossed casually on a chair, a rumpled bed, no human form in the picture. But the painting yet seems drenched with the presence of someone who has just left the room. I felt in that moment the presence of Jesus Christ in my life, reaching out across the millennia towards me, someone who had had the experience of betrayal and agony. Was that a mystical experience? I don't know. Was it something triggered by a psychological need? Perhaps. What of the divinity of Christ? What of it indeed? That day it didn't matter to me. In some ways I felt it would be even more poignant if Christ were fully human and not divine at all, but still the experience of one human being transmitted through tradition had become a living experience in my own life.

The same is true of the mystery of the Holy Communion. Is

it, as some of the evangelical churches believe, merely a memorial commemoration, or is it, as Anglicans and other Catholics believe, a sacrament? That wise woman Queen Elizabeth I certainly resolved the dilemma for me with her little quatrain:

> *His the hands that break it,*
> *his the lips that spake it,*
> *for what so e'er that doth make it,*
> *for that shall I take it.*

A recent poll showing that eighty per cent of Irish Roman Catholics do not understand the theological distinction between transubstantiation and consubstantiation, and in fact agree with the Anglican position, suggests that centuries of warfare, torture and misery were all for nothing.

Unfortunately a sense of openness has been replaced in the churches by concrete laws, rules and regulations that require us to obey what they see as the will of God. God is often made the blasphemous excuse for the basest political instincts of mankind. A great deal of damage is done by people who presume to know the mind of God and inflict their perception on other people. This is particularly dangerous when done in a political context.

The tragedy of the Roman Catholic Church is that it cannot seem to make up its mind what it should render unto Caesar and what it should render unto Christ. It pretends to be both a church and a state, thereby trying to have it both ways. This gives it the political entitlement, as it sees it, to interfere in the internal affairs of other states, in a manner that would be tolerated of no other entity. Instructing democratically elected representatives of the people as to how they should vote on social issues, which the Vatican regularly does, is an inexcusable interference. This is a Church that, under the last two popes, continually spoke about dialogue. The whole meaning of the word 'dialogue' has been turned on its head and it now appears to mean 'Sit down, shut up and do what you're told because I'm the Pope.' We've witnessed the gagging of the greatest intellects and spiritual influences within the Church: Leonardo Boff, Hans Kung, Charles Curran and John McNeill – and in our own country the silencing of Fathers Seán Fagan, Tony Flannery and Brian D'Arcy. I can think of no better way to alienate and hurt ordinary decent Catholics.

Even after the succession of child-abuse scandals, the obsession of the Vatican concerning sexual orientation continues unabated. In June 2012, the excuse of an apostolic visitation prompted by clerical sex abuse was used by Cardinal Timothy Dolan as an indirect key to suppressing independent thought and any deviation from orthodoxy in the historic Irish College in Rome. In an amazing turn he both raised and dismissed homosexual smears. The cardinal 'exonerated' the college from the 'unjust perception' that it had a reputation of being 'gay friendly'. The language is instructive in its blatant but apparently unconscious homophobia. Should the Church not be welcoming, as indeed Christ is, to all fallible mortals?

Perhaps it's time for a level playing field, because after all most homophobia springs from fear deep inside the subject. So let's hear it from the top – the cardinals, the Curia, the Pope himself. After all, fair's fair and it's over to you now in Rome: since you're so interested in *our* sexuality, why not be honest and divulge *your own*? As you ought to know, truth and openness, wherever they lead, are cleansing.

I do not gloat in the self-destruction of the Roman Catholic Church – it is close to my heart and my very genes – but I deplore that it has been placed in the hands of such mediocrities as the Vatican clique and their collaborators. I very much hope that the Holy Spirit does guide the next conclave and that we go back to the humble, life-enriching spirit of someone like John XXIII. The tragedy of the last election was that the great Cardinal Martini of Milan was actually modest and humble, and therefore did not facilitate his own candidacy. Anyone who can fill Milan Cathedral with young people and discuss with them the meaning of the gospels is someone to be revered, and I wish with all my heart that he had become Pope. In contrast the machinations employed to get Josef Ratzinger elected would do justice to the Borgias, and his open jubilation on the balcony of the basilica on that fateful day gave the lie to any suggestion that he was dragged unwillingly to the throne.

I was once invited to give a talk in St Thomas's Church entitled 'What I Believe'. Afterwards the vicar told me that I seemed to believe an awful lot more than he did. His name was Patrick Semple and he was a delightful, civilised and honest man. He subsequently withdrew from the Church and wrote a marvellous book entitled *The Rector Who Wouldn't Pray for Rain*. The reference in the title came from the fact that he was approached by some big farmers who asked him to pray for rain but he didn't see why they needed it more than the people in the Sahara and thought it a bit of a cheek to be petitioning God in this manner.

The thing that interested me most in his book was when he referred to the Anglican Communion service, where the prayer book says, 'There are two great commandments, the first of these is thou shalt love the Lord thy God with all thy heart, with all thy soul and with all thy mind. This is the first and great commandment, the second is like unto it, thou shalt love thy neighbour as thyself. Upon these two commandments hang all the law of the prophets.' As I understand it, Patrick Semple's idea was that the injunction to love God represented the perpendicular, the eyes heavenward, so to speak, and it was this that had created the Church with its intricate filigree of dogmatic theology and canon law, binding rather than liberating the human spirit. Whereas the horizontal, the love of one's fellow creatures and the attempt to render them only good, to regard everyone as one's neighbour just like the Samaritan of the gospel, can be enough of itself, because it automatically brings into life the genuine perpendicular, and this is God at work in the community. A lot of it simply revolves around language. What does one mean by 'God', the 'divine', 'sacrament', etc.? The more people in the Church are removed from practical realities and understandable language, the more atrophied the soul becomes.

In April 2006 I spoke at the annual conference of the Irish Theological Association in Limerick. The subject of my paper was civil partnership and the main Christian churches' political opposition to this. I did not pull my punches, with the result that, for the first time ever, the proceedings were not subsequently published. During a coffee break I met a troubled young man who claimed to have been sexually assaulted by a member of the Roman Catholic priesthood. He felt he had never been able to find justice and that nobody would listen to him. I returned to Dublin after the weekend and discovered within a couple of days that this young man had taken his own life.

The Pope has frequently launched vitriolic attacks on gay people, and the Vatican attacked their rights in employment and housing while employing the language of hatred in phrases such as 'objectively evil' and 'intrinsically disordered'. I do not swallow the usual pap about hating the sin and loving the sinner. I know damn well when I'm being hated and I detect hatred of the gay community from sections of all the main Christian denominations, including my own. The old adage comes to mind: 'If you want to know if the shoe pinches, you don't ask the shoe, you ask the foot.' It is also extraordinary and ironic that those very persons and groups who used to decry gay people for being promiscuous now attack them for wanting to have recognised stable relationships.

Moreover, I have never confined my strictures to the Roman Catholic Church. When I was invited to give the talk from the pulpit of Christ Church Cathedral in 2009 on International Day Against Homophobia, I opened my homily by saying I had come not to bring peace but a sword, and brought to their attention the problematic career of the seventeenth-century Bishop Atherton. More recently we have seen the unseemly politicking by bishops and others at the 2012 Church of Ireland Synod on the subject of same sex marriage.

On the other hand, I have no time for people like the equally dogmatic Professor Dawkins. Apart from anything else, science itself is nowadays much more mysterious than religion, with its dark matter, black holes and parallel universes. That puts at least as much strain on credibility as the idea of God's existence. The whole of science is in fact built on nothing more than observation and an acceptance of the first item in the scientist's creed, the law of cause and effect. As I've said, all we know is our own consciousness. We observe the world through that consciousness. As we develop we notice certain patterns emerge: the same act is virtually automatically followed by the same result. If you twist a handle and give a pull, the door is likely to open. We know that because we have done it so many times. But there is actually no reason apart from blind faith in our experience of cause and effect that the door shouldn't decide to surprise us by turning into water or bursting into flames just for a change.

The real mystery is consciousness. Machines can indeed be designed to perform apparently intelligent tasks but they remain totally unaware of doing so. So-called artificial intelligence is nothing more than a glorified abacus. The computer can only do two things, add and subtract. It has no intelligence; even if it can beat a chess grandmaster, that is only because it has been programmed to include the findings of human experience. The machine cannot be conscious of its own existence.

I believe that what is traditionally described as 'heaven' exists outside time and place for the refined parts of our consciousness, to be absorbed back into the underlying universal consciousness. And if heaven is not there it can hardly hurt me that I believed in it, because in the end I will know nothing of it, which is in itself a kind of heavenly peace.

I am, I suppose, *à la carte* as an Anglican, as I always would be also in a restaurant. This is how you get the best items on the menu and have a really satisfying meal. If you take the *table d'hôte* (especially depending who the '*hôte*' is) and surrender your choice to them, you risk not enjoying the meal at all. I resisted the trend within both the Roman Catholic and Anglican Churches to force people to say 'We believe' when saying the Creed. I haven't the slightest idea what the person next to me believes, and it's their business. I cannot speak for them, so I say 'I believe'. Although I do believe in the survival of the human spirit, I do not believe in the resurrection of the body, nor do I want to. It's bad enough being stuck with this clapped-out old thing of nearly seventy years' vintage for the next couple of decades or so, getting more and more creaky, but the idea of being landed with it for all eternity would be beyond endurance. And since I've never signed up to anything I didn't believe in, I am thoughtfully selective.

Like a lot of intelligent people I have difficulties with the various contradictory and bloodthirsty elements of the Old Testament. The Bible is riddled with contradictions which only a fool would believe, but it also contains a repository of vital and permanent truth. Picasso was right when he said, 'Art is a lie that reveals the truth,' and this is also true of some aspects of religion. To my mind we are very closely related to the animals. The most distinguishing human feature is imagination and the capacity to laugh. When we abandon those, we become less than human. If humour had been a predominant national characteristic in Germany, they might never have let the Nazis in. After all, Hitler's bunch of thugs claimed to be the super-race, the Nietzschean *Übermensch*. But look at them. What a bunch. The Austrian corporal Adolf Hitler who, according to the popular song and some supportive medical evidence, was testically challenged; Himmler the chinless chicken sexer from Bavaria; Goebbels with his diminutive size and gammy leg; and Goering, a heroin addict the size and shape of a barrage balloon. Imagine a poster with photographs of that group with the legend MEET THE SUPER-RACE? Yet these misfits were the people who systematically gassed the elements of their own society that didn't come up to scratch, and then did the same to the Jews, homosexuals and Gypsies.

There is of course another very uncomfortable fact that has rarely been faced because it is too delicate, and that is that virtually the entire top hierarchy of Nazism consisted of southern German or Austrian Catholics, some of whom had entertained ambitions for the priesthood: Hitler, Himmler, Goebbels, Bormann and the infamous doctor of Auschwitz Josef Mengele, as well as Heydrich and Eichmann, the architect and the implementer of the genocide committed by the Nazis against the Jews of Europe. Isn't it strange that the only Lutheran among them was Goering, even though it was a predominantly Lutheran country? Goebbels' diary must also make uncomfortable reading for traditionalists, with his avowed admiration for the Vatican's military organisation and ruthless capacity to spin the truth. The Vatican has certainly perfected the art of dissimulation over the years, and interestingly has recently appointed a Fox News reporter and Opus Dei member as chief spin doctor. Even before his arrival in Rome, a classic case in point was the effort to rehabilitate the Vatican's reputation in the light of the notorious concordat concluded with Hitler and the assistance given some of the leading Nazi war criminals. In an attempt to positively blur the issue, they excavated the stories of Father Maximilian Kolbe and Sister Edith Stein. Fr Kolbe valiantly sacrificed his life in Auschwitz to save that of a man who had a family, and Sr Edith was gassed in the same death camp. Significantly missing, however, were the troubling and recurrent suggestions that Sr Edith, who was a Jewish convert, was betrayed by her own community, and Fr Kolbe had been editor of an anti-Semitic magazine. I relished the irony when Rupert Murdoch was made a Knight of St Gregory by Pope John Paul II in recognition of his services to family values, shortly after a multi-million-dollar donation to the Church but shortly before he dumped his wife and married an employee thirty years his junior.

Some newspaper once asked me to name a book that changed my life, but instead of the predictable *Ulysses* or *The Great Gatsby*, I selected *The Book of Common Prayer*. My mother gave me my first copy of this missal of the Anglican Communion when I was ten, and inscribed it with her beautiful copperplate writing. In my family, prayerbooks were handed down lovingly from generation to generation, retiring after every revision to an obscure place in a bookcase. I have dozens of these ancestral items, some late-eighteenth- or early-nineteenth-century.

I principally cherish *The Book of Common Prayer* for its wonderful history, beautiful language and continued spiritual relevance. The prayerbook is in itself a testament to change, as the 1549 preface makes clear. It set out to give us, in the contemporary style of the sixteenth century, what is in effect a simplified translation of the Latin Mass. Of course good was intended by the latest linguistic revisions, the idea being to make it more accessible to an ever-diminishing congregation, but I do feel sad that this little volume, which has changed my life subtly by enriching me with its melody and meaning, is now itself changed at the hands of 'those who must be obeyed' within the Church. I also mourn the loss of the universality of the Latin Mass in the Roman Church.

Among my greatest friends are books, the nearly ten thousand volumes in my personal library. Great writers, or political leaders, or musicians, make you see your own world with new eyes. Ireland has been blessed to have had so many great writers, particularly of short stories. The greatest was arguably Frank O'Connor, who I was lucky to be taught by for six months in Trinity. Few adult writers had ever understood children in the special way that he did.

Another great story writer, Seán Ó Faoláin, asked me to give some tuition to the son of one of his friends, and afterwards invited me out to his house. He was just back from Tulane University and offered to lend me some jazz records. I knew Seán was a republican of the diehard Cork school which didn't give up after the Civil War, so when I went to his house for the first time I couldn't believe my eyes. I could have been visiting an English country gentleman. He wore a cravat and straw trilby, and was sitting in his rose garden, puffing on his pipe, listening to John Arlott's commentary on the cricket.

Ó Faoláin was a devout Catholic intellectual, but his priests tend to be nasty, bitter people. On the other hand Frank O'Connor, an atheist, drew them as warm, understandable, fallible human beings. Ó Faoláin and O'Connor were deeply involved in the Rising and the War of Independence, but the minute the new state was formed they became strong critics and got themselves banned. Ó Faoláin said it was the same old horse, just different arses in the saddle.

Subversion is so important with people like O'Connor and Ó Faoláin. Plato banned poets from his republic because they were politically unreliable – but they are supposed to be, that is their value – to question, to challenge.

The wonderful thing about the human spirit is that as a result of such challenges it can reach out across all preconceptions. An impressive thing about Ezra was that he was able to reach out from his Jewishness towards the oppressed Palestinian community, even when they found out he was gay. One poor family whom we had visited in their wretched little house made a living picking up scrap metal, and one day three of the youngsters picked up a twisted lump of metal that turned out to be an unexploded mortar bomb and it blew up in their faces. One son was killed instantly, another was blinded and a third lost a hand. We raised funds to get him a prosthesis but before it could be fitted he took his own life. Ezra was invited to help lay out the body, an enormous honour in that society. They knew he was Jewish, they knew he was Israeli, they knew he was gay; but they recognised the humanity that he had shown them.

I had developed a terrible fear of death after my mother passed away, but my aunt's death took away the final remnants of that fear. It made me realise that, at the end of the day, everybody is alone amidst the eternal spaces which, unlike Pascal, have ceased to frighten me. The reason people are afraid of death is because they fear the sense of loss and being separated from people they love. I've already been separated from most of the people I have loved, so for me there is little left of which to be terrified. I have always maintained in any case that you never lose the person you love, even if they die or you never see them again. The fact that you love somebody is because you have perhaps unconsciously identified, and are responding to, something in them that corresponds to an element in yourself, which as the relationship develops continues to blossom, so that a part of their reality is still left inside you whatever happens.

After my mother's death my aunt moved into the space she had vacated in my life and gradually took over the emotional role of mother. I had always loved my aunt, who was a stylish woman of remarkable intelligence, poise and courage. My affection for her took on a new intensity.

When she was ninety I moved in virtually full-time to her house in Sandymount Avenue, spending one night a month in North Great Georges Street. It was like being a teenager again: she would come downstairs in her nightdress to complain that I was staying up too late watching television – at half-past nine, and even though I was nearly fifty.

At ninety-five she had a series of falls and decided it was best to move into the wonderful ambience of the Alexandra Guild House. When she applied initially she was rejected, and was afraid it was because of her age. I wrote asking them to reconsider and saying that whatever the decision I would be happy to help in any way and at any time because of the special caring service they provided. I got an immediate invitation to meet some of the organisers. It transpired they were in financial difficulty and had been advised by their accountant to close down. I suggested they hold a board meeting and make two decisions: one, not to close, and two, to bring the board to a meeting with me in Leinster House. We met over lunch in the restaurant and I brought in Anne Byrne, a wonderful woman who was Brendan Howlin's adviser in the Department of Health, and Bob Joyce. We put together a package which saved the place. Although to many it might seem marginal and modest, this is one of my proudest achievements, for it was indeed a truly wonderful and homely place.

In the Guild House my aunt had her own small suite of rooms with her own furniture, private bathroom and a bay window looking out on a herbaceous border. I visited her there every day until she died in July 2000 at the great age of 103. She was happy to have fulfilled her ambition to live in three centuries, the nineteenth, twentieth and twenty-first. I brought her to the cathedral every Sunday until she was over a hundred years old.

When my aunt died she appeared to do so not once, but twice. I had been allowed to move into the Guild House and provision was made for me to sleep in a spare room so that I could be with her constantly. I was reading to her on her birthday when she coughed gently and stopped breathing. I called the nurse who examined her, believing her to be dead. However, a minute later, as some adjustments were being made, she emitted another cough and within half an hour she was sitting up having a cup of tea with a little birthday cake – and delighting me with some mildly scandalous stories of village life in the midlands before the First World War. But this was the last rally; it was clear that now she was dying in earnest. I sat with her for a week throughout the night and read to her passages from the Bible and some of the beautiful collects from Cranmer's *Prayer Book*:

O God, who art the author of peace and lover of concord, in knowledge of whom standeth our eternal life, whose service is perfect

freedom; Defend us thy humble servants in all assaults of our enemies; that we, surely trusting in thy defence, may not fear the power of any adversaries; through the might of Jesus Christ our Lord. Amen.

I read this repeatedly like a mantra, which acted as a balm for both of us. I also told her of a prayer of my own which she found very comforting. I had adapted it from a prayer of the Rosary in the Roman Catholic tradition: 'Jesus, be with me now and at the hour of my death. Amen.' I always repeat this to myself when I take communion every week in St Patrick's Cathedral.

One night around 4 a.m., when she seemed to be either asleep or unconscious, I said, 'Well, I expect you are tired now so I will stop for a while.' She opened her eyes and murmured, 'No, please go on,' so I did. Ten minutes before she died she regained consciousness and said very gently, 'My love to them all.' These were her last words. Hers was a genuinely happy death.

I have been lucky to have had good health, although I am at an age where inevitably a certain element of decay sets in. It's a perfectly natural process: things stop working, get rusty and fall off, and when enough of it happens you say goodbye, they put you in a nice box and off you go.

It was a prostate examination which almost cut me off in my prime about ten years ago. The doctor seemed clumsy and insensitive, and I should have been suspicious when he reassured me that the investigation he proposed would be done using a fibre-optic camera. When they had me on the slab they must have stuck an entire RTÉ outside-broadcast unit up my flute because I awoke in absolute agony and was dispatched half an hour later without so much as an aspirin.

Within twenty-four hours I was almost incoherent and could barely hold the telephone. I rang a medical friend and was advised to call 999, but by the time the ambulance arrived I was in a poor state. It was half-past one in the morning, and a crowd had gathered in the street outside to observe the drama. I was halfway out the door in my pyjamas and dressing gown when I realised I might be gone for a while, so I ducked back in and grabbed an armful of books. This got a cheer from the crowd, and one lad piped up, 'Fair play to ya, Norris, ye're the only man in Dublin who'd be at death's door and he'd be going back for his bukes.' I was taken first to the Mater Hospital, where because of a staff go-slow I was rejected and had to cross the river to St James's Hospital, where I was diagnosed with rigor and septicaemia, and remained there for three weeks.

I finally had the procedure painlessly and successfully – with a different doctor – and, just as I was about to go under, the anaesthetist said, 'Relax, you'll just feel a floating sensation,' which is exactly what happened as I wafted away without a care in the world. When I awoke I asked the nurse what they had given me, and asked her could I book to come for three armfuls of the stuff when I am in my last hours. She was a bit shocked and asked me did I not want to go to heaven? I told her, 'I don't think there's any doubt about the destination, I just want to be in a first-class carriage on an express train.'

I have various exit strategies planned, one of which first emerged during a live radio chat show. There was a discussion about burial versus cremation, and I suggested that I might have my mortal remains taken to a good local butcher to be boned and rolled, my hide flayed and nozzles fitted to the various apertures so that I could then be inflated and sold as a sex toy in New York. I could then enjoy post-mortem all the pleasures that a credulous public had imagined I enjoyed in my lifetime. And, for me at least, it would be safe sex.

That gave someone an idea and RTÉ made a whole programme about my funeral plans, mixing my script with footage of the funerals of King George V and President Douglas Hyde. I told them that I was having a full Haydn Mass, with weepy Victorian hymns such as 'Oh Love That Wilt Not Let Me Go' and Mozart's 'Ave Verum Corpus', which I see as the very heart of the Christian faith. I also decided I would as usual have the last word myself. I will have holes drilled in the side of the coffin and a little loudspeaker playing my last speech, which I shall record in advance. It will be along these lines: 'Well, I don't suppose you expected to hear from me quite so soon, ladies and gentlemen. I am happy to report that I have arrived in heaven where the weather is glorious. The Almighty sends his regards.' I will then go on to say some serious things about what going to St Patrick's Cathedral every Sunday meant to me.

As the service ends and my remains are carried through the heartbroken throng, an old-fashioned Dublin lorry will pull up at the west door. On board will be a jazz band (with cornet, clarinet and tailgate trombone) and they will strike up 'Just a Closer Walk with Thee' before the cortège heads for the canal and the Naas Road on the way to Laois.

I have already purchased my last resting place, in the little eighteenth-century churchyard at Roskelton, where I am related to every occupant bar one. I bought the grave some years ago and the last time I was there I found they had very considerately and practically marked it with a concrete pillow with my name upon it. I took that as an invitation to try it for size, which I did. The view, while not over-dramatic, does take in the woodlands and rolling fields of County Laois.

For my obituary I thought of combining a few elements. One was the remark of a cousin of the eighteenth-century novelist Henry Fielding, who said, 'I was greatly saddened to learn of the death of H. Fielding,' and the other Joyce's very human tribute to his father: 'He was the silliest man I ever knew but in his own way strangely wise.' So perhaps, if I am lucky, what might appear from the obituarist's pen is 'I was greatly saddened to hear of the death of D. Norris. He was the silliest man I ever knew but in his own way strangely wise.' I think that would sum me up quite well.

I have decided that what will be on the tombstone will not be from the Bible, but from Shakespeare's The Tempest: 'We are such stuff as dreams are made on, and our little life is rounded with a sleep.'

No one, whatever their religion (or lack of it), can argue with that.

I am in fact one of the few people to have been able to write their own obituary. I rang the *Irish Times* one day many years ago to ask a favour, and the lad on the other end of the line asked for one in return, which was to cast an eye over the obituary of me which they held in their archive ready for the fateful day. I hadn't realised that such things were done in advance, or that I was important enough to warrant a *Times* obituary. It was a bit out of date so they asked me to update it. I had a full weekend's fun rewriting it. What I submitted began:

> Last night, to the inexpressible grief of an inconsolable nation, one
> of the greatest spirits of this island, nay this continent, perhaps even
> this planet, passed to what is undoubtedly his eternal reward.
> Crowds gathered around his principal residence in North Great
> Georges Street, while police had to hold back grown men overcome
> with emotion. The rosary was recited and the wailing of his neigh-
> bours could be heard as far away as Croke Park . . .

It was completely unusable, but I cried with laughter writing it.

I have had a marvellous life. I have always been moved by the singing of the Little Sparrow of Paris, Edith Piaf, and like her, '*Non, je ne regrette rien*' – I regret nothing.

I did not get elected President – but I do not regard that as failure. Whatever good you do you hope it lives on. The presidency was just not part of my destiny. I have been exceptionally lucky to have the support of family and friends during a very turbulent time. I have the wonderful community in North Great Georges Street, its good friends and institutions like Lucky Duffy's, Foley's the family chemist, Tops in Pops the vegetable shop and Carneys butchers in Parnell Street. My brother and his family were of great comfort and assistance to me, as were my wonderful nephew John and niece Margaret, of whom I am very proud. I will say little of any of them as I respect their privacy. I also have a great friend in Mary Fletcher-Smith, who I met some years ago in Cyprus and who I still see both here and on that beautiful island. Her sister-in-law Louise McKeon painted a magnificent series of portraits, one of which she generously presented to me.

In addition to my neighbours, there are also some wonderful casual acquaintances. Among my favourites are the two consecrated virgins of the Pro-Cathedral. They are identical twins and I always enjoyed my chats with them when I met them on the street. When I asked them their names they giggled and one said, 'I'm Gin, and she's Tonic,' and they are known locally by this appellation. Once when I told them I was having dental problems, which involved a lot of pain, the two enfolded me in an embrace, bowed their heads and said an improvised but lovely prayer. They are truly the people of God.

I also enjoy my visits to Jude in his basement tailoring shop in Middle Abbey Street. He has African connections and works tirelessly for charities on that continent, as well as doing all kinds of repair jobs on my clothes. When my shoes need attention I go around to an immaculate little shop, Rapid Shoe Repairs, off Marlborough Street where the owner, Oliver McNamee, and his two cheery sons not only rescue almost unrepairable shoes, but give me the benefit of their wisdom.

I have a warm friendship with Tevfik, who has endured a great deal because of his friendship with me. We do not live together but care deeply for each other – how could it be any other way? He works hard as a nursing assistant in a Dublin hospital. When I was seriously ill after a non-malignant tumour became infected, he came twice a day, on his way to and from work, whether he was on night duty or day duty, to dress an unpleasant wound. Was this not love? Of course, for sensational purposes, every thought, action and deed of mine has been sex-ualised by sections of the media. He is a very private person and one of the best, most moral individuals I have ever met. On several occasions when we were out we noticed people making a beeline for us, and I thought in my vanity they were coming to talk to me; but instead they were coming to tell Tevfik how his nursing skills had saved their life. I am glad to say the injustice done to him has been partially rectified; one newspaper has already apologised and paid him a substantial sum in mitigation of a scandalous defamation.

In Cyprus, Nora has been a most stimulating friend and I have loved her as much as I have loved any man. As I told a newspaper some years ago, the hormones have settled down and I am now on that beautiful plateau where I can love men and women equally. The grubbier sections of the media sensationalised this and it was suggested that such an avowal was a betrayal and shock to the gay community.

So I'm lucky in my friends and I have enjoyed their company and the laughter that goes with it on the rare occasions I have been available for them. For the last forty years my private life has been sparse indeed, as I devoted myself remorselessly to the interests of the public and neglected many of those close to me. Indeed it got to the stage where my family complained that they had to make an appointment with Miriam to see me. Now my priorities are altering. As I approach the rich autumn of life I hope to rekindle those bonds of affection.

There was a marvellous film released early in 2012 called *The Best Exotic Marigold Hotel*, in which the Indian hotel manager comes out with a wonderful piece of wisdom: 'Everything will be all right in the end, and if it's not all right, then it's not the end.'

When the end does come, as Hilaire Belloc wrote, all that really matters is that your companions along the way have included laughter and the love of friends, and in my case I am fortunate to be able to say they have.

ACKNOWLEDGEMENTS

As Dylan Thomas said, to begin at the beginning. But where is the beginning? The first I heard of the idea of this book was from my good friend and neighbour Muireann Noonan, who has been a constant inspiration to me and secular equivalent of Our Lady of Good Counsel. Then I discovered that an earlier Damascene moment had occurred to my some-time neighbour and now good friend and agent Sharon Bowers; as she told me, as she crossed 42nd Street in New York she realised that 'David Norris must write a book.' I could almost sense the lightning strike, the sudden cessation of tap-dancing in mid bar. Then there are my publishers, Transworld, who have been kind, intelligent and understanding, all necessary qualities when dealing with me. Any raised voices were on my side; Brian and Eoin were models of decorum and were extremely helpful.

As in everything I do, I must mention the unfailing encouragement of my PA, Miriam Gordon Smith, and the tolerance of her wise and kind husband, Noel.

I am grateful to Douglas Appleyard for his invaluable research on my family tree.

But perhaps the most important person of all was Ger Siggins, who listened endlessly to my stories and, because I can neither type nor use a computer, had the grim job of transcribing my barely literate handwritten notes and myriad tapes. However, his marvellous wife Martha did tell me that she often heard laughter coming from the room where he was typing things up. Together we made endless revisions to the text and Ger also proved to be an invaluable researcher, checking facts for me and miraculously finding photographs whose existence I had been unaware of, showing the Queen Elizabeth clinic where I was born and the actual ship on which my mother, my brother and I returned from Africa. What started as a collaboration ended as a friendship and I am grateful to him and his entire family. However, the thing I appreciate most about Ger is that I managed to arrive, with unfailing regularity, with new work for him to type up or corrections or amendments to go through just at the moment when he was removing his celebrated fish pie from the oven. I think I must have developed an unconscious instinct for knowing when it was ready to be devoured.

Lastly, but from the bottom of my heart, I would like to thank all those who so generously gave me their support during my recent presidential election campaign. You know who you are.

PICTURE ACKNOWLEDGEMENTS

First Section
pp. 2–3: Dean Lamb © Bill Blue, courtesy of Harry Fanning.

Second Section
pp. 2–3: Protest march in 1974 © Gareth Miller; *Last House* © RTÉ Stills Library; cast of *Mister X* courtesy of Tonie Walsh and the National Library of Ireland.
pp. 4–5: Marshall of the Gay Pride Parade, 2009 © Martina Malone; Gay Pride march, 1990 © Derek Speirs; Gay Pride, © 2011 Barbara Lindberg; hanging of Iranian students © Iranian Students News Agency.

Third Section
p. 1: With Dean Victor Griffin and Dr Noël Browne © *The Irish Times*

INDEX

Senator David Norris has been an independent member of Seanad Éireann since 1987. He won a historic constitutional challenge in 1988 to the laws criminalizing homosexuality in Ireland. Senator Norris was a candidate in the 2011 Irish presidential election. He is a former lecturer at Trinity College Dublin, a Joycean scholar, a conservationist and a passionate defender of human rights.

Mail Clippings –
A cluster of critical corns

I have done many different things in a varied life and I recall my aunt describing me as being in danger of becoming a jack of all trades and master of none. One of the trades I practised for a while was criticism. I was an occasional critic of restaurants, opera, theatre, literature and the visual arts. I got tired of it when one of our serious newspapers said that all that was necessary to read when reviewing a book was a paragraph or two from the beginning, the middle and the end and to form my judgement on that. I felt that this showed a lack of respect to even second rate writers. So for those critics of a lazy disposition who in addition to this disability are required by insensitive editors to review this book at short notice without reading it, I hereby provide a few useful notional quotes which they may feel free to use.

What the Critics Might Have Said

'Would you permit your wife or your servants to read this book? I think not!'
– SIR CLIFFORD CHATTERLEY J.P.

'We no longer speak of Mr Norris at Trinity College.'
– PROVOST (EMERITUS) REVD SIR JOHN PENTLAND MAHAFFY

'A great read – I like a man with balls.'
– MAE WEST (DECEASED)